Desire beyond Identity

SUNY series in Gender Theory

Tina Chanter, editor

Desire beyond Identity

Irigaray and the Ethics of Embodiment

WESLEY N. BARKER

SUNY
PRESS

Cover Credit: *Uterine Western*, Erin Yerby, oil, acrylic, ink, and red dirt on canvas, 34 × 45; used by permission of the artist.

Published by State University of New York Press, Albany

EU GPSR Authorised Representative:
Logos Europe, 9 rue Nicolas Poussin, 17000, La Rochelle, France
contact@logoseurope.eu

For information, contact State University of New York Press, Albany, NY
www.sunypress.edu

Library of Congress Cataloging-in-Publication Data

Name: Barker, Wesley N., 1979– author
Title: Desire beyond identity : Irigaray and the ethics of embodiment /
    Wesley N. Barker.
Description: Albany : State University of New York Press, [2025] | Series:
    SUNY series in gender theory | Includes bibliographical references.
Identifiers: LCCN 2024039395 | ISBN 9798855801446 (hardcover : alk. paper) |
    ISBN 9798855801460 (ebook) | ISBN 9798855801453 (pbk. : alk. paper)
Subjects: LCSH: Irigaray, Luce. | Desire (Philosophy). | Identity (Philosophical
    concept). | Philosophy, French—20th century.
Classification: LCC B2430.I74 B37 2025 | DDC 194—dc23/eng/20250114
LC record available at https://lccn.loc.gov/2024039395

To my mother and all my grandmothers

Contents

Acknowledgments

When I was a graduate student at Emory University, my then advisor, Dr. Mark D. Jordan, signed my copy of his book, *Blessings of Same Sex Unions: The Confusions of Christian Marriage* (University of Chicago, 2005): "Until you write your own, better." I knew my scholarship would never approach that of Mark Jordan's, and, per the typical graduate student imposter syndrome, I still remember how humbling (and a bit confusing) it was to entertain the possibility that he thought I might actually be *that* good! Incidentally, that was also the first book in which I ever appeared in an acknowledgment section. I was grateful to my overly generous mentor for the nod, especially since I had been a mediocre research assistant at best. My dad was even more enthusiastic; he immediately went out and purchased a copy of Jordan's book just to see my name in print.

Prior to that first recognition, I had always bypassed the acknowledgments sections of books. Sure, I had noticed dedications, but I always looked forward to the main act. After Mark's book, I began reading acknowledgments, which I now understand are formal recognitions of some of the most intimate aspects of authorship—the relationships that make it possible at all. Although this book took two years of dedicated writing time, as I sat down to pull together my acknowledgments, I felt the weight of twenty years of gratitude for friends, family, and colleagues, some no longer living, who have supported me up to this point.

To begin I want to note that one of the most important resources for writing books, one that seems all too scarce these days, is time. *Desire* would not have been possible were it not for a year-long sabbatical, and I am thankful to Mercer University, the Office of the Provost, and the College of Professional Advancement for that all-important time and space. I owe special thanks to my dean, Priscilla Danheiser, and my former department chair, Fred Bongiovanni, who have consistently advocated on my behalf for course releases and research funds to pursue my scholarship. I am also grateful to Don Redmond and the Center for the Study of Narrative, which provided financial support for me to travel to Paris to join Luce Irigaray for a colloquy in March of 2023 that helped me clarify how I understood my contribution to Irigaray studies. I hope the work of this book reciprocates in some way the rich resource of Luce Irigaray's thought, whose work continues to inspire, and without whom this particular project would not have existed.

The seeds of this work, particularly my interest in questions of ethics and subjectivity, emerged during my graduate coursework at Duke and Emory. Professors Mary McClintock Fulkerson, Kathy Rudy, Pamela M. Hall, Claire Nouvet, Jill Robbins, Cathy Caruth, Diane M. Stewart, and especially Mark D. Jordan, were critical to my intellectual formation. My focus on Luce Irigaray began in earnest during my dissertation phase, and I am indebted to Carolyn Denard and my dissertation committee—Wendy Farley, Bobbi Patterson, Andrea C. White—for their commitment to my formation. Years later, at a time in my career when I was drowning in self-doubt about my scholarship, I was prompted by my friend (and fellow scholar) Emily Holmes to submit a proposal to the Irigaray Circle meeting in Winchester, UK. Participating in the Irigaray Circle for the first time felt like coming up for air, and I will be forever grateful to the members of the circle—especially Mary Rawlinson and Gail Schwab, Athena Colman, Sabrina Hom, Jena Jolissaint, Phyllis Kaminski, Ruthanne Soohee Crapo Kim, Rachel Jones, and Emily Anne Parker—for welcoming me and for making me a better scholar. An earlier version of chapter 2 was published in the Irigaray Circle's edited volume *Horizons of Difference* (SUNY, 2022) thanks to Ruthanne and her coeditors Yvette Russell and Brenda Sharp.

When I finally started to write this book in earnest, bringing together years of presentations and musings to say something coherent seemed daunting. Thanks to philosopher Kathryn Belle (formerly Gines) and her writing group, La Belle Vie, I was able to cultivate a new relationship to writing. The women of that group inspired me to push through the most frustrating days of the process; they have my deepest gratitude for including me in their collective. I am especially grateful to Katy Scrogin for her keen editorial eye and her wordsmithing, which helped me through the multiple stages of revisions and edits. I am grateful for the women who joined me to write daily in the spring of 2024 as I finalized revisions. I cannot wait to read their books! Thank you to Camille Hale and the production staff at SUNY for the care they have taken in copyediting the manuscript. Special thanks to Rebecca Colesworthy, my editor at SUNY, for her guidance and belief in this book. LeRhonda Manigault-Bryant was incredibly generous to offer her personal time to review parts of chapter 5, and her validation of my interpretive work inspired me to press forward with my analysis. To my anonymous readers: the generosity of your time and thoughtful engagement with the manuscript made this a much stronger book; your careful reviews are a model that I hope to follow for others.

Outside of my writing time, I have often been loath to discuss my project; theory can sometimes feel more like a quagmire than a conversation. There were times it seemed that with every verbalization of a particular dimension of this work, some other piece would slip farther away. Nonetheless, there have been certain friends and colleagues who pushed me past the rabbit holes and toward clarity: Neil Van Leeuwen, Jared Champion, Hollis Phelps, Nathan Digby, Mickey Moreland, Whitney Phillips, and especially Louis Ruprecht. Between Wilmington and Atlanta, I have also made some incredible (and talented) friends who have helped me materially and emotionally at various stages in this process: Tasha, Natasha, Laura, Molly, Maya, Christina, Nate, and Cameron. A special thanks to those who have shared your guest rooms and couches over the years! My "framily"—Ana, Candace, Parker, Doug, Katie, Banks, and Wanda—for years has been my refuge when I needed fresh air, perspective, a good laugh, or a good cry. This book was the occasion for reconnecting me with my dearest friend Erin Yerby, whose gorgeous artistic engagement with identity and ontology graces its cover. What a gift! Truly the generosity of my friends and family is humbling, and to those not listed above, know I am grateful for your kindness, patience, and support.

Throughout this entire process, my family members have been *the* stabilizing force. If they doubted me, they never let me know it. Rich, I don't know what I would have done without you those days and nights where the process felt more like defeat. Wilson, my constant companion of eleven years, resumed his same spot in my office every day during the two years of writing this book. To other loved ones who have passed while this volume was still developing, I no less write to you to thank you for your part in this journey.

Introduction

Desire beyond Identity

Desire arises from the void opened in us by taking our difference from the other into account. It contributes to our holding in ourselves, to unifying our self from what is particular to us, but also to longing for the other as the one who is needed for us to become ourselves. . . . Desire also connects the most intimate with the most remote. And yet, desire does not overcome opposites, it does not know them. Perhaps contradiction has no sense for it and results from its ignorance, its repression, its being reduced to instinct and drive, or to an abstract energy already cut off from its natural source. Life knows an absolute without opposites and contradiction. . . . But this absolute requires us to respect difference(s) and each to be faithful to its particularity.

—Irigaray, *Sharing the Fire* (2021), 4

Identity, Irigaray, and the Question of Desire

"Identity" appears in many forms and multiple registers. We have learned to think and speak of ethnoracial identities, gender identities, sexual identities, religious identities, class identities, and so on. Being a political subject continues to require recognition at the individual, social, and institutional levels. State governments commonly issue identity cards and conduct census surveys in which some (though not all) of these identity categories may be salient. Citizens are free to self-name and to self-identify in their speech, on their application for an identity card, and on the relevant census forms. Yet such self-identification also requires recognition by others, and their positive assent, if it is to be fully granted. The application form is an appeal; the presentation of the card is a (cor)responding assent.

1

For complex political reasons, some citizens—and perhaps more importantly, noncitizens—may be hesitant to participate in the governance of self-naming. They may not wish to be recognized, preferring to remain unseen, unacknowledged, or invisible on the census. For complex moral and ethical reasons, other citizens and noncitizens may object to the choices they have been offered on the requisite forms, whether because they judge the category of "mixed" to be inadequate (or even offensive) or because they are demanding more and better categories, more and better categorical choices than are currently available. Being a political subject continues to require such complex modes of recognition at the individual, social, and institutional levels. What's more, questions about the discourse of identity and the on-the-ground demands of marginalized bodies invoke questions of philosophical, ethical, political, and religious significance that extend beyond the academy, to a place where scholarship matters to contemporary life and politics. Whether or not, and how, one should be counted in the census is just one example of how recognition impacts individuals and their communities—bracketing the psychological impact of which box one must check.

Indeed, the challenges of identity far exceed the problem of identity politics, as identity broadly invokes questions about becoming, freedom, responsibility, belonging, and recognition in the midst of difference. This book is based on the premise that contemporary ethical, philosophical, and political debates about identity and representation reflect the unresolvable tension between materiality and discursivity in late twentieth- and early twenty-first-century theories of subjectivity. My proposal is that Luce Irigaray's work offers resources for tending to the complexity of this contested terrain in a way that thinks the embodiedness of living without relegating that embodiedness to a totalizing system of representation. My conclusion is that by building on Irigaray's particular notion of desire, at once similar to and different from those of Freud, Lacan, and Levinas (and others among her interlocutors), desire could provide an ethical and embodied mode of relation beyond identity.

Irigaray published *Sharing the Fire,* a book focused on desire, in 2020; however, the thread of desire can be traced throughout her work dating back to her 1974 publication of *Speculum of the Other Woman* (*Speculum de l'autre femme*). Reimagined apart from phallocentric theorizations, desire in Irigaray's work engages the time and space of life and death beyond binaries and recasts a relation of differences that is dynamic, always enriching, and risky. Tracing this thread of desire, particularly its emergence through the visceral language in her earlier work but also in her sustained thinking about touching, I elaborate a theory of desire as an at-once embodied, ambiguous, and generative space and time of relation. And I contend that if we think *through* Irigaray's sexual difference, we might begin to *displace* sexual difference and look toward the indeterminacy and ambiguity of an othered desire. This othered desire would be capable of reimagining the relation between discourse and matter that refuses to resubmit embodied living to identity and the prison of recognition.

Throughout, I argue that such desire embraces the riskiness of eros as a relationship between two, in order to transform the becoming of subjects, their relations to each other, and therein what it means to dwell in worlds that we create together.[1] Eros here is not the eros of Lacan's psychoanalytic readings of Plato; it is not based on desire for that which one lacks, such that the other is that which fills me up with that which I do not have. And difference is not constituted through lack or negation. Here, a desire made possible through both the irreducible difference and specificity of every desiring is constituted through a proximity that generates, to borrow from Irigaray, "wonder" between others. Put simply, thinking through the question of sexual difference leads us to the question of desire as that which extends far beyond sexuation itself. By reading through and beyond Irigaray's notion of sexual, or as she later terms it sexuate,[2] difference, I argue that the dynamic flow of desire cultivates a space-time for both specificity and difference, without reducing specificity to matter and difference to transcendence. This desire radiates from a reimagining of the difference itself as embodied, irreducible, and most importantly radically indeterminate.

Desire and Identity

For Freud, the question of becoming a subject was theorized through an examination of human development, where development was a negotiation of libidinal drives. The ethical in Freud is also a moment of eros; it emerges when one decides how to act in relation to the other—when I realize that the other can satisfy or thwart my desires. Insofar as the other appears to the one as an instrument for satisfying or an impediment for repressing one's desires, relation is never more than the satisfaction/realization of one's subjectivity.

Freud's depiction of development, and its role in the becoming of the social-psychological subject, has been framed in relation to a distinct reading of desire, exemplified in his interpretation of the Oedipus complex.

Not only is the male child the original subject of his study; he also casts the development of girls through the same lens. The movement toward becoming described above is therefore not only a movement of the one securing its oneness through the other; it specifically extends from and is oriented toward the satisfaction of male libidinal desire.

Because of this reading of relation, Irigaray insists that the ethical in Freud is reduced to a phallic desire, where desire of the one in its becoming a subject is oblivious to if not altogether violating the other's becoming. Irigaray sees the problem thus: there cannot be two if there are only ones whose relation is reduced to satisfying one. While Irigaray, like Freud, wants to think the relation between two (which ancient Greek philosophy framed in terms of eros) as ethical, she does not want the relation of two to be about satisfying the desire of one; rather, she wants the two to meet in the fullness of their own desires—only then can ethical relation take place.

The ethical response, Irigaray insists, is not to satisfy one's desire but to give space to the other's desire—to let desire flourish between two. For two to be two, they must be irreducible to each other. But what makes two irreducible to each other more than just two phallocentrically oriented ones? What makes two irreducible for Irigaray? Herein lies where/why psychoanalysis is most significant for Irigaray: it is what Freud has ignored and/or repressed that is precisely what could save us: female sexuality (Irigaray's phrase). If psychoanalysis has only been able to think of desire as a totalizing relation to one, for ethical relation to exist, desire itself must not return to one as though neutral, untroubled, or unaffected.

For Irigaray, the implications of a phallocentric theory of desire are not simply limited to psychic development. Building off the work of Jacques Lacan, Irigaray argues that Freud's occlusion of female sexuality in his phallocentric framing of desire is part of a broader social and cultural symbolic (primarily linguistic and discursive) representation of desire for oneness. Because of her Lacanian linguistic psychoanalytic inheritance, Irigaray views the very concept of worlds as constructed through the representation of desire.[3] Here, Freud's description of human development in terms of a desire for oneness is not the explanation of *the* world as a natural fact or forgone conclusion. Rather, human development and Freud's interpretation of it are both symptoms of a culture that prioritizes singularity as wholeness and oneness, secured through the annihilation of difference. Irigaray believes that new worlds are possible. The world of Freud, where phallic desire becomes the fact of human becoming, is a world where language has been oriented around a system of differentiation through negation and exclusion to secure sense and meaning—to secure an untroubled identity between the projection of self and the realization of self. The scope of the problem highlights the stakes of thinking about desire as between two and the necessity of irreducibility to their twoness in order for desire to remain between two. Consequences are not simply limited to outcomes for the individual and its relation to the social; the stakes are the sociality of life itself.

To confront a world constituted through a desire of one for one, Irigaray ultimately turns to the question of generativity and to the sexuation that is necessary to generate human life in order to posit irreducibility. From Irigaray's perspective, she isn't reifying the association of women to reproduction; instead, she is reimagining what it means to be human in terms of natality. In other words, how can we become if we are not born? And how are we born? We are born of two who are always already born of two. We are always already at least two. Irigaray views her philosophy of sexuate difference as constituting a radical reorientation of thought and living in the world—one she insists has never had an opportunity to exist. If the two were to be sexuate, the sexuateness of their desire would be expansive and irreducible beyond binary conceptions of desire that Irigaray inherits from Freud. Here, "female sexuality" gestures toward desire other than that found in the phallocentric male sexuality of psychoanalysis—a desire that, in its openness, its always at least twoness, would be capacious enough for rethinking all relations as encounters of openness and possibility.

Irigaray contends that a female sexuality might cultivate a language that is generative rather than representational and therein produces horizons for new worlds. It was her use of language that helped put her on the map as a formidable and controversial figure in gender studies in North America. Her references to wombs, placentas, labial lips, mucous, and other visceral language have served as part of a mode of writing intended to critique associations of women with carnality and materiality associated with reproduction, associations that she argued were symptoms of phallocentric philosophical and psychoanalytic discourses. These invocations were also constructive insofar as in their critical mimicry, they transformed those associations and attempted to cultivate a space-time for thinking through the othered desire of a female sexuality as embodied differently. As Maggie Nelson describes Irigaray's lips in her genre-bending memoir *The Argonauts*: "They are not one, but also not two. They make a circle that is always self-touching, an autoerotic mandorla."[4]

I expressly turn to Irigaray's figure of lips, as a figure of the irreducible gap between discourse and matter, to harness the rhetoricity of flesh that the othered desire of her "female sexuality" might cultivate. Irigaray's controversial and yet surprisingly undertheorized invocations of lips gesture to the embodiedness of desire in her work, and they shape my effort to think beyond a phallocentric logic. I am drawn by this desire that the morphology of touching lips evokes. Indeed, the very language of Irigaray's texts arouses this embodied desire—a desire that I recognized decades ago when I first read *Ethics of Sexual Difference*—a curious and awakening desire of touch as a condition and expression of difference. This is the desire in Irigaray's texts that Nelson describes on first reading Irigaray's "When Our Lips Speak Together": the desire to contemplate her own self-touching lips and the ways that "every woman in the class" might be doing the same. Drawing on the embodiedness of desire that Irigaray writes *through* in order to write beyond phallocentrism, *Desire* insists that these lips are an invitation to consider the capaciousness of a philosophy of embodied, indeterminate, dynamic desire for imagining radical change in the very world in which one lives.

Irigaray's appeal to sexuation to frame an other sexuality that emanates from an *other* desire establishes a relational ontology.[5] Yet Irigaray's casting of sexuate difference as ontological and a precursor to establishing a "female sexuality," and her framing of desire through a morphology of labial lips, as well as through other logics based on morphologies such as wombs and placentas, has rendered surface readings of her philosophy low-hanging fruit for decades of criticism and in some cases outright dismissal. But simply attacking Irigaray's sexuate as cisbinary or heteronormative oversimplifies her philosophy by reducing her use of terms to the very conceptual worlds she is attempting to refuse.[6]

Some of these criticisms can be and have been dispelled by readers of Irigaray who frame her appeal to the ontological (as what seems most "natural" to the possibility of being human), as part of her broader critique of ontology vis-à-vis Heidegger. Irigaray has long engaged Heidegger, from her notable 1983 monograph published in English in 1999 as *The Forgetting of Air in Martin Heidegger*, to her 2019 coauthored *Toward a New Human Being*. She often invokes Heidegger's work to frame the problem of metaphysical assertions about Being and also to differentiate an ontology of sexual difference from what she deems the false neutrality of Heidegger's Dasein.[7] And, as I will discuss in chapter 1, Irigaray follows the ethical turn in Emmanuel Levinas's criticism of the universality of ontology to frame sexuation as an otherwise than Being that is not reducible to negation of Being or the negative of the universal man. It is from the most nuanced defenses and extensions of Irigaray's critique of ontology that the most interesting potential challenges to Irigaray have emerged, particularly in relation to questions of ontological violence percolating in contemporary engagements with race and gender. I insist that understanding the fullness of desire in Irigaray is impossible without careful consideration of her critical revision of ontology and embodiment. And it has become nearly impossible, if not outright irresponsible, to appeal to embodiment without considering the extent to which what it means to be and become in and through bodies is constrained by discursive norms that are part of deeply rooted modes of relation. My appeal holds together an Irigarayan insistence on embodiment as ontological insofar as it is foundational for a philosophy of living, but not in a way that is determinative or takes Being for granted as universal.

Desire and the Question of Sexuate Difference

Irigaray's efforts to hold the agency of women's becoming together with ethical responsibility hinge on a dynamic notion of desire that disrupts its isolation or dissolution in either carnality or transcendence. Both descriptive and constructive in its attempt to clarify the relationship between desire and ontology, ethics, and politics in Irigaray's work, *Desire* aims to think a materiality and alterity of desire as a horizon for disruptively engaging the relationship between bodies and discourse, without devolving into a philosophy of immanence or a religion of transcendence.

Since the 1970s, Irigaray's work at the intersection of philosophy, psychoanalysis, and ethics has insisted that thought is an embodied enterprise of being in the world with others in relation to one's own desires. Desire in Irigaray is predicated on a difference between one and another (two beings), and she asserts that sexual difference is the irreducible difference through which this twoness is constituted. Particularly in her early works, Irigaray theorizes sexual difference in a way that is both discursive and material, refuting classical oppositions of spirit and matter, as well as philosophical binaries that align matter with immanence and language with transcendence. And the capacity of sexual difference to invoke this alternative space hinges on the centrality of desire in her theory of subjectivity. After all, the emergence of differences produces space for desire, and in psychoanalysis it is through navigating desire that one becomes a subject.

The radical philosophical dimensions of Irigaray's explorations of sexual difference in language and her assertions of an irreducible "sexuate" difference prior to discourse are often overlooked by Anglo-American audiences because their framework for interpreting sex and gender diverges from the context of Irigaray's continental and psychoanalytic entanglements. It is this different context that shapes the crises of representation in contemporary American politics. Anglo-American feminisms of the 1970s and 1980s in particular separated gender from biological sex in an attempt to overcome the notion that women's roles in society were expressions of some ontological essence of woman. Pushing Simone de Beauvoir's famous phrase that "one is not born a woman" to its logical conclusion, some later feminist theorists, most notably Judith Butler and Linda Alcoff, emphasized that not only were the gender roles attributed to women constructed and performative, but so too was the idea of sex difference according to which gender had been ascribed. While theories of sex and gender, including Gayle Rubin's famous sex/gender system and Kimberlé Crenshaw's "Intersectionality," became increasingly more nuanced, related conversation and criticisms continued to fall into two major camps: one holding on to the reality of certain material aspects of life and body, and the other insisting that the body itself is constituted in and through discourse, such that it is in a sense free of any preordained or predetermined biological/material reality.

The tension between these camps and the reduction of lived experience to either one or the other may be useful for critique, but they do little to address modern political realities (regardless of how real they are) in which actual bodies both perpetuate and suffer under the power of normalizing discursive regimes. Lynne Huffer, who takes what she calls a "queer feminist" position, argues that the prioritization of either discourse or materiality has divided feminist political commitments and radical queer theory for decades.[8] Recent and rather bitter political and philosophical debates about transgender rights and the implications of thinking trans* bodies in relation both to questions of racialization and to feminist political commitments remind us that these tensions are not going away any time soon.[9]

The friction has led to unfortunate hostilities among groups and persons who should otherwise be working together to think critically about ways to address gross inequities and reimagine being in the world with others. In 2017, the prominent feminist philosophy journal *Hypatia* published a peer-reviewed article entitled "In Defense of Transracialism" by Rebecca Tuvel. Tuvel's article used as a point of departure Rachel Dolezal, the disgraced NAACP official who had been pretending to be a Black woman, despite having been born and raised white. Tuvel's consideration of how trans* functions in identity was severely criticized by some of the journal's readership, the most vociferous of whom read Tuvel as analogizing race and sex. The fallout from this article, which included an open letter to the journal demanding the article's retraction, as well as an apology from *Hypatia's* board of associate editors, raised questions about academic freedom, about what trans* is and means, and for whom the term is operational. The controversy was even scintillating enough for popular media. On May 2, 2017, *New York* magazine's online news spinoff, *Intelligencer*, published an article largely defending Tuvel on the basis that interrogating processes of identification should never be taboo for philosophers. By May 18, the controversy had made its way to the *New York Times*.

Such controversies result in part from a lack of clarity around the terminology and discourse of trans*, queer, and feminist, as well as discourses of race and racialization. All have always been in flux, and, often by relating to norms through negation, they disconnect from particularities of persons' lived experiences, such that differences remain threatening to ideas about solidarity. Although such proliferations are intended to make space for particularities of experience, to find ways of addressing racist, sexist, and heteronormative systems, identity itself must be rethought in order for the particular to avoid becoming more of the same. Questions about feminist and queer commitments must be rethought in light of the discursive and material demands of nonbinary and trans* thought—*and* all must take seriously the implications of identification and disidentification for social and political existence. Unfortunately, politics doesn't typically make the time and space for philosophical investigation, and philosophy doesn't often compute the immediacy of persons' experiences.

Confusions about terminology and frustrations about political alliances are bound up with tensions between discourse and materiality that constrain how the body is imagined and how identity is conceived.[10] Technologies and practices can change the body such that questions about its material limits do in fact seem bound only by the limits of discourse, by the limits of what is imaginable in language. And yet, death is not simply a discursive limit, as is tragically evident in a world where identity is based on representation, where the materiality of the body has reasserted its significance in everything from transgender rights and politics to reproductive rights to #BlackLivesMatter, in often unpredictable ways. As Sara Ahmed writes in *Living a Feminist Life*, systems of sexism and racism "support and ease the progression of some bodies," and I would emphasize that this means some bodies over or at the expense of other bodies.[11]

This ability of bodies to reassert themselves over and against discourse challenges conceptions of the body as either exclusively discursively

constituted or as merely an effect of discourse. Indeed, bodies here constitute new discourses. Postmodern disruptions of discursive determinations of
bodies are the condition of possibility for materiality to assert itself anew.
Yet such reassertions of the materiality of the body are not without risk; as
theorists emphasizing the discursivity of bodies would insist, such appeals
are suggestive of an ontology of bodies that risks reinforcing normalizing
discursive regimes of identity.

Taxonomies, by definition, place individuals in groups; thus, naming
is an activity that thinks identity in terms of a recognition of similitude.
Most important, these debates about identity and recognition—about *what*
and *how* bodies are recognizable within a particular social and political
worldview and even what it means to be recognizable to oneself—involve
living beings. Because living beings and their differences are at stake, these
issues, and the bodies around which they circulate, are fraught with complexity. And for good or for ill, it is precisely because these debates involve
living beings with concrete and often immediate needs that complexities
get simplified for the sake of expediency. So, in a political landscape in
which the recognition of violations too often requires one to disavow the
uniqueness of one's spirit and flesh by identifying with that which can be
seen—where police brutalities meet #BlackLivesMatter and sexual violence
meets #MeToo—how does one call for justice while simultaneously calling
attention to the precarity of a politics built on alliances of visions to come,
on futures in which our dreams and our bodies are one?

Thinkers in critical theory including Lynne Huffer, Gayatri Spivak,
Saidiya Hartman, and Karen Barad reimagine discursive limits in the tradition
of deconstructive philosophy while remaining attentive to the particularities
of embodied living. They are, in this sense of their various efforts to think
life, engaged in the ongoing negotiation of the relationship between ethics
and politics. I believe their investments in rethinking politics share an antimoralizing ethical framework that problematizes identity on the one hand
but that is grounded in manifestations of embodied difference on the other.
I view these contemporary theorists' efforts as a reflection of the tensions
of our current era; I read them as inheritors of a postmodern subjectivity
that recognizes a certain arbitrariness of worldmaking and also of a reality
in which bodies cannot simply remake their worlds as easily as they can
be theorized. It is in the tensions between the discursive and the material
that questions of ethics and politics in critical theoretical discourses of the
current moment are situated.

I turn to Luce Irigaray as a profound resource for thinking through this tension in innovative ways. From within her criticism of the phallogocentrism of Western thought and culture, I interpret her prioritization of the question of sexual difference as an effort to highlight the deleterious impacts of a way of thinking that is divorced from the psychic and social impacts of worlds constructed through not simply the exclusion of identities, but through the annihilation of bodily existences that stand in the trace of those identifications. I embrace, therefore, the extent to which Irigaray's call to think through the question of sexual difference is a call to think through an as-yet-unrealized, embodied, fleshy space and time of the othered bodies that would transform acts of thinking themselves. And the task I begin is to consider what worlds might be imagined if we engage in such fleshy thinking.

Irigaray may seem an odd choice to locate any sort of liberatory political message for the modern landscape of gender theory. Indeed, she is often left behind in conversations related to identity because her insistence on the irreducibility of sexuate difference would seem to threaten a politics of self-determined becomings, especially becomings that transcend cisbinary-gendered identities and heteronormative couplings or becomings. And though many Irigaray scholars have insisted that race and/or racialization must be considered in any philosophy of sexuate difference, her thought has been relatively insignificant for philosophies of race more broadly. Irigaray, for whom race is a secondary difference, is an easy target for critics in this regard.

As a white European woman of an educated class, Irigaray's lack of reflection about her own subject position is troubling given that she privileges sexuation uniquely as the means for thinking irreducibility, potentially recreating a totalizing philosophical position. And as George Yancy and Calvin Warren have added, an anti-Blackness undergirds her efforts to reimagine a sexuate ontology apart from metaphysics. As Warren writes in "Improper Bodies," Irigaray's unthinkable woman relies on the "abject Black Belly as the bridge to her Being."[12] Still, Irigaray remains defiant that these conversations are secondary to the question of sexuate difference; for her, they represent struggles within a symbolic realm of culture and discourse always already constructed without attentiveness to sexuate difference. Such a symbolic includes a politics that constrains our imaginations and our capacities to be in our own bodies in relation to our others; such a politics, where representation gives us a sense of being, deprives us of our becoming beyond such constructs. The challenge, for many of Irigaray's readers, has been how to bring to bear the most innovative aspects of her work into conversation with a type of political philosophy with which Irigaray wants little to do.

For some readers, Irigaray's turn to an ontology of sexuate difference may be unsatisfying, even irresponsible, insofar as it risks returning human becoming to a certain materiality (albeit beyond metaphysical distinctions) of the body and nature.[13] In this regard, her work is somewhat at odds with a freedom of bodily self-determination. And as previously mentioned, Irigaray no doubt exercises a certain level of privilege as a white European woman of a comfortable class, a condition that allows her to move about unaware of the ways certain of her embodied differences (like whiteness) don't actually matter (as in become relevant) because they transcend matter. It is worth remembering, however, that having experienced being in the world as a woman/other, Irigaray has not been immune to the oppressive effects of regimes of power grounded in differentiation through reduction and exclusion. Irigaray has been denied the adoration and accolades of ceremony received by many of her male contemporaries, including Jacques Derrida.

As I see it, conversations surrounding identity require a shift in order to attend to the materialities of living, as well as to the transcendence of our flesh. I therefore attempt to consider the tensions between a politics that prioritizes the capacity of discourse to create the world on the one hand, and on the other, an ethics of embodiedness that resists the transcendence afforded discourse. While recognizing the role of categories, of identity, of taxonomies even, in becoming subjects, I insist that, from an ethical perspective, putting our stock in either proliferation or negation does not radically remake the binaries that impede relational ways of being with others. Rather than thinking sex and gender as either discrete or synonymous categories, Irigaray's work on sexual/sexuate difference frames subjectivity as a process of becoming in relation to the sociosymbolic order, a process in which self-recognition is always limited in relation to that which is recognizable. For Irigaray, self-recognition does not happen within the constructs of sexuality or of discourses of sex or gender. Self-recognition happens through an embodied experience of living in relation to one's own flesh as a possibility for being with others.

For me, turning to Irigaray's work is an opportunity to register becoming as an embodied tension of discursive possibility—that is, to think the relationship between materiality and discursivity without prioritizing either one or the other. Through (what is intended to be) a provocatively generous reading of Irigaray's work, I frame the becoming of sexed and raced subjects in relation to the embodied tension between the imagined and the real, at the limits between experience and that which is recognized. I am interested not in naming the self-recognition as sexed, raced, or even sexuate but rather in the power of Irigaray's notion of sexuation to remind us that there is no living in this world without being in our bodies as they constantly change and create new spaces for being in relation to others, spaces for encountering beyond our being through our becomings. This space, where identities are exploded in an instant that is simultaneously a suspension of the experience of time and space, is a space of embodied desire.

To be clear, I am not critiquing the sexuate by resubmitting it to a particular difference between an idea of men and women—a move that would return us to a cisbinary construct for thinking the sexuate. And, in defense of Irigaray, I think that if we truly appreciate the "at least twoness" of her notion of sexuation, the particularities that constitute sexuate becoming are not binary.[14] This book is not invested in either defending or criticizing the implications of Irigaray's sexuate philosophy for leftist politics—which have been thoroughly critiqued—in order to make her fit within my own politics. I am quite aware of where my own politics and the idealism and privilege of Irigaray's philosophy diverge. As such, I prioritize close readings of her work that are faithful to what I retrieve as the most radical dimensions of her thought—readings that refuse many of the categories of critique to which Irigaray's work is often subjected.

I locate in Irigaray's thought the fleshiness of an antimetaphysical materiality fundamental to a desire that is itself a possibility of being *in* and *with* radical transcendence. This, I argue, engenders a desire capable of reimagining worldmaking, of refounding a "politics" that might be rooted in individuations beyond identity. From these efforts, my work attempts to imagine the possibilities of what it would mean to think through the radical desire that Irigaray's sexuate portends. Irigaray's invocations of lips, mucous, porosity, openings, and touchings are not evocations for carnal titillation. Nor are her occasional seemingly circular logic and speculative thinking a rapture of the mind, in some eros of a different, disembodied order. I would venture that as Irigaray sees it, her writing elicits this desire because she writes through the space of her own sexuate becoming. Hers is a writing in and through a certain continued awareness of oneself as always in relation to the world and all its others, uniquely, in the particularity of one's flesh.

Irigaray's fleshy invocations cease operating within the constructs that constrain our politics not because of the absolute discursivity of bodies but because of the fleshiness of relations that desire ignites, and the lips gesture toward this aim. Her controversial invocations of the lips in particular, especially in her early work, occupy the tension between discourse and materiality that she struggles to reimagine. Going back to this foundation is, I think, a starting point for informing an onto-ethico-political way of becoming and living and thinking that can contribute to the conversations in critical theory today. Lips are therefore my point of entry for thinking through desire in Irigaray.

Both individualism on the one hand and a universalism on the other serve different extremes of a binary logic that impinges upon freedom and, relatedly, locates a promise of freedom in representation rather than in the embodiedness of relations. By arguing for a radical return to Irigarayan desire as a source for reimagining materiality and discourse toward a nonbinary ethic of relational becoming, *Desire* makes a decisive intervention into impasses of gender, sexual, and racial identity that continue to confound contemporary discourse and politics, both of which often lean too heavily on either ontological or intersectional arguments. The theory of desire I propose in contrast to these identitarian impasses is a possibility of becoming in the world with others apart from the binaries of nature/culture, matter/spirit, male/female, interior/exterior—those binaries that limit the dynamism of living.

In *Writing Beyond Race*, the late bell hooks writes, "Living in dominator culture we are often trapped by language that imprisons us in binaries, either/or options that will not let us claim all the bits and pieces of ourselves, our hearts, especially the pieces that do not fit neat categories."[15] hooks's decision not to capitalize her pen name was a rejection of the individualism that feeds a logic of identity; it was and is a call to solidarity through collective, shared work beyond an investment in identities informed by the logic of a phallocentric and anti-Black discourse. Here, I embark on a disruptive reimagining of the crisis of representation precisely because I do not take the proliferation of categories that have led to our current cultural impasse as a writ-large win for progressive ideas about life; proliferation of identifications does not empty taxonomies of the consequences they have on the ground for real bodies. At a time when it seems that choosing sides feeds the logic of "dominator culture," I insist that Irigaray's work offers a critical intervention not because she resolves the tensions between bodies and discourse in relation to how we live and imagine our worlds, but because she gives us pause, and suspends materiality with thought in the realm of eros of real and imagined pasts, presents, and futures.

Desire and Method: The Critic and the Theorist

Hortense Spillers, one of the most impactful thinkers in critical theories of psychoanalysis and race, opens her essay "Critical Theory in a Time of Crisis" by delineating two separate foci of early critical theory: on the one hand, methodological emphases on literary critical practices of close reading; on the other, broader theoretical engagements with the philosophical canon. Referencing Martin Jay's *The Dialectical Imagination*, Spillers argues that, in attempting to respond to the entangled social, political, and intellectual dimensions of a particular time, critical theory incorporates practices of analysis by the "critic" and reflection by the "theorist."

Spillers insists, however, that the academy has lost touch with this "desire" of early critical theory:

> In our work today, we have not only abandoned the powerful engines of *criticism*, having reified *theory* as the imagined pure locus of a writerly practice, but we've abrogated from any desire, it seems to me, for a vantage point onto a larger sociality that shapes our becoming. These lapses suggest, quite frankly, that the critical theoretical ferment of the 1970s to the beginning of the new millennium boils down to a standard operating procedure that provokes text after text of textual production, but entirely predictable in the moves it makes, the conclusions it draws.[16]

Spillers's warning about textual production and its relation to administrative "bean counting" in the academy brings to mind Foucault's critique of the proliferation of discourses about Victorian sexuality as producing increasingly ahistorical and disembodied limits for regulating bodies and pleasures, but with a capitalist biopower bent. To what extent has theory lost touch with a desire for engagement in the world that acknowledges one's responsibility in, with, and for living with others in the making of worlds?

Though Spillers, in this brief essay, refers to desire almost in passing, it is hard to read her invocation as a purely semantic choice. Spillers's use of the term *desire* in relation to *abrogated* (which invokes an evasion of ethical responsibility) and her reference to "sociality that shapes our becoming" (which invokes the psychoanalytic) suggest that the problem of critical theory lies in its abandonment of the radical ethical desire capable of imagining new worlds. As poet/theorist/classicist Anne Carson suggests in her essay *Eros the Bittersweet*, "In any act of thinking, the mind must reach across this space between known and unknown, linking one to the other but also keeping visible to difference. It is an erotic space."[17] I take Carson's comment that this space of thinking is erotic as a gesture to the materiality of desire, its embeddedness in the living and dying of life in relation to others. In the preface to his book on desire in Carson, *Reach without Grasping*, Louis Ruprecht Jr. writes that for Carson, "Hands, not just minds, reach and grasp."[18] I would add that for Irigaray, it is not hands, but the self-touching of lips, wombs, eyelids, and so on, that constitutes a movement toward the other through the self as the ground of what we might call the erotic, thinking of/in/through desire—where thought emanates from the alterity of our irreducible materialities (always touching) to make space for and with the other. But more on this later.

As to the radical desire suggested by Spillers, and Carson's erotic bittersweet of eros that reaches without grasping, such desire demands a willingness to open oneself up to the ambiguity (to borrow from Beauvoir) or perhaps the tragedy of desire in all its transcendence, in all its risk and its possibility. If engaging desire *without* desire has rendered desire a construct, Irigaray's work, which overflows with a "sweetbitter" erotic reaching-without-grasping (to channel Carson) approach to thinking, offers an alternative to the cold calculus of desireless critique or the desireless theory of egoistic projection. I hope that my efforts attest to the radical space of desire that thinking about desire demands—a work about desire that cultivates desire.

Heeding the gauntlet Spillers throws down, to engender a space for desire in thinking about desire, I attempt to bring together discourses of contemporary significance through practices of critique and theoretical reflection; its focus is at once narrow, and yet its appeals at times quite broad. Here, desire is cultivated through the entanglements with the philosophical, psychoanalytic, religious, literary, and political efforts to imagine ethical ways of being in the world with others. Emphasizing the role of the critic, I engage Irigaray's work through close readings, almost exegetical at times, to establish a theory of desire reflective of her uniquely speculative project. All the while, prioritizing the role of theorist, I reflect on broader ambitions by interweaving avenues of her project as they relate to embodiment and questions of identity in contemporary conversations in religious studies, queer and trans* theory, decolonial thought, philosophies of race, and posthuman thought.

As my brief time spent with Irigaray at a colloquium she held during March 2023 has convinced me, I am treading water by all accounts in dangerous seas. I anticipate that Irigaray would argue that many of these contemporary identifications I engage exist within a construct that participates in a masculine logic to which her sexuate ontology cannot be submitted. As such, my effort to place her work into conversation with these discourses might seem to her unfaithful at worst or pointless at best. Still, I persist because Irigaray's work has long taken seriously the complexities of living that remain driving points of contention in critical-theory discussions about materiality and ontology today. Living, for Irigaray, is embodied living in accordance with one's "natural" sexuate being such that one is always living in relation to one's self and others through desire. She prioritizes individuation and particularity rather than singularity (which devolves into neutral universals) as necessary to maintaining desire. My return to Irigaray, however, is neither a full-throated embrace of her conception of living, nor is it a rejection of her sexuate ontology. I want to locate a position that is truly *heteros* in the sense that Irigaray's reading of the Greek middle voice evokes—that is, a middle way of an altogether different kind beyond binary oppositions.[19] As a critic and theorist, I offer a reading of Irigaray that is at once charitable and also provocative, careful, and ethical in its effort to transform the implications of her work. Moreover, I read Irigaray herself as a critic and theorist (in the spirit of Spillers's description)—one whose thought about difference was shaped primarily through engagements with the political, social, and academic churnings of the twenty-first and late twentieth centuries, especially the 1960s and 1970s and their repercussions in the early 1980s and beyond. Irigaray's investment in deconstructive undoings of discourses of psychoanalysis, of metaphysics, of religion, and of ethics, I cautiously suggest, partakes in what Spillers refers to as the "interpenetrative" work of the critic and theorist.

Although Irigaray has lamented the extent to which readers often overlook her more recent work, I have decided nonetheless to prioritize Irigaray's earlier thought, where I locate greater nuance in her struggles that help ground her more recent and sometimes quite enigmatic writings. I would note, however, that her 2021 *Sharing the Fire* and her 2024 *The Mediation of Touch*, the latter of which I began reading during final revisions of this book, have in many ways validated my initial sense that Irigaray, first and foremost, is a writer of desire. Desire is a useful concept for Irigaray because it situates the multiplicity of pleasures (embodied for her in female sexuality) in relation to the generativity and creativity of life. Irigaray aims to reimagine human relations—as well as relations between humans, animals, and the environment—in terms of sharing in the becoming of self and world. Desire constitutes a thread that runs throughout Irigaray's efforts to reimagine these relations, from early entrenchments with eros in its philosophical and psychoanalytic implications for subjectivity (as in *Speculum of the Other Woman* and *An Ethics of Sexual Difference*) to later works on the need for love of self and other as necessary for cultivating more ethical and democratic worlds (such as *The Way of Love, Sharing the World*). Bracketing the significance of these different representations of desire in Irigaray's work, the overall character of desire in her thought extends from her notion of sexuate difference.

I interpret Irigaray's sexuate difference as naming a materiality of radical alterity, beyond discourse and beyond the language of causality and temporalities of metaphysics. This notion of sexuate expresses a proximity of material relations beyond reductions in discourse. Read through the question of sexuate difference, desire becomes a relation of indeterminacy, ambiguity, and uncertainty, that disrupts the self-sameness of subjectivity and therein the economic orientation toward difference. And herein lies what I hope is less a provocation and more a gesture as critic and theorist: I perceive the need to engage the question of politics *in relation to* the question of a radical ethical desire (like that of the sexuate) rather than *in spite of* it. In order to offer a meaningful intervention in what might be perceived as an impasse, I turn to the tensions between a politics of recognition and a sexuate ontology as questions of the relationship of discourse to materiality.

By prioritizing the role of desire in Irigaray's work, I locate a mode of relation that is embodied in ways that reimagine materiality beyond the limitations of discourse. And, insofar as essentialism must be recognized as a problem of reducing the body to a particular discourse, a materiality reimagined in relation to desire would be irreducible and infinitely differential in its particularity. Desire, like that risky, even tragic desire Irigaray elicits in her engagements with philosophical ideas like eros and wonder, and through the visceral, fleshy discourse of touching lips, is the possibility of becoming in the world with others apart from the binaries of nature/culture, matter/spirit, male/female, interior/exterior that limit the dynamism of living. Accepting the demand of Spillers's call to hold together the critic and theorist, and in a nod to Irigaray's interrogation of and reimagination of pleasure apart from psychoanalytic associations of female *jouissance* with passivity presumed by a phallic/polar/singular notion of desire, I intend to retheorize the space of desire as the horizon of worldmaking, of reimagining the intimacy of interconnections—beyond humanist constructions of the human, the animal, the vegetal, beyond the metaphysical constructions of the immanent and the transcendent.

Structure and an Outline of the Book

By placing Irigaray's notion of sexuate difference in relation to current political and theoretical contestations of sexed, raced, and otherwise classified bodies, this book argues for a vision of desire that reimagines the embodied space of materiality in relation to the discursive, but apart from its reduction to an essentialist-constructivist binary. To achieve this aim, *Desire* embraces the roles of both the critic and the theorist, using close readings to provide a nuanced understanding of desire in relation to discursivity and materiality and to theorize how such desire might reframe processes of identification and disrupt identity.

Chapter 1, "The Anatomy of Desire," offers an imminent reading of Irigaray, in which I situate my interpretation of desire in her work in relation to broader currents and concepts that permeate her œuvre. This chapter frames Irigaray's notion of desire in relation to her interventions in philosophy and psychoanalysis, prioritizing Irigaray's figure of lips as reimagining immanence and transcendence together through the question of sexuate difference. The chapter explores the extent to which Irigaray's lips offer a new ethical desire by way of sexuate difference—a remedy to the annihilation of difference that plagues both the ethics of Emmanuel Levinas and the linguistic psychoanalysis of Jacques Lacan.

Lips provide a way of desiring differently because they figure a relation to difference that is never absorbed into oneness. They are always two, never one. And in this twoness, the lips disrupt the phallocentrism of desire that drives Lacan's reading of the subject who becomes in relation to the symbolic order. The lips note a desire that was never singular, such that the relation to the symbolic order, including the order of thinking, would be one of openness to difference rather than reduction to sameness—it would be a mode of relational desire, not selfsame desire. Furthermore, these lips will expose Levinas's use of sexual difference to posit transcendence as a disembodied philosophical exercise that ultimately occludes difference and resubmits both the alterity of God and of woman to masculine desire.

Insofar as sexual difference frames a relationship between materiality and discourse that embraces alterity in the borders where bodies touch themselves and others, I argue that Irigaray provides a structure for thinking about embodied desire as the foundation for becoming in and through alterity. She probes the material-discursive tension in the becoming of woman in a way that is useful for thinking of other othered bodies struggling to live in a world where the very grammar of "being" is founded on their lesser, outside, or even nonbeing.

To begin articulating Irigarayan desire as an embodiedness of radical alterity that disrupts prevailing notions of transcendence and materiality, chapter 2, "The 'Matter' of Lips: Incarnating the Transcendence of Desire," explores Irigaray's efforts to "speak" feminine desire through the language of lips and the extent to which the lips are the occasion to reimagine the verticality of transcendence with the horizontality of immanence. Lips constitute a morphology of self-touching, a desire of and through space and time reimagined through the relationality of difference. Lips figure this desire without instrumentalizing it in some crude reduction of pleasure to a particular outcome; lips never speak exclusively excess on the one hand or sameness on the other. Within this continuous saying and unsaying of feminine desire, lips evoke a territory at the limits of philosophy and critique. It is in this space that religious language becomes useful for Irigaray and her readers. Specifically, Irigaray's intermingling of lips in relation to the Christian Incarnation becomes an opportunity to explore the morpho-logic of lips by attending to the unique materiality and alterity that emerges as part of her efforts to express the radical transcendence of sexuate desire.

By holding together Irigaray's play on the Christian mystical associations of vaginal imagery with the wounds of Christ in *Speculum*, with the performativity of the lips in *This Sex Which Is Not one*, and Irigaray's entwining of lips with the Incarnation in *An Ethics of Sexual Difference*, I interpret Irigaray as pressuring the slippage between the materiality associated with immanence and the transcendence associated with logos to summon a new space-time of sexual difference—an embodied temporality of desire. I conclude the chapter by suggesting that in their self-touching that is open, lips present a self-affection and other affection in which the particularity of fleshes, in their irreducible differences, is the condition of desire, as well as the occasion for approaching transcendence. Lips, I insist, can mark a radically material-discursive temporality beyond being and nonbeing—and rethinking sexual difference in relation to an embodied temporality of desire is an important move in connecting Irigaray's call for a new imaginary to radical constructive and/or operational projects in queer theory, decolonial theory, and critical race theory, projects that challenge the metaphysics of promise underwriting the present sufferings of BIPOC, colonized, and queer bodies. Such expansion of Irigaray's thought opens space for thinking of desiring flesh beyond sex and gender and pushes back on the slippage in Irigaray's own work between sexuate difference and a "nature" attributed to male and female bodies that makes that space less hospitable for thinking about the ways other bodies relate to the symbolic realm.

Following chapters 1 and 2, the book proceeds by placing the above notion of a multiple, nonassimilative, ethical desire of becoming in conversation with queer theory, decolonial thought, philosophies of race, and new materialism, using Irigaray to move beyond the limitations of her own work. Here, I am both balancing my insistence that Irigaray's sexuate is ontological and thus irreducible to a cisbinary depiction of bodies and acknowledging that Irigaray appeals to a natural order as one in which we are all born of two who are different. To consider the potential of radically disruptive desire that the materiality and alterity of the lips as a figure of desire evoke, I put forward a phenomenology of desire that posits alterity as an erotic touching beyond the limits of both being and its alternative by negation, nonbeing. It is within this space of radical touching beyond contradiction that the desire capable of sustaining a new mode of relation, and therein a new way of perceiving ourselves and the world, would be possible. Subsequent chapters therefore push Irigaray's work into conversation with those who have similarly challenged the radical alienation of othered bodies who cannot account for the desires of their becoming within the prevailing symbolic order. Specifically, chapters 3 through 5 read structural (not lived) similarities between feminine, colonized, Black, and queer bodies with regard to the alienation of desire in the becoming of subjects. Considering the potential of Irigarayan desire to disrupt metaphysical distinctions that undergird the material-discursive binary, these chapters suggest that when read in relation to the demands of queer life, decolonial life, and Black life, desire (as ontological) rather than politics could be a better category for thinking about and resisting the limits of thinking about being. Desire as a relation in alterity radically reframes the impasses generated by a sociality of differences that materialize in and through discourse.

For example, Chapter 3, "Queer Lips, Queer Wombs, and the Temporality of Desire," frames tensions between queer theory and feminist theory in terms of broader questions about the relationship between materiality

and discourse as constrained by a discourse that cannot account for differences. I turn to Judith Butler's direct engagement with Irigaray's language
of lips and wombs to think through sexuate matter. In their introduction of
"Bodies that Matter," Butler examines Irigaray's understanding of matter in
order to argue that the materialization of difference is manifested through a
heterosexual regime, dependent on sexuality and disciplined performances of
self-regulation, whose discourses create the body as a discursive concept—not
a thing.[20] Butler differentiates Irigaray's depictions of the lips and womb
respectively, arguing that while Irigaray does in fact disrupt the transcendent
value afforded form in Platonic thought, her resistance to penetrative desire
remains beholden to a heterosexist specter of desire (where penetration is
always seen as heterosexual penetration) that limits the potential of matter
to disrupt the social order.

Registering criticisms of the heterosexism found in Irigaray's work, and
also taking seriously antisocial queer theoretical critiques of social recognition,
I differentiate Irigaray's notion of desire from sexuality and rethink the lips
and the womb as queer spaces that disrupt the dichotomies of performativity
and body. Drawing on and differentiating from Lynne Huffer's queer-feminist
erotic ethics, as well as José Esteban Muñoz's queer practices of desire, I
register assertions that Irigaray's work is heteronormative and transphobic
in order then to consider the most promising dimension of her work: its
focus on embodied desires as the generative source of an other imaginary.
Inspired by Huffer and by Maggie Nelson's reference to Irigaray's lips in *The
Argonauts* (2015), chapter 3 interprets Irigaray's mimetic employment of lips
as fleshy spaces of disruptive desire that challenge the ethics of obligation
and the politics of autonomy that constrain queer and transgender politics.
I therefore turn attention to the performative potential of lips to usher in a
queer temporality—to establish a space-time where agency and responsibility
are redefined through the disidentifying materiality and alterity of desire. [21]

I continue to explore the relevance of Irigarayan desire for the tensions
between discourse and materiality in contemporary questions of politics and
justice in chapter 4, "Decolonizing Desire: Reading Spivak's Postcolonial
Echo and the Problem of Resistance." This chapter establishes the fact
that Irigaray's notion of desire remains entrenched in psychoanalytic and
philosophical frameworks that not only have alienated women from their
desires but also have effaced the differences of other beings whose desires are
unrepresentable within the logic of a phallic symbolic. In a nod to the critic,
this chapter analyzes Irigaray's linguistic psychoanalysis in relation to Gayatri
Spivak's decolonial thought. Through a reading of Spivak's decolonizing

interpretation of Echo in Ovid's *Metamorphosis,* I describe Spivak's double bind, that precarious position of theorizing and living resistance from a space of radical displacement from the political, social, and cultural life of empire, and from the deeper psychic consequences of ontological violence at play in such displacement. I draw on my exploration of Irigarayan desire to evaluate the question of desire in Spivak's reading of the double bind of the subaltern subject. Desire, I argue, has the potential to decolonize what seems like an untenable, unthinkable position of the double bind that does not view the ontological labor of resistance in terms of lack. Spivak and Irigaray share a sense of the potential of language to expose cracks in (respectively) a colonizing or phallocentric symbolic, and desire is the force that exposes such cracks and opens space for difference.

Whereas colonialism and its extended epistemological imperialism (masked as neutrality) perpetuate subjectivities based on narratives of mastery, desire has the potential to reimagine becoming through a space of difference that tells an/other story. Decolonizing critiques of ontology (by Julietta Singh and Zaynab Shahar), read alongside appeals to affect (made by Sara Ahmed), resonate with the extradiscursive materiality of Irigarayan desire. In its embodiedness, its ambiguity, and its dynamism, I argue that desire offers a decolonizing force that does not require the recognition of a selfsame discourse in order to constitute an alternative "resistance" to the colonizing logic of sameness. By thinking of desire as a materiality of alterity, I conclude the chapter by exploring desire as a decolonizing, nontotalizing force of the double bind, but one that does not render the ontological labor of resistance a lack.

It is precisely this question of lack and the potential of Irigarayan desire as generated through the becoming of those beyond being (as conceptualized within the masculine symbolic) that fuels the engagement with Afropessimism and the need to think a relationality *beyond* lack. As chapter 5, "Desire beyond (Non)Being: Toward a Black Feminist Labial Logic," suggests, there has been significant crosspollination among religious studies, critical race theory, and queer theory, particularly as it relates to tensions between ethics and politics. The predicament is how to argue on behalf of underrepresented persons without recapitulating the norms and institutions of a recognition based in sameness that constitutes an underrepresented status. Or more acutely, as Jared Sexton writes, "The question is how to theorize and to politicize violence in the midst of violence, to indicate the wetness of water while being submerged in it."[22]

In light of the tensions that thinking subjectivity as recognition poses, scholarship in philosophies of race has increasingly focused on experience and living over identity, and here the question of desire as a framework for imagining the experience of raced subject positions offers promise for resisting anti-Black violence. Fred Moten, for instance, ends his essay on his distinct phenomenology of "Black mysticism" by suggesting that the alternative space between the Being of white civil society and the nonbeing of its alienated other is a space of eros.[23] In the Afropessimist discourse of Frank Wilderson III, anti-Black violence—not primarily masculine desire—is the very ground of the symbolic through which subjects are formed.[24] Indeed, both race and sexual difference present us with conceptual and ethical challenges insofar as they pose questions about the relationship between the discursive realm of the symbolic and the material existence of bodies, past, present, and future.

Chapter 5 examines the way different epistemological positions hinge on the ontological question of desire. Without analogizing a concept of Black life and gendered life, this chapter holds the concerns and tensions of intersectional analysis together with ontology by focusing on the eros of material-discursive tension that constitutes lived experience. Attention to desire is an attention to the volatility of bodies, a volatility that is constitutive of a world that renders those bodies especially vulnerable. This attentiveness is also an awakening of and to the fleshiness of ethics—a *touching* that refuses identity as sameness, in the space of a hold that refuses Blackness as social death.

What is needed for ethics is a concept of desire not as lack, but as an eros of an altogether different order. Responding to LeRhonda Manigault-Bryant's interrogation of eros as a category radical enough for Black living, I return to the significance of embodied alterity as a morphology—a dynamic, fleshy logic of relation that is rooted not in the touch of the other but in the self-touching that constitutes one's becoming. I therefore conclude by engaging Amber Jamilla Musser's reading of Irigaray's lips to address the antagonism of psychoanalysis to Black women's sexuality and to reimagine the radicality of a Black labial logic of touching in relation to Saidiya Hartman's historical reimaginings of archives as a thinking through desire that disrupts the realm of visibility (and the anti-Black metaphysics of presence upon which that realm lies). Hartman's work extends Irigaray's efforts to reimagine the materiality of alterity, but in a way that holds the ontological and intersectional demands together for the twenty-first century—toward an eros of the unthought, in a labial logic of Black women's desires, beyond the presence and absence of the archives that delimit the real.

Though we cannot resolve the tensions between ethics and politics, we must no less face them by prioritizing the cultivation of desire between us as an always at least two that we embody plurally. I do not think that a philosophy of imagining a different world is a substitute for action. Nor do I think that proliferating categories of identity has proven to break any systems of identitarian politics. Bracketing my subtle disagreement with philosopher Emily Anne Parker's reading of Irigaray's sexuate difference as engendering a two-sex model of the human, I endorse her emphasis on the decentering of the human without abnegating human responsibility as critical for thinking the future.[25] A more nuanced approach to the body, and I would add to materiality more broadly, is needed, in order to stop reinforcing the same impasses.

Life today faces the effects of a globally warmer planet that will likely produce increasingly hostile environments, which will in turn lead to increased competition for resources and lay bare our societal entanglements with a natural world that does not need us, as well as the beings whose survival is now intertwined with our own. How do beings live in an entangled, dying world? Can there be an onto-ethics of an entangled *anthropos* that thinks the specificity and contingency of living and of responding? Despite tensions between Irigaray's work and the discourses of posthumanism and new materialism, chapter 6, "Horizons of Touch: Desire and a Reimagined Anthropos," reads the sexuate in Irigaray as an important reminder that while thinking beyond the human is important, a post-Anthropocene might require a new theory of the anthropos that takes seriously both the irreducible difference that conditions life as well as the desire that makes living possible.

While androcentric and anthropocentric conceptions of embodiment have mapped/framed the limits of existence in human terms at the expense of nonhuman others, I consider theories of touching that contest normative notions of materiality to deterritorialize such mappings. Modifying Rosi Braidotti's emphasis on sexual difference as the ever-expansive space for thinking through the semiotic-material tension in relation to feminist theories of new materialism, I contend that desire animates and ensures difference and therefore enables a material-transcendental relation to remain "touching" (a proximity that is at once a meeting and an interval) in and through difference. Critically reading Irigaray's lips in relation to Karen Barad's theory of touching, I argue that lips can articulate a robust concept of material becomings made possible through a theory of the touching of/in/through desire. Holding together reimagined notions of both touch (vis-à-vis Barad) and desire (vis-à-vis Irigaray), relationality refuses the anthropocentrism (white and phallic) nature/culture distinction and therein opens space for embodied relations in and with all others, at once beyond the human and in the midst of the specificities of human becomings. The chapter therefore concludes by rethinking the possibility of "touching desire" for an ethical relationality beyond notions of becoming as either absolute freedom or obligation, beyond guilt or innocence, beyond presence and absence, beyond the real and the imagined. This ethical relation entails persistence in the ambiguity of desire as a perpetual touching that never grasps, where the gap between at least two is the space of perpetual transformations.

Receiving and Reciprocating with Irigaray

In his essay honoring the work of Emmanuel Levinas, "At This Very Moment in This Work Here I Am,"[26] Jacques Derrida implies that the ethical "gift" of Levinas's legacy was an imperative to refuse the return to sameness and suggests that the ethical response to a gift is to refuse to give back or return anything to the giver. By Derrida's reading, Levinas's act of radical generosity places one under an obligation to respond with equally radical generosity—generosity that in that very radicality may not at first feel so generous. So, instead of uncritically praising Levinas, Derrida composed an essay that, in part, critiqued his colleague's notion of the Saying of the Wholly Other, by highlighting that notion's forgetting of sexual difference. Derrida's homage *was* that act of engaging in critique and expanding Levinas's philosophy in new directions—rather than simply submitting to the limits of Levinas's fallible thought world.

Derrida signaled his praise of and sense of obligation to the thought of Levinas, while and *by* pointing out the ways in which that thought had failed to address or anticipate certain matters. In this spirit, I lift up the work of Luce Irigaray as a resource just as critical now as it ever was—and make that offering partially by pointing out where Irigaray's work creates space beyond the limits of her own perceptions and perspectives. In doing so, I show how contemporary questions and circumstances, related especially to ideas about race, gender, and sexuality have made fruitful use of her thought and also broaden that thought by critiquing it. But I show as well how her work continues to provide profound tools for addressing the present moment—a polarized moment in need of reminders that no school of thought or assertion of identity is ever complete or without fault—and that it is often in exploring what is missing or misguided that we are able to come to a richer vision of moving forward. I attempt therein to engage in a praxis of desire as a labial logic that engages without reducing Irigaray or other interlocutors to homogenize their differences in service of my aims.

Reading the limits of Irigaray's philosophical explorations of an irreducible "sexuate" difference as a radical fleshy horizon, I hope this book pushes Irigaray's work beyond her normal audience, creating space for thinking about her work in relation to current questions of identity that demand consideration by critical theory—while also providing critical theory with the means of remaining in touch with that desire that Hortense Spillers insists is its lifeblood and is crucial to maintaining "a vantage point onto a larger sociality that shapes our becoming."[27]

My turn to the limits of Irigaray's work includes a recognition of the potential violence that can emerge through the vulnerability of desire and an acknowledgment of the danger of this project for all those bodies whose vulnerabilities become an occasion for theorizing. But I contend that in Irigaray's work, lips, for example, are the possibility of self-touching, of self-becoming in and through desire. Lips are neither graves nor tombs where desire is a movement/will to death; lips have the potential to gesture to the slave-ship hold—a space beyond being and nonbeing, an embodied space that refuses representations of Blackness or the feminine that constitute the embalming of vulnerable bodies upon which white supremacist and patriarchal civil societies and their idols are erected.

Moving with to move beyond Irigaray, I want put forward an erotic ethic of alterity in which lived bodies, whose flesh signals a deep vulnerability/volatility in relation to the sociosymbolic order, offer a phenomenology of flesh where desire is beyond wounding or pleasure; theirs is a space of wonder that touches and ruptures and must remain without suture in order to be ethical. Thinking through sexual difference may not save us as Irigaray says it will—but thinking through sexuate/sexual difference might offer a phenomenology of embodied becoming (where the wound of desire is not erased or healed but perpetually open and closed, welcoming and touching) that might inform an ethic of desire beyond discursive notions of sexual difference.

Chapter 1

The Anatomy of Desire

Toward a Morphology of Lips

Prevailing sociopolitical divisions, including renewed nationalism throughout the geopolitical landscape, have been intensified by myriad developments in artificial intelligence that undermine some of the most common sense of explanations about what makes us human. Despite the impacts of competition for resources and class conflict on these matters, such are not reducible to a neo-Marxist historical analysis. The questions we face are deeply philosophical, ethical—I would add psychical and religious—in their significance. And in this regard, when attempting to determine how to confront the realities of our world, I find that Irigaray's philosophy still has much to offer: the beginnings of a model of thinking, relating, and living otherwise in a "culture" of selfsameness.

As discussed in the introduction, Irigaray may not be the most obvious choice for a radical reimagining of living beyond identity that doesn't devolve into a neoconservative ideological purity. In one of the most oft-quoted lines from *Ethics*, she writes, "Sexual difference is probably the issue in our time which could be our 'salvation' if we thought it through."[1] Recalling Heidegger, though without acknowledging the problematics his politics poses to the language of salvation, Irigaray's suggestion that thinking through the question of sexual difference was the question of the age seemed directly at odds with prominent liberal feminist efforts in the 1960s and 1970s to articulate a politics of equality and sameness.

Still, to engage the questions of identity and difference that dominate moralizing discourses in contemporary ethics and politics, I turn to Irigarayan desire as a model for refusing the metaphysical distinctions that keep us in semantic knots when it comes to discussing the relationship between discourse and materiality. I argue that Irigaray's notion of desire is the source for her disruption of a metaphysical opposition between discourse and matter. In later chapters, I confront the potential limits of Irigaray's reliance on sexuate difference as a starting point for engaging questions of ethics and politics today. But in order to explain those limits without simply submitting Irigaray's work to the logic of opposition that she wants to overturn, and in order to establish the theoretical framework for the materiality and alterity of desire that I seek to develop, I begin by explaining why such a radical reading beyond Irigaray is possible because of Irigaray. I therefore situate Irigaray within her intellectual milieu: the ethical turn in French phenomenology and the linguistic turn in psychoanalysis. The point of this framing is to promote a nuanced interpretation of Irigaray's notion of the materiality and alterity of sexual difference (or sexuatedness) that engenders a relation of desire—one that would be capable of generating a critical dialogical partner with contemporary theoretical currents surrounding identity and difference taken up in subsequent chapters.

How does Irigaray's work on sexual difference remain relevant to contemporary questions about the ethical and political dimensions of identity, especially when identity is equated with unlimited individual autonomy? Insofar as I read ethics and politics as concerns of relation and recognition entwined with questions of discursivity and materiality, I locate in Irigaray's efforts to deconstruct metaphysics through the work of her thinking and writing as an innovative starting point for philosophy itself as an ethical and embodied praxis.

Decades before new materialism had been dubbed as such, Irigaray conceived of a certain bodily materiality that actively resisted the prioritization of discourse in ways that ran afoul of social constructivist moves dominating Anglo-American feminism in the late twentieth century—while also refusing charges of essentialism. Despite her sustained engagement with language, which was also indicative of the linguistic turn in continental thought, Irigaray has maintained that the sexuate is corporeal. Indeed, her criticism of the transcendence of discourse was at once a move both to disrupt modern assumptions that cemented the feminine as woman and also to critique postmodern appeals to a certain arbitrariness of discourse that could leave us floating in yet another construction. Because her challenge to the transcendence of discourse was also a challenge to masculine constructions of materiality, her "re"-turn to materiality is a return to an embodiedness, an enfleshedness that cannot be the matter of political, scientific, religious, or philosophical discourses that have brought us to this impasse.

Nor is Irigaray's notion of materiality simply an excess of discourse, its residue, or its gap. For Irigaray, the materiality that must be reimagined is prior to discourse. Note that this language of priority, which gives way in Irigaray's later work to her appeals to nature, has rendered Irigaray susceptible to criticisms that her turns to bodily language and embodiment, and to the sexuate couple, reinscribe women within essentialist/determinate linkages to matter. However, when read in relation to the ways Irigaray's references to bodiliness aim to critique metaphysics and reimagine space and time, such a notion of priority should not be trapped within a linear notion of temporality.

Lips are a primary example of this logic that disrupts materiality. Lips figure a materiality of alterity made possible through relation between at least two, co-arising in and through the dynamism of life. I contend that desire, figured by and through lips, persists in a plurality that Irigaray's overemphasis on the sexuate couple (and by extension the copula in language) abandons. Cultivating the materiality and intimacy of thought that the labial logic of these lips portend leads to a desire that is ethical in its unwavering commitment to the radical immanence of difference and the radical difference of immanence.[2] Interrogating the discursive-bodily relation within what Irigaray deems masculine models of subjectivity in philosophy and psychoanalysis is critical to understanding prediscursive desire and how it functions in her epistemological framework. To prioritize Irigaray's reimagining of materiality and alterity apart from discursive-material entanglements that characterize the process of selfsame subjectivity, I propose reframing the question of sexual difference as a question of differing desires. This reframing gestures toward the irreducibility of difference that Irigaray's sexually different "two" are meant to accomplish. In this space where two are continuously conceived together, flesh relates to alterity in and through the ambiguity and irreducibility of those desires.

This way of reading, emphasizing the irreducibility that sexuate difference names and the space that such difference creates as a generative, open, and relational desire, calls us to reimagine both sex and desire more radically, far beyond reductions of sex to gender (or to biology) and of desire to sexuality.[3] Significantly, a radical reimagining of desire that is dialectical yet not teleological, which is how I read Irigaray, begs the question of the purpose of reimagining desire at all. I will continue to pursue this more complicated question by locating the ethical in the ambiguity of desire, looking to the incapacity of identifications—personal and systemic—to testify to the particularities of living as the cost of an unethical response to alterity.

The Ethics of Desire: Lacan, Levinas, and Sexual Difference

LACAN AND SEXUAL DIFFERENCE

To begin to understand the complexity of desire (as embodied and ethical) in Irigaray's work, one must consider the breadth and depth of her engagement with psychoanalysis, in particular its framing of ethics and subjectivity in relation to the mediation of desire in the symbolic order. In his *Essays on the Theory of Sexuality*, Freud suggests that an entire world exists beyond conscious reality. This subconscious world includes innate, libidinal drives; consciousness is characterized by the repression of these drives out of fear (broadly construed) and social pressures. Lacan, who directed the Freudian School of Psychoanalysis in Paris from 1965 to 1980, charted the possibility of thinking about women's desire within its Freudian figuration as a construction of a male libidinal economy. Two related developments in Lacan's theorizing are especially significant for my reading of Irigarayan desire and my move to transform that notion of desire beyond the limits of Irigaray's thought: (1) his premise that subjectivity occurs by entering into the linguistic world, which is the space through which one re-presents one's subconscious drives, and (2) his subsequent framing of the social order as a sociosymbolic order in which the phallus is the master signifier.

Lacan's essay "The Mirror Stage as Formative of the I Function" is foundational to his understanding of subjectivity. Following Freud's studies of human development, Lacan suggests that when a child recognizes itself apart from its other (mother), the child desires to return to that originary union. The analysis goes as follows. In the mirror stage, the mother holds the child up to a mirror, and the child sees his reflection. In seeing his reflection, he receives an image of himself and comes to know himself as autonomous and separate from the mother who is holding him. The mirror presents the child with an illusion of totality, of symmetry between what he is and what he sees. The child's separation from this mother is constitutive of his self-recognition.[4] Prior to this recognition, the child's identity and his desires are tied to his mother; after the mirror phase, the child's identity will be based in being distinct from his mother as other.[5] Separation from the mother is therefore necessary to his subject formation, and from here forward, the mother threatens the totality of his image. The mother becomes an other who reminds him that his origins are not in his self-recognition but in a fragmentation, a difference. According to Lacan, this innate drive for the child to return to its origins cannot be reified in the world, so the child enters into a symbolic realm of language through which he can express his desires apart from this mother whom he wants but cannot have. The child's drive toward autonomy, as a separation from the mother, is represented in the symbolic order (of which language is part): the symbolic operates through a system of significations that produce meaning through reductions and exclusions of differences, replicating this prediscursive desire for certainty and wholeness.

The becoming subject, like the child, enters into linguistic relations to return to a condition of wholeness, to become whole by uniting the imaginary realm of the symbolic with the Real of desire (here Lacan is drawing on Freud's understanding of the Real). Importantly, Lacan suggests there is a fundamental failure here as it relates to the question of sexual difference: sexual difference constitutes a binary that is necessarily divided such that the Real can never be whole. Insofar as representation requires a movement toward sameness, sexual difference marks an irreducible difference of desire such that sexual relation is impossible to represent. The fundamental asymmetry of the sexes means that there is no oneness to represent; therefore, representation cannot make sense of sexual difference.

Signification thus feeds on an illusion or fantasy of wholeness. It is at this point of failure of signification to represent the binary of sexual difference that the subject negotiates its relation to its desire and lack of capacity to represent that desire in full. This movement of signification to wholeness does not stop because of this failure; rather this structure of representation Lacan describes opposes meaning with desire in a way that makes the "Real" of sex opposed to relation in the symbolic. Note, he is describing the system of linguistic representation in relation to a psychoanalytic understanding of the Real. If the Real, as an obsession with the illusion of wholeness, is a negation of the truth of our irrecoverable origin in two, the symbolic is the negation of the Real. The symbolic allows for us to escape the narcissistic movement toward this illusion of wholeness. In this context, representation is a fact of communication and relation; therefore, this "failure" does not change the fact that humans communicate in and through language. Insofar as language continues to move toward wholeness, the unity to which representation is ordered is a whole that is only half of the whole. And the half of the whole to which signification returns is the masculine half. Lacan thus depicts the relationship between desire and representation as an insufficiency or lack where the subject's becoming is something that happens only through a cutting off of oneself from one's other. It is the question of the other as constituted in this symbolic that will drive Irigaray's critique.

In his 1972 through 1973 seminars, Lacan expounds upon this relationship between the symbolic realm through which one becomes a subject and sexual difference in language. Acknowledging that Freud has left aside the question of women's desire, Lacan, echoing Freud's note to Marie Bonaparte lamenting a certain failure in his own thinking, asks, "What does the woman want?" This question initiates Lacan's discussion of the impossibility of "the" woman. There is no "the" woman, Lacan suggests. He writes, "She is incorrectly called the woman, since, as I have stressed before, once the the of the woman is formulated by means of a not all, then it cannot be written."[6] Lacan's point is that the singularity (read as a universalized other, not as an irreducible particularity or uniqueness) of the "all" is an effect of the phallic function of masculine desire.[7] The "the" implies a specificity that woman's relation to the system of language makes impossible. As such, woman is always already closed off from this specificity of her desire and cannot want anything apart from this idea of woman through which her desire is signified. She is never in direct relation to her desire because her position with respect to the "all" is mediated. Positing woman as in relation to a neutral universalized Other places the desire of woman outside the symbolic realm, ultimately silencing her desire. That woman serves as a placeholder for man's Other without a place of her own is a problem that Irigaray will take up in her delineation of sexual difference.

Sexual difference is thus represented through a masculine imaginary representing a male desire that secondarizes female desire and provides an illusion of wholeness or universality of that system of representation. In this movement of return to only one-half of the binary of sexual difference, there is no oneness to represent—and yet language serves the illusion of wholeness and the promise of desire's fulfillment, or jouissance, in Oneness. Insofar as representation requires a movement toward sameness, it cannot make sense of the asymmetry of sexual difference: an irreducible difference of desire such that sexual relation is impossible to represent.

Irigaray on the Problem of Sexual Difference

As his student, Irigaray follows Lacan's reading of the subject's becoming in relation to signification and the emergence of culture.[8] But as Ewa Plonowska

Ziarek notes, "Irigaray is suspicious of the symbolic resolution of imaginary violence"—that is to say, Irigaray will argue that the symbolic does not resolve the drive toward singularity of an imaginary Whole but rather repeats it.[9] Irigaray ultimately pushes Lacan's theories by emphasizing his suggestion that the linguistic realm through which one becomes a subject is a representation of masculine desire exclusively.[10] Both the becoming of the self and the recognition of the other occur in the symbolic—so not only is becoming a mediation, but, as Irigaray argues in *Speculum*, the other is constituted through the subject's becoming.

According to Irigaray, the subject that rules the world of discourse is always a masculine subject, because the symbolic order represents phallic desire.[11] Man, Irigaray suggests, "claims to be the whole" [se pretend le tout] and "constructs his world into a closed circle" [construit son monde en cercle clos].[12] Woman, as the other to the male subject, becomes a subject through a feminine that is inscribed within this masculine discourse that represents a masculine desire for subjectivity. A concept of the feminine is therefore always already dictated or predetermined by the masculine subject's frame of reference—himself. The feminine is, by Irigaray's description, a masculine construction of woman.[13] And woman is therefore rendered a mediated or secondary subject, denied the possibility of imagining the world.[14]

But beyond mediated desire or a secondarized subject, the feminine, Irigaray argues, also serves as a placeholder or marker of woman's assimilation. The feminine, used to designate difference, conceals the reduction of woman's difference prior to any assertions about subjectivity in language. Therefore, the feminine cannot represent a difference from the masculine because the feminine always already belongs to the masculine's projection of his difference.[15] The feminine is like a weathered gravestone marking woman's annihilated difference prior to discourse. The feminine subject is not woman; woman is not a subject. The feminine subject is an object of man's construction, and woman has been erased prior to any structuring of discourse. She is a mark of sameness and the proof that identity and assimilation, not openness and wonder, have been the basis for understanding the world and human others.[16]

The Lacanian understanding of desire as the foundation for subjectivity leads Irigaray to the conclusion that a new symbolic order, a new way of knowing in language, must emerge in order for women to become subjects in accordance with their own desires. At issue, however, is not simply this need for a new symbolic realm with a new worldview and a new language for representing desire. At issue, I would argue, is the structure of desire itself within the existing model of the subject. Insofar as the Lacanian subject becomes one in himself by conquering his desire for the other (mother) whose difference has awakened him to himself, the Lacanian model structures subjectivity through the sublimation of desire for the other in which the desire the other evokes is a threat. For Irigaray, this understanding of desire in relation to subject formation is not simply the depiction of a sociolinguistic reality; it is for all persons a fundamentally unethical way of being in the world and of theorizing its future. The structure of desire itself must be rethought.

In psychoanalysis, the two (man and woman) have been conceived in terms of one desire; therefore, if two constitute the realm of ethics, the ones who make up two must be rethought in a way that guarantees their difference, their twoness. Put differently, insofar as ethics is the realm of two, psychoanalysis allows Irigaray to rethink desire between two as the foundation of ethics. Irigaray ultimately argues for a relation between desire and subjectivity in which the resolution of desire, whether through annihilation or sublimation of the hold of the other, is not the condition of becoming subject. In the place of desire for oneness, Irigaray wants desire, not the resolution/annihilation/sublimation of that desire, to be the foundation of subjectivity. The tension between subjectivity (as a question of desire for oneness) and ethics (as a question of desire between two) is evident in Irigaray's work.

Irigaray's insistence that prevailing discourses from science to theology have marginalized women in concrete ways suggests that her attempt to rethink desire also reflects a political sensibility in her work. But Irigaray sees politics as a reflection of a culture that is symptomatic of a failure to take being into account. She therefore builds on the psychoanalytic framing of presymbolic desire to posit a relationality that grounds subjectivity as prior to the sociosymbolic realm of discourse. Psychoanalysis therefore allows Irigaray to imagine a subject constructed in and through language and therein to reject the marginalization of women as necessary or ontologically based.

Selfsameness and the Problem of One: Ethics and Prediscursive Relation in Levinas and Irigaray

The work of twentieth-century continental philosopher and ethicist Emmanuel Levinas (1906–1995) is integral to Irigaray's framing of the ethics of subjectivity. Much of Levinas's work criticizes what he sees as the prevailing model of the modern subject, such as the one Lacan describes. This "subject" of his discontent is one constructed through a movement of self-recognition, a movement of the self, in itself, for itself. This self is an egoism, an I becoming an I—a movement of sameness, of one toward the veracity of oneness.[17] In this model of the subject, difference impedes and threatens unity. Fearful that he might not be the singular and certain master of his surroundings, one whose subjectivity is secured through sameness projects his fear onto the other, displaying what Levinas refers to as an "allergy" to the other. The subject is sure of himself because he is not "other" and he proves that he is rid of the differences that would jeopardize his selfhood by establishing that the other is not like him. And the other becomes the receptacle in which the subject dumps his own self-doubt. The space of difference between self and other collapses into a hierarchical polarization by which difference is reduced or arranged according to the movement of power that substantiates the subject position. The subject that assures itself of its identity violates the other by erasing the other's difference. Nothing in the world can continue in otherness; all otherness returns to the self.

In contrast to the self-as-egoism model of the subject, Levinas asserts that alterity is the linchpin of the foundational principal of ethics. Alterity, understood as radical otherness, is the possibility for interrupting the egoism of selfhood. Welcoming alterity therefore constitutes a disruption of the selfsame subject. Levinas writes, "The relationship between the same and the other, my welcoming of the other, is the ultimate fact, and in it the things figure not as what one builds but as what one gives."[18] Levinas's statement confronts the reduction of the other to a medium of one's becoming, or building block in the construction of total self-consciousness. Instead, he suggests, the appropriate relationship between one's self and one's other will involve giving to the other, not using the other. For Levinas, the ethical relationship to the other is a relationship based in desire for the other in their otherness, not the necessity of the other to one's own becoming.

As we will see, Irigaray's debt to Levinas is evident not only in her explicit engagement with him in her works, especially in "Questions for *Emmanuel Levinas*" and *An Ethics of Sexual Difference*, but also in her emphasis that ethics ultimately requires an irreducibility of difference. In this sense, the realm of ethics provides a model of two in relation without consumption that Irigaray will use to rethink desire. The idea that subjectivity could emerge through an ethical safeguarding of difference serves as the foundation of Irigaray's ethics, and while Levinas's ethics of alterity envisions what should be, Lacan's psychoanalysis describes, in a sense, what is—a reality that discourse expresses a single, masculine symbolic of desire. For Irigaray, there is no man and woman who can stand before each other as two prior to discourse. There is no prediscursive ethical moment if otherness is a condition of linguistic representation, as in psychoanalysis. Because the world has been ordered only in terms of masculine desire, the encounter between men and women is one in which woman is perceived in terms of masculine desire. Woman's appearance to the masculine subject is without newness because he has already imagined her. To use Levinas's terms, she does not interrupt the drive toward oneness, of his desire; rather, in economic fashion, she fulfills his desire by returning to him that which he seeks.

Women have been framed as man's other and prevented from constituting their own otherness, and it is on the basis of this original violation of the difference of the other, Irigaray argues, that even Levinas's depiction of the ethical encounter violates the gesture toward radical alterity that it espouses.[19] For Irigaray, the problem with Levinas's two is that the two are not necessarily irreducible to each other because they stand before one another with a notion of relation and proximity that is already implicated in a particular notion of two—a notion of two that is one. The two who are face to face *in his* ethical encounter are always already masculine because Levinas himself, in positing a neutral, universal ethical subject-object relation, has failed to address the symbolic, prediscursive working of masculine desire. Depicting the ethical moment of the face-to-face encounter as gender neutral suggests that a universal way of being in the world is open to both men and women equally, which is just one more veiling of the mediation of female desire through a masculine symbolic, one more failure to see the occlusion of women's desire as the condition of entering into discourse.

Confronting this problem of neutrality in her "Questions for Emmanuel Levinas," Irigaray asks, "Who is the other, if the other of sexual difference is not recognized or known? Does it not mean in that case a sort of mask or lure? Or an effect of the consumption of an Other [Autre]?"[20] These questions engage the status of woman in the ethical relation, hinting at the aforementioned occlusion. After all, if there is no difference in sexual difference, if the feminine is a masculine representation of the other, then who is woman? If she is masked by a language that is not her own, then is woman really man's other who can encounter him ethically? Irigaray's questions are rhetorical, but the implications are that the erasure of women's difference constitutes an ethical breach because her difference is consumed. The selfsame is representative of masculine desire; therefore, an other desire must be a desire beyond selfsameness for there to be two who could stand in ethical relation. But this twoness cannot be conceived entirely prediscursively, as though language were merely an effect of desire. So, while Irigaray's homage to Levinas is the affirmation that two are necessary for ethics, the idea of two is not sufficient for irreducibility.

Irigaray's questions to Levinas are written in a way that suggests he has provoked these questions, leading the reader to gather that Irigaray finds promise in Levinas's description of ethics as being a relation between two that is prediscursive, immanent, and amorous. However, despite this promise, Irigaray suggests that by de-eroticizing the sexual relation between the amorous couple, Levinas closes off the very alterity of the third term—a transcendent Other—that makes ethical relation possible.[21] Irina Poleshchuk writes that Levinas abandons the power of eros because he perceives that "[t]he erotic relation is less radical than the ethical relation of the face-to-face" based on its tendency to "collaps[e] into the enjoyment of being touched."[22] Irigaray will posit the two as an ethical and erotic relation that doesn't seek fulfillment in a transcendence as radical alterity beyond the two but rather through that relation of two. For Irigaray, there can be no eros without the alterity of ethics, nor can there be alterity without the eros of relation.

An ethical model of openness to the difference of the other, an openness that does not attempt to conquer the other or assimilate the other, cannot occur without two who are irreducible to each other, and, for Irigaray, the two who encounter each other in an ethical moment are only irreducible to each other if they are sexually different. What sexual difference actually describes requires a more nuanced look at the materiality of difference. And it is in the play between desire and responsibility that one sees the relation between psychoanalysis and ethics most clearly in Irigaray's work. Who the two are and how they are constituted in relation to the world matters; two must really be at least two. In order for there to be two who encounter each other, the at least two of an othered desire must be allowed to emerge in and through difference rather than through the sameness of a symbolic realm that expresses a singular desire. Note the "at least" is important here because for Irigaray, despite her gravitation toward the language of the couple, there is the possibility that once we begin to think at least two to become in their twoness, other becomings are possible to imagine.[23]

The Materiality and Alterity of Desire

MATTER OF ALTERITY AND THE ALTERITY OF MATTER IN SEXUAL DIFFERENCE

The interplay between ethics and psychoanalysis in her own thinking leads Irigaray to a model of desire that is continually relational and without synthesis—a model of desire suspended in the tensions of eros, in the space of ambiguity without resolution. Irigaray's critical adaptations of Lacan and Levinas respectively generate an important contribution to the conversation about ethics and difference by bridging the gap between two philosophical trajectories of otherness and subjectivity that define her intellectual milieu.[24] John D. Caputo explains these trajectories as heterologies that can be contrasted according to their understanding of the relationship between the freedom of the human subject and its relation to the other: heteronomy points to investment in the otherness of the other, while heteromorphism is invested in difference. Those invested in projects of heteromorphism, such as Gilles Deleuze, prioritize the proliferation of differences as the means for becoming subjects. Those, such as Levinas, who prioritize heteronomy understand differences as interrupting the freedom of the subject, and they structure ethical obligation as the foundation of becoming.[25] I will continue to insist as I elaborate a concept of desire that it is this holding together of freedom and responsibility that challenges identity and the ethics of identification without rendering becoming a complete abstraction.

I have rehearsed the positions of Lacan and Levinas specifically because they both think about the question of sexual difference and the embodiedness of desire as important for ethics. But it should be noted that Irigaray, Lacan, and Levinas are theorizing responses to the legacies of Hegel's thought. Hegel's work has had an enduring impact on the concept of subjectivity, on questions of how it emerges in relation to and as part of the unfolding of history, and of how, arguably, the foundations of that truth of that becoming subject transcends the limits of the historical. Irigaray's turn to the sensual, embodied relation in order to critique the autological language of the same must therefore be read as a critical response to Hegel's structuring of subjectivity, Lacan's theorizing of the woman as lack, and Levinas's interrogation of the ethical stakes of a philosophy that reduces alterity to the subject's own becoming.

Irigaray's relation to Hegel, including discussion of her adaptation of Hegel's dialectic, has been well documented. Among Irigaray scholars, Mary

C. Rawlinson's rigorous reading of Hegel in relation to Irigaray demonstrates Irigaray's transformation of the dialectical relation from one that aims toward completion to one that remains open.[26] Laura Roberts traces this open dialectic in Irigaray's *Speculum*, *Ethics*, and *I Love to You*, emphasizing its implications for fostering an altogether different political subject.[27] And Alison Stone suggests that Irigaray's positing of the feminine as lack, while deeply entangled with Lacanian psychoanalysis, must also be interpreted in relation to the French philosophical tradition of interpreting Hegel.[28] I would add that Irigaray's engagements with Levinas's ethics are inseparable from both Irigaray's and Levinas's own distinct interpretations of Hegel.[29] Like Levinas, Irigaray aims to think transcendence through the ethical horizontality of human relation rather than through a Hegelian aspiration of self-transcendence, but she does so by insisting upon the uniquely singular embodiedness of sexuate difference.

I mention Irigaray's relation to these thinkers to frame her turn to the corporeality of the sexuate as a resistance to both the projection of alterity as immanence *and* to the reduction of immanence to a movement of a subjectivity that re-presents a phallic morphology as universal (and therein transcendentalizes that morphology). Indeed, Irigaray holds materiality and alterity together in sexual difference and insists that the desire cultivated in this difference could ground a new sociosymbolic and the possibility of new worlds of relation therein. So how might a charitable interpretation of the unique materiality and alterity in Irigaray's notion of the sexuate proceed?

As I read Irigaray, the very possibility of transcendence arises through an ontological reality of irreducible difference. But Irigaray does not attribute the prediscursive difference of the other to the trace of alterity, as Levinas does in his reading of the face-to-face encounter; rather, for Irigaray, flesh is the condition of alterity, not simply the condition of relation to alterity. There is no preexisting alterity that generates the flesh. She argues for a different temporality altogether. Ethics is not simply prior to flesh; it is within and part of flesh. Read this way, Irigaray thus locates alterity in the midst of a predicsursive, presymbolic relation of difference that is fleshy. The corollary is that she attributes the forgetting of flesh and the loss of transcendence as intertwined with the problem selfsame desire. For Irigaray, the unethical desire that drives toward singularity as a whole, uninterrupted one occludes the irreducible difference of an at-least-two as the sensible-transcendent source of life. The selfsame desire of Lacan's phallocentric symbolic has manifested in a history of Western thought that prioritizes transcendence through a dissociation of body and spirit, securing the illusion of universality.

This dissociation of body and soul leads to an aspiration for transcendence constituted through an overcoming of the body.

Irigaray locates this dissociation of body and soul, and its corollary expression of phallic desire toward wholeness, within philosophical framings (explicit and implicit) of sexual difference ever since Plato's differentiation of the souls of men and women in the origin of the human. The legacy of Plato is one in which the masculine gendered body is more closely aligned with the capacity for transcendence, and the feminine body is associated with carnality. Put differently, the symbolic of a masculine desire veils the irrecoverable difference of its sexuate ontology by debasing materiality and projecting a neutral/universal transcendence. Irigaray aims to overturn this framework by prioritizing a body that, in and through the discourse of the masculine symbolic, has been denied the transcendence of its own flesh, its own incarnation—the feminine body. Moreover, returning to the earlier point about materiality as necessary to alterity, Irigaray's focus on incarnation as the enfleshment of alterity is different from the notion that incarnation is a representation, discursive or otherwise, of alterity. Irreducibility is tied to incarnation, to the material otherness that makes the other, as she says, a "mystery."[30]

Insofar as Irigaray is challenging the symbolic form of representation while still operating within the economy of the selfsame, her writing incorporates a constant movement or play even within the use of the language of the feminine. She uses the feminine to expose the violence against woman that occurs in discourse. At various points in her work, Irigaray turns to the language of wombs, genital and oral lips, mucous, placentas, and flesh more broadly, reappropriating the carnality associated with women in the Western philosophical tradition. As almost ironic reappropriations, these evocative fleshy invocations foster the viscerality and spirituality that keep desire ambiguous and irrecuperable, the ambiguity of eros that makes the heart sick and the soul ache.

I will continue to foreground Irigaray's language of lips throughout this book as a figure of desire in her work, and as figures of the radical desire I want to put forward. These lips, which Irigaray introduced in *Speculum*, were made famous in her essay "When Our Lips Speak Together," which was published in *This Sex Which Is Not One* (Cornell, 1985 [1977]). When I was an undergraduate in women's studies in the US in the late 1990s and early 2000s, it seemed as though you couldn't find a reader on gender studies and/or feminist theoretical perspectives in other disciplinary contexts that didn't include at least an excerpt from this essay. The lips of "When

Our Lips Speak Together" became a representation of the pushback against liberal feminist perspectives that prioritized equality in terms of a sameness between men and women. Irigaray was counted among those feminists who advocated a reorientation of feminist politics that elevated the differences associated with what it meant to be a woman.

Given Irigaray's associations with a difference-based model of feminism, her lips have become a trope that is passé for many; they instantiate a physiological form that conjures associations between women and reproduction, which invites open season for critiques of essentialism. But Irigaray's invocation of lips, like her other visceral allusions, are meant to arouse such associations in order to deconstruct them. Although the lips of "When Our Lips Speak" are the most well-known or perhaps most infamous of Irigaray's labial invocations, I want to begin by turning to the lips in *An Ethics of Sexual Difference*, to emphasize the interrelatedness of Irigaray's ethics and her efforts to use her writing to cultivate a desire that disrupts the logic of sameness as manifested in metaphysics. By situating Irigaray's references to lips more broadly in relation to her aims in *Ethics*, I hope to demonstrate how the lips gesture to a nonselfsame desire. I insist that Irigaray's lips invite the other without consuming the difference of the other, and, I argue, these lips are erotic precisely because they evoke something that is at once real and indeterminate, embodied and dynamic in ways that present an alternative space of philosophical thinking.[31]

Lips: A Story of Sexuate Desire

An Ethics of Sexual Difference was first published in France in 1984 as *Ethique de la différence sexuelle* and later translated by Carolyn Burke and Gillian Gill and published in English in 1993. The book was based on a series of lectures Irigaray delivered on "The Ethics of the Passions" as part of an honorary chair position at Erasmus University.

In *Ethics*, Irigaray exploits the semantic tensions between flesh and spirit perpetrated by the forgetting of sexuate difference, offering a turn to the "threshold of the [labial] lips" as the figure that could usher in a new relation of space and time that would allow for the "remaking of immanence and transcendence."[32] The visceral dimensions of her writing are telling. Irigaray's turn to the lips here, which I revisit in greater depth in the next chapter, constitute a threshold that marks the space between her criticism of the masculine symbolic on the one hand and her cultivation of sexuate desire on the other. Irigaray writes that the lips are "strangers to dichotomy and oppositions," that "offer a shape of welcome but do not assimilate, reduce, or swallow up."[33] In refusing to allow their twoness to be dissolved, lips reject the selfsameness of phallocentric desire. They gesture to a different mode of relation between immanence and transcendence—offering a space that invites without consuming the other. Rachel Jones reminds us that this remaking of immanence and transcendence through the lips is part of Irigaray's sustained critique of the psychoanalytic model of subjectivity with which we began: "[T]he figure of the lips introduces a dissymmetry twice over: not only does each lip not simply mirror the other, but together they figure a process where self and other take shape in ways that neither reflect nor invert the oppositional process through which the male subject is formed."[34] Instead of filling the gap between the fundamental asymmetry of sexual difference by positing a transcendent God, Irigaray's lips insist on irreducible touchings cultivate a new relation to desire.

Irigaray's staging of the lips in relation to the figure of the cross lends further support for the assertion that the materiality and alterity of Irigaray's sexuate opposes and redefines metaphysical bifurcations of immanence and transcendence. In *Ethics*, Irigaray refers to the crossing lips "like the arms of the cross," invoking a distinctly theological register as the means to engage Heidegger's call for the reuniting of immanence (horizontality) and transcendence (verticality) in his philosophical disruption of metaphysics. Recalling Irigaray's assertion that "the link uniting masculine and feminine must be horizontal and vertical, terrestrial and heavenly," the image of crossing suggests that the fleshy lips engender the space of an indeterminate threshold—an entrance and exit between one and an other that guarantees the sanctity of the space and time of their respective differences while also facilitating their communion.[35] Because the crossing remakes the relation between horizontal and vertical, the entrance and exit is never just a sharing between humans on the one hand or between human and a transcendent God on the other. The crossing of two lips (mouth and genital) that are always already two gestures to a redoubling, such that the thresholds are multiple.

By recasting the horizontality and verticality of immanence and transcendence and the interiority of time and exteriority of space, the lips provide a new philosophy or manner of thinking—a morphologic wherein thinking is relation, aspiration of and through the body.[36] The morphologic is a logos that speaks to the transcendence of the form in and of itself. Here, morphe is a form that is dynamic, and logos is not merely discursive. It offers a way of thinking and creating worlds, in and through the forms of one's differences, understood dynamically. Importantly, what we might refer to as a "transcendence" of the morphe is embodied; it is, in Irigarayan terms, sensible transcendental, holding the being of beings and the conditions of their possibility together.[37] Irigaray herself has repeatedly emphasized the need for reclaiming morphology. The morphology of the lips figures the at least twoness of desire that will be necessary for ethical relation because their touching is predicated on the twoness of their materiality. They are material in a way that exceeds the materiality of metaphysical reduction, and their individuation is beyond relations within the symbolic, marked by an always already twoness as the occasion of their touching[38]

As previously note, Irigaray's invocations of fleshy language, including her imagery of lips and wombs and also the viscerality of placentas and mucous, has been a sticking point for many who argue Irigaray's fleshy language is essentialist at worst and overly optimistic in its radicality. But most scholars of Irigaray frame her linguistic play on materiality as an effort to create space for difference that does not essentialize the female body in the oneness of a particular reuniversalized body. As Penelope Ingram argues, "According to Irigaray, it is through the recovery of her imaginary morphology, her own body, that woman is able to establish her difference and her subjecthood."[39] Ingram's interpretation of the intentions of Irigaray's writing, consistent with readings by Tina Chanter, Ellen Mortenson, Gail Schwab, and Margaret Whitford, among others, emphasizes that morphology is not a static understanding of the body that creates a specific subjectivity; rather, the morphology itself is part of a silenced relation of flesh and spirit that must be recovered in order to be in one's body as an individuated embodiment. Read this way, Irigaray's disruptive adoption and adaptation of representations of woman in terms of flesh are the occasion for her to cultivate space for difference apart from which women can be other than the forgotten other to the one universal man and the sacrificed other necessary to posit a radically Other God.

My focus, however, on the remaking of immanence and transcendence through the question of fleshiness and desire pushes an interpretation of Irigaray's fleshy writing even further. Her fleshy language employs the sensuous carnality of Platonic and neo-Platonic constructions of women to refashion the fleshy borders of that materiality as the condition of alterity. Irigaray insists that this fleshiness that once held women to a lower level of love/eros, and therein, further from the otherworldly, divine, and/or transcendent good, now becomes the very thing that makes possible the alterity on which eros depends.

Precisely because Irigaray demands recognition of the distinct twoness as a condition of an ethics of sexual difference, the flesh is not merely a vehicle for experiencing transcendence. Nor is the world of spirit only significant in its incarnation. The boundaries of matter and spirit cannot simply be elided in an ethics of sexual difference; they can only touch. Both matter and spirit must be touching, intimately, erotically, with ambiguous boundaries, in order for the fullness of their fecundity to be realized. This embodiment, a dynamic of matter and spirit, is the essence of Irigaray's sensible transcendental—a dialectic of matter and spirit in which the eroticism, the ambiguity, indeed the indeterminacy of their embrace/union/touching, is the condition of ethical relations.

Beyond the Singularity of Desire: The Problem of One and the Promise of At Least Two

Ethical desire between the sexes will be, for Irigaray, a desire of attraction without consumption, and this desire can only occur if the sexes are so "unknowable" and irreducible to one another that theirs is forever an encounter of wonder. Irigaray writes, "The one who differs from me sexually is the one who elicits this wonder."[40] That sexual difference is constitutive of this irreducibility signals the embodiedness of desire and of the consequences of relating to the world disconnected from that desire. Indirectly addressing the significance of a material, embodied notion of sexual difference for an ethics of alterity, Irigaray ends *Ethics* with the following passage: "[T]he most intimate perception of the flesh escapes every sacrificial substitution, every assimilation into discourse, every surrender to the God. Scent or premonition between my self and the other, this memory of the flesh as the place of approach means ethical fidelity to incarnation. To destroy it is to risk the suppression of alterity, both the God's and the other's. Thereby dissolving any possibility of access to transcendence."[41] This passage not only concludes Irigaray's essay on Levinas but also serves as the final lines of the entire collection that constitutes *Ethics*. Irigaray's words are powerful, couching ethics, theology, and philosophy in terms of an embodied desire that is at once intensely visceral and personal at the same time it is transcendent and irreducible.

This desire that refuses dichotomies and also refuses synthesis in favor of dwelling in ambiguity is an erotic desire, understood in the fullness of a carnality that has been starved of the alterity it is due. Alluding to Levinas's notion of substitution, Irigaray contends a "memory of the flesh" of the other who is sexually different "escapes" any reduction in discourse and, she also implies, to ethics. This memory is one of a certain prediscursive freedom, in which flesh moves in relation to flesh, "prior to any construction of words, any enshrinement of idols or even of temples, something—not reducible to the ineffable aspect of discourse."[42] Irigaray's insistence on a "memory of the flesh" prior to discourse frames an encounter between two whose recognition of one another is unencumbered by the representation of their individual desires—it is a moment of recognition within a lost promise of unmediated desire. In other words, for this encounter to exist, there must be two who are irreducible to discourse such that their flesh, "with no discourse to wrap itself in," is touching in nakedness, where touch, not language, is the mediation of desire.

For Irigaray, at least two sexually differentiated fleshes are the ground of at least two desires, but the possibility of their difference has been covered over and forgotten, replaced by a single memory of a single perspective of a single flesh. Irigaray's early work critically mimes the discourse of a single flesh to expose its occlusions and erasures to gesture to this inexpressible memory of the fleshy encounter of two, to be in relation to it, to touch the other where discourse cannot, in a gap that discourse engenders—to remember in and through the flesh without deciphering its meaning. This is precisely what writing through the body of sexuate woman accomplishes for Irigaray: it creates a gap, a space of unintended consequences that exploits the limits of discourse and draws attention to the fact that one of the two bodies has been forgotten, that the touching of two has become the masturbation of one, that eros has become autoeroticism as opposed to self-affection.[43] Whether, for example, she is reading Diotima in *Ethics* or Antigone in *Speculum*, Irigaray attempts to remember that which exists only as a gap, an absence, or a mark of the feminine.

Seeking to cultivate a different mode of articulation, Irigaray's writing aspires to a *parler femme*, a distinctive mode of language, a poetics of speech (*la parole*) and writing (*l'écriture*) that extends from the morphologic of women's sexuate being.[44] This language institutes relation from a new symbolic order, to begin to express an other desire that only sexuate difference, she insists, could engender. Irigaray's own faith in the work of her writing suggests that feminine desire gives women the space they need to become subjects in accordance with their own desires such that they retain the freedom required for two to behold one another in wonder, "never taking hold of the other as its object."[45] The body (discursively marked) who speaks and who writes matters here, and this "mattering" fundamentally reflects Irigaray's emphasis on the psychosocial, spiritual, and political conditions of women, or, as I would parse this, bodies marked as other in and through the masculine symbolic.

Despite the disruptive intent of *parler femme* as a means of manifesting a sensible transcendental, Irigaray's depiction of sexual difference exclusively in terms of male-female difference continues to pose significant questions about her work and challenges to how it can, and should, be received. Further complicating the appeal of Irigaray's work, especially for those who are rigorously constructivist and/or postmodern, is that for her, sexual difference is not simply a semantic or symbolic difference; sexual difference is embodied difference. We cannot simply speak of the lips as operating on a semantic register or say that sexual difference is simply a linguistic marker for an irreducible difference that has nothing to do with the relationship between actual fleshes, their desires, and their becoming. And even if we grant that sexual difference is irreducible to biological or cultural depictions of sex or gender, Irigaray's description of the relation between two has itself been subjected to criticism. The complementarity of two different desires of two prediscursive fleshes has been critiqued for its heteronormative dualism of desire that is anything but different from heterosexist and therein phallocentric frameworks. The reality that bodies do not fit into existing sexed categories is nothing new, and with an increased visibility of trans* bodies and queer sexualities this reality is as apparent and important today as ever. What is Irigaray's place amid a current reality of embodiment that is perhaps more radical than she once imagined?

Secondarily, there is a question about the cost of the emergence of *parler femme*. Even the most charitable reader who sees within Irigaray's earlier works the seeds of a radically indeterminate concept of sexual difference may find her reductions of the "East" to deeply personal and arguably unnuanced interpretations of Buddhist philosophy and cursory invocations of yoga, Hindu cosmology (as in *I Love to You, To Be Two,* and *Between East and West, To Be Born,* and *A New Culture of Energy: Beyond East and West,* and *The Mediation of Touch*) as effects of her continued insistence on male-female coupling that are difficult to reconcile.[46] How does one square a reading of a radical sexuate as opening a new way of thinking with what teeters on orientalist appropriations?

Despite such trappings of Irigaray's emphasis on sexual difference, I maintain that her writing refuses any necessary correlation between the sexuate and the discourse of gender, opening a quite radical space for disrupting the categories of man and woman.[47] So while Irigaray's emphasis on male-female difference, sexual difference, sexuate coupling, and variations on the theme may keep some from returning to her work, I contend that amid her relentless reliance on a notion of sexuate difference lies a more promising notion of the irreducibility of desire as the basis for an ethical theory of human becoming. Indeed, Irigaray's ethics of sexual difference is a destabilization of or a *question* of sexual difference, and in her particular use of this very questioning as a means to cultivate space for thinking through a prediscursive fleshy difference, she re-eroticizes eros.[48] Doubling down on the embodiedness of sexual difference in Irigaray might seem a counterintuitive approach to challenging identity, but it is also within this question of embodiedness that the tensions between a sexuate ethics and the limits of political discourse are most obvious. If ethical desire is nonidentical, then how can it remain a desire between a specifically differentiated idea of male or female, or even between masculine or feminine bodies?

I want to insist that reducing Irigaray's sexuate to man and woman as the only sexuate morphologies undermines the dynamism and relationality that make the sexuate an irreducible ontological relation and thus of a different order of logic than that of a politics of representation. In his essay "Irigarayan Ontology and the Possibilities of Sexual Difference," James Sares writes that sexual difference "incarnates an ontological relationality through distinct morphological forms."[49] Sares argues, and I think rightly, that for Irigaray, a sexuate morphology, if read as the incarnations of a relational ontology, can "open us to possibilities for new forms of embodiment."[50] In Irigaray's ethics of sexual difference, the two who are irreducible to one another, and therefore the two whose relationship creates the space within which alterity exists, are not reducible to a concept of cis male and cis female bodies that would undermine the dynamism of sexuate morphology.

Sares offers a compelling vision of the potential radicality of Irigaray's sexual ontology, and one that I embrace as his own important reception and furtherance of Irigaray's thought. But even as Irigaray has continued to emphasize the irreducibility of the sexuate as fundamental to the radical desire that allows one to become in oneself and with one's other as they aspire toward transcendence, her "suggestion of rebuilding the world from a relationship of desire and love between a man and a woman" explicitly privileges the cis heterosexual couple as a materially unique relation of sexuate alterity.[51] And while I will make the argument in chapters 2 and 3 that the sexuate, because it signals a register beyond negation, could and should deconstruct gender identity and sexuality entirely, Irigaray has continued to make statements that because some forms of sex are different, featuring different forms of penetration for example, they are more conducive of radical touching and sharing that cultivate the sort of dynamic relationality for which she calls.

I will not try to "rescue" Irigaray for liberal political purposes, making her say something she does not want to say. These are challenges in her work that still make me cringe but also make me curious. To borrow from Sares's diagnosis of Elizabeth Grosz's comparison of Irigaray and Darwin, I think it is clear that Irigaray is stuck in the "actual" in terms of how she imagines the sexuate. She might even concede this. But I would add that what Irigaray cannot quite reconcile is precisely what her writing accomplishes—eros as prior to ethics and subjectivity. I reluctantly note a latent irreconcilability between Irigaray's actual statements and the radicality of her philosophy; this conflict informs my more literary than philosophical approach because it allows an exploration of the rhetoricity and fleshiness of the lips in Irigaray's morphological writing to move beyond the limits of her work.

This Self Which Is Not One:
Desire, Becoming, and Politics

Thus far, this chapter has situated identity as an ethical problem from the perspective of both philosophy and linguistic psychoanalysis. I have offered above a cursory explanation of the materiality and alterity of the sexuate and how Irigaray invokes this concept in her thought and writing to establish a nonselfsame desire. To summarize here: I want to link the ethical questions of identity to politics by virtue of the question of sameness. I do so by returning to questions of the binary relation that opened this book, to the relationship between discourse and matter that cast politics as a movement of selfsame desire, and to the need to reimagine an othered, nonselfsame desire to disrupt such a politics.

Irigaray's relationality draws on the psychoanalytic and the phenomenological insofar as she is part of a philosophical tradition that reframes the question of Being as a static, given truth—seeing Being instead as a question of becoming through the dynamism of relation with one's human and nonhuman others. One becomes a subject through relation to others. From Irigaray's perspective, however, both psychoanalytic and phenomenological accounts of the relational character of becoming have posited the irreducible difference that is the condition of at least two, and therein the condition of relation, without thinking through the material difference that is necessary for two to exist. As I have explained in the introduction, that material difference of two is sexuate difference for Irigaray.

An ethical becoming is a becoming that does not attempt to recuperate the other in one's own becoming—it is, like the lips, a nonapporpriative becoming in which desire opens to and invites the other without consumption. At least semantically in keeping with psychoanalysis and phenomenology, Irigaray's sense that one becomes a subject in relation to others is the foundation for an ethical subjectivity. One of the most integral interventions of Irigaray's turn to the sexuate is the insistence that becoming one is never becoming through reification into a singular one and that a return to oneself in relation to the dynamic particularities of living, "the dynamism conforming to [. . .] living being," is necessary for rethinking the world.[52]

A notion of a becoming subject as always at least two is not a divided subject but an individuated subject whose individuation is not limited to the differentiations made possible by discourse. Irigaray asks us to rethink the at-least-twoness of the sexuate, like lips and their self-touching, as the condition for a multiplicity of desires at the foundation of being in relation. As Irigaray writes in *Divine Women*, "Everything is given to us by means of touch, a mediation that is continually forgotten."[53] Relationality is not just about reaching out to the human other here; it is about being in and with the particularities of oneself as relation. Being in relation is not just about being in relation to an other; it is about understanding one's self as relational at its core, from its birth. The becoming subject is never simply a one becoming in relation to an other; it is an individuated "self" whose individuation is neither singular nor static nor proscribed by culture or language.

In her 2022 essay "Dreaming of a Truly Democratic World," Irigaray frames impediments to a democratic society in terms of the impasse created by materialist-versus-idealist views of materiality. The materialists, she contends, are so caught up in metaphysical thinking that they cannot imagine materialism beyond matter. In their forgetting of air, for example, as "more necessary for life than any solid, any object or possession, materialists do not think the relationality of subjectivity."[54] She adds, "[Materialists] do not imagine enough that the material needs do not suffice to make blossom a human being and to build a human community."[55] Idealists, on the other hand, are bent on "overcoming materiality towards/by abstraction."[56]

I view Irigaray's words quoted above as emblematic of her longstanding refusal of an either/or relation between discourse and bodies—a false dichotomy that informs a politics of recognition based on desire for sameness. Irigaray continues "Dreaming" by making claims about the types of relations that must be transformed in order to establish a truly democratic order; however, in the abstract to the essay, she raises the importance of desire for engendering a space-time wherein the materiality of differences generates non-neutral and nonbinary worlds to further nurture the plurality of material differences.[57] Desire, she suggests, is the possibility to "transcend oneself" and imagine more; desire is also "what brings people to each other and is the most important agent in the formation of a democratic community."[58] I interpret Irigaray as suggesting that the materialities of differences and the differences of materialities are possible because of irreducibility of one to the other, and this irreducibility is the possibility of a desire of relationality that does not attempt to consume or appropriate.

Insofar as institutions and ideologies are constructed around visions of a particular subject, and those ideologies reinforce the certitude of those subjects, they are complicit in the drive toward oneness of a selfsame subjectivity. Identity is therefore not just a question of the individual psyche. It is bound up in the sociality of being itself. Politics, in which sociality seems to be given, is classically understood as a relation of three or more, as different from the relation between the two of eros. Freudian psychoanalysis challenges the model of ethics and politics because it thinks the ethical as the relation between two as a movement of the individual's becoming. And Lacan further disrupts this understanding by positing the ethical as a movement of the individual's becoming in relation to language as the space of relation to one's others.

Political recognition recapitulates the selfsameness of this representational thinking. One projects one's identity, and political recognition constitutes an affirmation of this projection. Whether we imagine the political as a relation that happens between two or three or more, politics today remains a realm for re-presenting that which is already imagined. Because representation within a masculine symbolic is part of a movement of sameness, and because politics is an institution in which inclusion is based on recognition of differences as part of a same, universal whole, politics too is a relation of and in sameness. Even various social constructivist (including performativist) understandings of identities as arbitrary, provisional, or fluid do not undermine the processes of identification as the foundation of relations. As Emily Anne Parker notes, despite its various permutations, "social construction takes the origin of political differences to be politics itself."[59]

The question of the ontological becomes integral to the discussion of a radical reimagining of politics precisely because it refuses the selfsame economy of representation, wherein recognition is merely a reification of representation. In chapter 4, I will acknowledge postcolonial criticisms of the imperializing work of ontological thought on the grounds that it ignores the sociality of becoming. Here, though, I want to emphasize that Irigaray's ontology has the potential to offer something different from a quasi-essentialist, neoconservative political philosophy. I propose that we read Irigaray's ontology as a disruption of the materialist and constructivist-type tensions that she criticizes in "Dreaming" and that we hold this disruptive ontology alongside her critique that the two in both Lacan's and Levinas's notions of relation are always already masculine. By weaving together these threads of her theorizing and critique, I believe we can posit Irigaray's ontology as refusing the stasis of Being and as thinking materiality and living, together, in a becoming that is possible through desire as a dynamic ground of life itself.

Here I offer a distinctive reading of Irigaray that is not so much a defense as a nuanced and charitable interpretation of her position. Irigaray attributes the forgetting of sexual difference in the history of thought and culture to the movement toward selfsameness. And representational thinking, the notion that the world is described as it though it is given, has resulted in the delusional view that a masculine, undifferentiated notion of sexual difference marks an actual, determinate difference. Therefore, although Irigaray invokes language of sexuation as natural to life itself, she has remained steadfastly critical of the totalizing project of representational thinking. In her corrective to the selfsameness of representational thinking, she interweaves the question of the becoming of a subject with the erotic relationship with the other and the complexities of ethical and political relations to multiple others. Rather than separating the spheres of the individual, the couple, and the collective, Irigaray's sexuate philosophy intertwines the becoming of one, of two, and of more than two. Her turn to ontological language of sexuation is not simply a reduction of all of these aforementioned dimensions of relation to the becoming of one; she is thinking all becomings as relation that happens because of the irreducibility of difference.

In *To Be Born*, Irigaray writes, "It is through the unfolding of our desire to be that a new word can arise, full of a meaning restored by the incarnation of the relational being of humans."[60] Refusing to reduce becoming to the limits of language in culture or politics, Irigaray's ontology, where relationality is a matter of desire, rejects the representational thinking of political recognition and aims to establish an altogether different concept of becoming that emerges "through the unfolding of desire." Indeed, in Irigaray, the irreducible materiality and alterity inform the relation of self and of other as a dynamic desire, one that resists a politics and sociality based on binary understandings and appeals instead to something more liberative, intimate, and relational—a certain personhood of becoming that doesn't require recognition within a system of reductivist representation. The desires of this relational becoming are beyond representation in the language of politics, and yet they are entrenched in the embodiedness of living in and beyond and perhaps at the limits of social and political discursive-bodily relations.

Conclusion: Desiring and Becoming Differently

Articulating desire in terms of Irigaray's sexuate is an effort to disrupt the structures that currently constrain our imaginations (through discourses of sex, gender, and sexuality, among others) and our capacity therein to describe the "actual." And I would argue that following the most radical thread of Irigaray's ethics of sexual difference links her emphasis on desire with a nonselfsame subjectivity that irreducible difference makes possible. For Irigaray, different desire(s) is a condition of possibility for two to be in their at-least twoness; consequently, differing desires are the ground of an ethics grounded in the relationality of individuation itself, where individuation is a "being with oneself free from representation or knowledge already determined."[61] Irigaray's fleshy writing pushes us to think through the dynamism of irreducibility that is material and materiality that is irreducible.

This is a fleshiness that I would argue is irreducible because it is always a flesh born in relation to the ambiguity of desires for self and other that is the condition of relation. Again, one is never just one. This materiality of the flesh is a space of possibility between a feminine that has never properly speaking existed and an other "language" or symbolic that would emerge from making a space for that indeterminate feminine as a continually imagined, desiring subject. This is not a discursively constituted body but something altogether unnameable in language, a visceral experience at once beyond the edited versions of ourselves that emerge through the regimes of truth of a discursive existence and yet also simultaneously unnarratable, even nonexistent, without those regimes.

Taking seriously the relationship of ethics to subjectivity requires rethinking the difference between two in relation to the irreducibility of difference within ones. If alterity is the ground of ethics, and if the point of establishing a different way of knowing and being in the world is to find a more ethical way of knowing and being (in a different way), then the ethical encounter of two is inseparable from the ethical becoming of one. Both demand a relation to alterity such that if the two in relation are irreducible to each other, so too must their oneness be irreducible even unto their own desires. Rethinking of one not only in relation to an other but also as one in relation to the other within itself in the space and time of one's own desires thinks a materiality and alterity of becoming beyond the discursive-bodily tensions of politics.

Sexuate individuation, as Irigaray refers to it, is not singularity as a one-universal but as the uniqueness of irreducible difference. Her notion of the irreducibility of the sexuate is more akin to Jean-Luc Nancy's "on being-singular-plural" or Adriana Cavarero's ontology of uniqueness.[62] Cavarero's ontology of uniqueness emphasizes that uniqueness is a condition of being that is not universalizable.[63] For Nancy, the notion of singularity is part of a co-essence and coappearance of existence grounded in the alterity of origin. Speaking of this alterity, Nancy writes, "This 'other,' this 'lowercase other,' is 'one' among many insofar as they are many; it is each one, and it is each time one, one among them, one among all and one among us all. In the same way, and reciprocally; 'we' is always inevitably 'us all,' where no one of us can be 'all' and each one of us is, in turn (where all our turns are simultaneous as well as successive, in every sense), the other origin of the same world."[64] What these concepts gesture to is the importance of thinking a certain interdependence of becoming in the world together.

If we are open to thinking the radical alterity as uniquely embodied, we can read, with Irigaray, the lips as a figure of desiring differently. Lips disrupt the idea that pleasure is ever one, that becoming is ever just one in isolation. Lips convey the dynamic dimensions of desire—such as touching, openness, interval, and dynamism, to name a few. Lips, in the context of Irigaray's efforts to think and write otherwise, are a morphologic of a desire that, in their at least twoness, offer a model of relational becoming that resists the reductive logic of phallocentrism—that refuses to be the debased carnal matter of someone else's pleasure.[65] In their morphology, the lips embody a relation of materiality and alterity as the possibility of an other desire, beyond the metaphysics of the masculine symbolic and beyond therein the legacies of identitarian thinking that make ethics and politics so difficult to think together. And, as I suggest moving forward, this is why the lips become so integral for revisiting Irigaray's notion of sexuate desire and for thinking this desire (or way of desiring) within contemporary questions of identity that have become so important for how we understand difference.

Chapter 2

The "Matter" of Lips

Incarnating the Transcendence of Desire

In the opening of *An Ethics of Sexual Difference*, Irigaray writes, "Sexual difference is probably the issue in our time which could be our 'salvation' if we thought it through."[1] This line is often cited to emphasize the importance of sexual difference for Irigaray's speculative philosophical reimagining of the world. That she uses the religious language of salvation, however, is not merely hyperbole; in *Ethics*, the language of salvation is accompanied by multiple references to incarnation and sacrifice in general and allusions to the Christian Incarnation and Crucifixion in particular. This language of incarnation, including Irigaray's repeated suggestions that the Incarnation is partial, signifies a crucial aspect of Irigaray's ethics of sexual difference: an embodiment uniting both flesh and word has yet to happen but remains necessary for a sexuate relation to exist.[2]

In *Ethics*, Irigaray repeatedly uses the term *incarnation* (*l'incarnation*) and/or alludes over two dozen times to the Christian Incarnation of Jesus as the son of God.[3] Irigaray's invocations of the specificity of the Christian Incarnation are in part her means of framing a world that has lost appreciation for the sexuate body as part of what it means to be human.[4] But as is characteristic of her disassimilation (*déassimilation*), she will locate, within the language of the Christian Incarnation, the promise of a union of flesh and transcendence that reimagines both in terms of their embodied specificity—incarnation as a materiality of radical alterity. Given that Irigaray's use of Chrisitan theological terms is always already entangled with the philosophical, ethical, and psychoanalytic genealogies of her thinking, it is no wonder that her work continues to present an inexhaustible source of inquiry beyond the bounds of disciplinary thinking.[5] In this chapter, I consider the language of incarnation in relation to Irigaray's efforts to rethink materiality and transcendence beyond metaphysics.

As I suggested in the first chapter, materiality in Irigaray's work is not synonymous with a metaphysical concept of matter. In invoking the language of bodies, of bodily parts, Irigaray is not simply redefining woman and matter with a positive bias, which would only leave structures of division in place, constituting at best a reversal of the masculine-feminine position that leaves the economy of sameness untroubled. Contrary to the assertion that Irigaray's employment of visceral metaphors essentializes male and female difference, her use of mimesis actually disrupts the connection between the flesh of which she speaks and the words used to speak that flesh. Irigaray's writing thus plays with the space between the flesh and discourse in a way that resists the idea of an essential truth of bodies that can be captured by discourse. Her writing attempts to create space for difference—a difference that could ground a nonselfsame mode of representation, as well as the possibility of subjects becoming through an irreducible desire that might ensure the mutuality of recognition.

In relation to incarnation, the lips, I have argued thus far, are one of Irigaray's earliest and most famous, albeit still undertheorized, invocations of the antimetaphysical prediscursive materiality of the sexuate that would engender such a space of and for a radical relation in and through differ-ence. With the language of lips, Irigaray engages in a serious play with the limits of language, summoning a gendered visceral representation in order to articulate the *possibility* of a desire of what she deems an othered, unthought female imaginary. If we read Irigaray charitably, that is, with the knowledge of these grand aims of her project in mind, we can view the lips as part of the process of cultivating the desire that is always at least two—the desire necessary for a radical reimagining of the world. Indeed, as part of a mimetic process of cultivating an other, nonselfsame desire within a selfsame system of representation, the language of lips mimes the association of woman with matter, using the language of the feminine to engage in the disassimilation of a sexuate other from the "feminine." The lips elicit an othered imaginary, to a desire beyond sameness that can only exist if difference is allowed to be difference, fundamentally, materially, "naturally" at its core—beyond discourse. Lips press the limits of representation in language, revealing that every representation of feminine desire as the other to masculine desire will involve the trace of a more primary unthought difference of an othered desire. These lips therefore never exclusively speak excess on the one hand or sameness on the other.[6]

As I discuss in chapter 1, the lips are not merely a rhetorical device used to gesture to some transcendent excess in Irigaray; the lips are material in a very fleshy sense. The mimetic force of the lips in her writing is an extension of what Irigaray identifies as a prediscursive reality. The lips' irreducible difference is embodied (otherwise) as a sensible transcendental, refusing metaphysical binaries of a masculine selfsame; therefore, lips not only disrupt meaning making through their mimetic play; they also invoke this embodiment beyond sameness. Within this continuous saying and unsaying of feminine desire, as that which is real and yet remains unthought, as that which is at once hidden and revealed, the language of lips manifests a territory at the limits of philosophy. It is precisely in this space at the limits of thought that religious language and imagery become useful for Irigaray and for her readers. Irigaray's lips are at once ethical and religious insofar as they move in/with eros to evoke a fleshy alterity, an abstraction that is not a figment.

Christian theological narratives provide Irigaray with a vocabulary (of God, angels, incarnation, salvation, and Parousia, for example), that holds flesh and radical alterity together beyond the metaphysics of immanence and transcendence.[7] Reciprocally, Irigaray's work has provided feminist theologians in particular a significant framework for rethinking Christological concepts such as the Incarnation, for reinterpreting accounts by/about women in the Christian tradition, and for reimagining the possibilities of Christian life and community today.[8]

Adding to this conversation, my interest here is in Irigaray's specific interweaving of the language of lips with the language of incarnation, as well as in her evocations of the crucifixion as a critique of the sacrificial economy of phallogocentrism. I contend that Irigaray's iconic lips, as always more than one, give a sexuate specificity to incarnation, figuring it as a dynamic embodiment of irreducible difference that refuses the phallocentric desire for singularity and unity. By virtue of the radical desire in the space of this irreducible difference, these incarnate lips remake immanence and transcendence and also remake the space and time of becoming and dwelling in and with the world in one's singularity and in relation to others in their singularities. This chapter therefore examines Irigaray's interweaving of the lips in relation to the language of incarnation and crucifixion, probing the slippage between materiality and discourse to give shape to a more radical desire.[9]

The chapter concludes by examining Irigaray's invocation of lips that are crossing in *An Ethics of Sexual Difference*—a crossing that leads toward a notion of desire as a continuous incarnation of the ambiguities found in the generative slippage between flesh and word. This crossing ushers in the space-time of sexual difference as an embodied temporality of desire, remaking immanence and transcendence to present a new incarnation, a new materiality of the space and time of an othered desire.

A Theology of Lips: From Salvation to Incarnation

Irigaray's dialogue with religious discourse is both explicit and sustained, from her earlier *Speculum, Marine Lover of Friedrich Nietzsche*, the *Forgetting of Air in Martin Heidegger*, and the essays in *Sexes and Genealogies* to her writings in the 1990s and 2000s such as *I Love to You* and "The Redemption of Women" in *Key Writings*, *Between East and West*, and *To Be Born*, to her most recent endeavors in *A New Culture of Energy*, *The Mediation of Touch*, and her personal reflection "God Becoming Flesh, Flesh Becoming Divine."[10] Through the juxtaposition of Christian theological allusions with the visceral language of her sexuate morpho-logic, Irigaray invokes an alternative imaginary for inhabiting the logical tension of the discursive-material divide. With its emphasis on the specificity of the Incarnation of Christ as God and man, and on the sacrifice of that Christ in the Crucifixion, one can interpret Christianity as narrating a preoriginary unity of the sensible and transcendental realms, of the flesh and spirit, as the fulfillment of some ideal. Irigaray appeals to this theological narrative both to diagnose the forgetting of the feminine in sexual difference and identify a lost cultural sensibility about embodiment that the Incarnation at least partially captures.[11]

While philosophers and theologians alike have explored the complexities of Irigaray's invocations of the language of transcendence, of flesh, of the divine, and so on, for decades, Irigaray's invocations of Christian images and themes have resulted in her being a particularly significant interlocutor in constructive feminist Christian theological debates.[12] Her significance for feminist theology is due in no small part to her 1984 lecture published as "Divine Women." The lecture has served as a foundational essay for interpreting Irigaray's understanding of the relationship between sexuate becoming and transcendence. It emphasizes the cultural, social, and psychical significance that having a transcendent other has for men and women.[13]

Irigaray opens "Divine Women" with literary representations of mermaids, gesturing to the Women's Center on *Melusine* that was cited in *Sexes and Genealogy* for organizing the lecture. She reflects on *Melusine* as part of a larger folklore of mermaids, emphasizing that these representations are "a stage in our imaginary" in which our passions confront the limits of how we have conceived humanity. Irigaray says that our dreams about who we could be confront "certain identity crises experienced by humanity and the world."[14] She asks, "What lies behind these partial incarnations, these monstrously composite women?"[15] Irigaray answers her own question by suggesting that the partially human incarnations of women in the myths (as mermaids for example) are both symptom and cause of these stories of "couples who give birth to offspring but have difficulty with love."[16] The myths, she says, can only imagine love as ill-fated because they are never between two. And there are never two who can love each other because there is only one in culture whose incarnation is complete—one human who becomes divine: man.

Drawing on the nineteenth-century Christian theologian Ludwig Feuerbach, Irigaray proclaims that the divine is the ideal to which one aspires and that would allow for a transfiguration of values necessary for remaking the world.[17] She proclaims, "In order to become, it is essential to have a gender (*genre*) or an essence (consequently a sexuate essence) as *horizon*."[18] And in order "to posit a gender, a God is necessary: *guaranteeing the infinite*."[19] Here, implicitly critiquing Levinas's rendering of the feminine other as one whose body is only given to her by man, Irigaray alleges that one cannot become if she is always the "Other of the other" and not in herself; she cannot become if one does not have an essence of her own. For Irigaray, humans need the divine because the divine is the possibility of becoming in one's uniqueness, and only then can two be in relation to the other in the fullness of their own embodiedness.[20]

Irigaray's critical miming of the Christian tradition throughout her work, using explicit references to Christological language like *incarnation*, *parousia*, and the *cross*, is meant to expose the ways in which the feminine has been used in elaborating a God of and for men. Simultaneously, she engages in this play to use the revelation of woman's occlusion to articulate a way of knowing and being through sexual difference. In this double work of critique and cultivation, Irigaray's employment of theological language certainly offers opportunities for both critiquing and reimagining the phallogocentrism of Christianity. Here, however, I am interested in Irigaray's use of theological language, not as a primary or privileged space for reimagining the masculine symbolic, but as a "narrative site" that opens onto a broader conversation about Irigaray's work—as a window into the extraphilosophical, extradiscursive, yet fully material thrust of her writing.

In this regard, my reading of Irigaray's use of incarnation follows Ada Jaarsma's suggestion that "the story of the incarnation in Irigaray's work does not occupy a foundational role that excludes other stories, traditions, or practices, but rather constitutes a narrative site at which to glimpse complex inter-related problems of Irigaray's project."[21] Because it is inherently problematic to reduce countless theological debates across geographically and historically diverse communities to a "Christian tradition," and because I am not interested in making a claim about right belief, I will borrow those dimensions of the language of incarnation that seem most normative in the context of Irigaray's European Catholic background. Further still, without complete "fidelity to a single discourse,"[22] I read the Incarnation from a literary rather than a theological perspective, as I cannot, in the time and space of this chapter, address the centuries of debate about the status of the Incarnation (as though they are ever settled by doctrine). I therefore offer a depiction of incarnation that supports the very critique of the Incarnation that Irigaray provides in order to highlight what the lips attempt to accomplish in her work.

Within Christian systematic theology, both Christ's Incarnation and Crucifixion, as well as his death, resurrection, and ascension, collectively inform the concepts of salvation, or soteriology. As such, Irigaray's claim in *Ethics,* that sexual difference would be our salvation if we thought it through, appeals to this tradition of seeing the masculine representation of divine-human Incarnation as the possibility of salvation. But it also points to the importance that the sacrifice of this divine-human flesh has had for at once reflecting and shaping Western perceptions of matter. The corporeality of matter that is worthy of divinity has been that of man, such that his body is transcendent. Irigaray contends that the maleness of this sacrifice is bound to a veiling of Mary/mother's role in bringing forth the corporeality of Jesus that makes the Incarnation possible. "Without the mother of God, there can be no God."[23] It is to this prior sacrifice of the mother as an other who gives flesh to spirit that Irigaray's invocations of the lips orient us in her texts.

Within the context of Irigaray's use of incarnational language and its relation to the sacrificial economy of the Crucifixion, there are two specific places I consider where the lips relate directly to the question of the relationship between discourse and matter as space of desire: the first is in *Speculum*, and the second is in *Ethics*. In both of these examples, Irigaray's lips elicit the ambiguities of the Christian theological tradition when it comes to interpreting the relationship between word and flesh and human and divine.[24]

In *Speculum*'s "La Mystérique," Irigaray appropriates the voices of female mystics, most directly that of the thirteenth-century Angela of Foligno (ca. 1248–1309),[25] situating the sensible flesh and the transcendental divine, elicited by the wounds of Jesus, in relation to the embodied eros of Angela's feminine lips.[26] "La Mystérique" begins with a mournful, if not disturbing, tone; there is a longing here. This tone of longing is at once emblematic of the desire expressed in the courtly love tradition of medieval mysticism, in particular that of the Beguines, women mystics including Teresa of Avila, Mechthild de Magdeburg, and Hadewijch, who were members of Christian lay orders between the thirteenth and sixteenth centuries. That longing not only conjures the general Christian desire for (re)union with God; in the context of Irigaray's work, it also suggests that these women mystics are alienated from their own desire. Irigaray's obscuring of the specificity of the women who formed part of this tradition will ultimately serve to complicate readings of desire for union with God.

Scholars have noted the layers of voices that seem to speak from this haunting text. Emily Holmes reminded me in our work together that "Irigaray almost certainly had in mind two early 14th century women writers: Marguerite d'Oingt, a Carthusian nun and author of *Speculum*, and Marguerite Porete, burned as a heretic for her book, *Le mirouer des simples âmes*."[27] And Ann-Marie Priest emphasizes that in addition to the many voices that Irigaray interweaves, there are also three epigraphs from three different mystics—Meister Eckhart, John Ruysbroeck, and Angela of Foligno—that open Irigaray's essay. These epigraphs further complicate the question of voice, as well as the extent to which the mystical tradition represents a universalized notion of desire for union—a notion that obscures a desire for radical alterity that might be relational in a different way.

This multivocality, and with it a dehistoricizing layering of images and voices across time and space, is consistent with Irigaray's citational practices in her mimetic writing. Irigaray is reimagining the specificity of Angela's experience in order to mime the broader history of interpretation of (here) women's mystical experience. Indeed, devotion to the wound of Christ and associations of that wound with motherhood, menstruation, and the vaginal were not uncommon between the twelfth and fifteenth centuries.[28] Theologian Janet Soskice explains that the descriptive and visual representations of Christ's body in relation to motherhood were meant to emphasize "the tender, nurturing aspect of God's care for souls."[29] But as feminist theological historian Amy Hollywood suggests, Irigaray's use of the Christian mystical tradition muddles the historical specificity of primary texts and the experiences of individual mystics.[30] Relative to historical theological accounts of the lives of female mystics and the stories of their devotion, Irigaray's writing cultivates an ambiguity and almost ambivalence surrounding the mystical tradition that can be frustrating. Despite this important criticism from the perspective of historical theology, I turn our focus to how Irigaray uses the language of wounds and lips within a broader disruption of the word-flesh relationship that she probes by appropriating the mystics.

Irigaray's use of the language of lips to mime the Christian mystical tradition will ultimately transform the Crucifixion from a site of phallo-centric triumphalism to a space of an othered, feminine, desire. In a stark example of miming the tradition to resurrect the sacrificed othered desire, Irigaray meditates on the kissing of Christ's side wound, playing upon medieval mystical associations of the wounds of Christ with the bodily parts of women.[31] Specifically, she elicits the vulvic nature of Christ's wounds (*vulnus*), especially the wound of his side, as represented in Angela's medi-tations (as reported in the collection of her writings, commonly referred to as the *Book* [*Il libro*], 1248–1309). Invoking history as layers to be mined through miming the representations of the historical, Irigaray interpolates the devotional narratives and imagery with psychoanalysis—to disassimilate the feminine from what she portrays as a totalizing thrust of a phallocentric history of thought and to then reimagine an othered desire. Irigaray attends to Angela's *kissing* of Christ's side wound in part to critique Freud's notion of desire as penetrative, which she sees as reducing women's pleasure to a phallocratic economy. Invoking a female mystical experience by way of Angela, Irigaray writes:

> And she never ceases to look upon his nakedness, open for all to see, upon the gashes in his virgin flesh, at the wounds from the nails that pierce his body as he hangs there, in his passion and abandonment. And she is overwhelmed with love of him/herself. In his crucifixion he opens up a path of redemption in her fallen state.
>
> Could it be true that not every wound need remain secret, that not every laceration was shameful? Could a sore be *holy?* Ecstasy is there in that glorious slit where she curls up as if in her nest, where she rests as if she had found her home—and He is also in her. . . . In this way, you see me and I see you, finally I see myself seeing you in this fathomless wound which

is the source of our wondering comprehension and exhilaration. And to know myself I scarcely need a "soul," I have only to gaze upon the gaping space in your loving body.[32]

Irigaray suggests that the mystic recognizes herself in the wounds of Christ. In looking at him, "she is overwhelmed with love of *him/herself.*" I add emphasis here to Irigaray's use of the masculine and feminine as interchangeable and mutual in the eyes of the mystical experience of "Angela." This identification has at least two dimensions. First, within the history of the tradition, and in relation to "Angela's" earlier mournful tone that marks her double alienation (from God and from herself), her identification with Jesus Christ as a male universal savior gestures to the collapsing of sexuate difference. After all, these are not the wounds of any man; they are the wounds of a God-man. Read mimetically, this God-man of the metaphysical tradition has wounded Angela by mediating her access to the divine through a masculine symbolic that frames the fulfillment of her desire in terms of penetration.

But there is another, more complicated, relation we can read in that same moment. The mystic relates to Christ's suffering by seeing herself in him and him in herself, but this is not a reductive identification that results in an annihilation of human flesh so often associated with the ascent of the soul. Rather, Irigaray's depiction of the ecstatic union insists on the irreducibility of Christ and the mystic's coupling by way of the lips: "Ecstasy is there in that glorious slit where she curls up as if in her nest, where she rests as if she had found her home—and He is also in her." Although the lips are entrances and exits which would connote movement in and out of these passageways from one place to another, the ecstasy that Irigaray's Angela experiences is not, on first read, the pleasure of penetration. Rather, her ecstasy comes from the pleasure of touching, kissing lips. The focus on lips kissing the *vulnus* is a part of Irigaray's effort to reconstitute images and symbols to inform a culture based in a female imaginary.[33]

By focusing on the lips as the means for kissing and self-touching, Irigaray redefines the pleasures as multiple. In kissing the wound, the two do not dissolve into one; they remain open ended for one another, offering a place to move into and out of freely. For Irigaray, these lips—of wound, vagina, and mouth—provide a symbolic wherein the relationship between men and women will not be the annihilation of the woman's (or the mystic's) selfhood but rather a becoming of their (and her) ecstasy. And furthermore, this ecstasy, this jouissance conceived as a deeper way of knowing rather than the Lacanian unknown, becomes the possibility of a way of speaking through sexual difference as/by women (*parler femme*) and therein a new symbolic register for becoming.

This image of "that glorious slit" is a precursor to the speaking, kissing, and touching lips in Irigaray's *This Sex Which Is Not One*, for which she is perhaps most well known, at least in an Anglo-American context. In the book, Irigaray develops an erotic scene of feminine lips, both oral and genital, whose touching boundaries are constitutive of their twoness, whose touching offers infinite points of sharing, touching, and pleasure—foundations of an expansive horizon of desire. In an early translation of "When Our Lips Speak Together" in the journal *Signs*, Carolyn Burke notes the play between blood and meaning/sense given in Irigaray's statement "Your blood becomes their meaning." In a footnote, Burke writes, "The play on *sang* ('blood') and *sens* ('meaning,' 'sense') extends the analogy between sexuality and writing. Blood is at once metaphorical and literal, a source of female sense and sexuality."[34] As Burke suggests, embedded in Irigaray's play between *sang, sens,* and sacrifice, is the notion that the blood of the feminine interlocutor's difference is sacrificed for the sake of the masculine world of meaning making; yet insofar as Irigaray's linguistic play associates feminine blood with meaning itself (rather than simply a means to some particular end), she ultimately resists the determinacy of that sacrifice.

It is no accident that the reader senses, or makes meaning from, the materiality or fleshiness of Irigaray's writing. In and through these visceral invocations, Irigaray probes the depths of the sacrificial economy to relocate an othered desire. Indeed, as the lips begin to speak and an other way of knowing emerges, Irigaray writes: "Wait. My blood is coming back. From their senses. It's warm inside us again. Among us.[35] Their words are emptying out, becoming bloodless, Dead skins. While our lips are growing red again. They're stirring, moving, they want to speak. You mean . . . ? What? Nothing. Everything. Yes. Be patient. You'll say it all. Begin with what you feel, right here, right now. Our all will come."[36] Meaning in the text manifests through the senses awakened in the experience of reading the punctuated rhythms and stimulated by Irigaray's erotic language of the sensations of feminine lips and the implication that the readers who partake in this meaning making do so as kissers and lovers of those lips. This meaning is tied to the becoming of a desire not as lack but as animation and energy, signaled by reinvigorated lips—whose blood has returned to them through the mimetic manipulation of language and a different way of knowing, sensing, and meaning. Against the singularity of the phallus, the multiplicity of the lips inspires a subjectivity that defies reduction to sameness, rejecting a notion of desire oriented in relation to a single organ. Lips disrupt the linearity of sense making, insisting instead upon a fecund expression of desire, opening previously foreclosed possibilities for ethical relation between the sexes within and through language.

Though the lips of the mouth typically mark the doorway to speech, and labial lips present the passageway of reproduction, for Irigaray, the possibility of language and sex, sexuality (not as an identity but as an expression of one's sexuate being) and subjectivity, comes from the touching of these lips that are always "at least two."[37] As Irigaray claims, "For in what she says, too, at least when she dares, woman is constantly touching herself."[38] Here, Irigaray associates saying and touching, touching and saying together, hinting at the uniqueness of a *parler femme* as an embodiment of lips. In this self-touching, desire is never lacking. It is always available in and for itself and capable therein of expressing a language otherwise than the masculine *le langue*. Emerging from at least two lips, and perhaps more, this is a desire beyond the singular desire of one sex; they are constitutive of a new horizon of knowing and becoming subjects beyond the singularity of a masculine symbolic. These lips constitute a convergence of the ambiguities of orality and the multiplicities of pleasure, to disrupt the oneness of meaning toward which language is aimed.

Irigaray's deliberate transition from the language of sacrifice to pleasure in *This Sex* is also useful for interpreting the *vulnus*/vulva beyond the wounding of desire in *Speculum*'s "La Mystérique." Like Irigaray's later portrayal of the lips in *This Sex*, Irigaray's mystic/hysteric vulva-to-*vulnus* touch is a mystical union signaled by the simultaneous relationality and irreducibility of their two fleshes. In kissing, two who are already at least two touch continuously without ever being reduced to one *vulnus or* vulva. And to borrow from Irigaray's even later references to lips in *Ethics*, the two create an open-ended envelope for each other, a space where the other can dwell and yet move freely in relation to their desires. "La Mystérique" performs this sort of openness by playing with theological notions of the wound of Christ as a symbol of his passion and the vulvic image of "openness" that express the desire of a female imaginary.[39]

As the passage from "La Mystérique" quoted previously suggests, the *vulnus* and the vulvic are the marks of bodies wounded by a discursive tradition, but whose wounds become the possibility of their ecstasy, their mystical, thoroughly enfleshed pleasure. Irigaray describes the intense love that the mystic experiences as she gazes upon his wounds. The wounds are revealing—they are part of his nakedness. The "gashes in his virgin flesh" suggest that the wounds attest to his innocence.[40] The language of "virgin flesh" reminds the reader that, consistent with the theological tradition's insistence on Christ's sinlessness, these wounds are not the consequence of guilt or sin. The language of virgin flesh also echoes with Irigaray's earlier lines that he is "that most female of men."[41] In the theological tradition of explicating salvation, the sinlessness of Christ provides a rational basis for the redemptive power of his sacrifice. Irigaray writes, "In his crucifixion he opens up a path of redemption in her fallen state."[42] But the power of this meditation on the wounds of Christ will not be redemption for sins; it will be an interrogation of the state of her fallenness. In fact, Irigaray immediately follows the identification of the crucifixion and redemption with two rhetorical questions: "Could it be true that not every wound need remain secret, that not every laceration was shameful? Could a sore be *holy*?"[43] The scene of love has moved beyond agapeic love for Christ's sacrifice. In keeping with the notion that the multiplicity of feminine desire rejects making sense in language as ever a singular endeavor of a male body, the play between *vulnus* and vulva dances erotically at the limits of pleasure and pain, fullness and lack, openness and secrecy.

In addition to the mystic's rhetorical rejection of the shamefulness attributed to women's flesh, a sense of shame that haunts the early tone of the text, her questions—"Could it be true . . . ? Could a sore be *holy*?"—mime the wound of Christ like a doubled mirror that disrupts the certainty of representation. In these questions, she invites interrogation of the phallogocentric myth of the sacred and profane that differentiates what is holy from what is shameful. The slippage between *vulnus* and vulva figures the site of this contestation.

As Kathryn Stockton writes in her intriguing literary interpretation of this text, "Woman's 'slit,' here pronounced 'glorious,' mirrors Christ's 'fathomless wound.' The wound itself acts as mirror(s), enabling 'woman' to reflect upon her material folds."[44] Here, Stockton is playing on Irigaray's call for women to make a mirror that they might be double unto themselves—such that their recognition would not depend on man. I would add that this slippage between *vulnus* and vulva means that the glorious slit elicits woman as a wounded sexuality and a flat empty mirror, only to transform her woundedness by rethinking the space of lack, the abyss (attributed to the feminine in philosophy and psychoanalysis), as a fecund, multiple, fleshy space. In other words, the vulvic imagery enters the conversation as a question of sexual difference that will transform the annihilation of the feminine self, an annihilation that must happen in an ecstatic union with a masculine God. Furthermore, rather than a penetration of one into another that results in the annihilation of difference between the human self and the divine other, here ecstasy is one of mutual touching. And this mutual touching is the possibility of her self-recognition becoming through her own desire, "*Outside of all self-as-same.*"[45]

The play between the *vulnus* and the vulvic in the passage mimics and disrupts theological moralizing of feminine desire that would depict women as dangerously carnal by virtue of their open genital and oral lips—yet without the promise of fulfilment in the form of transcendence typically afforded matter. Theirs is an erotic coupling of two bodies whose slits attest to their mutual transcendence. Irigaray thus transforms the *vulnus/*vulvic relationship into a sensible transcendental erotic coupling that plays upon the fleshiness of Christ's wound in order to share in the fleshy lips of women's "nonthematizable materiality" (per Judith Butler) or "material opacity" (per Irigaray).[46] In this erotic coupling of *vulnus* and vulva, their fleshy "slits" affirm their mutual transcendence such that the specificity of their flesh is irreducible and yet never fixed. The fleshiness of the mystic and Christ's mutual ascent is a reminder that eros is an embodied desire of irreducibly differentiated flesh and spirit in incarnation. Irigaray writes, "But if the Word was made flesh in this way, and to this extent, it can only have been to make me (become) God in my jouissance, which can at last be recognized."[47] As Irigaray and her mystic suggest, meditation on Christ's wounds will give her access to self-knowledge that will also be, for her body, a mark of redemption and not sin.

Wounding, Penetration, and the Remaking of Immanence and Transcendence through an Othered Desire

Although the interplay of the *vulnus* and vulvic disrupts associations of women's sexuality with woundedness—of women with carnality and carnality with sin—in a way that restores eros to the incarnation, this play remains risky. Citing Irigaray's critique of Lacan in *Marine Lover of Friedrich Nietzsche*, Hollywood notes that, in the works that follow *Speculum*, Irigaray shifts away from the language of wounding.[48] Hollywood acknowledges that this shift ultimately dissociates the penetrative attributes of Christ's wound from the vaginal to "reject an understanding of the female sex as wound-like."[49] In other words, Irigaray makes this shift in order to avoid associating feminine desire with woundedness more broadly. Hollywood is critical of Irigaray on this account. She claims that Irigaray's rejection of the penetrative space of a wound results from her insufficiently critical adoption of the psychoanalytic framework. By Hollywood's account, Irigaray's abandonment of the penetrative quality of the wound casts the othered desire of woman as exclusively antipenetrative, thus conceding to a framework that associates penetration as belonging exclusively to the masculine sex.

Hollywood adds that Irigaray's turn away from the wound reinforces Judith Butler's criticism that Irigaray's lips present a "rigorously anti-penetrative eros of surfaces."[50] According to the logic of Butler's critique, Irigaray's erotic scene is not just antipenetrative; its identifications are sexed such that even if one wanted to explore possibilities for rethinking the penetrative apart from a heterosexual matrix, it is now impossible by virtue of this sexing. However, Hollywood adds that the mystical texts themselves destabilize "gender positions" so as to exceed reductions of penetration to the masculine and antipenetration to the feminine.[51]

In other words, by Hollywood's reading, Irigaray has missed the potential radicality of the tradition itself, and therein she has missed an opportunity for thinking beyond the limits of the heterosexual matrix. To dissociate the language of penetration from heteronormative desire, Hollywood draws on medieval devotional literature and art to locate spaces of difference that imagine Christ's wounds apart from a fatalistic notion of penetration that she thinks Irigaray is attempting to avoid. Hollywood concludes, "Perhaps the Christ of 'La Mystérique' is better read as refusing gender binaries than as feminized and so as refusing the distinctions Irigaray herself continues to desire, even as she calls for their radical reimagining."[52]

While I agree with Hollywood that this tension exists in Irigaray, I insist that it is not just the wounding in "La Mystérique" that can disrupt metaphysical binaries that limit the making of worlds. This disruption is in fact available in the force of attraction that constitutes the space-time of desire, that irreducible materiality and alterity of lips—the boundaries themselves that constitute the threshold of *vulnus*/vulva. Put simply, the radicality of desire that Hollywood suggests is available by thinking the *vulnus*/vulva alongside the tradition is also offered in Irigaray's later renderings of the lips beyond the language of wounding as a penetration. In fact, I would argue that prioritizing penetration as an act of fleshy impalement or breaking of surfaces, which then transcends the limits of fleshy surfaces upon which discourse writes a body, has its own risks of reinscribing meta-physical binaries.[53]

Indeed, the power of the mimetic work of Irigaray's writing—of the writing that the lips foster—rests in its appropriation-as-refusal of binaries of interior and exterior of a masculine time and space of the subject and its becoming. Reading Irigaray's mimesis as a radical philosophical, linguistic, theological, and ethical endeavor, the eros of the lips cannot be reduced to *either* surfaces *or* wounds, nor can it be said that the lips are *either* exclusively antipenetrative *or* penetrative. As Anne Caldwell has insisted, Irigaray's efforts to disrupt the sacrificial economy, in which the materiality of differences is sacrificed for the sameness of identity, involve a reimagining of materiality altogether that dwells in the passageway of the material to the intelligible, in the space of a sensible transcendental.[54] I would add that reading the lips as emblematic of Irigaray's sensible transcendental means we cannot resubmit them to a language of antipenetrative versus penetrative that is itself based on a logic of inside and outside upon which materiality is excluded from intelligibility in the sacrificial economy.[55]

Lips hold together the discursive/intelligible/transcendent and material to create a gap (an embodied catachresis), providing an eroticism that rede-fines the inside-outside that marks the language of surface and penetration.[56] I want to rethink the lips and the radicality of touching by revisiting the remaking of materiality and alterity that the eros of the lips invokes. In order to consider how the eros of flesh and language transcends the language of wounding in terms of penetration, I therefore propose turning to the previously described embodied alterity of Irigaray's eros that the mimetic lips elicit.

Crossing Lips: Salvation beyond a Wounded Desire

In "When Our Lips Speak Together," Irigaray insists that love does not demand wounding. Playing with the autoeroticism of the lips and the possibility of a nonsacrificial love of self and love of other, Irigaray writes, "I love you: body shared, undivided . . . There is no need for blood shed, between us. No need for a wound to remind us that blood exists."[57] The suggestion that there is no need for a bleeding wound implies that pleasure, not reduction, is the possibility of life. The pleasure that would be a jouis-sance of the lips of feminine desire is not reducible to a particular notion of the feminine, or of her flesh, as lack. What is more, read in relation to "The Power of Discourse and the Subordination of the Feminine" (the interview also published in *This Sex*), this pleasure of the lips is perhaps the "'elsewhere' of feminine pleasure . . . found only at the price of *crossing back through the mirror that subtends all speculation.*"[58]

Irigaray asserts that the purpose for articulating this "'elsewhere' of feminine pleasure" would be to disrupt the logic of identity given in the specular economy of the masculine symbolic. Exposing those "conditions under which systematicity"[59] emerges and potentially "threaten[ing]" the logic of the system will require a recrossing or "*crossing back*" (*retraversée*).[60] This crossing back is precisely what mimesis continuously performs, and it is insofar as Irigaray's mimetic lips engender an erotic space capable of holding word and flesh together in this "'elsewhere' of feminine pleasure" that they are worth revisiting apart from the language of a fatalistically wounded eros. Furthermore, if as Irigaray writes, the "'*elsewhere*' *of female pleasure* might rather be sought first in the place where it sustains ek-stasy in the transcendental . . . where it serves as security for a narcissism extrapolated into the 'God' of men," then lips are especially worth revisiting as the figure of "*crossing back through the mirror*" of Christian theology.[61]

Irigaray's lips, as they appear *An Ethics of Sexual Difference*, initiate this crossing, calling forth theology, ethics, and the horizon of feminine desire in a way that disrupts the relationship of female desire to wounding. Allow me to trace the rationale. Irigaray contends that prevailing images of a Father God posit the divine as "the immutable spokesman of a single sex" such that women have been left without access to a "horizon . . . of the gods"; therefore, she evokes God, the lips, and incarnation at multiple points in the text, bringing these terms together in the chapter "Sexual Difference" to reimagine the space and time of sexual difference apart from the masculine discourse that has deprived women of access to divinity.[62] Remaking the world apart from the universalized masculine *one* requires reimagining space and time, transcendence and immanence, to make space for women to create their own places to inhabit, places that would have their own borders, their own horizons, their own limits, and therein access to a new horizon of other gods.

This "remaking of immanence and transcendence" occurs, Irigaray says, via "the threshold of the *lips*."[63] She writes that the *lips* are "strangers to dichotomy and oppositions. Gathered one against the other but without any possible suture, at least of any real kind."[64] Here, lips figure a relation both within the self and between self and other that does not collapse into sameness, and the horizon of their touching without collapsing has a spatial and temporal reality that literally and figuratively reimagines immanence and transcendence in relation rather than in opposition. Irigaray continues, "In this approach, where the borders of the body are wed in an embrace that transcends all limits . . . each one discovers the self in that experience which is inexpressible yet forms the supple grounding of life and language."[65] Lips thus call to an ethical horizon at the threshold of an irreducible difference of desire that separates as it connects them, that gives them boundaries as they give contours to each other; they link the materiality of flesh in all its senses with the indeterminacy of transcendence, refusing to reduce word to flesh or flesh to word.

After invoking the threshold of the lips and their capacity to reshape immanence and transcendence and reimagine the horizon of the divine, Irigaray sets off the following in parentheses: "(Two sets of lips that, more-over, cross over each other like arms of the cross, the prototype of the crossroads *between*. The mouth lips and the genital lips do not point in the same direction. In some way they point in the direction opposite from the one you would expect with the 'lower' ones forming the vertical.)"[66] Irigaray's lips conjure images of female genitals and the mouth, suggesting that feminine desire is sexual, symbolic, and irreducible to either. That the relationship between desire and representation emerges from the crossing of lips is telling.

The lips of pleasure and speech figured in the cross could seem like *dis*membered body parts, suggesting a sacrifice wherein women's bodies are deprived access to the difference of their desire. And while alienation from one's own desire is a familiar trope in Irigaray's mimetic use of the feminine, the lips "crossing over each other like arms of the cross" connect this alienation from self with alienation from the divine.[67] In the Christian tradition, this alienation is intensified by Jesus's maleness, which comes to represent a troubling mark of Christ's *universal* humanity, heightening the invisibility of feminine genital lips and the silence of lips of orality.[68]

Within normative Christian theological claims, the Incarnation links the Logos of creation to the Logos of salvation. The Gospel of John opens with the verse, "In the beginning was the Word and the Word was God and the Word was with God."[69] The theological concept of Incarnation and its doctrinal formulations are founded upon this statement. Echoing the introductory words in Genesis, the Word that will become flesh a few verses later in John 1:14 is explicitly linked to the Logos that creates the world. The notion of the word becoming flesh in the male Jesus who then dies to offer salvation for humanity makes man inseparable from this divine economy. The possibility for salvation, which in most Christian traditions involves bodily resurrection, is tied to this male body, the incarnation of a masculine logos of creation. Inasmuch as the cross is synonymous with sacrifice in Christianity, the lips reveal a veiled erasure of feminine desire concomitant with the becoming of a masculine God. These lips represent a sacrificed other, silenced and displaced from the logos of creation and the discourse of world making.

I recognize that such a reading potentially returns lips to the language of wounding sacrifice that undermines the eros lips have engendered through their remaking of the space and time of transcendence and immanence; however, I also think the crossing of the lips invites yet another reading. Returning to the passage in *Ethics*, in crossing, Irigaray's lips reappear from this sacrifice, resurrected in a space between—literally, parenthetically—transforming the sacrifice into an affirmation of othered desire, a desire that refuses the Oedipal desire for oneness of a masculine model of the subject. This othered feminine desire becomes the condition for resurrecting/reimagining the division between immanence and transcendence that marks the distinction between the material and discursive realms. The sexed specificity *and* indeterminacy of the lips allow Irigaray to reframe the cross's image of sacrifice as an ethical image of an incarnate otherness (and an other incarnateness) that emerges through the irreducible alterity of eros, rather than through the oneness of a wound. Here, the absence of a wound is not a rejection of penetration but of that universalized oneness, of the universalizing of its singularity.[70]

In sum, Irigaray's evocative lips play upon the slippage between the discourse and materiality that the Word-made-flesh of Christian language of the Incarnation enables by virtue of its occlusion of the body of woman—a meaning making that occurs through an overt sexing of matter that dematerializes woman's desire. The lips exploit this occlusion, gesturing to the materiality and alterity of an as-yet-unthought desire; they at once articulate the sacrificial economy of a phallomorphic culture and open toward a new incarnation.

The Space-Time of Incarnate Lips

Although they are beyond the purview of this book, Christian doctrinal formulations about the Incarnation involve a contentious history of debate about what it means for Word to be made flesh. And the debates about the specificity of the Word-flesh of Jesus's incarnation are inseparable from other theological claims about the meaning of crucifixion, resurrection, and ascension. Representations of these events are the occasion for worldmaking. Irigaray has harnessed this radical religious imaginary, which in so many ways defines Christian theology's notion that the Incarnation changes the world, to stage an intervention into how that world has been imagined.

In religious studies, Christianity is, along with Judaism and Islam, often dubbed a "religion of history." This classification is used to denote the historical time, that is, the unfolding of the religion in relation to human history, that dominates narratives of Christianity. The linearity of time in Christian theology is emblematic of its debt to historical time. Though there is a significant ambiguity of space-time in the divine economy that preexists Creation, normative Western Christian theological formulations, which owe much to Plato's cosmic order, frame God's relation to creation, and therein the Word in relation to flesh, in both linear fashion and teleologically in terms of a beginning and an end.[71]

By miming the language of the Incarnation and of the Crucifixion (as well as of Pentecost and Parousia, which mark the progression of God's time), Irigaray rejects the casting of the tradition in singular formulations that erase the traditions that precede it. Irigaray's writing retraverses the space and time of the Christian Incarnation in order to reimagine the relationship between word and flesh in a way that gives a nod to the question of history in the creation of a cultural symbolic. Mimetically drawing on the disruptive force of sexed material/visceral imagery to play upon the relationship between matter and language, she is "crossing back through the mirror" of the specular economy to articulate the " 'elsewhere' " of female pleasure."[72] If thinking through sexual difference will save "us," that thinking will be incarnate in the fullness of desire.

A different incarnation capable of reimagining the scene of the Crucifixion beyond an economy of sacrifice is offered in the eros of the lips. Lips propose an other desire, a desire of a feminine imaginary, as the possibility of an incarnation in which sacrifice is not the ultimate demand for salvation to occur. Here, the lips, as cross and/or crossing, gesture toward the incarnation of an othered/elsewhere desire that disrupts the binaries of the space-time of metaphysics and therein refigure the space and time of incarnation (beyond *the* Incarnation) differently.

Irigaray refigures the sacrificed God-man of metaphysics through the crossing lips, which touch and speak differently because of a space between them such that their borders constitute horizons of othered desire. Horizontally, the lips refuse the linearity of time and the telos of representational language; vertically, they refuse the hierarchy of space that prioritizes spirit over matter, word over flesh. The "lower" genital lips of sexual pleasure here are replacing the verticality of the phallus, upsetting the orientation of a world that separates and hierarchizes the heavenly over the terrestrial, the symbolic over the concrete. The lips of the mouth, which are above the lips of the genitals, point horizontally, articulating the horizon of desire that emerges through this resignification. Lips thus constitute an incarnation that crosses over metaphysical distinctions of terrestrial and heavenly; they constitute the specificity of a materiality suspended beyond the space and time of signification and open therein to radical alterity.

In discussing Irigaray's refiguring of the Hegelian dialectic, Laura Roberts reminds the reader that the "linking together of the 'terrestrial and heavenly' or 'horizontal and vertical' is not a synthesis of the two terms or subjects."[73] Keeping in mind the uniqueness of this relation with the other that refuses synthesis, we can read crossing lips as holding the relationship of word and flesh together in a different space-time of that " 'elsewhere' of feminine pleasure."[74] Crossing through and over one another in a radical touching, perhaps the crossing lips mark that "ceaseless exchange" that "increases indefinitely from its passage in and through the other" of the multiplicity of woman's pleasure that disrupts the economy of sameness.[75] Perhaps their *traversée* is constitutive of their *croix*; their crossing and moving through one another is the possibility of their word-flesh dynamic of incarnation as an "elsewhere." These lips are neither bleeding wounds nor impenetrable surfaces; they are marked more by their behavior than by some fixed idea of their matter. These lips begin to reconstitute, close, and go past the gap that they create in and through their crossing.[76] Refusing the wounding universalized oneness of a Christology marked by the reduction of time, space, and maleness of the Incarnation in a particular telos, the lips form the contours that transform space and time, suspending incarnation in a different temporality—one that refuses to put off the incarnation's value in a future and/or in a transcendental other.[77] And perhaps, more importantly than whether or not the lips are rigorously antipenetrative (and I don't think they necessarily are), it is worth thinking about the lips in the materiality of their radical alterity—in the specificity of their continuous incarnations of multiple desires.

I am insisting that the ethical dimensions of Irigaray's erotic lips are not reducible to a disembodied desire for some radically other transcendent.

The connection between heaven and earth is no longer represented by the oneness of an arguably disembodied phallic signifier. Instead, this link is represented by the multiple folds in female genital lips—lips that challenge notions of a disembodied movement between heaven and earth. In the crossing lips, the border between one and the other and between one and the same is now reframed as an interval of time and space made possible by the erotic space of two, which are always more than two, reaching toward each other, touching, without grabbing hold. These lips are absolutely fleshy, and the specificity of this flesh shapes the contours of the space between them that constitutes their crossing.

By virtue of the layers of those touching folds that confound the space of inside and outside, the lower lips of feminine desire figure the vertical stretching between transcendence and immanence as an extension upward and downward, inward and outward—giving depth and dimension, giving flesh to that body on the cross, refusing to allow the specificity of its flesh to become a disembodied, masculine universal. In this fleshy resignification of Christian language of Incarnation and Crucifixion, lips perform nothing short of the resignification of the order of the universe: a resurrection that would redeem a world constructed through the annihilation of the feminine other.

Becoming and Dwelling, the Space-Time of Lips

If the specular economy that enables the "'God' of man" also attributes transcendence to language and immanence to matter, this is precisely the space-time of the cross that Irigaray's lips retraverse or penetrate in order to articulate an "'elsewhere' of feminine pleasure."[78] In the interval created by their rhetoricity and fleshiness, the lips offer the type of "playful cross-ing" that Irigaray states in "The Power of Discourse" would refigure such distinctions between language and matter.[79] Irigaray again borrows from Christian theology to initiate this play that could make space for just such an elsewhere. Invoking Christian foundational language of the Incarnation as word becoming flesh and dwelling among us in the Gospel of John, Irigaray interweaves with the language of woman's "becoming" (devenir) and the sexes "dwelling" (habiter) in her enunciation of an ethical horizon.[80]

According to Irigaray, women need to be able to dwell within their own flesh, have a logic of their own morphe, in order to incarnate the divine in themselves. And, as her later critique of Levinas's positing of the divine in relation to male and female lovers in Ethics suggests, divine love cannot be thought until love between two exists; and love cannot be reimainged between two unless there are at least two incarnations; and two incarnations require two different fleshes. Irigaray writes, "The entrance into the dwelling, or the temple, where each would invite the other, and themselves, to come in, also into the divine."[81] Her use of the feminine *la demeure* as a dwelling/place of living is followed by her use of the masculine *le temple*.[82] This quote from "The Fecundity of the Caress" in *Ethics* encapsulates an entire universe of Irigaray's concerns about the need for women to have a place from which to imagine a divine that could mediate their fleshy becoming.

Irigaray's association with the temple as a place of inhabiting plays with the tension between man having a home or dwelling in language and the placelessness of woman that she also articulates earlier in *Ethics* in her critique of Aristotle as the consequence of relating woman with matter. A new incarnation is necessary for ethics, for alterity to be truly other, for a touching that is reciprocal rather than selfsame (and here she is playing with Levinas's own distinction between touch as primary and caress as constituted in subjectivity). Furthermore, insofar as "Fecundity of the Caress" was delivered in December of 1982, we can locate here the seeds of Irigaray's depiction of the relationship between partial incarnation and failed love presented in "Divine Women" in 1984. And in this critique, we might read her demand for women to have a place in order to cultivate a divine, to access a transcendence that their difference might generate. As Irigaray writes decades later in *Sharing the Fire*, "As humans, we lack roots of our own, and incarnating our union is that which can provide us with a place suitable for our dwelling."[83]

Irigaray's incarnate lips aim to cultivate such a space and time for becoming and dwelling. This space-time, this embodied temporality of lips, holds flesh and radical alterity together in a way that the God-man of the Christian Incarnation cannot. As always more than two, the crossing sets of lips reject a symbolic order governed by a single male signifier. The lips disrupt the selfsame structures of masculine discourse, and this disruption creates a space/gap/interval from which an other desire can emerge. Lips therefore stand in contrast to the gendered male body on the cross, but not as a simple reversal. The crossing lips are constitutive of a materiality of an interval or passageway, a crossing, beyond inside and outside, refusing the linear temporality of teleological time and its logic of satisfaction in a particular future. The lips embody the dynamic materiality of an othered desire. Crossing lips thus transform the word *became* flesh into a labial logic of word *becoming* flesh—in a continuously open, nonlinear temporality—as an ethical intervention into the sacrificial economy of the selfsame.

Recalling the introductory opening to *Ethics*, if sexual difference could be the "salvation" of "our time," an ethics of sexual difference cannot be simply a conceptual exercise. It requires actively offering words that speak with the wisdom of the materiality and alterity of desire between at least two, "at home" in their difference. This is a salvation from the economy of thought through attentiveness to incarnation. Lips refuse to be either immanent or transcendent, either material or representational, and crossing lips mimic the Christian cross to reorder the relationship between immanence and transcendence altogether, insisting instead that incarnation is partial—always open even as it may be sealed, always changing even in its specificity.

The lips' rhetorical capacity to resignify the Incarnation apart from a selfsame economy is inextricably bound to this irreducible relationship between pleasure/genitals and speech/mouth that indicates a differentiated desire. The lips may be rhetorical, but if they are not really lips, if they are not really fleshy or material in some way, then the ethical force of Irigaray's writing is lost. It is this embodied alterity in the space of writing that evokes an eros irreducible to its potential wounding. Beyond the time and space of the historical specificity of the Christian Incarnation, the incarnate lips mark the embodied tension of desire at the limits of word and flesh, or discourse and matter, where bodies struggle to see and be seen without reifying the specular economy. To borrow again from Butler's analysis of the distinctly nonphallogocentric materiality of Irigaray's feminine, Irigaray's lips constitute "a nonthematizable materiality" precisely because they refuse the binaries of metaphysics.[84] Perhaps a desire belonging to an "nonthematizable materiality" allows the possibility for thinking *through* sexual difference to get beyond sexual difference.

In the space between rhetoric and flesh, the embodied alterity of the lips engenders a nonphallogocentric logos of some other sort of nonmetaphysical alterity. Here, the lips are an invitation to lived reality at the crossroads of what is imagined and what is real. Because they are mimetic and bound to a discourse of sexual difference that is itself a repetition of sameness and difference, they invite meditation on the gap where their fleshy edges intimately meet. To borrow Anne Carson's imagery, the space of reaching without grasping, of touching without holding, desire without consuming, ensures that the desire these lips evoke is erotic.[85] As a rhetorical and material terrain for exploring the contours of this in-between space, the lips mark the pleasures of flesh becoming words in speech, insisting that incarnation is not simply a descent of the divine to the human but an ascent of the human to the divine. That Irigaray uses these lips, a certain flesh-made-word, to turn to the word-made-flesh of incarnation is an invitation to recall that bodies are sites where flesh and signification are bound up with one another in the sameness and difference of the space-time of living.

Bodies live, die, and are resurrected where flesh and signification meet. The coding of flesh into bodies—old bodies, young bodies, Black bodies, male bodies, female bodies, transgender and cisgender bodies, abled bodies and nondisabled bodies—has real effects, even if that coding is impermanent, dynamic, and to some extent arbitrary. Such is the challenge of a politics of recognition based in the repression of difference. In this context, returning to Irigaray is compelling because, as the lips reveal, her work operates in the tension between the material and the discursive, between the present and the future that these living, flesh-and-blood bodies inhabit. She intervenes in the sacrificial economy to imagine lips on a cross—a nonsacrificial economy of the sensible transcendental—that dwell in the eros of ambiguity rather than through a telos achieved through exclusions and repressions. Most significantly, this irreducible space of desire constituted by the lips neither fetishizes the wounding that can accompany the experiences of living amid this tension, nor does it close off, or suture, every hole as though it were a wound. Rather than the deep wounding of a desire resolved in the separation of the soul from its body or the annihilation of the self in becoming divine, an ethics of the lips inhabits the sinuous networks of intertwining of flesh and signification that reach for one another and also separate one another in the sweet bitterness of eros, redefining the space and time between them altogether differently.

Chapter 3

Queer Lips, Queer Wombs, and the Temporality of Desire

Modern liberalism is generally characterized by an association of subjectivity with autonomy. An autonomous subject is self-determinative, naming oneself apart from others. Put another way, liberalism ties subjectivity to a freedom of self-determination or autonomy, or at least the illusion of it. A politics based in liberal notions of subjectivity, as is evident in most contemporary democratic nations, recognizes persons as political subjects based in their capacity to perform their subjective identity, to be one in the same with the ideal subject. Under these conditions, the very possibility of political identification is based on recognition of categories within social life. And social life further conforms to the categories that are recognizable within the political. These recognitions are based on the capacity to create something familiar through differentiation from something else. They are, in short, recognitions based in an economy of the selfsame—the movement of subjectivity writ large.

Divisions within queer theory and politics are often due to different ideas about how to respond to the challenges of liberal politics—namely, whether it is possible, or desirable, to imagine queer collectivity without reifying a selfsame politics of identity. "Transgender" (or "trans*") and "non-binary" constitute contemporary discourses that arguably challenge binary determinations of gender identity and, relatedly, concepts of sexuality amid a sociopolitical discourse of sameness. Indeed, trans* and queer are much more than identities; they are affirmations of embodiedness beyond the limits of the binarisms of discursive representation, resisting the dimorphic understanding of bodies. However, political identifications too easily lose

81

their radical edge because of the potential (by associating cisgender categories with specific bodily enhancements and treatments) to follow a logic that reifies gender in particular biologisms that can feed transphobia and trans-misogyny.[1] Indeed, paradoxically, efforts to disrupt cisbinary gender identity and its counterpart of heterosexism risk reinforcing rather than disrupting these binaries. So while creating new categories might decenter normative or privileged identities, the more pervasive logic of identity remains intact, and new norms with their own forms of moralizing will doubtless emerge. The logic of heterosexism, of white supremacy, of patriarchy, of imperial exceptionalism remain because they belong to a more fundamental structural problem. As Lee Edelman suggests (in a way that gives me pause in my endeavor to reimagine ontology through desire) even the most seemingly radical positions reinforce the world they intend to disrupt, destroy, or flee.[2]

The paradoxical position in which queer and trans* politics and eth-ics find themselves speaks more broadly to the consequences of how one understands the relationship between discourse and the framing of bodies, between language and materiality, and how one conceives therein the prospect (or impossibility) of resistance to the norms that this relationship brings to bear upon subjectivity.[3] How does one negotiate an ethic (that resists identity) with politics (which demands identity) when one's ethical efforts are undone by political demands for recognition, in which identity is the means of solidarity?

I do not have the space and time to do justice to the complexities and differences found within the many theoretical engagements with the tension between discourse and materiality that informs the split between ethics and politics—but I do want to highlight dominant voices whose work interfaces with Irigaray's efforts to inhabit rather than accept this perceived impasse. It is my intention to explain the shared concerns in a way that highlights how radical Irigaray's aims actually are, to think Irigaray as foundational to queer and trans* theory. I do this not to absolve her of some of her disappoint-ingly unreflective statements related to nonbinary and trans* politics, but rather to consider the radicality of her notion of sexuate and how writing through the lips offers a way of thinking through the discursive-material tension in the becoming of subjects—one that neither fades into abstraction nor resubmits bodies to a stale, static ontological vision of reality. In short, we cannot think radical queer or trans* theory in relation to a phallocentric liberal subjectivity based in selfsame identity.

Like feminism, queer and trans* thought and politics cannot be reduced to a byline.[4] My aim in this chapter is to highlight key tensions represented by a handful of thinkers who take seriously the dangers that espousing a new category or new identity may have for remoralizing new norms (think virtue signaling and policing identity within communities in ways that hierarchize intersectional demands for justice). There is significant resonance between Irigaray's disruptions of autonomous subjectivity and anti-identitarian queer and trans* efforts to think through the discursive and material realms and their relation to the individual and the social.[5] This chapter thus frames tensions between queer and trans* theory and politics in terms of broader questions about the relationship between materiality and discourse and the "natural" and "sociohistorical" dimensions of subjectivity.

Reading the work of José Esteban Muñoz, Judith Butler, and Gayle Salamon, I consider the status of materiality in various queer and trans* theories of performativity. Following these theorists, I register criticisms of Irigaray's sexuate, as expressed primarily in her references to lips as reinforcing sexual dimorphism. But I argue, by way of Lynne Huffer's reading, that the lips hold materiality and alterity together, inhabiting the discursive-material tension in order to gesture beyond it. Pushing Irigaray beyond the limits of her own work, I reinterpret Irigaray's mimetic employment of lips as fleshy spaces of disruptive desire that challenge the ethics of obligation and the politics of autonomy that constrain queer and transgender politics. I therefore conclude by turning attention to the performative potential of lips to usher in a queer temporality[6]—to establish a space-time where agency and responsibility are redefined through the disidentifying materiality and alterity of desire.

Foucault and the Foundations of Queer Performativity: Discourse and the Possibility of Subjectivity

Contemporary divergences in queer theory, which I argue extend to a particular way of reading transgender theory, may be traced to the various receptions, interpretations, and manifestations of Michel Foucault and his legacy. How one interprets Foucault on the questions of discourse, embodiment, and the becoming of subjects impacts how (or if) one conceives of individual or collective resistance. On a fundamental level, Foucault's work challenged the foundations of knowledge, of self-knowledge, and of discourses that extend from and inform the social foundations of knowledge through which one becomes a self. In his early works in particular, Foucault submitted the foundations of knowledge to an analysis of their historical transformations in order to situate or contextualize those knowledges. This contextualization has resulted in a destabilization of the determinative power of discourses. Furthermore, Foucault's historicization of the category of sexuality, and in it his interrogations of the discursivity of sex, destabilizes any sense of an ahistorical essence to sexuality. And this disruption opened a way to imagine acts in terms of desires and pleasures rather than in terms of categories, which could be labeled and policed in the becoming of subjects in their discursive worlds.

So what is the connection between the proliferation of discourse and the problem of identity? The more categories one has, the more mechanisms one has to discipline oneself, to regulate and differentiate oneself as a self. From Foucault's perspective, then, proliferation is part of a cultivation, not destabilization, of self. Foucault's writings prior to and over the course of *The History of Sexuality*, and the development of his thought therein, have resulted in different interpretations of his understanding of the subject, his processes of cultivation and subjectivation, and those processes' implications for differentiating a religious ethics of pleasure from moralizing discourses of sex. Nevertheless, a central thesis of this work is that the modern subject has been imagined in relation to a discourse of sex that focuses on sex practices, practices framed through moralized and/or medicalized discourses. As Foucault writes in volume 1, "with the great series of binary oppositions (body/soul, flesh/spirit, instinct/reason, drives/consciousness) that seemed to refer sex to a pure mechanics devoid of reason, the West has managed. . . . to bring us almost entirely . . . under the sway of a logic of concupiscence and desire."[7] Furthermore, in this context, sexuality is a discourse that becomes based on sex practices and then reinforces the veracity of those practices and their relations through its own discourse. In service of this chapter's turn to a desire that is irreducible to the sociohistorical subject, and irreducible therein to sociohistorical identifications, I sketch a brief summary of Foucault's extended historicization of the emergence of the modern sexual subject as presented in his four volumes devoted to the topic: *The History of Sexuality*.

In his series of volumes dedicated to historicizing sexuality, Foucault applies early poststructuralist and linguistic psychoanalytic understandings of how meaning is established through differentiations and considers therein how differentiations are less a form of resistance than they are recapitulations of the exchange economy of discourse. In volume 1 of *The History of Sexuality: The Will to Knowledge* (*La volonté de savoir*, 1976), Foucault places Freud's repressive hypothesis within a broader history of the production of discourses on sexuality.[8] In the repressive hypothesis, desire is predicated on lack, and the law constitutes this lack that informs desire. The repressive hypothesis is based on an entire economy of interests that are served by its promulgation, which is precisely how Foucault understands the workings of discourse.[9] Tracing psychoanalytic discourses on sex back to Christianity, Foucault likens the proliferation of discourse to the form of the sermon. Like the sermon, Foucault writes, the proliferation of discourse on sex proclaims certain truths, rebellions, and futures such that the proliferation of discourse about sex, rather than engender a liberation from sexual repression, ultimately reproduces the knowledges that exert power in relation to the regulation of bodies and their pleasures. Some individuals benefit from these exchanges, but the proliferation of discourse has a silencing effect overall, and moreover, that proliferation is not neutral—it is a movement in and through power.

Foucault begins his analysis in volume 1 by establishing the conventional arguments regarding sexual repression as arising out of Victorian bourgeois society and the rise of capitalism. He writes that while this is "the" story of sexual repression, the discourse surrounding the suppression of sex and the silencing of sex talk has not taken into account the proliferation of its own discourse in the retelling of that silencing. In the repression hypothesis, and with the proliferation of discourse on sex in general, society castigates itself for ignoring or repressing sex and talk about sex. Society proliferates the discourse for talking about sex, but this proliferation of discourse about sexual repression is ultimately no less moralizing—because it creates more discursive opportunities, and therein, more categories for framing, and impinging upon, one's becoming a subject. So even if a period like the Victorian era gave the appearance of sexual austerity, that does not mean that that appearance corresponded to a self-denial in the same sense we see it today. Returning however to his focus on the question of the psychoanalytic subject, Foucault concludes volume 1 by insisting that the rendering of sex as a discourse during the nineteenth and twentieth centuries means that sexual desire serves the broader discourse of sexuality and cannot, therefore, be that which grounds the possibility of "liberation."[10]

In volume 2 of *The History of Sexuality* (*L'usage des plaisirs*, 1984), Foucault turns to the transitions from seventeenth-century practices of confession to psychoanalysis as a nineteenth- and twentieth-century form of confession. As part of his investigation, Foucault argues that through the increased focus on the relationship between sex, sin, and the body, the church forced an increasingly detailed confession onto its members, which amounted to a transformation of all/any desires into discourse. Here, the proliferation of discourse informs a certain power of self-discipline. This speech mill, with its censorship, was projected in literature via "scandalous" literature. The scandalous literature that emerged named and differentiated these desires, "making" more desires that gave rise to an even greater need for confessional practices. As Foucault framed it, the more desires were named, the more things there were to confess. Furthermore, even in the self-disciplining turn back to God and away from these desires, the very naming of these desires intensified the desires themselves. In the final chapters of volume 2, Foucault more precisely discusses the deployment of sexuality as a product of particular movements of power. The deployment of sexuality was a subsequent shift that included the proliferation of discourse surrounding sex, beginning with the confession and moving to the analyst's couch.

In volume 3, *The Care of Self* (*Le souci de soi*, 1984), Foucault traces the cultivation of a self as a sociodiscursive practice to the Greeks. For the Greeks and Romans, he writes, the care of self was a deeply embedded "true social practice." Foucault states, "Around the care of the self, there developed an entire activity of speaking and writing in which the work of oneself on oneself and communication with others were linked together."[11] Foucault discusses the historical transitions of this Greek broad-based care-of-self model to one focused on looking to specific disciplines to generate a notion of self-knowledge. He goes on to explain the relationship between shifts in discourses about the self and transformations of the care of self. Foucault writes that as the focus on the care of self becomes increasingly preoccupied with medicine, it moves away from its association with practices for correction and training and education of the body (like the Greeks), gives way to the notion of the ill soul that must be treated (philosophy and religion), and then moves on to a certain self-care. Of the transition, Foucault writes, "The improvement, the perfecting of the soul that one seeks in philosophy . . . increasingly assumes a medical coloration."[12] Self-care develops into subjecting oneself to the discourses of medicine (psychology included) that enabled one to become a self.

Here, educating oneself and taking care of oneself are interconnected activities."[13] The art of self-knowledge develops, and with it a more schematized subject which must submit itself to practical tests (such as deprivations) as well as self-examinations or evaluations of one's progress.[14] Foucault writes that in self-knowledge, one must have a constant attitude of laboring in thought in order "to accept in relation to the self only that which can depend on the subject's free and rational choice."[15] The individual, now self-possessed as a result of these tests, practices, and examinations, is now an object of pleasure for himself—pleasing to himself.[16] Such is the pleasure of the modern subject in its illusory autonomy.[17]

Foucault suggests that understanding the cultivation of the self is necessary to contemplating ethics. The ethics of pleasure, according to Foucault, arises out of a cultivation of the self that develops into a pleasure in the self. "The development of the cultivation of the self produced its effect not in the strengthening of that which can thwart desire, but in certain modifications relating to the formative elements of ethical subjectivity."[18] The mechanisms through which one becomes a self are not, Foucault insists, an overcoming (or sublimation) of one's desires but a more dynamic and complex navigation of one's desires. Foucault's writings over the course of *The History of Sexuality*, and the transformations of his thought therein, have resulted in different interpretations of his understanding of the subject. What is evident in Foucault's reflections on his earlier examination of the discursivity of the subject—and his focus on the modern subject as cultivated through a discourse of sexuality—is his correlating suggestion that a "hermeneutics of desire" constitutes an enduring lens through which selfhood has been cultivated.[19]

Notwithstanding the question of desiring "man" as the subject of Foucault's inquiry, which Eve Kosofsky Sedgwick took up in the 1990s, there is little doubt that Foucault's depiction of the relationship between discourse and the cultivation of a self has impacted how the body has been figured in more contemporary conversations about the "body" and its relation to discourse. His contextualization of bodies and discourses within historical periods and trajectories has led some to think of the body as a malleable site through which one becomes a subject in the world. Thoughtful and talented scholarly engagements that address the rich complexity of Foucault's legacy abound. And the posthumous publication of *Volume IV: Confessions of the Flesh* (2018, 2021 in English) has invited further consideration of how Foucault's conceptions of the sociality of embodiedness changed over the course of his work.[20]

Foucault's analyses of both the sexual subject and, later, the desiring subject remained focused on their emergence through discourse as a socio-historical unfolding. Lingering questions about Foucault's legacy have shaped divergences in queer theory, especially regarding the question of power and the possibility of resistance to the moralizing force of discursive norms. For example, if one becomes a subject by subjecting oneself to the discourses of one's time and place (where resistance is just another dimension of power in the discursive economy), what is the possibility of resistance? What is the consequence of such a totalizing reading of the relationship between bodies and discourse, between pleasures and discourse, between desire itself and discourse? On the one hand, if one embraces the totalizing relationship of self-cultivation through discourse, multiplying categories and identifications offers an opportunity for agency to disrupt existing norms. On the other hand, if within this discursive-bodily dynamic that Foucault articulates one locates a call to think beyond the selfsame economy itself, to resubmit the modern self to the scrutiny of its foundations, they may turn to a more fundamental transhistorical or even perennial desire. Furthermore, Foucault's suggestion that desire is fundamental and irreducible to the sociohistorical self relates to questions about how to conceive embodied desire apart from sociohistorical identifications.

Returning to the question of ethics and politics posed at the outset of this chapter, I will focus on inheritors of Foucault's legacy. In these theoretical visions, how one understands embodiments and the relationship of embodiment to social and historical norms shapes the sense of their inevitability or their malleability. Such readings of the relationship between discourse, materiality, and subjectivity will also inform how theories of performativity imagine the possibility or impossibility of embodied antinormative practices. As my engagements with Muñoz, Butler, and Huffer will also suggest, how one inherits Foucault will also impact how one reads Irigaray. In particular, the idea that for Foucault, the perennial subject is a desiring subject resonates with Irigaray's ontology of becoming as always a relation of desire. And for both thinkers, I argue the question of desire should be read as a question of ethics, radically reimagined through the strange asymptotic touching of lips, rather than a question of identity.

Queer Performativity in the Work of Muñoz

The tension between ethics and politics is in part a tension between the notion of the individual and the social, the autonomy or freedom of the self versus responsibility to one's others. With Levinas's efforts to make ethics the first philosophy, the ego emerged out of responsibility to one's others, rather than out of an autonomous self-naming. This meant that ethics became a responsibility to others, and the politics of identity began to look like a will to self through recognition and belonging within the social. The perceived impasse between ethics and politics as a question of the individual's relation to the social order has rendered it ripe for psychoanalytic intervention. Indeed, psychoanalysis has been useful for rethinking the relation between ethics and politics by allowing for consideration of an agential self that is not always already and/or exclusively an effect of the social and political discourse of self.

José Esteban Muñoz stands out as one of the most incisive thinkers of a subjectivity that is not constituted exclusively by capitulating to the selfsame sociocultural matrix of which politics is part. Balancing political recognition with the desire for belonging, Muñoz does not locate resistance in new identifications (or proliferations of identities therein); rather, he locates in the psychoanalytic a sphere of agency that stands outside and is yet always in relation to the social. In Muñoz's landmark book *Disidentifications: Queers of Color and the Performance of Politics*, the late author brings together ethnography, psychoanalysis, and performance theory to engage the interstices of race, sexuality, and identity. He examines identification and disidentification as a performance that is also a survival strategy for queer persons of color; for Muñoz, disidentification is a radical position that challenges political liberalism's elision of autonomy with identity.

Muñoz posits an ethical space of racial performativity not as the consequence of a particular essence, but as the effect of racial belonging and recognition—not an essential condition, but a function of the condition of alterity, of antinormativity, of not belonging or being recognized. Analyzing Marga Gomez's interviews of lesbian truck drivers, as well as reading James Baldwin's depiction of Bette Davis on the silver screen in *The Devil Finds Work*, Muñoz articulates identification, counteridentification, and disidentification as paths that a subject negotiates in relation to the discursive and ideological norms within society. He says that in identification, the good subject "chooses the path of identification with discursive and ideological forms."[21] This makes the good subject synonymous with the obedient subject, that is, the one who locates identity in the universal or ideal subject—for example, being a good girl, a good boy, a good woman, a good man, and so on. In counteridentification, one rejects those forms in a way that risks reaffirming the dominant ideology. Counteridentification operates as a negation of the normative or ideal identities. As such, it appears as a resistance, but it relies on an antagonistic framework for structuring categories, an antagonism (between self and other, same and different) upon which the politics of recognition is already based.[22]

Muñoz establishes a third option: disidentification. In disidentification, one chooses a different path, of neither identification nor rebellion. This choosing to engage identity and disrupt it, he argues, enables marginalized persons to transform the confines of their cultural expectations, effectively remaking worlds. This practice of using identity to disidentify provides a resistance to the subject's interpellation of the symbolic and to the dominant ideology of wholeness toward which that symbolic is ordered. Disidentification aims for a possibility of agency in the radical refusal of identity.

As a rejection of liberalism and the politics of autonomy that is grounded in a complex embodiedness, I think it is useful to read Muñoz's disidentification in relation to Irigaray's lips. For Muñoz, disidentification is an embodied practice. Like Muñoz's work, Irigaray's lips combat the logic of identity and exclusion that mark liberalism, and liberal politics,[23] with their emphasis on an individual's ascent to universality. Muñoz posits queerness as "something whose mourning is a condition of possibility for other modes of sexuality that are less problematic," less disruptive to the norms of social and political existence.[24] It is in turning to psychoanalysis in particular that Muñoz establishes this queer performativity, a performativity rooted in "modes of sexuality," that is the condition or grammar upon which normative categories are deconstructed. Irigaray's notion of a prediscursive materiality, I think, inhabits a similar structure with respect to the psycho-analytic model of the subject and the possibility of being in relation to the symbolic without being determined by it. Her turn to a sexuate materiality is in some ways similar to Muñoz's notion of queerness, insofar as it is a desire that has not been thought through that must be recovered.

The collective agency that Muñoz attributes to queerness as a materiality of alterity (his words) further resonates with Irigaray's efforts to imagine the materiality of alterity in relation to an irreducible sexuate as the possibility of women's subjectivity.[25] In other words, disidentification locates the agency of the queer and/or sexuate other in the materiality of their alterity. The question of materiality thus pinpoints Irigaray's sustained interest in the symbolic as a space of discourse into which one enters to become a subject. It also highlights her investment in reimagining that symbolic in order to conceive becoming in a more ethical way, beyond identity as the sacrifice of difference. As I will argue, Irigaray's attempt to rethink materiality reflects her interest in agency and the possibility of politics, topics that emerge in her later work.

On this point, I agree with Anne Caldwell and Alison Stone that Irigaray's efforts to think through materiality are aimed at (1) the broad effort to reimagine subjectivity as a relational mode of being beyond an economy of sameness that sacrifices difference for identity and (2) the effort to ground some sort of viable political position based on a different model of the subject. And as suggested in the previous chapter, Irigaray's lips remake materiality apart from the sacrificial order of the selfsameness that drives identity in language as well as in liberal politics. But are Irigaray's lips radically queer in the sense that Muñoz's queerness suggests? Can Irigaray's lips exercise an agency in/of a materiality that truly disidentifies, as I think Irigaray's resistance to the selfsame aims to do? To answer these questions in the affirmative, with an appended "and then some," I want to focus on the materiality of the sexuate as a queer space in Muñoz's understanding of queerness in (dis)relation to the social, to suggest that prediscursive materiality is not essentially sexed.

In the following sections in this chapter, I explore feminist and queer readings of Irigaray's project as they relate to reading materiality in relation to discourse. I begin by focusing on Judith Butler's reading of Irigaray to articulate a key difference between their conceptions of materiality. I emphasize that there is a radicality to Irigaray's efforts to rethink materiality that gets foreclosed in her efforts to articulate a present politics in terms of a sexuate future. I then argue, based on Lynne Huffer's criticism of queer performativity, that Irigaray's lips offer not only the impetus for disidentification, but that they do so in a way that is mindful of the continuous reimagining of the present that avoids framing specific sex acts as subversive. In fact, I will argue that Irigaray's lips abide in a notion of desire beyond sex and sexuality and locate desire in a much more radical space and time of the materiality and alterity of the sexuate.

Butler and Irigaray:
The Prediscursive Materiality of Irigaray's Lips

Irigaray is both loved and reviled by feminists and queer theorists, and more recently trans* theorists, for a variety of intertwining but different reasons. For some feminist theorists, Irigaray is too abstract to support feminist politics; for some queer theorists, her abstraction risks reinforcing heteronormativity; for some trans* theorists, her notion of sexuate difference can be criticized as cisnormative. The vast majority of these critics focus on the political implications of Irigaray's thought, arguing that her constant interweaving of discursive representations of the female body in order to make philosophical critiques conflate the feminine with materiality. But Irigaray's work, including her language of lips, placentas, membranes, and womb, is an effort to re-embody language, including the linguistic psychoanalysis of Lacan.

Judith Butler is among the theorists who both acknowledge the dense theoretical deconstruction that Irigaray's use of the feminine attempts and criticize Irigaray for getting in her own way, so to speak, by not going far enough in her deconstructive project. Butler's efforts have long engaged the theoretical tensions between ethics and politics, and they have engaged Irigaray rather extensively.[26] Butler has been invested in reimagining a more ethical subjectivity beyond sameness, while also attempting to avoid the moralizing that too often accompanies ethics. Butler, too, is an inheritor of Foucault's poststructuralist legacy and is similarly invested in antinormativity. Their own project argues for an ethics and politics of performativity that interrogate the relationship between bodies and discourse.[27] Butler's particular vision of performativity owes much to Foucault's work, especially its destabilization of the relationship between gender and bodies and highlights the embodied effects of discourse as constituting a sociohistorical imagining rather than an intractable reality.[28]

Butler, like Foucault, looks toward antinormative embodiments of gender and sexuality in order to disrupt seemingly inevitable relations between bodies and discourse. This work not only highlights an arbitrariness found in the inscription of bodies in discourse; its disruption of identity also suggests a certain agency (even if passive) inherent in performativity.[29] In other words, in a dynamic and inevitable engagement with social life, through which one becomes recognizable to oneself and one's others, there is at once a necessary loss of what/who one might have been as well as a possibility of agency that one can exercise within the sociocultural matrix. Butler's work has inspired queer and feminist theorists of performativity, including Muñoz, who emphasize the power of discourse in order to unshackle the body from essentialist binds.

In the introduction of "Bodies That Matter," Butler examines Irigaray's understanding of matter to argue that the materialization of difference is manifested through a heterosexual regime. Butler frames sexuality as a regime wherein discourses engender disciplined performances, or self-regulation (i.e., Foucault's subjectivation). The body—not as a thing, but as a concept given in discourse—becomes a reality, becomes some thing, because of this debt to sexuality. In this essay, which opens with a quote by Irigaray, Butler notes that conceiving the material-discursive relation of lived bodies as an either/or proposition oversimplifies the dynamism of the space that constitutes their limits at any given time. They hint at the seemingly obvious question that lingers with respect not only to the discursive-material relationship in the wake of performative theory but also to the Foucauldian vision of the subject.

What does it mean to speak of matter, and how is speaking of a materiality prior to masculine discourse any different from suggesting that a natural or real prediscursive body exists? That Butler turns to Irigaray to think through the question of matter and materiality in the wake of post-structuralist disruptions of bodily determinism is a testament to the ways Irigaray's thought intersects with queer theory's engagement with ethics and politics. It is also confirmation of how Irigaray's work converges with the effort to think about the possibility of agency for those who are marginalized, without that "agency" being simply an effect of submitting oneself to an identity, to a subjectivity that is recognizable within the politics of a particular present. Indeed, Irigaray's efforts to think sexual difference prior to politics is, for her, a possibility of thinking a subjectivity for women that is not based in a notion of the feminine.

Butler's reading of Irigaray is sympathetic but also critical, and it is within the context of their own prioritization of discursivity that Butler embarks on this critique. Their charitable criticism does not reduce Irigaray's work in terms of a simple essentialism or heterosexism, and they acknowledge the aim of Irigaray's project. Reading *Speculum*'s "Une Mère de Glace," Butler acknowledges Irigaray's play between woman as womb and mother and Plato's notion of *chora*; the Aristotelian distinctions between form and matter; and those distinctions' subsequent redeployments for grounding existence in a way that places woman as mother as womb on the side of a particular originary, but also placeless, materiality.[30] Referring to Irigaray's miming of the feminine as part of a "penetrative textual strategy," Butler writes, "This textual practice . . . penetrates, occupies, and redeploys—the paternal language itself."[31] By this reading, Irigaray's use of the maternal-feminine to engage metaphysics empowers sexed matter to disrupt the illusion of woman and remake that difference anew. Butler thus recognizes that Irigaray's intertwining of the forgetting of the feminine with denigration of matter is part of Irigaray's critique of the power of discourse.

However, Butler locates a fundamental philosophical failure in Irigaray's framing of matter in relation to the problem of sexual difference, which prevents Irigaray's work from being sufficiently radical. Butler describes efforts to use an irreducible prediscursive sexuate to move beyond a masculine symbolic as constructing a totalizing circularity that undermines Irigaray's philosophical project. Butler writes that Irigaray's mimetic engagement "enacts the theory of flesh that it also interrogates, installing itself in a hermeneutic circularity from which it cannot break free and in whose hold it appears quite willfully to stay."[32] Butler contends that Irigaray's insufficiently critical adoption of psychoanalysis limits the radicality of her efforts—trapping her in a circularity of language and a heterosexuate concept of desire. Butler explains this heterosexism that is latent in Irigaray's efforts to think materiality as prediscursive by differentiating Irigaray's depictions of the lips and womb, respectively, arguing that while Irigaray does in fact disrupt the transcendent value afforded form in Platonic thought, the lips' resistance to penetrative desire remains beholden to a heterosexist specter of desire (where penetration is always seen as heterosexual penetration) that limits the potential of matter to disrupt the social order. As such, Irigaray's efforts to rethink matter by way of lips might not undo the sexing of matter.

The proof of this inescapable paradox appears, Butler suggests, in Irigaray's depiction of the lips as "rigorously anti-penetrative." As I discussed in the previous chapter, Butler contends, like Hollywood, that Irigaray's insistence on framing the lips as antipenetrative is insufficiently radical because its antipenetrative position assumes that penetrative desire is inherently selfsame, phallic desire. In other words, Irigaray's antipenetrative desire assumes that penetrative desire is the desire of a phallocentric psychoanalysis, without considering that penetrative desire could be otherwise. The lips, by this argument, are insufficiently radical because they cannot remake materiality without already subjecting materiality to an antipenetrative notion of desire that is ultimately a concession that penetration is the desire of a masculine selfsame. *For Butler, it would seem that the problem of returning to matter through antipenetrative lips is that there can be no notion of matter itself that is not always already caught up in a discourse of dehistoricized sexuality. In attempting to resist penetration, the lips might kowtow to it.*[33]

Based on Butler's reading, because the lips resist penetration, Irigaray overlooks the sociohistorical situatedness of interpreting desire through a psychoanalytic framework. Reading lips as exclusively antipenetrative risks reducing desire to a homosexuate touching as a reversal of heterosexism that capitulates to the heterosexist binary. By positing an irreducibility in antipenetrative lips, the prediscursive desire that would be the space of those lips loses the multiplicity of desire. In a powerfully succinct charge, Butler contends, "Indeed, if it can be shown that in its constitutive history this 'irreducible' materiality is constructed through a problematic gendered matrix, then the discursive practice by which matter is rendered irreducible simultaneously ontologizes and fixes that gendered matrix in its place."[34]

Butler's allusion to the "irreducible" is a reference to Irigaray's positing of the sexuate as an irreducible difference prior to discourse. Butler contends that Irigaray's notion of irreducibility is so radically dehistoricized that it ignores the conditions of its own theorization. Here, Butler warns against grounding a feminist vision of "bodily life" in a prediscursive notion of materiality because that materiality assumes and therefore (potentially) reinscribes a particular irreducibility that is divorced from its sociohistorical situatedness.[35] Butler therefore critiques Irigaray's reading of prediscursive materiality of an irreducible difference of the sexuate as dehistoricizing the question of materiality—rendering the question of materiality a question of sexual difference as an ontological question.

For Butler, Irigaray's reliance on a prediscursive notion of sexual difference cannot sufficiently trouble the discursivity of matter itself as a construct for imagining the limits of political life.[36] In a cautionary assessment of grounding sexual difference in a prediscursive materiality and a grounding of materiality in sexual difference, Butler writes, "We may seek to return to matter as prior to discourse in order to ground our claims about sexual difference, only to discover that matter is fully sedimented with discourses on sex and sexuality that pre-figure and constrain the uses to which that term can be put."[37] Here, the concept of materiality is itself an effect of discourse with which one cannot easily dispense. Butler's critique pushes us to consider the more entangled dimensions of Irigaray's notion of matter with heterosexism. And their challenges to Irigaray remain an important reminder that matter itself must be continually rethought in relation to the available discourses for speaking of the surfaces of the world at any given moment. Until these entanglements are considered, it becomes difficult to locate an agency of materiality that is not always already an agency of heterosexist identification. After all, Irigaray's sexuate is an irreducible difference behind all possibility of relation.

I take these criticisms of Irigaray's work seriously, but I think there is room in her ethics to establish a generous reading of her project that would highlight the potential bubbling at the surface of her work, rather than its limits. Irigaray's turn to the lips to disrupt the relation between matter and maternality is an attempt to make space for an other, as-yet-unarticulated desire. I would add that reading the lips as "rigorously antipenetrative," as Butler does, overlooks the active remaking of inside and outside in the radical touching of lips, as a touch that reimagines surfaces as porous folds rather than flat mirrors.[38] And I would also add that Butler's own resistance to articulating materiality as anything but discursive/cultural leaves us with a materiality so abstract that it defies certain commonsense notions of physical existence.[39]

In regard to Butler's critique, is there a way in which a reading of materiality in Irigaray stands up to the question of history without dehistoricizing materiality, that is, without rendering the materiality of alterity a complete abstraction, without any attention to specificity? How might we read Irigaray in relation to her efforts to rethink what Butler calls "the history of sexual difference encoded in the history of matter," without simply rethinking the history of matter as a history of sexual difference?[40] Against Butler's charge that Irigaray's notion of matter dehistoricizes sexual difference, I would argue that Irigaray's notion of sexual difference operates beyond the binaries of the real versus the imagined or the historical or ahistorical. As Irigaray reminds us in "Dreaming of a Democratic Future," this capacity to think the materiality of sexuate difference uninscribed by the symbolic is precisely the possibility of its relation to queer disidentification.

Like Butler, Gayle Salamon, in her book *Assuming a Body: Transgender and the Rhetorics of Materiality*, considers Irigaray's reading of Aristotle as a starting point for thinking materiality. But unlike Butler, Salamon argues that Irigaray's notion of place is relational and indeterminate in ways that are productive for thinking through materiality beyond gender and heteronormativity.[41] Salamon articulates Irigaray's insistence that place is constituted through a (material) proximity of difference. She writes, "Whereas what secures place in Aristotle is the substitutability of one kind of body for another, Irigaray points here toward the limits of that substitutability and suggests that the form and shape of the body secure for it an identity, though not a sameness, that allows and enables proximity."[42] According to Salamon's reading, Irigaray's notion of place engenders a reading of relationality capable of thinking materiality beyond the receptive, passive, empty matter of metaphysics.

Salamon, however, departs from Irigaray, turning to place over sexuate difference as a site for thinking through a queer materiality. Her departure is based on her reading of Irigaray's sexuate as fixed in terms of male-female. Salamon suggests that Irigaray's notion of irreducibility is based in the unsubstitutability of a man's body for a woman's body in a way that flattens the radicality of their specificity and universalizes their irreducibility. Salamon writes, "The logic by which the male body is unsubstitutable for the female body is the same logic that would posit every male body as able to stand in for any other or viewing women, in some sense, as interchangeable parts of Woman."[43]

Salamon's criticism of the sexuate echoes part of Butler's concern that within Irigaray's framework of sexual difference/the sexuate, materiality remains caught up in a sexed binary (male-female) notion of matter. And, as with Butler, I follow Salamon's reading of Irigaray up to this point of the fixity of the sexuate. Salamon claims to depart from Irigaray when she asserts that Irigaray's thinking of sexual difference ultimately remains trapped in a binary notion of sex. Salamon writes, "If one thinks sexual difference in other than binary terms, the category can become unyoked from determinative bodily materiality in a way that makes it easier to resist the temptation to posit genital morphology as essentially determinative not only of sexual difference but also of the self. If sexual difference is categorically and functionally indistinguishable from genital difference, which is itself understood to manifest (as) a binary, then sexual difference is genital difference is genital dimorphism."[44] Salamon argues for a move from sexual difference to transsexual difference in order to get past this potential for sexual difference to become dimorphic.

The sexedness or not sexedness of matter in Irigaray's notion of sexuate/sexual difference remains a topic of debate among Irigaray scholars. Emily Anne Parker's *Elemental Difference and the Climate of the Body*, for example, provides a compelling reading of how and why Irigaray's sexuate remains cisheteronormative. Following Salamon's argument and Sylvia Wynter's reading of biocentrism, Parker argues that Irigaray's sexuate relies on a notion of a two-sex model of morphology that reveals her reliance on a biocentric (i.e., consistent with discursive constructions of nineteenth-century biology) notion of relationality.[45] In other words, according to Parker, Irigaray's emphasis on the need for women to become sexuate subjects in and of their own morphology (a morphology that is not phallocentric) assumes the sexuate is two, excluding a nonbinary morphology that could otherwise sustain a trans* feminist and posthumanist notion of sexuate relation.

But this is not an entirely fair reading of Irigaray with regard to the sexuate, particularly with regard to materiality. I would argue that Irigaray's reading of place in Aristotle is part of her broader remaking of space-time, by thinking through sexual indifference toward a truly different sexual difference/sexuate. Reimagining the space and time of the sexuate means reimagining materiality as relational (as Salamon suggests), and, I would argue, without resubmitting that materiality to a cisnormative heterosexist discourse representative of selfsame desire. There is no doubt that the potential cis- and heteronormativity of Irigaray's work is not easy to bracket, especially in light of her pursuit of materiality through the sexuate. Even charitable and careful readings of Irigaray, like those by Butler, Salamon, and Parker, have contested the capacity of her work to move into more radical spaces for thinking about the more complex questions of gender and of sexuality posed by noncisheteronormative binaries. However, I maintain that the radicality of Irigaray's work that has drawn imminent scholars in queer and trans* theory is too often abandoned because of a submission of her notion of the sexuate to the demands of a phallocentric logic and discourse that burden scholars. This abandonment results in an unwillingness to think the sexuate in relation to Irigaray's larger speculative project—to cultivate the desire that remakes the space and time of materiality and alterity and is capable of sustaining relationality of becomings beyond sameness. This means reading Irigaray's sexuate in terms of the dynamism of its irreducibility—a dynamism based in desire. And here I agree with Stone, who suggests that Irigaray's sexuate is not sexed.[46]

To push back on criticisms of the cisbinary heteronormativity in Irigaray's work, while taking seriously antisocial queer theoretical critiques of social recognition, I argue we must be diligent about differentiating Irigaray's notion of the sexuate from biological sex and/or gender and desire from sexuality; we must rethink the lips as radically queer. If we focus less on pinning down the status of the sexuate and more on this dynamism of the materiality and alterity of desire in Irigaray's framework, we must consider the real and the imagined together, beyond the priority of presence and yet not completely divorced from the language of and in the present that binds us and limits our imaginations. On this point, I contend that, despite the precarity of grounding difference in prediscursive materiality, there is still value in interpreting Irigaray's prediscursive materiality on Irigaray's terms. To say "on Irigaray's terms" is to think of the materiality of the sexuate in relation to Irigaray's prioritization of ethics—to think materiality in relation to her prioritization of alterity. And yet to think of prediscursive materiality is also to insist on Irigaray's demand to acknowledge the alterity of one's other as material. Indeed, for Irigaray, the prediscursive "matter" of sexual difference has a material specificity; it has a substance all its own that is the condition of its resistance, the reminder of its presence in the midst of its attempted erasure.

Together, this materiality and alterity of the irreducible difference of the sexuate are suggested in the labor, the mimetic work, of the lips.[47] And most importantly, for this project, this irreducible difference of the sexuate refigures materiality in the space and time of desire. For in touching lips, it is desire that remains (rather than is filled as though it were a lack) and desire that frames and sustains the interval between *at least* two.[48] And in positing lips as a material embodiment of the alterity of the sexuate, the desire they invoke flows and bubbles up in/between/among the spaces of bodies-who-are-not-one (to riff on both Muñoz and Irigaray) touching in their alterity. This is a Muñoz-inspired queer reading of the lips; it is the remaking of space and time through the dynamic materiality of Irigaray's work that ushers in this disidentification. Beyond sameness, it refuses freedom as some self-same autonomy that forgets its debt to the other/mother and instead imagines an embodied practice that is always at once agential and relational. Lynne Huffer has taken up a similar vision of desire in adopting and adapting Irigaray's lips, focusing on the way Irigaray's lips are antifoundationalist, antimoralizing, antinormative embodiments by virtue of their materiality and alterity.[49] *I therefore turn to Huffer's efforts to read Irigaray's lips in relation to a queer feminist ethic of performativity that does not render the physicality of matter a complete abstraction, but rather locates an ethical demand within materiality.*

Queer Lips: A Materiality and Alterity beyond Sexuality

Huffer's engagements with Irigaray on questions of ethics and politics span more than three decades. And Huffer's own interest in conceiving a sort of intersubjectivity in terms of an ethics of eros responds to the question that I think Irigaray's work inspires. At the heart of Huffer's sustained interest in Irigaray is, I would argue, a deep engagement with lingering questions of the relationship between ethics and politics—of questions of self-determination, of the contingencies of history, of the specificities of material embodiments and the relationality of existence. In Huffer's early work, *Maternal Pasts, Feminist Futures*, Irigaray's evocative language of labial lips leads Huffer to the question of the relationship between ethics and politics. She writes that "it's those lips that keep tempting me, that I want to go back to, that are begging to find their place on this map."[50] In this text, Huffer suggests that the relationship between ethics and politics hinges on a way to think of subjectivity emerging at once ethically beyond sameness and yet in a way that attends to that emergence as part of a matrix of discourse and sociality. Irigaray's two touching labial lips—as a trope for women speaking their becoming through a desire that is bound to the other without occluding the pleasures of the self—gesture toward the subjectivity beyond sameness that Huffer is looking for. It is these lips, divorced from their "service of reproduction," that provide the liberating possibility of a becoming in the materiality of desire that can resist the sameness of identity.[51]

Irigaray's lips are particularly useful for Huffer insofar as they inspire and inform a focus on ethics as a radical openness to alterity. Huffer reads Irigaray's "When Our Lips Speak Together" as "an exemplary feminist interruption, at the point of collapse where woman and mother are hinged as impossible metaphors of truth."[52] Huffer emphasizes that through mimesis, the lips disrupt the gendered epistemologies upon which knowledges are grounded. Specifically, Irigaray's casting of lips as sites of pleasure without reproduction constitutes a refusal of the antagonisms of the oedipal economy, a refusal of a psychoanalytic history framed in terms of an irrecuperable desire for origins that breeds fear and contempt for woman as mother.

Because the genital/oral lips touch without being absorbed into oneness, they serve as a physical representation of relation without assimilation, of desire without *telos*, a mediation of a perpetual gap. Huffer reads Irigaray radically, writing, "Irigaray uses the two lips to theorize and to perform a relational model of subjectivity that would allow for the irreducible difference of the other."[53] These lips do not trap woman in a particular modality of her flesh, such as reproduction; Irigaray's lips are erotic. Accordingly, for Huffer, "Irigaray's lips are lesbian, overtly nonreproductive, and therefore antinostalgic."[54] For Huffer, lesbian desire, inspired by Irigaray's two lips, provides a way to think of the historicity of the subject without collapsing that subject into the realm of a universal actor. A feminist politics of lesbian desire challenges the social and historical limits of understanding women's desires through a symbolic that casts them as mothers, and yet it also places women's bodies, by way of the lips, as primary to the signification of that desire.

Irigaray's lips speak to Huffer's own sense that the relationship between ethics and politics hinges on a way to think of subjectivity emerging ethically beyond sameness—and that yet attends simultaneously to that emergence as part of a matrix of discourse and sociality. In *Maternal Pasts*, Huffer writes that "without access to a past from which we draw meaning, we can never live as ethical, future-oriented beings."[55] By this reading, the other to whom one is in ethical relation is not an ahistorical other but a political other whose identity is contextually embedded in metanarratives.[56] This would be an ethics without the violence of morality; perhaps we could say a possibility of genealogy without nostalgia.[57]

In *Maternal Pasts*, Huffer is not however convinced that the alterity of Irigaray's lips is sufficient for thinking through the question of politics.

With an eye to the political implications of a poststructural disruption of identity, Huffer attempts to think through the subject's relationship to a sense of history and/or origins without the nostalgia of a masculine economy of sameness. In her statement about the need to access a meaningful past in order to live into an ethical future, Huffer grapples with the tensions between a radical ethics in which alterity is unbounded by the sociality of historical specificity and the demands of politics fully entrenched in such specificity. Interestingly, Huffer's criticism resonates here with Butler's criticism about the ahistoricity of the materiality of the lips. But whereas Butler will argue that any materiality that does not consider the specificities of history recapitulates the primacy of a heterosexist worldview, Huffer problematizes the radical alterity of Irigaray's ethical other. In other words, the problem with the lips, for Huffer, at least in *Maternal Pasts*, is that their abstraction is insufficient for political action. Huffer ultimately contends that the other to whom one is in ethical relation is not an ahistorical other but a political other whose identity is contextually embedded in metanarratives. As such, ethics involves a political responsibility to recover the stories of marginalized persons without feeding into identity politics, insisting that these narratives must be continually interrogated in order to avoid reifying the process of selfsame identification through which this marginalization emerges.

Huffer's interest in the question of ethics and of the embeddedness of the subject and the other in the contingencies of history leads her to a sustained engagement with Foucault—which focuses on Foucault's turn to the voices of history that exist only as silences and occlusions.[58] In *Mad for Foucault*, the first book in her trilogy on the thinker, Huffer begins to develop answers to questions about ethics and politics that she raised at the end of her engagements with Irigaray in *Maternal Pasts*. In the second book in her Foucault trilogy, *Are the Lips A Grave?*, whose title plays on the implications of Irigaray's famous use of the trope of the genital/oral lips for queer theory and the notion of the rectum as a grave (referencing Leo Bersani's famous essay), Huffer elaborates on subjectivity as a question of ethics and ethics as a question of the self and other in relation to the sociohistorical production, reproduction, and transformation of truth.[59] In this text, her interest in Irigaray's lips becomes more clearly a new way of imagining subjectivity as a question of freedom and ethical responsibility that is best perceived through an exploration of eros.[60]

Huffer begins the text by insisting there has been an unnecessary split between the concerns of queer theory and feminism. She describes that split thus: feminists tend to moralize sexuality and remove eros from the political; the queer camp might be said to miscalculate the radicality of asocial practices of freedom that rely on discursive structures that always already privilege the masculine speaking subject. This split has resulted in a thoroughly unerotic feminism and an asocial, self-referential queer performativity—both of which are potentially moralizing in their own ways (even when in the form of antinormative bodies of pleasures).[61] Huffer traces these tensions between queer theory and feminist theory through what she deems as certain shortsighted interpretations legacies of Foucault (in queer theory) and Irigaray (in feminist theory).

In critiquing queer theory on the basis of its somewhat ironic moralizing, Huffer draws attention to the "normative force of queer antinormativity," which emerges even in the seemingly most radical places, in order to caution against the limits of prevailing notions of queer performativity.[62] For instance, discussing David Halperin's *Saint Foucault*, Huffer notes that Halperin's use of fisting as an ethical practice of freedom, indeed a "queer praxis" of undoing subjectivity in the cultivation of an "impersonal" genderless self, is a practice that he claims is "invented" by gay men.[63] According to Huffer, this "slippage" reveals that this queer praxis of fisting as an undoing of gender and sexual norms depends upon Halperin's stated reliance on a masculinist subject position. Huffer notes, "In Halperin's queer disavowal of his own investment in masculine subjectivity, the act of erasure through which the genderless 'queer' becomes gendered as 'gay men' is rendered invisible."[64] Any attempts at asserting identity in politics, even through assertions of antinormativity, recapitulate the moralizing power of discourses of sexuality and gender.[65]

Huffer attempts to reclaim the space of tension between queer antinormativity and "French" feminist positions by thinking Irigaray and Foucault together. Specifically, Huffer embarks on a sustained reflection on the relationship between Irigaray's lips and Foucault's desubjectivation in order to reframe the queer and feminist positions. In her chapter "Foucault's Fist," at the end of a discussion of what she sees as the unnecessary, though not entirely inaccurate, characterizations of feminists as sexphobic moralists and of queers as self-referential, egoistic closet misogynists, Huffer provides the reader with a compelling intervention into the moralizing tendencies of this unnecessarily bifurcated rhetoric.[66] Arguing that both Irigaray and Foucault provide antifoundationalist notions of the subject, Huffer brings the two theorists together to start a "conversation" that "would embrace, together, both the feminist insistence on social sexing and the queer challenge to normative sexuality as immutable truth."[67]

In order to reframe the queer and feminist positions as a "queer feminism," Huffer insists on rethinking both Irigaray's reductions to the female, heterosexual, psychoanalytic, and visceral in feminist theory *and* the reduction of Foucault's legacy to the male, homosexual, subversive, and historical in queer theory. Huffer argues that Foucault and Irigaray share an "antifoundationalist" disruption of epistemology.[68] They critique the "rational-moral foundations of Western knowledge" in order to think an ethical subjectivity beyond sameness. Furthermore, this particular "antifoundationalism" emerges through an interpretation of desire in which alterity is primary; this is an ethical desire not bound to sexuality.[69]

In terms of Foucault's work, desubjectivation is this antifoundationalist promise. Huffer contends that the sexual moral subject is a subject that emerges in relation to the limits of his/her own psychosexual subjection; it is a subject-producing subjection (*assujetettissement*). *Assujettissement* is a selfsame process of subject formation. Through the moralization of sexuality, the modern subject becomes intelligible (even unto itself)—creating a reality of subjectivization that must be "retraversed" in order to ensure not only that the subject is non-self-identical, but also and therein that the subject would not be linked to others in the production of a selfsame, egoistic model of relations.[70] Huffer notes that Foucault's process of desubjectivation is a turn to history as part of a self-undoing. And it is within this "dissolution of the subject" that alterity is an inherently relational and social act, at once ethical and erotic.[71]

Contrary to interpretations of Foucault's notion of desubjectivation as antisocial, Huffer maintains that what is often overlooked in Foucault is that alterity is embedded in the historical and social, not outside it.[72] Huffer insists that desubjectivation is an act of freedom in relation to the social and historical other.[73] She writes that Foucault's work demonstrates an "ethical attention to the alterity of the past" that is also "an attention to the exclusions of our historical future."[74] Thus, the alterity of Foucault's notion of desubjectivation is an inherently relational practice because the relation to alterity emerges through a practice of freedom that is *also bound to the concrete, social other*. And this relation is ethical insofar as the undoing of the subject also consequently renders as vulnerable the narration of the subject's genealogy, refusing to reduce that genealogy to a moralizing justification of a present subject position.

Not unlike Foucault's desubjectivation, Irigaray's lips are antifoundationalist in their focus on alterity. Consistent with her earlier readings, Huffer grants that Irigaray's lips prioritize alterity, a read that resonates with

Irigaray's ethical aims. As Huffer writes in *Are the Lips a Grave?*, in *these* lips, Irigaray is able to "theorize and perform a relational model of subjec- tivity that refuses the closure of truth, allowing the irreducible difference of alterity to emerge."[75] As with Foucault, Huffer suggests that both queer and feminist theory have misread Irigaray's lips. Queer theory she says, has largely read Irigaray incorrectly, unwilling to see the underlying radicality of Irigaray's move to sexual difference as cognizant of the question of history.[76] Huffer notes, "Irigaray's project appears not as a metaphysics, idealization, or essentialist ontology, as so many of her critics have argued, but rather as a historically situated project of ethical desubjectivation within the modern episteme of 'man' as a sexual moral subject."[77] Irigaray's ethics of sexual difference is *a question of sexual difference as a historically situated discursive constraint of women in the feminine*, and therefore, its very irreducibility is relational. Here, Huffer's reading of Irigaray is quite different from Butler's; she suggests that Irigaray's focus on sexuate irreducibility does not abandon the specificity of history in a way that dehistoricizes matter. In fact, for Irigaray, the sexuate, in its materiality and alterity, is always in relation to the work of her project.

Read with Huffer, Irigaray's lips insist on a relation to alterity that emerges through the simultaneously fleshy and representational experience of difference. Her lips negotiate a tension between accountability and the possibility of a non-self-identical subject that comes quite close to the way Huffer describes the ethics of Foucault's desubjectivation. To return again to Huffer's reading of Irigaray, it is clear that the queer feminist theoretical space that Huffer is cultivating is one inspired by the way Irigaray's lips insist on holding together the ethical and the erotic, where one's undoing is a condition of becoming. If queer and feminist perspectives are split, the lips allow them to touch.

Lips, appropriately, seem to mediate the queer and the feminist because they figure a gap, a space of difference, whose condition of possibility is the erotic self-touching of one flesh that is always already two. Huffer writes that "the Irigarayan lips . . . perform both self- and other-oriented forms of lovemaking in the infinite and funny combinations of mouth to mouth, mouth to labia, labia to mouth, labia to labia, inner labia to outer labia, outer labia to mouth, outer to outer, inner to inner, outer to inner, to mouth, to labia."[78] Irigaray's lips provide a way to bring the feminist together with the queer, as evident in Huffer's retracing of women's erotica to suggest possibilities of "mutuality, reciprocity, and respect for difference—that would weave together a new ethics of love."[79]

In bridging Irigaray and Foucault (and *Maternal Pasts* and *Mad for Foucault*), *Are the Lips a Grave?* insists on alterity as something that is immanently relational. Huffer's moves from Irigaray to Foucault and back perform the radical alterity of ethics in a way that recognizes embodiment itself as part of a sociohistorical production, reproduction, and effacement of truths. This "conversation" that aims to "embrace, together, both the feminist insistence on social sexing and the queer challenge to normative sexuality as immutable truth" establishes a "queer feminist ethics of alterity" that attempts to be both "kinky and relational but attentive to harms."[80] In essence, Huffer is redefining performativity apart from its asocial self-referential deployment in queer theory toward a narrative performance that, through its antifoundationalist desubjectivation, is ethical in its relation to alterity.[81]

Insofar as Foucault's desubjectivation demonstrates an "ethical attention to the alterity of the past," which is also "an attention to the exclusions of our historical present," Huffer's juxtaposition of Irigarayan lips with Foucauldian desubjectivation allows us to read the lips and their struggle within the dynamism of an ever-changing historical narrative, making them at once free and fleshy, capable of such an anti-identitarian, antifoundationalist performativity.[82] Huffer's reading thus highlights the materiality and alterity of Irigaray's lips, speaking and touching, as part of an economy of bodies and pleasures—experiences that are irreducible to the sociohistorical constructions of gender and sexuality—gesturing toward the unmaking of subjects as a new mode of becoming with one's others.

It is, I contend, precisely because of the lips' embodied alterity that Irigaray's evocative language of genital lips enables Huffer to submit the question of ethics to the demands of politics in order to establish a queer praxis of freedom that also attends to the question of history. As Huffer's reading of Irigaray suggests, and as I have argued throughout this book, the lips are not just linguistic interruptions. Lips constitute a praxis of desire that is based in a materiality and alterity that refuses metaphysics. The alterity of the lips is based in the always at least two in relation without assimilation; their relation remains dynamic because of the material specificity and irreducibility of this twoness. This dynamic touching in alterity and materiality attends to the historical specificity of the subject without collapsing that subject into the identity of a universal actor. Herein lies the possibility for these nonreproductive lips to frame the ethical performativity of decidedly queer politics.[83] Lips bring together the antinormativity of queer and feminist politics because they figure a space of difference whose condition of possibility is the erotic self-touching of one flesh that is always already two—an embodiedness of multiple desires. Bringing Foucault and Irigaray together as Huffer has done connects the radical indeterminacy of a poststructuralist Irigaray with the questions of what fostering alterity actually looks like as a way of answering the question of how to live. That Huffer's performativity borrows from the lips in order to create this space is a testament to the untapped theoretical potential of Irigaray's lips—to think the prediscursive materiality to which Irigaray refers without resubmitting it to the discourses of sex, gender, or sexuality.

I locate a sense of queerness in these lips that is also influenced by Vicki Kirby's convincing exposition of the uses of queer in theory (and politics)—one that rewires notions of "normativity" as queer such that it resonates with the ambiguity, alterity, and complex embodiedness of desire that I have put forward.[84] As Kirby notes, categories, both queer and trans*, are as broad and diverse as the experiences of trans-identifying persons. But read through a queer, nonlinear time of lips, these experiences invite questions about the personal and the political, about the power of discourse to shape and transform lives, and about the power of bodies to utter desires for transformative becomings, beyond gender binaries toward a queerness of sexual difference, where queerness is a refusal of reification in identity. It is precisely in the capacity of such desire to think experience that transcends the historicity of categories of gender and sexuality that I think desire offers possibilities for trans* theory.

The lips are just such a morphological expression of a desire that gestures to becoming in our individuate uniqueness *together*, beyond self-same identity. As Athena Colman writes in her brilliant essay "Tarrying with Sexual Difference," Irigaray's morphological thought challenges the language of identity (even as implicated in some trans* political discourses) that risks undergirding transphobic discourses and transmisogyny. Thinking with Irigaray, Colman articulates how thinking the irreducibility of difference as embodied actually affirms trans* experience as a more radical way to think subjectivity in terms of dynamic becomings of difference.[85] Colman has developed this argument further by drawing on Jules Gill-Peterson's criticism of the history of sexology's framing of trans* bodies in accordance with images of idealized conceptualizations of gender. Colman contends that Irigaray's morphology doesn't idealize gender; it reveals gender's ideality. It reveals the ways that gender identities, and sexing of the body as images of that ideal, are wedded to a masculine morphology.[86]

For me, an interpretation of the lips that embraces their dynamism and desire as a condition of their disruption is the possibility of thinking of a certain "agency" of a prediscursive materiality of sexuateness beyond sexuality. I want to conclude by registering queer challenges that mark Irigaray's work as heteronormative and transphobic in order to push Irigaray beyond the limits of her own thought. I frame the prediscursivity of materiality figured by Irigaray's lips as fleshy spaces of disruptive desire that challenge the ethics of obligation and the politics of autonomy. This is a space where both agency and responsibility are rethought through an embodied othered desire.

Agency, Ethics, and Disidentification: Disidentification and the Lips as an Embodied Praxis of Relational Becoming

Foucault's attention to the social and historical situatedness of truth claims inspired poststructuralist reimaginings of gender in feminist theory and sexuality foundational to queer theory. How one inherits this relationship between the discursive, the individual, and the sociohistorical—whether one interprets the sociohistorical situatedness of bodily becomings as a prison house, as a never-ending possibility of disruption, or both—shapes both the "type" and promise of performativity.

Butler's performativity, with its prioritization of discursivity, can feel oppressively totalizing at times. As their critique of Irigaray's materiality shows, for Butler, any appeal to materiality beyond its figurations in discourse is always already entrenched in discourse's false promise that there is some neutral, universal space beyond its reach. Muñoz's performativity, on the other hand, can seem more promising in attempts to locate freedom in acts of disidentification. He, like Butler, acknowledges intertwining in the sociality of becoming but locates within the individual a capacity for desire that remakes the world. Both of these thinkers are attempting to grapple with the simultaneous promise and demand of the postmodern condition—as well as its implications for philosophy, for ethics, and for politics.

Despite her resistance to moralizing, Huffer's aim is to think through the either-or—to acknowledge that there are limits to resistance while also acknowledging that there are real, material crises that demand action. There is a certain pragmatism to Huffer's work in this regard. And, as in her "later" philosophical engagements with ecology and politics, Irigaray too ought to be read as one who refuses to let the totalizing philosophical frameworks of discourse absolve her from the demands of acting and thinking.

My return to Irigaray is therefore, like Huffer's, an acknowledgment that the entanglements of the symbolic and material ways of being in this world are inescapable; however, it is also an insistence that the symbolic is not all there is. As Stephen Seely suggests in his reading of Huffer and Edelman and noting the radicality of Irigaray's sexual difference, calling it "a queer ethics of the other," Irigaray's sexual difference imagines an ethics that is beyond the questions of representation as a totalizing dialectic. Seely writes, "For Irigaray . . . the negative is beyond the dialectic altogether; it is precisely the registration of the impossibility of any system to fully enframe its other(s), that is, it is the trace of sexual difference."[87] I would add that in attempting to disrupt an epistemology based in the selfsame, lips, in particular, imagine an ethics of alterity in which one's capacity to become a subject, and therein one's agency, is constituted in the openness to an other who is irreducible to the self in and through their difference. And this relation to alterity is also thoroughly embodied, such that alterity is not the difference of an entirely otherworldly Other. The sexuate lips embody this materiality and alterity—they inhabit and generate it continuously in the space of their touching to cultivate a different symbolic order (rather than bowing to the totalizing reading of the symbolic as all there is that would render any alternative a mere negation).[88] As this *threshold of the "radical immanence" of alterity and the radical alterity of immanence*, the lips *disidentify beyond negation* in the working of their fleshiness beyond the limits of the symbolic reductions, gesturing toward difference where there was none, disclosing the ethical labor of Irigaray's writing.[89]

If we read embodiment as an embodiment of a sexuate that, though indeterminate (i.e., not gendered as in discourse), still involves an irreducible difference, discreteness, or specificity, then the relationality of the irreducible two could seem to delimit alterity by fixing it in a specific type of relation. At best, such an effort to hold ethics with embodiment risks radical alterity, detracting from the ethical in order to provide a strategically dynamic ground for politics. At worst, it risks ethics by normalizing the ground for a particular gendered relation that is fundamentally heterosexuate (even if not heterosexual) insofar as the two in relation are irreducible because of their sex. These tensions between ethics and politics are constitutive of a condition of trying to imagine relationality beyond identity without allowing that relationality to become so abstract that it is completely divorced or disembodied from existence. After all, what does it mean to think about embodiedness without resubmitting that body to a symbolic that inscribes the body and its limits within a sociality that is historically constituted?

Despite these concerns, I locate in the antifoundationalism of Irigaray's lips a way to think of her materiality in terms of the eros of relations between two or more that reimagines agency beyond autonomy and the politics of identity. Read in terms of desubjectivation, lips gesture toward a presymbolic materiality of ambiguous desire (perhaps uncultivated?) that is inherently antinormative and therefore refuses to limit embodiment to a particular body (or identity between discourse and matter). And disidentification gestures to the agency of this prediscursive materiality as an active, dynamic embodiment. As desubjectifying and disidentifying, lips actively reject a liberal notion of freedom wherein freedom is achieved through self-naming, through autonomy, becoming one and the same as the universal or ideal subject.[90]

In prioritizing the desire of Irigaray's lips as an embodied ethical relation, a queer praxis of desubjectivation through disidentification, the lips figure a space where agency and responsibility are redefined through the unraveling of subjectivity that occurs in the ambiguity of desire. Furthermore, by thinking the irreducibility of this desire in terms of the dynamism of a materiality itself as a relation to alterity beyond the sexuate, its specificity cannot be frozen in a particular embodiment that can be deployed for a normative politics or its negation. Lips are epistemological interventions, in the flesh, and the queerness of Irigaray's lips lies in the embodiment of their alterity. And here, queer is not a sexuality; queer is a radical ethical reimagining of sameness, whose radicality is in its embodiedness. To conclude, I focus on how lips, read as disruptions of identity, function like prediscursive material agents of disidentification. I contend the lips reframe the ethics of obligation and the politics of autonomy in terms of an agency of the materiality and alterity of desire constituted in a radical touching.

Lips, Wombs, and the Revolutionary Time of Queer Freedom

Irigaray frames liberalism's pursuit of a subjectivity grounded in autonomy as tied to the exclusion or repression of the materiality of differences. Discussing Irigaray's critique of the selfsame's "sacrificial" economy, Anne Caldwell writes that liberalism's universal and/or ideal subject is "a subject guided by an abstract ideal [that] defines itself through the process of disavowing materiality."[91] Caldwell articulates Irigaray's efforts to rethink materiality as a specific reaction to the selfsame's positing of a universal by way of sacrificing the particularities, or material differences, of life. In other words, the turn to materiality in Irigaray is always part of her interrogation of universality as an abstraction that veils its transcendentalization of a particular (i.e., masculine) singularity. There is something about materiality that calls to Irigaray but that Butler will not concede—a certain specificity of embodied life prior to discourse. If we grant that Irigaray is always interrogating the ways universals become neutral, we must concede that this notion of materiality is never trapped in a particular concept of the natural. In fact, for Irigaray, nature, and with it the materiality of life, including the very elements that facilitate the relationality of existence, is irreducible to concepts, including of the natural: "'Nature' does not exist."[92] Desire, in this materiality, is everywhere; the world itself is fecund with desire. Read this way, the lips gesture to this materiality of desire that is so dynamic that it is irreducible to discourses of gender and sexuality.

I read this viscous dynamism of desire in Maggie Nelson's *The Argonauts*. There, Nelson interweaves reflections on feminist and literary theory and philosophy with intimate portrayals of her life. Her stories of reading theorists like Irigaray, Foucault, and Eve Kosofsky Sedgwick are as intimate as her personal accounts of mentors; of her meeting icons like Anne Carson; and of the love-letter-like address chronicling her courtship and romance with Harry, a trans* man, and her pregnancy with their child, Iggy. Nelson's memoir is genre busting and gender busting. It refuses the reductions of her own lived experience in what I would argue are radically queer terms—through disidentifications. These disidentifications are rooted in her experiences of desire, sexual and otherwise, and in her experiences of this desire in relation to Harry (and including Harry's transition to a trans* man) and in relation to her own body, including the transformations of her pregnant body. They are material disidentifications of lips and of wombs but also of the entanglements of bodily life, in and of desire that includes sex acts and reproduction but that also exceeds sex acts and reproduction.

In her encounters with the demands of identity and the absurdity of its demands, Nelson's words (which, in honoring Sedgwick, buck the notion that the unsaid is ever sufficient for answering the questions of life) portray the eros (in its bittersweetness) of the postmodern condition—the endless struggle to overcome the categorizations and labeling that limit life, and yet the demands of living and the longing for representation that just can't relinquish those attachments.

Following an interlude in which she reflects on her college mentor Christina (which includes an aside therein where she considers the performativity of her own writing), and immediately preceding a reflection on attending an art porn film while pregnant, Nelson remarks on her first encounter with Irigaray's work:

> In Christina's feminist theory class, we also read Irigaray's famous essay "When Our Lips Speak Together," in which Irigaray critiques both unitary and binary ways of thinking by focusing on the morphology of the labial lips. They are the "sex which is not one." They are not one but also not two. They make a circle that is always self-touching, an autoerotic mandorla.
> [. . . .]
> While we were discussing Irigaray in class, I tried to feel the circle of my labial lips. I imagined every woman in the class trying to feel it too. But the thing is, you can't really feel your labial lips.
> It's easy to get juiced up about a concept like plurality or multiplicity and start complimenting everything as such. Sedgwick was impatient with that kind of sloppy praise. Instead, she spent a lot of time talking and writing about that which is more than one, and more than two, but less than infinity.
> This finitude is important. It makes possible the great mantra, the great invitation of Sedgwick's work, which is to "pluralize and specify."[93]

Following Sedgwick's lead, Nelson thinks and writes through the finitude of the experience, including the experiences with irreducibility. This emphasis on finitude insists on a specificity of materiality that is indeterminate, beyond discursive categorizations that might otherwise transcendentalize or universalize these experiences.

Within the context of writing about (to borrow from Huffer) the "strange eros" of her experience of her own body in pregnancy, Nelson describes watching art porn with her trans* lover. In this reflection, she stages a scene in which she is pregnant—but the pregnancy is not the centerpiece of her reflection. Nelson sits in a theater surrounded by bodies and their pleasures. And her very presence—sitting in a theater—is one that is also fecund with desire—in her gaze but also between her legs in her silence.

She reaches out to the other and to herself in this moment in ways that transform the space and time of her intimate experience of her own flesh, of the child in her womb, of her lover whose hand she can touch, and of a world of desires and pleasures at which she can gaze in wonder but which also look back at her and call her outside of herself. In one moment, the space of intimacy, of touching, is not only transformed beyond the limits of her interior and exterior, but in relation to other worlds as well.

That Nelson invokes the Irigarayan lips of orality and pleasure immediately preceding this scene speaks to the transformative capacity of touching lips to remake the space and time of existence by their evocation of a materiality that holds together the sensible and transcendental experience, the horizontal and the vertical of immanence and transcendence. The material specificity of her own pregnancy, as both an intimacy and an estrangement of the body, is the occasion for connecting with her memory of a collective imagination of jouissance (of hidden touching lips in the classroom), and it is the occasion for recounting the experience of a film of eros and art at their limits. The space between Maggie and Harry is one of shared relation without sameness, of a relation in the erotic silence of the art-porn theater, in the strangeness of relation to her own pregnant body, in the distance between Harry's experience of his body and Maggie's. This distance, strangeness, and eros constitute a relation of difference that makes possible the bittersweetness of their love and their becomings (beyond political identifications). It is also the space and time of Maggie's own becoming—a becoming in and through her body that alerts her to the ways expectations of gender desiccate the experience of the body's fluidity, its very life.

Nelson turns to Sedgwick to insist on specificity and pluralization as parts of a practice of disruption. But it is no accident that Irigaray's lips inspire this dynamic between commonality and specificity, between the social and the individual. I would argue that in their plurality, Irigaray's lips maintain a certain specificity that is porous and dynamic. Lips as two in relation to the space between them are never the same, even in themselves. The lips are not a new universal—they are the morphological mark of relation—of a touching that is beyond the active and passive nature of the autonomous subject who exteriorizes the other as object. Nelson's reflections include a pregnancy without sex, sexual desires she shares with Harry without the possibility of reproduction, the longings of love and of life. It is a work of lips and wombs—literally in the communal and individual self-touching labial lips of the feminist-theory classroom and in Nelson's pregnancy, carrying Iggy in her womb. This is also a space of lips and wombs in the Irigarayan sense, beyond figurative and literal distinctions. These wombs and lips are morphological—not as forms of words but as forms in relation to words. Lips and wombs are, like the moments in Nelson's life that are interwoven in a nonlinear narrative, spatiotemporal transformations of bodily life lived in desire.

There is a radical dimension to the lips and wombs as thresholds opening onto a new space-time of fecundity. Whether that fecundity is the jouissance available in the porous folds of the vagina or the passageway to a womb that redefines the dimensions of interior and exterior, the touching lips are the threshold of a new language, a new tongue, a new relation. These lips and wombs lead us to a radical remaking of space and time, reframing the present demands of politics in relation to the constant historical undoing of the self, or desubjectivation. By this reading, the lips are not as different from the womb in Irigaray, as Butler claims they are in "Bodies that Matter." Both remake the space of interiority and exteriority to imagine pleasures beyond a penetrative/antipenetrative economy. The lips and wombs, both, are a new materiality—fleshy thresholds of an unthought space and time.[94]

Though I have focused almost exclusively on the lips as the marker of materiality in Irigaray by tracing Butler's and Huffer's engagements, I think it is important to remind ourselves, as Caldwell does, that the larger issue for Irigaray is the reimagining of materiality itself. Furthermore, it is the transformative materiality that the lips and wombs engender that remains most significant in regard to thinking Irigaray's relevance for a queer performativity. Indeed, the dynamism of materiality, which lips and wombs offer in the inherent dynamism of their fleshy signification, enables an antifoundationalist and antimoralizing queer ethical praxis. If we return to Irigaray's lips with this reimagined notion of space and time, the radicality of lips becomes clearer. The lips remake the temporalities of time and space that manifest in dichotomies of internal and external respectively. Desire, here, is never about an external one longing for an external other. The one and the other are always already in relation beyond the interiority of time and externality of space; each is the possibility of the other's desire and therefore the other's becoming. And the borders of their touching are fleshy thresholds that remake the relation of space and time. The lips thus undermine the world of metaphysics, with its binary that frames matter, maternality, and specificity and sensibility on the one hand, against the world of intelligibility, paternality, universality, and transcendence on the other. Lips gesture toward a reimagined materiality that refuses binary separation. They gesture toward a materiality grounded in the relationality that thinking through the sexuate demands—a relationality of an othered desire of an other space and time.

And with these lips, desire is always between at least two, who are irreducible in their difference, prior to an irreducibility framed in discursive reduction. That irreducibility is itself constituted through the proximity of relation that constitutes desire, a proximity whose dynamism ensures the ambiguity of desire (rather than identity or sexuality). This is a proximity of reaching without grasping, of the radical touching that constitutes the space or interval between us—a radical touching beyond inside and outside, beyond past and future. We might frame the lips as the open-ended beginning (to borrow language from Fanny Söderbäck)—a new materiality of a queer futurity.[95]

In the radical touching of a revolutionary time and space (again borrowing from Fanny Söderbäck), lips resist a present politics of identity in favor of a materiality that exists in relation to the past but is not swallowed up in it. In this performance that is also ethical practice, the radically touching lips invoke the agency of a new materiality—an agency essential to interpreting the prediscursive materiality of lips as queer acts of freedom.[96] What could be more queer than rethinking materiality altogether, beyond sex and sexuality, through the infinite permutations of desire? Than harnessing the ambiguities of desire, in its constant reaching but never grasping or consuming, to disrupt the discursive foundations upon which sex and sexuality are structured? Might this rethinking gesture to the queer temporality of Muñoz's *Cruising Utopia*? A "queerness as a temporal arrangement in which the past is a field of possibility in which subjects can act in the present in the service of a new futurity?"[97] And because Irigaray's lips locate alterity in a material specificity that is dynamic, that is transformative, might the lips also avoid the tendencies toward remoralizing that universalize certain behaviors as antinormative (that is, freezing particular acts in a transcendent space and time that would seem to owe nothing to materiality for its existence)?[98]

Returning then to the question of identity and its entanglements with sex and sexualities, proliferations of identifications of sex, gender, and sexuality do not necessarily radically remake the space and time of subjectivity. In terms of ethics, the proliferation of gender identities and sexualities does not necessarily get us any closer to that which exceeds the limits of discourse; it does not invariably take us toward an alterity of relational living. Nor does multiplying identities necessarily destabilize the normative framework (or the frameworks of normativity for that matter) for a particular identity or the logic of a particular binary (e.g., man and woman). At worst, such proliferations might even reaffirm the model of accumulation that drives biopower and leads to the sort of rampant individualism that lends itself to a culture incapable of empathy. To disrupt identity as the foundation for becoming subjects, something more "lipcentric" is required—something capable of resisting the binaries that support a selfsame economy by which the bodily is a commodity of discursive exchange.[99]

If we think Irigaray's lips in their prediscursive materiality, they gesture toward a "deesentialized embodiment" that is less a willful act of self-naming (to borrow from Rosi Braidotti) and more an embodiment of an asymmetrical antinormativity that remains opaque within discourse.[100] Lips challenge the discursive-bodily entanglements of sex, gender, and sexuality, locating an othered desire that is dissociated from binaries and the negations that constitute binaries altogether. They hold alterity and materiality together, attending to both the historicity of desire's embodiments *and* the ways in which such embodiments are irreducible to the discourses of a particular history. These lips are trans* refusals of gendered binaries; these lips are queer rejections of regimes of sex and sexuality. They are embodiments of disidentification beyond negation that speak to the depths of an Irigarayan ontology of an othered desire. In subsequent chapters, I will explore what thinking through and writing through the materiality and alterity of the lips could look like in relation to the demands of ontological and political others.

Chapter 4

Decolonizing Desire

Reading Spivak's Postcolonial Echo and the Problem of Resistance

In her essay "More on Power/Knowledge," Gayatri Spivak reads Foucault with Derrida, describing the two philosophers' investment in thinking beyond the limits of liberalism (including the entrapments of ethics and ontology) in order to consider power and resistance in relation to the impositions of colonial logic. In an adaptation of Foucauldian resistance, Spivak insists that the position of the oppressed is often framed by the logic of the oppressor such that resistance constitutes a reversal that recapitulates the oppressor's logic.[1] So while for persons whose daily lives have been defined by imprisonment, oppression, and marginalization, the process of recreating or reimagining one's identity beyond a tragic context of dehumanization and marginalization would seem to constitute an act of freedom and resistance, the investment in identification is not as radical or disruptive (or free) as one would hope. Spivak writes,

> The political claims that are most urgent in decolonized space are tacitly recognized as coded within the legacy of imperialism: nationhood, constitutionality, citizenship, democracy, socialism, even culturalism. In the historical frame of exploration, colonization, decolonization—what is being *effectively* reclaimed is a series of regulative political concepts, the supposedly authoritative narrative of the production of which was written elsewhere, in the social formations of Western Europe. They are thus being

reclaimed, indeed claimed, as concept-metaphors for which no *historically* adequate referent may be advanced from postcolonial space.[2]

Spivak cautiously maintains a critical concern with the imposition of colonial power while also acknowledging the ontic peril of what she describes as the subaltern, "previously" colonized position. The subaltern is in the position of a double bind: attempting to subvert the legacies of imperialism while caught up in the demands of a colonizing logic. The very language of decolonization presents itself in relation to a narrative of colonization that, Spivak insists, belongs to a Western European story. By this reading, to imagine one's becoming apart from an imperialist sociocultural order without resubmitting oneself to the "concept-metaphors" of that order is to find oneself in an impossible position.

Despite her criticism of colonial logic, and the impossibility of the double bind, Spivak insists that this "does not make the claims less urgent."[3] Her writing attempts to disrupt colonialism by continuously deconstructing colonizing logic, exposing its failures to enact its totalizing claim.[4] I suggest that through this work of perpetual critique, Spivak refuses to think resistance as a "countermastery" narrative (as described by Julietta Singh) that would recapitulate colonizing logic.[5] Taking a cue from Spivak's early attention to Irigaray's work on the sexuate, this chapter reads Irigaray's linguistic psychoanalysis in relation to decolonial thought, arguing that the economy of sameness undergirds epistemological imperialism (masked as neutrality), perpetuating subjectivities that are based on narratives of mastery.[6] I conclude by considering how decolonizing critiques of ontology, read alongside appeals to affect, resonate with the extradiscursive materiality of Irigarayan desire.[7] Reading these discourses together, I argue that desire, in its ambiguity and dynamism, is a decolonizing force that does not require the recognition of a selfsame discourse in order to constitute an alternative "resistance" to the colonizing logic of sameness. By thinking of desire as a materiality of alterity, I hope to offer a decolonizing, nontotalizing reading of the double bind that does not read the ontological labor of resistance in terms of lack.

The Double Bind and Catachresis in Spivak's Echo

For decades, Gayatri Spivak has incorporated the particularities of her subject position as an Indian woman engaging with continental philosophy in a postcolonial context in order to write through the position of the double bind and rethink the modern subject without either rendering the postmodern subject an abstraction or recapitulating colonizing logic.[8] Continuously critically interrogating the double bind, rather than looking for a way to (re)solve it, exposes the limits of the system of identification of a dematerialized and disconnected notion of self and other or oppressed and oppressor—and claims the position of the double bind as a way forward. To this end, Spivak's work has been foundational for postcolonial feminist thought and its inheritors. Spivak asserts that the double bind of colonized subjects is marked by a crisis of representation—the demand to articulate one's subjectivity by participating in the very discourses that colonize them. Spivak's 1988 essay "Can the Subaltern Speak?" famously frames this crisis by interrogating the difference between speaking and being heard. She suggests that Western scholarly discourse makes its world by excluding the voices of others in order to establish universal truths. It further perpetrates that exclusion by requiring the othered to speak one's difference, and one's claims to subjectivity, using the language of the colonizer. She draws attention therein to the incongruity of the postcolonial subject's position with respect to discourse: Western discourse creates a condition in which the subaltern can only assert subjectivity by participating in the very discourse that alienates her from her difference. If she speaks otherwise, she is not heard.

Spivak engages this decolonizing work in her essay "Echo," a deconstruction of Ovid's classic text *Metamorphoses* that I also read as a postmetaphysical narrativizing that attends to the crisis of representation. Spivak begins her essay by citing Christopher Lasch's *A Culture of Narcissism*, noting that the author, much like Freud, frequently frames narcissism in feminine terms and/or uses women as examples of the condition.[9] It is this uninterrogated sexism in the use of the term *narcissism* that leads Spivak to discuss her own cautionary incorporation of psychoanalysis in cultural critique. In Freud, Spivak writes that she finds a way to challenge Western moral philosophical framings of ethics. Spivak differentiates moral philosophy's "talking about doing" from Indian practical ethics, which draws on "narrative instantiations of ethical problems," as demonstrated in the Hindu epic the *Mahabharata*.[10] Spivak juxtaposes her Derridean- and Freudian-inspired interpretation of ethics as an aporia with the Indian ethical tradition to criticize the imperializing imposition of the Western moral philosophy. And she turns to Echo to read the colonized position as both one of occlusion within the history of construction of an ethics of subjectivity, and a demonstration of an ethics as aporia.

Spivak turns to *Metamorphoses*, and "The Story of Echo and Narcissus" in particular, to expose the double bind of the colonized position with respect to the law and the possibility of resistance. "Echo and Narcissus" begins where "The Story of Tiresias" concludes: Juno punishes Tiresias for taking Jupiter/Jove's side in an argument about the pleasure of love, an argument that the two gods asked him to arbitrate. Ovid reports that Juno, whose ego was a casualty of Tiresias's judgment, "said that umpires were always blind" and therefore "made him [Tiresias] so forever."[11] But Jove compensates Tiresias out of pity, granting him the ability to foretell the future. Significantly, Tiresias's punishment has not simply been mitigated by Jove's intervention; Tiresias has received a gift that constitutes a bestowal of "some honor."[12]

"The Story of Echo and Narcissus" begins by mentioning that this gift brought Tiresias notoriety. Ovid proceeds to corroborate the veracity of Tiresias's new power by telling another story—a story about a nymph of the river, Liriope, who was among "the first who tested" Tiresias's ability to foretell the future.[13] Ovid then offers a brief account of Narcissus's origins, describing that he is born from Cephissus's rape of Liriope. When Liriope asks Tiresias if her beautiful boy, Narcissus, will live to old age, Tiresias responds, "Yes, if he ever knows himself." The story of Narcisuss's death will be the story of his coming to know himself, and collectively this will serve as a demonstration of Tiresias's "honor" and therein, a testament to the law of Jupiter. My point: Tiresias's powers are thus the occasion for the story of the nymph Echo and Narcissus such that it is embedded in the narrative about justice. And Echo emerges in the story only in relation to this broader narrative of a death-driven selfhood as the attestation of divine justice.

Spivak's reinterpretation of Echo offers a literary representation of the subaltern in "Can the Subaltern Speak?" Arguing that the colonizing discourse of Western thought is both masculine and imperializing,[14] Spivak suggests that Echo's perspective is subordinated to the fate of Narcissus in dominant interpretations of the text, asking, "Where was Echo, the woman in Narcissus's story?"[15] Her question implies that the condition of colonized subjects, like Echo, is marked by a crisis of representation. It alludes to the disconnect between speaking and being heard and the tensions therein between presence and absence, between difference and its materialization in discourse. This crisis of representation is doubled insofar as Echo's voice will be mediated by Ovid's words, just as colonized subjects are forced to speak within an imperializing discourse that is not their own. To build a case for the analogy between Echo and the subaltern, Spivak describes the punishment and dispossession of Echo by opening her reading with an examination of the conditions under which Echo is punished. Spivak emphasizes that Ovid refers to Echo as *garrula*, a talkative girl. Echo is labeled thus because she talked to Juno excessively in order to keep Juno from discovering Jupiter's sexual escapades with the other nymphs.

When Juno discovers that Echo's talkativeness has been masking Jupiter's affairs with the nymphs, she punishes Echo by condemning her to make only "brief noises of the fewest words."[16] From here forward, "Echo only repeats the last of what is spoken and returns the words she hears."[17] Spivak interprets this punishment as Juno effectively telling Echo that she can no longer speak for herself. The words she utters from here on will only be responses. Spivak paraphrases the punishment by appropriating Juno's voice, writing, "Talkative girl, you can only give back, you are now the respondent."[18] An originary word will never again fall from Echo's lips. From here on, Echo can only give back; she can only respond.[19]

Through her status as respondent, Echo signifies the other who returns the desire of the addresser. Each time someone speaks to Echo, she must respond; she is not only subjected to the other's representation, but she must also return that representation like a mirror that affirms an incomplete image as whole. In repeating the addresser's words, Echo both constructs and affirms the normative "self," whose words will silence her desires as she utters them. Spivak suggests that in a way similar to Echo, subaltern persons, and subaltern women in particular because of the impacts of colonialism's phallocentric renderings of ethics, are not heard in their own voice. Those persons not accounted for in hegemonic discourse can only speak the language of those for whom they are other. The discourse and language that have been imposed upon them do not provide the space for the desires or the utterances of the subaltern. Like Echo, the subaltern is forced to occupy a position by which she returns the desire of a hegemonic discourse, becoming the sacrifice that enables an imperialistic and patriarchal culture of narcissism.

But Echo's punishment alone is not what makes her position analogous to the colonized. Spivak proceeds to expose the colonizing workings of the text, in its movement to create a closed universe, and to highlight the ruptures that exceed efforts at such closure. Through her deconstructive reading, Spivak highlights the juridico-political character of colonizing discourse and its assumptions about agency, which reveal that agency only belongs to those whose desires are already representable (and therefore recognizable) within that discourse. Spivak frames the position of the subaltern as an inherently gendered "other" position with respect to a patriarchal discourse—a position that entails an asymmetrical gendered relation to the application of the law of the text. After all, Echo's punishment comes on the heels of Tiresias's punishment by Juno. However, in the case of Tiresias,[20] Jupiter intervenes to mitigate the sentence by offering the seer intuitive powers. Echo, Spivak emphasizes, receives her penalty without obtaining any sort of clemency from Jupiter, to whose service she owed her demise. Jupiter does not intervene on her behalf. Unlike Tiresias, Echo receives no compensation, no "honor" to mitigate her suffering.

Reading the juxtaposition of Echo as the female signifier and Tiresias as the male signifier demonstrates the asymmetrically gendered exercise of a law that expresses the tongue of the patriarch. The inconsistent application of punishment shows that the universality of discourse cannot account for the difference it effaces in order to posit itself as universal, whole, or neutral. The asymmetry of the positions with respect to the law is both revealed in and further discloses the incapacity of the language of the law to consider the very difference it has constructed. To this end, Spivak suggests that while Juno's punishment would seem to doom Echo to the role of respondent, the punishment itself assumes that Echo spoke for herself at some point. But Spivak reminds the reader that prior to Juno's damning, Echo had been speaking for Jupiter, protecting his pleasures and his desires. Echo's prepunishment utterances were made to protect Jupiter. Thus, her incessant talking had been a sort of parroting representing another's desires, the *desires of the patriarch*. Echo is not punished for her own words; she is punished for talking on Jupiter's behalf, for representing his desire. She is punished, in short, for the very thing that she is already destined to do. And Echo's punishment is to continue to repeat the desires of others, desires represented in their utterances that she will then echo. Spivak's reading implies that a grave irony exists in the position of the colonized. She interprets Echo's punishment as an obligation to take the role of respondent; however, Spivak also suggests, the concept of response implies agency, and Echo is never afforded volition of her speech.

Herein lies a secondary paradox in Echo's punishment as it regards the impossibility of her agency: her punishment attributes to her an agency over her crime that never existed and, in turn, imposes an obligation upon her that she cannot fulfill. Echo has been placed in the position of respondent, but the notion of response implies some sort of responsibility, which requires agency. To respond would imply that one gives a response willingly by one's own volition. If ethics, in the Levinasian tradition, is the opportunity to be responsible to one's other, one has the potential to become an ethical actor by virtue of exercising a certain agency involved in how one responds to the other. But Echo's response does not resemble this definition of ethics. The only way to name Echo's situation as response that would grant her some sort of agency would be to reframe the relationship between response and responsibility. Paradoxically, such reframing places an obligation on the respondent in which they are forced to respond in a particular way. For Echo, to be the respondent means that she can only reiterate the desire that is given to her. Analogizing Echo and the subaltern in this paradox, Spivak writes, "In her own separate enclosure, the subaltern still cannot speak as the subject of a speech act."[21] Echo's position is one of unintentional response and servitude rather than that of an ethical agent.

In relation to the colonized subject, Spivak's reading of Echo suggests that the colonized are paradoxically judged as though they were equal agents in the discourse of crime and punishment to which they are subjected. In reality, the form of response decreed by Echo's punishment, as is the case for the colonized subject, and for "woman" in a phallocratic symbolic, becomes an obligation that seals her off from her capacity to become a subject in the juridical world of this colonizing discourse. Echo, like the colonized subject, is forced to participate in a discursive universe (and its juridical force) without ever having been an agent, without ever having spoken and been heard (had her words recognized) in her own voice, in the echoes of her own desires. *By considering the punishment as a double dispossession of Echo's voice, Spivak thus asserts the complexity of the double bind in which the colonized are denied their own agency in discourse through the imposition of an assumption of agency and then rendered "the other" to be sacrificed in securing the self-sufficiency of the whole, singular, or universal truth.*

The seemingly totalizing depiction of discourse suggests that, insofar as Echo represents the position of women and the subaltern, even exposing such dispossession of the agency of one's desires does not constitute resistance as counteridentification with the law. After all, how can Echo speak her dispossession? While Echo is forced to respond, others receive her response under the conditions in which response implies volition. She can never warn the addressee that her words are not intentional and that they do not speak her desire. She can only echo. The literary play in which Spivak engages suggests the impossibility of resistance being anything but an exercise within the prevailing norms of discourse.

In the midst of this troubling reading of dispossession, Spivak is performing a deconstructive analysis of the text, suggesting that the text cannot fully account for the juridical scene it has created. It is by reading gaps in the text that Spivak offers a sense of what resistance looks like for the colonized. Specifically, Spivak suggests that insofar as Echo's punishment is given through the juridical commandment, that punishment structures Echo's life by ordering her desire. Spivak asserts that when the punished Echo encounters Narcissus, the differences between Echo and Narcissus as gendered subjects and as juridical subjects (i.e., in relation to law and punishment in this narrative) creates a crisis of response. In Ovid's telling, Echo had been following Narcissus, burning with desire for him: "She wanted to come near with coaxing speeches, make soft entreaties to him! But her nature sternly forbids; the one thing not forbidden is to make answers."[22] Because of her punishment, the only way Echo can speak her desires is through the words that Narcissus would offer her. Spivak notes that there is a moment in the text when, repeating Narcissus, Echo is able to fulfill her punishment and still speak her desire. When Narcissus cries out, "Come," Echo responds, "Come," returning the hunter's desire but also uttering a truth of her own desire. This truth is unintentional to the extent that the utterance is forced, but it nonetheless represents her own passion for Narcissus.

Despite this coincidence in Echo's and Narcissus's utterances, Spivak reminds us of the incongruity of their positions with respect to language. "Her desire and performance are dispensed into absolute chance rather than an obstinate choice, as in the case of Narcissus."[23] Echo's words are not spoken as a subject of her own desire through some agential claim. Though Echo utters words that mimic the truth of her desire, the words are *his* words representing *her* desire; they are her desire veiled by Narcissus's representation of—his words for—his own desire. Thus, Echo's desire remains unspoken in her own voice, through a mode of representation that gestures toward her desires. The coincidence of Narcissus's words with her desires is a violence in the text that veils the way Echo has been alienated from her desires and deprived of subjectivity.

Narcissus becomes frustrated by Echo's repetition and finally asks her, "Why do you flee from me?" (quid me fugis).[24] Echo, forced to utter the words in which her own desires are veiled by words that are not her own, must say "flee from me." But this is the point at which language fails. In Ovid's text, Narcissus has been calling out into the woods, and until this question is asked, Echo repeats Narcisuss's calls verbatim. But when this question is asked of her, Ovid simply writes that Narcissus "receives the same words as he speaks."[25] Spivak highlights the reason for this silencing of Echo: when Narcissus calls out "me fugis," Echo cannot respond directly because the grammatical form of *me fugis* cannot be changed from an interrogative to an imperative and remain the same, an echo.[26] As a respondent who cannot respond in her own words but must instead repeat *the ends of the words given* to her, Echo is at an impasse.[27] She cannot say "flee from me" because the grammatical form would have to change to the imperative, fuge me, in order for her to repeat the end of the phrase properly. And if Echo says "fuge me," she changes the end of the question Narcissus's asks (me fugis).

An aporia occurs in Echo's inability to respond. Unable to speak *for* herself, she is forced to speak a version of herself in a language that is not only not hers but also in a grammar that is not available to her. Her position designates a double suspension. Spivak writes, "Caught in the discrepancy between second person interrogative (*fugis*) and the imperative (*fugi*), Ovid cannot allow her to be, even Echo."[28] In this moment, Echo cannot speak her desire, nor can she speak against her desire. Her voice cannot be her own, and the limits of the law of language cannot represent the position in which they have placed her as Echo, defined by her echo. Echo's "subjectivity" becomes a subjectivity framed by uncertainty.[29] Her difference cannot be accounted for, and therefore her difference fails to exist.

This catachresis of language registers Echo's position as respondent with an asymmetrical relation to the law of the father god and patriarch (Jupiter). From the perspective of the law of the gods, the seemingly totalizing discourse of punishment cannot fully exercise the reverberating echo as a punishment, for in doing so, that punishment contravenes its own law, its own grammar. After all, to respond with an echo, the nymph would have to utter a phrase that cannot exist according to the language that has defined her imprisonment within the role of respondent, of echo. The text, as the very grammar that constitutes Echo's being, cannot account for her. And yet the text, with colonizing force, proceeds despite this internal inconsistency, enacting a cover-up to hide its insufficiency, submitting Echo to further violence. Echo's response, and in it her punishment, is deferred through Ovid's report.[30] Compounding the violation further, Ovid compensates for the paralysis to which Echo has been subjected by responding *for* her. Because Ovid acts as Narcissus's respondent, Narcissus receives the same words that he utters (reenacting a specular logic in language). Ovid's attempt to cover the juridical failure marks a colonizing obliteration of Echo's difference.[31] Spivak's reading of Echo suggests that the logic of identity that informs the egoistic imperialist logic of liberalism is colonizing in part because of its juridical force; it establishes law through exclusions, creating punished others who are at once exteriorized by the law even as they are constitutive of it.

Catachresis as Resistance

Echo's situation might seem hopeless, but Spivak does see possibilities for something that resembles resistance to the selfsameness of discursivity, and therein the possibility of ethical agency. She points to the catachresis to show that the system is not an indomitable totality. According to Spivak, Echo's *deferred re*sponse *points to a différance* in Derrida's sense of the word.[32] In regard to Echo, *différance* can only be known through the failure of her punishment, which presents itself as a failure of language—a failure that Ovid attempts to hide by reporting Echo's me fugis as "receiv[ing] the same words as he speaks."

Her deferred response, as *différance*, is the mark of the system's failure. Though the juridical function of language is based on a universal and is applied to all, the linguistic catachresis that results from the crisis of response reveals that the embodied particularities of the colonized/punished Echo do not allow that function to apply to all universally, as intended. Echo cannot abide in her punishment; she cannot speak the precisely mimicked response. She cannot respond to Narcissus's call and speak in her voice as her discursively constituted body would demand (she is, after all, written as a woman). Echo thus transgresses the laws of representation. Echo's inability to respond to Narcissus results in an inability of Narcissus to fulfill both his assigned role and hers, as respondent/echo of his desire.[33] When Ovid reports that Narcissus receives the words he has uttered, Spivak suggests that Narcissus, in Echo's deferred response, does not receive the perfect reflection of his desire.

In addition to reading Echo's crisis as transgressing the law of the text, Spivak decolonizes the eros of Echo and Narcissus's relationship, at once highlighting the relationship between the linguistic and the psychoanalytic subjects and deconstructing it. At first, the law reinforces the imago as ego, as a projection of masculine desire. Narcissus, who had previously thwarted the desires of others through his nonresponsiveness, receives an unintentional "nonresponse" from Echo. In receiving the words he delivered, he receives the representation of his desire. Echo had been returning that imago as ego, that self-fixation as self-knowledge, to Narcissus. But in the moment of her deferred response, Echo defers that return. This moment, in which no path existed for Echo, this aporia, might create a brief death of Narcissus's imago—his ideal image. It interrupts the return of his voice, his discourse; it interrupts the return of his image to his ego. Echo's deferred response, as a "truth not dependent on intention," thus undoes the promise of narcissistic self-knowledge.[34]

Referring to the predicament in which Echo is placed under an ethical demand to respond and yet rendered incapable of fulfilling that demand, Spivak says, "A difference and a deferment together are, strictly speaking—. . .—a *différance*."[35] The incongruity of Echo and Narcissus's relationship with respect to language results in this *différance*, and it will be their mutual undoing. Spivak describes the relation as a "deconstructive embrace."[36] Doomed to fail, the punishment cannot account for the difference that the deferment marks. The resistance in the deferred response exceeds the text because it violates the rules of representation—there is a gap between what is meant and what can be said.

The deconstructive embrace is an undoing of the law and of the structures that frame the relationship between Echo and Narcissus, a relationship that itself frames their asymmetry with regard to the law. The deconstructive embrace is also, importantly, signaled in a botched physical embrace that at once mirrors this linguistic and conceptual undoing while also hinting that the embodiedness of subaltern difference is the possibility of resistance. After Narcissus poses the question "Why do you flee from me?" that becomes the catachresis, the desirous Echo leaps from the woods in an attempt to throw her arms around Narcissus's neck so that her physical gesture might "help her own words."[37] But Narcisuss indignantly rebuffs her approach. When he does so, Echo is left with the realization that his desire was never for her and that her utterance inviting him to "come" was never on her terms. Echo mourns the return of her desire that never existed, and she pines for Narcissus until her body wastes away and she becomes nothing but a voice—fulfilling her fate as an echo. Echo, in her inability to speak her own desire and upon her rejection by Narcissus, remains only as the unintentional respondent, whose "bones are turned to stone."[38] Though reading the deconstructive embrace paints a picture of Echo's loss, Spivak's reading of the text emphasizes the mutuality of embrace and in this case, its deconstructive dimension.

The grievous corporeal embrace is thus the manifestation of a catachrestic tension that is also the suspension of Echo and Narcissus's collective undoing. Narcissus rejects Echo because his voice, not hers, is the one he has fallen for. He fears her in her own desire. Echo has been giving back Narcissus's words, but now that he must contend with her flesh and not simply the repetition of his own desires, she is threatening. Her embodied presence forces him to contend with a *real* other who is not simply the projection of his desire for sameness. Echo's flesh, beyond the utterances through which she has signaled her "presence" up until this moment, confronts the absence of Narcissus's self-knowledge. In the embrace, her embodiedness, not her echo, refuses the perfect reflection of his desire. Rather than being used in the formation of his subjectivity, she gives back to him in a way that disrupts his subjectivity, challenging the selfsameness of his identity.[39] Narcissus's rejection of Echo exposes the incapacity of the selfsame to embrace the embodied alterity that it can neither recognize nor hear. But it also suggests that this inability involves a fear and anxiety that can perhaps be its downfall.[40]

The deconstructive embrace transforms the condition of Echo's lack to a condition of resistance; however, Spivak gives us pause. Because the deconstructive embrace results in a physical unmattering of Echo, catachresis *might* seem an unsatisfying, textual reading of resistance for subaltern subjects.[41] Spivak does not equivocate about this precarious position of the colonized. She writes, "Claiming catachreses from a space one cannot want to inhabit and yet must criticize is, then, the deconstructive predicament of the postcolonial."[42] But, to return again to the question of ontology at the heart of this chapter, I insist that the particularities of the predicament need not be eternal if the ontological is read as a structural position of lack with respect to the law and/or the political, such that the ontological can then be reimagined by reframing desire beyond lack.

Coloniality, Phallocentrism, and the Question of Ontology

In *Irigaray and Politics: A Critical Introduction*, philosopher Laura Roberts writes that "Spivak finds Irigaray's positive articulation of desire as double—that refuses phallocentric logic and the categorising of woman as sex or reproductive object—ways in which we can connect women across the globe."[43] Roberts, whose own work integrates indigenous thought worlds as part of a decolonizing political philosophy, juxtaposes Spivak and Irigaray to articulate a philosophy of solidarity against the structural violence of liberalism's imperialist logic.

In her reading of Spivak's 1993 "French Feminism Revisited," which Spivak suggests is in part a retrospective of her 1991 "French Feminism in an International Frame," Roberts emphasizes Irigaray's influence on Spivak's "reworking of female pleasure."[44] Roberts's reading of Irigaray and Spivak together carefully and clearly articulates their shared investment in a radical remaking of politics that is rooted in the Levinasian aspiration to a nonselfsame ethic of their shared philosophical genealogy. Roberts offers a succinct description of Irigaray's "sexuate other" as the one who gives subjectivity its limit and further philosophically frames Irigaray's notion of desire as the "third space" in this relation between two through which their subjectivity emerges.[45] But before positively asserting sexuate relation as the emergence of a new subjectivity and before articulating desire as an excess of this relation, I want to take a deeper look at how these two thinkers diagnose the logic of discourse to better understand their positive assertions about the importance of female pleasure's ability to reshape desire.

Both Irigaray and Spivak share critical theory's investment in interrogating connective threads between philosophical ethics, literary theory, and psychoanalysis; however, Spivak's critique of the psychoanalytic framework insists that it is not only phallocentric but also colonizing.[46] Irigaray, on the other hand, understands colonialism as an effect of the phallocentrism of the psychoanalytic framework. Tension therefore remains between the "postcolonial" and what Roberts refers to as the "metropolitan" feminist positions that emerge in Spivak's and Irigaray's respective interpretations of the mechanics by which one becomes a subject in and through language. Roberts argues that Irigaray's insistence on the doubling of women's pleasures engenders a retrieval and re-formation of social bonds between and among women; this doubling inspires Spivak to adopt Irigaray critically — that is, to "problematize, destabilise and refigure" the relationship inspired by the touching lips as an invitation to engage in "non-hierarchical dialogue."[47]

I find Roberts's assessment of the Spivak's debt to Irigaray quite helpful for thinking through the political resonances and discontinuities of Irigaray's and Spivak's aims; however, here I am interested in a deeper theoretical pressure point related to Irigaray's theoretical allegiance to sexuate difference and *how* that remains at odds with Spivak's adaptation of her work. That tension, I insist, is an effect of the problem and promise of ontology. In what follows, I will explain how the colonizing and phallocentric are similar with regard to the movement toward sameness and how they are different with regard to the question of ontology. I offer this foundation as a means to advance a decolonial ontology of desire.

In continued support of my argument that an "ontology" of desire conceives relation between discourse and materiality somewhere between becoming and subjectivity, I begin by emphasizing the two theorists' shared investment in using language to disrupt the logic of the same. Indeed, both

Spivak's notion of the double bind and Irigaray's depiction of women's relation to the symbolic operate on the assumption that language mediates subjectivity such that one's relationship to language offers insight not only into one's relation to the social order but also to a more fundamentally to the structuring of that mediation itself.[48]

Irigaray, I have argued, insists that women are in the impossible position of representing their desires through the masculine symbolic. Their desires are therefore doubly mediated, and their subjectivity thus amounts to a double alienation from any authentic self. This mediation further results in "failures" of women to speak "correctly," in a way that is consistent with masculine desire. The double alienation of women from their desires is the condition of possibility of signification (as representation) in language. The fate of woman and the fate of the colonized with respect to the selfsame law of the text is a deconstructive embrace—an embodied pining for self that results in a disembodied voice and a relegation of corporeality to an image of inert materiality, of "bones turned to stone." We might extend this embrace to Irigaray's reading of the disembodiedness of thought that produces and reproduces an alienation of discourse from the radical alterity of materiality (of Echo's flesh) such that bodies are mere objects of discourse itself. Perhaps bodies and discourse are in this state of a deconstructive embrace today? Are discourse and bodies not entangled in the production and reproduction of categories of identity, whose proliferations create more opportunities for disruption but also more occasions for exclusions, as Foucault's reading of the discourses on Victorian sexuality suggest?

For both Spivak and Irigaray, the work of their writing is the starting point for imagining some sort of alternative or resistance to the selfsame logic of colonial imperialism and phallocentrism, respectively. For Irigaray, mimesis, written through the position of a woman, disrupts the logic of the symbolic in its movement toward the self-sufficiency of thought, just as catachresis in Spivak's "Echo" creates an interruption in language that must be covered over for the law to maintain the sense of its wholeness and consistency.[49] Catachresis, like Irigaray's mimesis, is an interruption (however unintentional and unwanted) of the otherwise totalizing logic of sameness in language.[50] It is the effect of the other's double alienation within the symbolic—an effect of the gap between the difference assigned to the other in the symbolic and the alterity that is excluded (i.e., the difference for which the law, or the symbolic, cannot account) in order for the machinations of the selfsame economy to continue. So while mimesis is a condition of women for Irigaray, and while Echo's unintended response is the position of the subaltern for Spivak, their respective readings of woman and the subaltern suggest their positions are also the possibility for disruption. In linguistic terms, the mimetic "failures" in logic constitute catachrestic interruptions in language.[51]

Spivak's reading of the catachresis resonates with the structure of "Irigarayan" mimesis; the "ventriloquisms" of women as other, speaking this otherness within a masculine symbolic, is similar to Echo's subjection to the law of the gods.[52] Echo's punishment signifies her difference in relation to the law, as its violator, its criminal. Women in mimesis are subject to the law of language, participating in its movement toward truth. But the difference of their proximity to this truth and its movement is, like Echo's echo, not entirely affirming of the law's truth, of its self-projection, of its imago. Irigaray similarly insists that women relate to the selfsame symbolic differently. And this is revealed in part in the different ways Irigaray says men and women use language.[53] Just as Echo's catachresis shows the insufficiencies of the law of language to account for this other, mimesis reveals cracks within an otherwise totalizing logic of sameness—evidenced in the crossing lips that create a space and time suspended in ambiguity.[54] For Echo, and for women (as other), "resistance" resides in the incapacity to fulfill the mandates of the juridical force of language in the symbolic.

Both Spivak's reading of the colonized in relation to the law of text and Irigaray's reading of the symbolic conceive the sociocultural (and juridical) as operating according to a logic of reduction to sameness that is perpetuated in and through the order of language. For both thinkers, the logic through which worlds are constructed is therefore selfsame. They present language and social and cultural artifacts and/or symbols as simultaneously the effects and instruments through which this logic is perpetuated. Acknowledging that they are writing in a way that claims a position-as-predicament, Irigaray and Spivak write nonetheless, performing a labor of resisting sameness in and through their writing.

Spivak locates resistance within the failure of the system to enact a complete enclosure: resistance is the unintentional response that creates a catachresis. Spivak's reading of Echo demonstrates that colonizing logic is gendered in ways that reveal a disconnect between representation of difference and any sort of difference excluded through that representation.[55] Irigaray reads the selfsame symbolic as phallocentric because she relies on a psychoanalytic framework for imagining identity as a reflection of desire for singularity. Irigaray insists that it is the violation of sexuate difference, which is prior to any entrance into the law, that makes these exclusions, and juridical expulsions, possible. Both Irigaray and Spivak provide a depiction of the symbolic order as operating according to a logic of identity, and both depict this position by focusing on mimicry/echo as a condition of being other within the symbolic order. However, despite the similarities in Spivak's and Irigaray's assertions that the logic of discourse exhibits a movement toward sameness, and despite their thinking and writing from the position of the other, depicting discursive logic as phallocentric is not entirely analogous to depicting that logic as colonizing. This difference is especially evident in how they conceive resistance/disruption and the question of ontology.

Irigaray's emphasis on the sexuate as an extradiscursive difference rings with a certain appeal to ontology that Spivak avoids. Although Echo's position as feminine engenders this crisis, Spivak doesn't locate the disruption in Echo in an ontological way. Spivak portrays Echo's double bind as an effect of language that shapes Echo's reality, not a representation of a necessary ontological reality but rather something more along the lines of a political ontology.[56] As Johanna Oksala describes it, political ontology (as distinct from an ontology of the political as separate domains) is an "understanding of reality" that is "achieved in social practices and networks of power rather than simply given."[57] Contending as she does that the being of Beings is constitutive of the very question of Being, what we might call Spivak's political ontico-ontology is not a description of a fixed reality; her analysis of Echo is not meant to fix the reality of the subaltern as eternally Other. Rather, Spivak's analysis of Echo is meant to diagnose that Otherness in relation to the problem of colonialism and the law of empire.

Irigaray, on the other hand, appeals to the sexuate as an irreducible difference that is the possibility of a nonselfsame desire of a feminine imaginary. For Irigaray, then, the sexuate invokes an embodied extradiscursive reality whose difference is the possibility of a relational subjectivity. Admittedly, this sounds like a reification of sexed ontologies; after all, asserting a materiality of the sexuate difference without situating that materiality in a sociohistorical context implies that it is somehow outside systems of discursive representation. This formulation is precisely why some have argued that in Irigaray, "woman" is resigned to the ontological condition of lack. Ontology can empower, but it often does so at the expense of reifying, even concretizing, the position of the excluded in a specific notion of the body that reductively freezes the "everydayness of being."[58]

Oksala warns that one of the most enduring and "disastrous" problems of ontologies is their implications that the "right ontology would furnish the right political order."[59] Reading Foucault at the crosshairs of foundationalist/antifoundationalist arguments (like those I raise in chapter 3), Oksala proposes an alternative ontology that does not appeal to an ultimate foundation. I argue that Irigaray's invocation of the sexuate is, not unlike Spivak's catachresis, an "ontology" that disrupts the phallocentric/colonizing logic of sameness; it is disruptive of a pure ontology that would reify sameness. Indeed, the turn to some form of extradiscursivity that is also material is part of Irigaray's appeal for my own project because it does not think discourse as an inescapable totality; rather, she provides space for thinking beyond the colonizing logic of identity.[60] Irigaray perseveres in her writing with a certain hopefulness about the demand, the need, and the possibility of changing the world, of imagining a way of becoming otherwise.

Despite the hopefulness of Irigaray's vision, I want to acknowledge the dangers of any sort of turn toward a presymbolic or extrasymbolic existence as the ground of such efforts. After all, it seems disingenuous writing, in this time and space of Israel's war with Hamas and the catastrophic humanitarian consequences of countless assaults, to attempt to raise the problem of ontological violence without acknowledging that while Levinas advocated the possibility of radical alterity as the trace of the divine in the face of his other, not all of his others were really wholly other in practice. As Andrés Fabián Henao Castro notes, "Writing in the context of the settler colonial occupation of the Palestinian territories by the newly founded state of Israel after the end of the Second World War, Levinas regarded Palestinians as faceless, and his theory fares no better in relation to Black people."[61] And while Irigaray insisted that Levinas's other was never neutral, she did so by prioritizing the sexuate as that which his face-to-face encounter sacrificed. She never attended to the possibility that there might be other wholly others. As Henao Castro writes, "Irigaray remained focused almost exclusively on the universality of sexual difference without troubling the ways that colonialism also complicated the universalization of the feminine she considered exclusively a masculine construction."[62] Henao Castro's interpretation does not sufficiently grasp the psychoanalytic foundations of Irigaray's understanding of sexual difference as entrenched in a Lacanian reading of sexual difference that is prior to the symbolic (such that colonialism and masculine constructions are always already names given to phallocentric logic); however, it does remind us of the entanglements of attempting to describe a future by appealing to a presymbolic embodied difference marked by its exclusion in the present without occluding other corporealities that make the appeal possible.

The Imperialism of Ontology

The neoimperialism of liberalism expressed in the narcissism of the sym-bolic—through its assertions of benevolent universal truth claims—is perhaps most totalizing when it appeals to ontology. Ontology, as an appeal to Being, easily becomes an opportunity to dehistoricize and decontextualize a situation, such as when speaking of the equality of creation. Within the context of colonialism, ontological difference supports the narratives of differentiation that define and orient a subject. It becomes the means for normalizing the ontic otherness of the discursively constituted Other. But as I suggested at the opening of this chapter, postmodernity's destabilization of ontology as a resistance to neoliberal universals is itself a potentially neocolonizing gesture.[63]

When Spivak first published "Can the Subaltern Speak?" she was addressing Western scholars who were engaging in cultural critiques of non-Western persons and people. Part of Spivak's criticism was that the West interprets others within a moral framework of liberalism. Pointing to the practice of sati in some parts of the Indian subcontinent, as well as to the British colonial government's outlaw of the practice, Spivak highlighted how scholars analyzed non-Western "subaltern" subjects without interrogating the imperializing force of liberalism's assumptions. Because liberalism is the dominant force asserting normative claims globally, Spivak's rhetorical title about whether or not the subaltern can speak highlighted the double bind in which a subaltern subject finds herself: forced to articulate her experi-ences within a sociocultural and symbolic discourse that is not her own. For critics of Spivak's radically deconstructive work, her depiction of the double bind risks articulating the position of the subaltern persons and/or women (in Irigaray's case) as a position of exclusion and raises questions about how the excluded can exert agency without appealing to the law/language that depends on exclusions.[64] If the position of the double bind is read as an unwelcomed space of catachresis, in the position of speaking without being heard, of asserting one's rights without being recognized, it is a position of ontological insecurity.[65] The obvious question for on-the-ground activists aware of the calamitous positionally of subaltern persons is how one overcomes this ontological insecurity without recapitulating colonizing logic. How does one fashion a subjectivity that decolonizes the selfsame?

Julietta Singh has taken up the question of ontological insecurity as an affective dimension of embodying the colonized position. Singh turns to postcolonial narratives themselves to articulate the colonial logic that continues to operate even within decolonial narratives of personhood. According to

Singh, ontological insecurity is manifested in countermastery narratives that invariably risk reifying the logic of mastery. In *Unthinking Mastery*, Singh examines Frantz Fanon and Mohandas Gandhi as anticolonial critics whose efforts to establish liberatory narratives of solidarity are complicated by the inevitable "remainders" in which "the subjection of other bodies appeared almost necessary to anticolonial recovery."[66] Singh argues that "other bodies" that get left behind, if not remastered, in the narratives of the "emergent master" are typically "colonized women, indigenous peoples, the 'uncivilized groups' of the emergent nation state, the animal, the cripple, and nature itself."[67] Singh acknowledges the predicament of the postcolonial position, and she reflectively and critically engages the reading of humanitarianism that informs her own personal narrativization of that position, recognizing that her desires for notions of justice and autonomy are rooted in the logic of imperialism. She thus extends her personal reflection in order to interrogate literary "narratives of humanitarian benevolence" that inform a "postcolonial" liberalism that doesn't recognize the role of these fictions in the perpetuation of global human inequality.[68]

Singh's interest in a constructive yet critical response to the double bind is, like Spivak and Irigaray, an attempt to think something like subjectivity without embracing the logic of sameness. According to Singh, postcolonial assertions of subjectivity are constructed through narratives that represent the values and logic of colonial oppressors. This representation results in the alienation and marginalization of minority positions within the narratives of countermastery. Ontological insecurity is, by Singh's reading, the condition of the colonized narrativizing their subjectivity within neoimperialist demands for recognition. Attention to the bodies that are "sacrificed" so that these narratives become political movements is the work, she suggests, of decolonization, the work that her critical readings of Gandhi's and Fanon's countermastery narratives perform. I would add that Singh is, in a sense, reading the Echo of/within an anticolonial narrative in order to resist the sacrificial economy through which one becomes a subject whose subjectivity is then validated in political recognition (wherein identification/solidarity flatten differences).[69]

In a 2019 article, Zaynab Shahar examines Singh's depiction of the emergent mastery within countermastery narratives in relation to the affective dimensions of ontological insecurity described in Sara Ahmed's work. Shahar begins by reflecting on how her admiration of Singh's efforts ended in frustration with what she views as Singh's replication of the affect of mastery in an effort to decolonize countermastery by rereading Fanon and

Ghandi among others. Shahar goes on to argue that the countermastery narratives of anticolonial thinking participate in a "politics of affect."[70] She writes, "The presence of mastery in the oeuvres of anticolonial thinkers not only orients readers towards their conceptions of masterful decolonial subjects but away from colonial subjects which provoke their own onto-logical insecurities."[71] In other words, countermastery narratives play upon the desire for sameness.[72] Shahar insists that affect therefore becomes an important lens through which to engage in the continuous decolonizing of both colonial and decolonial discourses. She writes:

> If we understand affects as at once incorporated into coloniality and decoloniality, then decolonial solidarities and discourses must necessarily pay attention to the proliferation of ontological insecurities through the transmission of affect. Anyone doing the work of decolonization has to question their affective relation-ships to gender, power, knowledge production—particularly the implications of theorizing gender through the lens of indifference to women, LGBTQ people, etc. Those producing discourses on coloniality/decoloniality and gender have to critically examine their affective attachments to colonial conceptions of gender.[73]

Shahar's interrogation of the affective dimensions of the coloniality of gender and decolonizing efforts is particularly significant insofar as it links discursive gendering with an ontological insecurity. Insofar as ontologies provide foundations for secure selfhood, they are entwined with affect and, therefore, entwined with discourse and exceeding it. I will return to the relationship between ontological insecurity and phallocentric desire later to insist that Irigaray's interrogation of the selfsame logic as that which gov-erns the relationships between men and women, as well as her turn to an imaginary born of a nonselfsame desire, operate according to a decolonizing logic that has the possibility for resisting countermastery.

Shahar interweaves contributions of decolonial and queer theorists who have attempted to think practically about ways to disrupt mastery narratives by exploiting the ways certain bodies fail within narratives of mastery. She emphasizes the resonance between Walter Mignolo's insistence on failure as an epistemic resistance to coloniality (which I would add resonates with Spi-vak's reading of Echo's catachresis)[74] and Jack (Judith) Halberstam's notion of queer failure.[75] Shahar also incorporates Gaile Pohlhaus's notion of "knowing without borders" to rethink the spatial dimensions between persons as the dynamism that undermines what is known.[76] Shahar insists that decolonial discourse and discourses of mastery, including "cisheteropatriarch[al]" and "heterosocial[l]" discourses, order relationships between gendered, raced, and sexed subjectivities at the expense of other relations, "sublimating the ways of knowing emerging from lived realities outside of that preview."[77] I would add that this ordering takes place with an intent toward sameness. Mastery and phallocentrism are describing a particular orientation of desire as a colonizing, dominating, consumptive relation to the other.

Shahar concludes by considering the relation of affect to queer and queer-of-color practices of disidentification (as an embodied narrativization of a nonselfsame subjectivity) as a way to address ontological insecurity without recapitulating mastery. Though Shahar is not entirely explicit about the connection, I read her turn to disidentification (in the work of Muñoz and Eric Thomas) as an effort to think through the embodiedness of failures to identify in accordance with cisheteropatriarchal and heterosexist social regimes (to become recognizable or—to draw on Spivak—to be heard). These "failures," not unlike the catachresis in Echo's narrative, create ruptures in the space and time between one and an other. This creation of space and time where there was none—between discourse and the bodies whose relations are figured through that discourse—illustrates the affective relation between the subject and the other. Similarly, Echo's catachresis at once reveals law's inability to account for her difference and also unveils a prediscursive, prejuridical, affective orientation of Echo to the gods that enabled the gods (and Ovid) to assume their law was a totality. As such, these failures expose the mobilization and/or weaponization of a prediscursive relationality or affect that enable discourses of mastery (which I insist are selfsame discourses).[78]

Singh's deconstructive reading acknowledges the mastery that governs efforts at resistance. And what I find most useful about Shahar's effort is the consideration of affect as both extradiscursive and in relation to masterful discourse that orients affect toward identity. It is precisely the suggestion that there is something beyond or behind the representations of conscious subjects (in politics and political movements) that makes engaging the psychoanalytic useful for thinking about how to imagine counternarratives that are not reemergent masteries. As this book has insisted throughout, Irigaray's linguistic adaptations of psychoanalysis have a longstanding engagement with notions of the subconscious and the prediscursive as a way both to combat the notion that worldmaking is not inherently a selfsame endeavor and to imagine an alternative that flows from the embodied alterity of prediscursive desire. Without completely analogizing affect and desire (though Irigaray too notes their relation in *The Mediation of Touch*), I suggest that desire captures the dynamism of affect's relation to discourse and the making of worlds. Irigaray has paved the way for thinking space and time beyond active and passive or inside and outside—and can therefore inform a notion of anti-identitarian embodiment that do more than resubmit embodiment to discursive reductions. It is here, in thinking about the relation between affect and desire that Sara Ahmed's reading of embodiment is helpful for considering that space between the logic of identity and the embodiments of alterity that are not simply effects of discursive exclusions.

In *Willful Subjects*, Ahmed differentiates her notion of willfulness from its historical associations with political subjectivity, and this depiction of willfulness helps to frame unintentional catachresis as a decolonizing of subjectivity. Ahmed writes, "Willfulness tends to imply a particular kind of subject, one that has intentions and knows her intentions."[79] She then interrogates this concept of will by creating what she calls an archive of its use, primarily in relation to its uses in legal discourse. It is through this particular historicizing of will that Ahmed differentiates the will as an intentional action (which assumes an agential, knowing subject) from a notion of willfulness as a feminist disruption of subjectivity. She continues, "Willfulness is a diagnosis of the failure to comply with those whose authority is given."[80] This statement, in particular the "failure to comply" that constitutes living a feminist life, evokes the disruption of catachresis that is an effect of living as a postcolonial subject, as a subaltern echo, and as a feminized other in a phallocentric discourse.

For Ahmed, willfulness is an affective and unintentional dimension of living that is also "a way of holding on, of not giving up."[81] In the idea of "holding on," Ahmed locates a discrete optimism in willfulness that could empower and motivate a way of being in the world without being of the world—a way of living creatively to imagine ways of being that resist putting one's hope in political identifications. She is aware that the language of optimism can result in a passivity vis-à-vis the world, and she insists that this optimism of willfulness is not the "cruel optimism" that iconic theorist Lauren Berlant criticizes.

Attentive to the ease with which optimism becomes sufficient in and of itself, Ahmed turns to Antonio Gramsci's warning that "optimism" can amount to "nothing more than a defense of one's laziness, one's irresponsibility."[82] Ahmed articulates her notion of the optimism of willfulness in order to address the abnegation of responsibility against which Gramsci warns. For her, the optimism of willfulness is not a hopefulness in optimism as an ideology, an optimism in optimism. Rather, optimism for Ahmed requires effort. And in this way, the optimism of willfulness evokes a certain ethical obligation. But the work of the optimism of willfulness is not a political labor; responsibility is not structured by a notion of the subject who becomes a subject through voluntary identifications. Rather, Ahmed insists that the optimism of willfulness is the possibility of "bypass[ing]" a subjectivity synonymous with political identifications.[83] This bypassing means that Ahmed perceives the effort of the optimism in willfulness as a disruption of the selfsame economy of political subjectivity.

There is an important affective dimension of willfulness that allows Ahmed to differentiate her notion of willfulness from the historical uses of willfulness entangled in notions of political volition that assume a "knowing subject."[84] In turning to affect while insisting on effort, Ahmed establishes a willfulness that implies a certain agency (my word, not Ahmed's characterization) without intentionality. This is not an "agency" that recapitulates political identifications and is thus only agential insofar as it is recognizable as a political subject. Rather, Ahmed's notion of willfulness suggests an agency that is baked into embodied living. Affect appeals to the unintentional without relying on the unconscious as an ontological condition of being in the world. Willfulness, as "a way of holding on, of not giving up," is therefore not a nihilistic hope for political recognition; it is the optimism of ongoing effort informed by embodied affect.[85]

Ahmed's efforts to think through willfulness beyond the political aim to theorize becoming in the world beyond identity, and thus to avoid the cruel optimism of willfulness. Willfulness encompasses an agency beyond volition, an agency that "bypasses" the demands for recognition within the social and political order of the symbolic, that bypasses the need to claim/concede being or belonging to a particular identity in order to be recognized.[86] Though not appealing to desire as an unconscious foundation of becoming, Ahmed suggests a relation of willfulness to desire. She is clear that she does not think of willfulness in terms of an unconscious that structures becoming. Instead, she wants willfulness to be something beyond a notion of the unconscious that she sees as entrenched in psychoanalytic discourse. I perceive her avoidance of the unconscious in part as an effort to think desire beyond libidinal drives and embodiment without the risk of ontologizing the "effort" of willfulness—that is to say, to affirm the embodiedness of living without essentializing particular modes of life.

Ahmed's depiction of willfulness highlights a notion of agency that is not constituted in and through political identifications. Her turn to affect and her particular association of willfulness with desire invite thinking about willfulness as a resistance not only to the politics of recognition, but also more broadly to the sociocultural and political discourses of the selfsame symbolic. I also perceive Ahmed's resistance to the symbolic as a resistance to the colonizing dimensions of ontologies. And I think, along with Singh, that we should resist instantiating being in particular bodies in a way that determines their fate as willful subjects by virtue of ontological exclusion. I want to heed the threat that ontologies pose while also embracing the need to think a mode of anti-identitarian activity that "bypasses" notions of intention that assume the singularity and coincidence of a subject. Beyond the structural analogy of phallocentrism and coloniality as selfsame, what I find interesting about Spivak in relation to Irigaray is the question of the position of the excluded from which to imagine resistance to sameness.

Becoming beyond Lack: Decolonizing Ontology

The works of Singh, Ahmed, and Shahar make me wonder what it would mean to think about decolonizing work beyond a place of ontological insecurity, if such a place exists. Shahar reminds us that Singh's deconstruction of anticolonial literature reveals how writing through the place of the othered, the excluded, is writing through a place of ontological insecurity. Countermastery narratives thus *overcome* this ontological insecurity by reasserting sameness. But I would argue that ontology only reifies narratives of mastery if that ontology belongs to a phallocentric notion of origins that informs metaphysical subjects. In other words, *there is the possibility of other ontologies that don't extend from a nostalgia for irrecoverable origins that motivates the selfsame economy.*

I contend that Irigaray's depiction of woman with respect to the symbolic and Spivak's reading of Echo in relation to the law of the text are not necessarily read as positions of lack with respect to discourse (to the law, to the text, to the symbolic) that would reify the logic of sameness. In fact, through their deconstructive writing practices, Spivak and Irigaray refuse to recapitulate the movement of sameness that exploits rather than reconstructs the wholeness of the world, of thought, of texts. In this refusal, I suggest, they radically reject the position of the other as ontological insecurity and lack. Put simply, both Spivak and Irigaray evoke a decolonizing way of thinking that challenges narratives of mastery without invoking a framework of countermastery.

Note that Spivak's reading attends to the fact that Echo's other-ness with respect to the law is not based solely, or even primarily, in her gendered position. Echo's fate is an effect of being in the position of the colonized—in the position of being the messenger, whose voice and body serve as mediators for someone else's (Jupiter's) crime and punishment. This gendered and "postcolonial" reading of the logic of language and subjectivity highlights the position of the excluded other as *relative to* the normalizing (and moralizing) force of sameness of the law and to whatever identity sits at the head of that totem. That the law is phallocentric means the other is gendered; that the law is imperialist means the other is colonized. But these are not ontologically determined positions; they are relative positions.

And yet Spivak's Echo is not a complete abstraction of lack with respect to the law; she has a certain materiality. On one level, Spivak's attention to the deconstructive embrace suggests that Echo's disembodiment is an effect of the failure of the law to make space for her desire. But Spivak's attention to the deconstructive embrace as a decolonizing act complicates the reading of Echo's body as an ontological fact. Rejected by Narcissus, Echo is confronted with the total loss of her desire in the world, and she wastes away in her pining.[87] But this is actually a second alienation of Echo from her body since the text has already submitted her to a punishment that she cannot fulfill because of her gender, because of the body the text has assigned her, her discursively constituted body. Therefore, her pining enacts a loss of a body that was never allowed to materialize in and of her own desire. Echo's body in the text is the materialization of her differences within the selfsame, totalizing economy of the law. Read in the context of Spivak's deconstructive embrace, Echo's pining leads to a disembodiment that is actually deconstructing the materiality of her colonized gendered existence. In the deconstructive embrace, Echo's discursive unmattering in the catachresis and her physical unmattering in the deconstructive embrace are intertwined.

A decolonizing logic, then, is one that resists the movement toward identity without reifying an ontology of lack, and Irigaray's notion of the sexuate as an alternative to sameness that is not its reverse is useful for thinking through such a notion of decolonizing logic. To appreciate the relationship between the sexuate and ontology, one must understand Irigaray's reading of the symbolic, the imaginary, and the sexuate. Irigaray portrays the economy of sameness as a representation of a masculine imaginary that has posited a universal as neutral and then erected an entire way of relating based in the forgetting of the extra/presymbolic other. In short, the masculine imaginary is defined by its forgetting of sexuate difference. For Irigaray, the movement toward identity is not biologically or ontologically male; rather, the movement toward identity is a phallic representation of a desire for oneness. That desire for oneness is *not* tied to the penis in a necessary way. Desire for oneness is not an effect of being ontologically male, nor is the multiplicity of desire an attribute of some female ontology. The sexuate is not sexed in this way. Rather desire for oneness is a consequence of forgetting the twoness of sexuate difference as the condition of becoming, and the multiplicity of desire is a possibility of relation in that twoness.

Irigaray's insistence on the sexuate as a relation in multiplicity also implies that there is an imaginary capable of a different symbolic relation beyond the movement toward reduction and sameness. Irigaray describes this imaginary as feminine. It designates desire between at least two. A feminine imaginary would be an imaginary that does not forget the twoness but rather abides in the ambiguity of this desire between two. While she labels this a "feminine imaginary," the point is that this imaginary flows from the irreducible desire that exists between two or more; it flows from the sexuate as a space of irreducible difference.[88]

It is this space of an ambiguous and embodied desire, of a radical eros, of wonderment, that generates an imaginary otherwise than a desire for sameness. This imaginary promises a different symbolic order for sociocultural and sociohistorical relations in order to reflect this ambiguity of desire. It is the threshold of a symbolic of openness and ambiguity for which the phallocentric model of sociality cannot account. Read this way, the sexuate should not be resubmitted to the gendered positions of a colonizing, cisnormative, and heterosexist discourse. If we read, as Allison Stone does, that the sexuate is not a representation of discursively constituted identities (such as sex), then the Echos of the world are not simply lack. They are only lack if we center the selfsame order. This reading makes Irigaray particularly useful in regard to the question of resistance: her ontology can be read as irreducible and dynamic because it is grounded in the materiality of alterity, not in a particular difference.

Put plainly, in Irigaray's work, desire for oneness is not a consequence of some prediscursive maleness. Desire for oneness is a consequence of the violation of sexuate difference, a violation that culminates in a binary gender hierarchy. The selfsame, in its sameness, prioritizes a gendering of subjects that privileges men over not-men, the latter of which becomes synonymous with women, gender-nonconforming persons, colonized subjects, and raced subjects. Similarly, colonizing logic is phallocentric, not because it has to be masculine, but because the logic of identity engenders a priority or sameness that is synonymous with the masculine (which is why the masculine stands as a representation of the universal and neutral). Read this way, the framing of a universal (e.g., white, European, rational man) as synonymous with particular sociocultural and political identities is an effect of the logic of identity, not its cause. As such, a decolonized reading of the position of the excluded beyond lack supports a reading of Irigaray's ontology as a fecund indeterminacy. Inspired by Irigaray's sexuate desire as decolonizing the universalizing orientations of pure ontology, I suggest that decolonizing ontology becomes a praxis of resisting new narrative of mastery that a universalizing ontology would recapitulate.[89]

The Subconscious and Unintentional Response: Reimagining Resistance through a Decolonized Ontology of Desire

Mindful of the dangers of ontology that Singh and Ahmed have articulated, this section considers the unintentional response in Irigaray's mimesis and Spivak's catachresis, in the context of their deconstructive projects, as rejections of the selfsame. Furthermore, this effort appeals to a certain materiality that does not relegate the other to a position of lack with respect to sameness. I contend that Irigaray's turn to an extradiscursive sexuate in particular articulates a materiality of radical alterity, manifested in the multiplicity of desire. I will argue that this appeal to the multiplicity of desire, and to the materiality of its irreducibility, has the potential to ground an nonphallocentric, or nonmastery, narrative of becoming that refuses to recapitulate sameness. In refusing not simply the reversal of phallocentric narratives of mastery, I offer a reading of (nonselfsame) desire as the affective labor of decolonizing ontology.

In order to interpret the unintentional response as a space of "resistance" reimagined, I want to draw attention to the affinity between Ahmed's notion of willfulness, Spivak's catachresis, and Irigaray's notion of desire as they relate to the turn toward embodiedness beyond its discursive prescriptions or exclusions. Before Echo became a disembodied voice that mimes the addressee, she was an embodied Echo, submitted to the law. The materiality that is violated and sacrificed in order for the selfsame logic to proceed is not simply the body of the talkative girl (which is an effect of Echo as defined in the discourse of the law, of Ovid's text).[90] Rather, the matter of radical difference, the difference effaced in order to constitute Echo the colonized and gendered subject of discourse, is the materiality that is violated as a condition of phallocentric discourse. If it were otherwise, we could simply speak it back into existence, voluntarily.[91]

Insofar as colonizing logic violates this materiality of radical difference or alterity, decolonizing work *abides in* the materiality of alterity.[92] As opposed to a recapitulation of the colonizing logic, Ahmed's notion of willfulness provides a lens for understanding the stakes of thinking the materiality of alterity only in relation to the logic that excludes them. It points to the problem of thinking of resistance only in terms of the logic of sameness. Reading Irigaray's mimesis in relation to Spivak's catachresis demonstrates how Irigaray's notion of desire interrupts, disassimilates, and operates according to a decolonizing logic. Because Irigaray locates this desire in a prediscursive materiality of alterity, it is at once grounded but also indeterminate. This desire offers a way to think about a certain (non-discursive) notion of embodiedness that is not limited by raced, sexed, or sexualized notions of bodily difference—a decolonized ontology capable of decolonizing. Returning to Ahmed, willfulness invokes a relationality that is neither entirely abstract nor relative because it is material, nor is it essential because it is always dynamic. Such a notion of willfulness beyond intention is helpful for considering a certain nonselfsame agency of desire in Irigaray; it invites a reading of Irigaray's desire as decolonizing. This in turn makes Irigaray's notion of desire much more radical and more capable of confronting the tensions between ethics and politics by redefining the limits of both.

If we grant that Irigaray's logic, including her notion of desire, is a decolonizing logic, then we can see a similarity in the aims between Ahmed's willfulness and Irigaray's desire. Ahmed's efforts to hold together a promise of agency, a promise of resistance, a promise of a different subjectivity, are not unlike Irigaray's aims. Ahmed's use of willfulness to address embodiments that are not merely constructions of political choices exhibits an anti-identitarian, decolonizing logic that we witness in Irigarayan desire. Furthermore, both are grappling with speaking of embodiments while critiquing the discourses through which bodies materialize. In light of this similarity, I think Ahmed's turn to affect cannot be overplayed here. It is in the affective that she locates a willfulness beyond political volition. It is without intention (though not "unconscious") that willfulness "pulses with desire."[93] Ahmed invokes the desire to frame willfulness as both relational and agential beyond the selfsame economy of identity. But rather than a "holding on, not giving up," I would argue that an Irigarayan-inspired reading of desire as a "reaching without grasping" more accurately speaks to the aim of a concept of "willfulness." Reading desire as eros that reaches toward the other without grasping captures the type of "optimistic relation" of willfulness that Ahmed says informs a "less intentional model of subjectivity."[94]

Thinking Irigaray and Ahmed together, a decolonizing desire is thus willful. It reaches out.[95] It keeps reaching in spite of itself. To riff on Ahmed and Irigaray, I would argue that "willfulness as an optimistic relation" is an erotic relation. In the eros that constantly reaches out without grasping, we get the sense of an ongoing effort, like that of decolonizing work, the type demanded by Ahmed's willfulness. The difference between reaching and holding, I think, has everything to do with how one wants to interpret embodied living and its relation to ontology. You can reach out if you have a place from which to reach. But holding implies that the object of your desire is what grounds you.

An ontology of desire is not about certainty. It does not extend from a place of insecurity or lack. Both Irigaray and Ahmed want to think embodiment beyond a condition of lack (which means to think embodiment on its own terms, not merely in relation to the colonizing logic of sameness and its notions of bodily subjects. Ahmed needs the notion of "holding" because she does not want an ontology to stabilize and orient willfulness. She wants to avoid the ontological argument because it too easily slips into essentializing. In this avoidance, she turns to affect to hint at an embodiedness that is inessential and that defies intentionality.[96]

Irigaray, on the other hand, does have a reimagined ontology to ground an alternative space for resisting the selfsame subject. And if, rather than reading Irigaray's ontology as a sexuate ontology, we focus on the ways the sexuate is used to mark a relation of irreducible differences, then we can even decolonize Irigaray's ontology by naming it an ontology of desire—capturing the dynamism of the materiality and alterity that the sexuate is meant to name. Irigarayan desire, like willfulness, defies the notion of intentionality synonymous with voluntary political identifications. It is an (un)intentionality beyond sameness. It involves, as Irigaray has suggested, a love of self that is not love of same. What we might describe as the intentionality of this other subjectivity, or a certain agency of a dynamic desire, is the possibility of radical resistance to identification. Resistance, then, would not be trapped in relation to sameness, but it would rather exist in a way of becoming that offers a sense of another way of being.

A decolonized ontology as a nonselfsame ontology is useful for thinking difference beyond its position of exclusion in the symbolic. Ontology provides a ground of being to which one can appeal in the face of an exclusionary logic that affronts one's very right to existence; it provides a ground for becoming that is not an effect of discursive exclusion but constitutive of it. A decolonizing ontology achieves this ground without resubmitting to the logic of identity, without the narrative of countermastery. And if the symbolic is a manifestation of an imaginary, and if that imaginary is constituted through desire, desire is the relation in and of this difference that can provide that dynamic ground (or that breath).[97]

Ahmed's turn to affect attempts to capture what Irigaray has done with sexuate difference, but without an appeal to ontology: a possibility of a subjectivity that can be imagined as not completely subject to selfsameness. Indeed, for Ahmed, reference to affect gestures to an embodiedness beyond intention—an embodiedness that would disrupt models of subjectivity based in self-naming.[98] For the self-naming subject, what would pass for "resistance" happens within or in relation to the economy of sameness. The willful subject, beyond intention, emerges differently, apart from self-naming. Resistance, I surmise, would be the work of optimism.

But what desire does in Irigaray, affect alone does not accomplish.[99] In Irigaray, desire constitutes a space for the unintentional becoming that happens from being in relation to one who is not me, from reaching out toward the other from the fullness of one's own desire. The desire that reaches out in its multiplicity and its dynamism decolonizes the logic of sameness of the symbolic. This desire decolonizes the symbolic order in catachresis as a disruption beyond the intentionality of a subjectivity that assumes a selfsame, knowing subject, and makes desire an unintentional resistance that resonates with Ahmed's notion of willfulness without being rendered the same as will. Furthermore, decolonizing desire is not simply embodied; rather, it is the possibility of embodiedness itself. I think this is where Irigaray's desire is actually more helpful for avoiding the resubmission of bodies to overdetermined facts of political ontologies. Whereas affect, as described by Ahmed, suggests a certain preexisting embodiedness, desire in Irigaray is the possibility of bodily becomings, not an effect of it. Lips, after all, exist, but they always already exist in their twoness. The very possibility of desire's decolonizing effort is grounded in the irreducibility of alterity to a static self-identical materiality. It is an embodiedness that is not reducible to a body of discourse, even as discursive exclusion or lack. This materiality of alterity is not the embodiment of political identities; it is not the body of discourses (whether voluntarily or involuntarily recognized).

In her text on desire, *Sharing the Fire* (Springer 2020), Irigaray articulates her vision of desire in a way that affirms my suggestion that her ontological turn is dynamic and interwoven with complexities of living. She writes, "Desire liberates us from the fetters of imposed requirements, habits and limitations, which kept us trapped, and it invites us to appear in accordance with our own limits."[100] Here, Irigaray emphasizes that the sexuate relation is one of being in oneself in a dynamic relation to both nature and culture. Desire, Irigaray contends, is a "bridge" that allows us to transcend the limits of culture by returning us to our bodies as sources of knowing beyond oppositions. As Irigaray describes it in *Sharing the Fire*, desire informs a dynamic ontology that I would argue potentially operates as a decolonizing logic—it is an ontology of the presymbolic materiality of radical alterity that is the constitutive absent "ground" of the symbolic. This dynamic ontology of desire is not the pure ontology of metaphysics.[101] Ontology here is not an ontology of sexual difference as biology or a religious origin story, nor is ontology a mere effect of discourse. It is radically other to the ontologies of selfsameness—the ontologies that, in thinking of "ground" of being as an inert, unshifting force, reinforce the imperializing logic of sameness. This also means that the position of the colonized other is a material, fecund indeterminacy, rather than lack.

Despite the promise of Irigaray's dynamic ontology, I want to conclude this chapter with a cautionary word. What I have attempted to suggest in this book is that by thinking through discursive significations of sexual difference as traces of the constitutive absence of the sexuate difference Irigaray points us to a fleshiness that exists but has not been allowed to be. I appreciate Irigaray's turn to being in one's body or in her notion of the specificity of bodies as the starting point for desire. I have found in the rhetoricity and fleshiness of her earlier writing a promise of a radical reimagining of both materiality and alterity that describes relationality through the dynamism of desire. Her more recent work, however, has seemed to me to prioritize a back-and-forth dialectic that reframes relationships between binaries rather than disrupts those binaries. In other words, despite her efforts to differentiate the mediating function of desire from Hegel's dialectic,[102] she seems to focus more on disrupting the selfsameness rather than on the terms of the dialectic. My own interpretation of the radicality of her early insinuations about materiality and alterity therefore depart from the ways that she speaks about the sexuate specificity in relation to this dialectic.

Again, in *Sharing the Fire*, Irigaray writes, "Our sexuate body operates as what enables us to overcome the split between matter and form—it produces matter with form, and form with matter. . . . Perhaps I could also suggest that it is the place which leads us to pass from immanence to transcendence, from an ontical to an ontological level—but also from the one to the other."[103] Irigaray is not departing from her earlier work here; she has long spoken of moving between self and other, and she remains committed to the dynamism of desire. But in reinvoking the binaries to clarify her views, she undercuts the power of irreducible differences' constitutive absence to generate a catachrestic disruption. Indeed, this is a similar issue that her relentless appeals to cisgendered language to describe the sexuate creates. And in foreclosing catachresis, we risk losing the trace of an unthought radical desire.

Relatedly, and perhaps more problematically, Irigaray describes the human in terms of a relation to the symbolic that universalizes that experience as one of "exile." She invokes language suggestive that desire would provide liberation from the captivity of the symbolic. Irigaray problematically writes that the experience of being in our sexuate bodies will "liberat[e]" us "from an exile partly constructed against our real being."[104] Irigaray's use of the sexuated specificity of bodies to frame the sociocultural and historical as a sort of imprisonment demonstrates a lack of interest in the ways that order impacts the capacity to imagine bodies. Furthermore, she makes such statements without acknowledging that both decolonial and the Black radical philosophical traditions have theorized the symbolic and, in even the idea of a presymbolic, as participating in a logic of colonizing carceralization.

I have therefore offered this chapter to appeal not to sexuate ontology as I think Irigaray understands it but to an ontology of othered desires as a decolonizing ontology that flows from the materiality of alterity, from the radical indeterminacy of material relations. An ontology of othered desire is thus based in the relationality of embodied differences whose material—though not determinate or static—specificities are not captured in discourse, in the language of political subjects. These differences are at once outside the symbolic but related to it as a constitutive absence of symbolic representations. Such an ontology of desire utters, in the catachrestic disruptions in discourse, a materiality of alterity prior to its materializations in discourse.

If we return to desire as ambiguous, where ambiguity is a consequence of bodily specificities, we can read that ambiguity as the possibility of jouissance, as a fount of pleasures with the other, not insecurities about the self. As such, an ontology of desire resists the narratives of mastery and reorients the space between one and another in an embodied affective relation (wonder) beyond identification.[105]Abiding in such desire amounts to a certain willfulness, to borrow from Ahmed.[106] It is an act of survival[107] that constitutes an insurrection—a radical resistance beyond intention in the midst of living—a resistance that is not trapped in the binaries of passive versus active that would render that resistance a mere relation to power, an effect of discourse, or a condition of lack.[108]

Within the context of colonizing discourses, catachresis is a disruption beyond lack, beyond passivity or its negation in mastery; it is a resistance baked into the exchange economy of meaning making.[109] Catachresis is Echo; it is the colonized subject who is capable (involuntarily) of this penetration. And perhaps we might suggest that with this penetration, which is never truly inside nor outside of discourse, but rather altogether elsewhere, is the possibility of disruptive pleasure in the midst of an attempted enclosure and erasure—a pleasure that is beyond intent but not banished to a place of lack—a pleasure of living "willfully" in the elsewhere of embodied desire for which the law can neither account nor fully absorb.

Chapter 5

Desire Beyond (Non)Being

Toward a Black Feminist Labial Logic

Women of today are still being called upon to stretch across the gap of male ignorance and to educate men as to our existence and our needs. This is an old and primary tool of all oppressors to keep the oppressed occupied with the master's concerns.

Now we hear that it is the task of women of Color to educate white women—in the face of tremendous resistance—as to our existence, our differences, our relative roles in our joint survival. This is a diversion of energies and a tragic repetition of racist patriarchal thought.

Simone de Beauvoir once said, "It is in the knowledge of the genuine conditions of our lives that we must draw our strength to live and our reasons for acting."

Racism and homophobia are all real conditions of all our lives in this place and time. I urge each one of us here to reach down into that deep place of knowledge inside herself and touch that terror and loathing of any difference that lives there. See whose face it wears. Then the personal as the political can begin to illuminate all our choices.

Audre Lorde, "The Master's Tools Will Never
Dismantle the Master's House"

For if Afro-Pessimism is defined by anything—a theory or theorem, a method or approach, a motley crew or citational network, an ensemble of questions or set of postulates—then it may be the motive force of a singular wish inherited in no small part from black women's traditions of analysis, interrelation, invention, and survival.

—Jared Sexton, "Afro-Pessimism: The Unclear Word."

151

My reading of Irigaray has been inspired by the struggles against neocolonialist, antidemocratic, racist, heterosexist, and misogynist institutions (social, political, and discursive) of the twenty-first century. But, as a white-presenting woman writing this book as critique, I am complicit in the white phallogocentric market of academic discourse. And so, although this project prioritizes a turn to the ambiguities of desires as an ethical response and alternative to becomings based on identity, I cannot avoid a certain "commonsense" notion that radically disrupting identification doesn't magically disrupt a world constituted through violations. In a political economy grounded in the mutual reinforcement of recognition and commodification of differences, social and political institutions too easily reabsorb radical reimaginings of society. Anti-affirmative-action cases in universities, conservative politicians championing decontextualized quotes from Dr. Martin Luther King Jr., and so on show that politics too easily appropriates the rhetoric of equality and reframes it as sameness, generating new universals that neutralize differences in the name of egalitarianism.

Regardless of arguments that gender or race are constructed, the #BlackLivesMatter and #SayHerName movements, for example, insist on a present reality that bodies are coded in ways that render them vulnerable unto death. It would be disingenuous to overlook these "real conditions of all our lives in this place and time" by completely dispensing with questions of race and sex to articulate prediscursive desire.[1] In the United States of America, it would be impossible to think through the ethical demand for radical disruption of identity without considering the onus that such a demand places on Black subject positions.[2] For example, there is an immediate acute violence of surveillance, policing, and incarceration of Black bodies in the United States. But there's also another violence that speaks to the question of prediscursivity, or extradiscursivity of ontologies (even if reimagined). That violence extends from the singularities of the deaths of Trayvon Martin, Pearlie Golden, Eric Garner, Michelle Cusseaux, Michael Brown, Tanisha Anderson, Tamir Rice, Natasha McKenna, Mya Hall, Walter Scott, Freddie Gray, Alexia Christian, Joyce Curnell, Ralkina Jones, India Kager, Kisha Michael, Alton Sterling, Philando Castile, Korren Gaines, Deborah Danner, Michelle Shirley, Charleena Lyles, Decynthia Clements, Stephon Clark, Pamela Turner, Atatiana Jefferson, Breonna Taylor, George Floyd, of Ahmaud Arbery, . . . a violence that is part of a broader discursive and material mechanism for dehumanizing persons to the point of their not constituting an ethical other.[3]

This chapter continues the trajectory of this book's reimagining of an ontology; I maintain that desire is the possibility for imagining a different ontological reality through a materiality of alterity that is beyond discourses of sex, race, gender, and sexuality, and yet also acknowledges the discursive impacts on how one can think life beyond it. However, if in reimagining the ontological one willfully divorces oneself from the question of the political, I would argue that one has failed to think the limits of appeals to even the most radical of ontologies. Critical philosophies of race, as represented in the works of the thinkers examined in this chapter, often trouble returns to ontology, focusing instead on articulating the totalizing force of anti-Blackness at work in philosophy. The cross-section of voices engaged in this chapter offers in some cases divergent perspectives for pursuing questions of ontology and epistemology. The diversity of these thinkers' aims and methodologies, including their varied framings of ethics and politics, presents theoretical challenges to the very processes for interrogating concepts like Being and subjectivity. I will not resolve these tensions for the sake of argument but rather flag them as fruitful spaces for thinking a radical Irigarayan desire beyond the limits of Irigaray's own thought.

Careful parsing of questions of ethics and politics, especially in relation to questions of history and ontology—as in the historicity of race and/or gender versus ahistoricized ontologies as well as the more nuanced positions—will no doubt be important to the future of thinking desire. Here, I will turn primarily to Afropessimist ethicopolitical contestations of Being (including the turn to sexual difference) because I believe such efforts unlock ways to read Irigaray differently and also highlight questions haunting the redefining of Being beyond Non-being. Rather than prioritize either the ethics of alterity to challenge Being or the political interrogation of Being that resubmits thought to an exercise in immanence, the engagements of this chapter hold the ethical and political together to pursue the nuances of how one figures the relationship of discursivity to the materialization of differences in the social and symbolic order and how that relationship relates to the desire of fleshy becomings. Afropessimism and its lineages do not therefore provide some test of my hypothesis about desire but a deepening of the work that must take place to think the radicality of such desire. I want to focus on the tensions between submitting anti-Black violence to a historical critique on the one hand and theorizing anti-Blackness as an eternal, totalizing truth of Being on the other—to consider a reading of desire that is reducible neither to the historical nor to an immutable transcendence.

This work brings sexual difference into conversation with the interrogations of ontology brought forth by Afropessimist discourse in order to shift the question from what constitutes irreducible difference to the relation of desire to reimagine becoming from beyond a being/nonbeing binary and to mark the dynamic materiality-alterity of embodiment. Registering the critique of ontologies raised in Afropessimist thought, I return to Irigaray's lips as an expression of such desire. I then turn to the question of touching beyond the visible, emphasizing the lips as a touching beyond the regime of visibility that typifies a metaphysics of presence.

Drawing on Kalpana Seshadri-Crooks's and Amber Jamilla Musser's respective interrogations of the whiteness and phallocentrism of psychoanalysis, I suggest that lips present a relation of desire that offers a "labial logic" emerging from the generativity of thinking through sexuate difference. I conclude by reading Saidiya Hartman's innovative work in historical studies as a confrontation of the ocularcentrism of the archive. Hartman does not prioritize the visual as the sphere of relation through which Black life is constituted; instead, she reimagines what is not immediately visible, what is not represented, the space of the unthought, as the fount of Black becoming. And by thinking through the position of Frank Wilderson's "unthought" (beyond unintelligibility and lack), Hartman, I argue, presents a Black labial logic in which a certain potential for confronting the violence of an anti-Black and phallocentric selfsameness lies in the materiality of alterity. Radical othered desire, I therefore insist, is that space of relationality of the unthought, a relationality beyond representation, capable of rejecting the hard and fast distinction between the ontological and the political, capable of asserting a nonidentitarian becoming wherein recognition is not the basis of one's being. Here, a Black labial logic disrupts not just the prevailing social structures that delimit bodies but a more radical starting point for theorizing becoming, one that challenges the anti-Black violence of metaphysics and its sacrificial economy that forgets sexual difference.

Sexual Difference and the Limits of Desire

For Irigaray, theorizing the problem of sexual difference extends from her assumption that language functions differently for men and women and that this difference strips women of access to their desire. Irigaray's early work has demonstrated how woman is relegated to a place of lack within the discourse of psychoanalysis. Her analysis of speech patterns among her analysands, which she documents in *Ethics*, for example, serves as her evidence that these differences exist. Because Irigaray starts with language as a representation of desire, she turns to language to think differently. Indeed, one of Irigaray's greatest contributions is her capacity to write and think through sexual difference as a perennial question—to name the work of deconstruction and reimagining in her writing as a continuous engagement with the philosophical root of inequalities in the world. Her allegiance to the linguistic psychoanalytic view of becoming leads her to the conclusion that language that is reductive, like a philosophical thinking that is motivated by a return to self, represents a desire of and for oneness. Referring implicitly to the Hegelian dialectic of becoming through re-cognition of oneself as the prevailing model of subjectivity in philosophy, Irigaray contends that philosophical discourse extends this reductive desire for sameness. Ultimately, in the discourses of psychoanalysis and philosophy, but also, she adds, in science and politics, the annihilation of what I am referring to as "othered desire" is the desire of woman.

Irigaray's framing of the indeterminate woman as "other of the Other," prior to any signification of alterity, is also the possibility, she suggests, of a multiple, nonselfsame desire. And this nonselfsame desire could reimagine the symbolic, and therein, reimagine subjectivity.[4] So although woman does not map onto sexual difference in any essential way, Irigaray still writes through the position of woman in her work to suggest that the subject position of woman relates to the irreducible difference of the sexuate, even if that relation is unclear and unarticulated.[5] Her deconstruction of the phallocentrism of discourse is a cultivation of the fecundity of an "elsewhere" via the disassimilation of woman from the phal-logo-centric masculine social and cultural order. She aims through this work to find a way of becoming in the world that was not inscribed in webs of meaning making based in the reduction to sameness (re-cognition).[6] As I have noted in the previous chapters, Irigaray has undertaken this disruption and cultivation through the work of her writing—through writing as a gesture of thought.

Irigaray's writing evokes the othered desire of a female sexuality, and that female sexuality is the possibility of more than a desire for oneness. As I have discussed in some detail in chapter 1 and will argue further in this chapter, Irigaray's notion of female sexuality is a critical extension of Lacan's description of feminine sexuality as the lack that is part of the subject's becoming. In Lacan's description of subjectivity, which turns to language to investigate the becoming of subjects, the subject emerges through an antagonistic dialectical relation to the irretrievable origins of their own being.

Irigaray extends the multiplicity of pleasures to which Lacanian feminine jouissance gestures to suggest that recovering that which has existed only as lack will be the recovery of a desire that could engender a discourse for thinking subjectivity beyond antagonism or negation. Hers is a notion of desire as a dynamic relation cultivated in the space and time of irreducible difference, beyond the limits of a phallogocentric psychoanalytic (or philosophical) reduction.

For Irigaray, this irreducible two must be sexuate, as sexuation is necessary for the generation of human life. And over the last five decades, Irigaray has unflinchingly prioritized sexuate difference as the irreducible difference that would be necessary for an ethical, nonselfsame desire to exist. But in noting this prioritization of sexuate difference, I cannot emphasize this point enough: sexual difference is not an effect of discourse for Lacan or for Irigaray. If for Lacan sexual difference is a fiction or a myth, for Irigaray, sexuate difference — an at least two who are required to become human — is precisely what Lacan forgets in theorizing that fiction of sexual difference. I will return to this in more detail later. Sexuation may indeed be necessary for life, especially if we bracket the technological capacity to alter generativity on some level. But perhaps what is more radically transformative is not Irigaray's positing of irreducibility to sexuation but her philosophy that emerges through the generativity of relationality made possible by the very idea of irreducible difference. Irigaray's effort to articulate embodied desire beyond metaphysics contributes to a presymbolic materiality and alterity as a possibility for rethinking difference beyond the logocentric materializations of difference through discursive (read phallogocentric) reductions within the symbolic.

Throughout this book, I have argued that thinking through the question of sexual difference as a question of desire opens up ways to reimagine the investments and entanglements of discourses, of entire worlds and values, of ethics and politics, of truth itself with gender difference (and here, I am referring to gender not as a fact but as naming a difference within the masculine symbolic). As chapter 1 suggests, Irigaray adopts Levinas's prioritization of the ethical to disrupt the selfsameness of Being, and she adapts his invocation of sexual difference to suggest that eros is the foundation of a sexuate encounter that would make ethics possible. And I have argued that turning to a new relational ontology of desire is radical insofar as, for Irigaray, it promises a different imaginary that might overcome the logocentric reduction through which differences materialize in a world constructed through selfsameness.

But is thinking through sexual difference the only means by which one can locate the prioritization of sameness and the desire for a universalized oneness? And perhaps more forcefully, what are the risks of asserting irreducibility through a notion of sexual difference that is somehow beyond discursivity? What does it mean to place the origins of discursivity beyond its historical manifestations? Problems of racism and sexism in the United States are entangled, and lumping these issues together as symptoms of a more fundamental problem of selfsameness might seem disingenuous at best. Is framing an extradiscursive materiality of desire really capable of sustaining such an imaginary by thinking exclusively through sexual difference? Is the sexuate the only decolonizing ontology capable of a dynamic, irreducible desire?

Considering these questions and concerns, I want to continue to press the question of desire—but I do so differently from Irigaray. What if we step away from Irigaray's prioritization of sexual difference and her doubling down in the appeal to sexuation as the natural order of being that risks presupposing a plurality of desires of only certain bodily meetings? What if we think more broadly in terms of othered desire as not simply an ethical but also a political interrogation of Being? And if we consider, as Gayatri Spivak and Frantz Fanon among others have demonstrated, that language is colonizing and raced, could we then turn to othered desire—not simply as an historical effect but as entangled with the possibility of history—to confront racial schematizations that promulgate racism and white supremacy within the social order, as represented in subjectivities built on serial identifications constructed through reductions of difference?

Eros and the Politics of Flesh

Ethics and politics are intertwined in radical desire insofar as such desire is capable of nonidentitarian becomings constituted through a materiality of alterity. That radical materiality, I have insisted, is not the same as the materialization of some shared "difference" that is represented within a social order; the materialization of difference through the symbolic is more accurately a reduction of differences. Within the selfsameness of discourse, which includes the discourses of thought itself, identifications are what makes "difference" recognizable, and within the context of the selfsame, such reduction is what makes "difference" possible. For Irigaray philosophy and psychoanalysis are the primary purveyors of such reductive representations of difference, peddling the illusion of difference.

This lack of difference is precisely what Irigaray's invocations of lips confront. The fleshy folds of touching lips express a multiplicity of desire, gesturing to a promise of pleasures of an untapped female sexuality—a sexuality sacrificed in the phallogocentric symbolic order. Importantly, this female sexuality is not the simple negation of the phallic order. After all, the positing of opposites feigns an ontology of the neuter; it attempts to posit origins through evading, avoiding, and covering over the fact that we don't have access to our origins.[7] The presymbolic space of desire toward which the lips gesture refuses to participate in the binary that would pit female sexuality as the opposite to male sexuality. Nor is this female sexuality an other to male sexuality reducible to Lacan's depiction of female sexuality as lack, which would plunge female sexuality irretrievably into an abyss and recapitulate the totality of the phallic order. Just as sexuate woman, for Irigaray, is not the "woman" who has been identified as other within a masculine discourse, the female sexuality to which the lips gesture is an other to the "female sexuality" that psychoanalytic discourse has imagined through its phallocentric imagination.

There remains, however, a tension about such an appeal to the capacity of desire to engender a relationality that is truly *elsewhere* in the midst of the sociocultural order. In her work critiquing the ethical interrogations of Being that prioritize alterity, LeRhonda Manigault-Bryant argues that the historical relationship of Black bodies to desire complicates the ability of radical queer desire to disrupt the norms that constrain Black life.[8] Specifically, she questions the capacity of eros, even as a radical undoing, to be politically useful for those defined through their "inability to escape the body."[9] Manigault-Bryant argues that Huffer's assertion that eros radically destabilizes notions of selfhood that make the body strange, anew, is, for Black bodies, an "estrange[ment]."[10] She writes, "Encountering black bodies remind[s] us of how synchronizing eros and political possibility challenges those whose bodies might be undermined by processes of politicization." [11] Here she reminds the reader that radical disruptions of identification can seem vacuous and disconnected from living, even though they are, for Huffer and Muñoz, for example, conceived through engagements with the world at its limits. So, although Huffer specifically links the alterity of eros to the historically constituted social other, Manigault-Bryant remains skeptical—effectively interrogating who Huffer's social other can be if eros is not thought together with the question of Black bodies.

Manigault-Bryant's challenge to Huffer's eros is not, however, an abandonment of eros altogether. Her concern is with an eros capable of grounding a politics that can speak to the demands of Black life. She contends that to reimagine "eros as political possibility," the dehistoricization that is necessary to Huffer's reading of eros as a radically destabilizing force must be rethought through the particular historical situatedness of Black bodies in relation to Black subjectivity. By reading #BlackLivesMatter in relation to its emergence as a social, political, and community response to the murder of Trayvon Martin, Manigault-Bryant demonstrates the significance of Black death for history and the very notion of Blackness. The "bodily fictions ascribed to blackness" are the making of an idea of Black subjectivity that "made" the unarmed teenage Trayvon Martin a threat, not only in the mind of his murderer George Zimmerman, but also in the institutions of jurisprudence that constitute the law.[12]

Ahistoricizing eros to articulate radical alterity that could disrupt the foundations upon which discourses reduce bodies misses an opportunity to think the radicality of historical corporealities.[13] Manigault-Bryant therefore proposes that the sort of radical destabilization that eros makes possible could offer a rehistoricization of bodies as sites of erotic power. She thinks eros in relation to the body as both historically situated and yet also exceeding its historical corporealizations. In a statement that conjures (for this reader) Audre Lorde's "Uses of the Erotic," Manigault-Bryant follows a quotation from Bibi Bakare-Yusuf's "The Economy of Violence," writing, "We must never underestimate the significance of creativity, individual and collective agency, the instability of subjectivity and their combined potential for resistance."[14]

While Manigault-Bryant shares with Huffer a desire for thinking of the radical liberatory potential of eros as an ethical and political possibility, her fundamental concern is admittedly the question of freedom that is a consequence of thinking through her own experience as a Black woman. Here the need to continue to think freedom is a reminder of the precarity of responsibility and of the ease with which appeals to extradiscursive ethical demands can reinscribe the historical forces of colonization, white supremacy, heteronormativity, and patriarchy. Manigault-Bryant concludes: "If we are honest in our historical ontology, then we must also face the fact of history past and present that there are some bodies in our midst—including those that look like mine—where history past and present does not recognize or acknowledge the possibility of eros—as life, as askesis, as freedom, as political possibility, or as love."[15] Her concluding statement suggests that recognition (in its historical and political particularizations) does not afford certain bodies access to a radical eros. And Manigault-Bryant ultimately asserts a Foucauldian suspicion of the ahistorical.

Her assertion that eros is not recognized among certain bodies does not mean that those bodies do not have the capacity for erotic desire. As Manigault-Bryant frames the emergence of #BlackLivesMatter Black bodies are engaged in an eros that radically disrupts the thoroughly unerotic "eros" of a politics based in the selfsameness of representation and recognition. After all, what is erotic about the known, the fulfillment of the expected? Manigault-Bryant's essay thus establishes a tension between Black death and Black eros. She concludes her essay with a warning about "ahistorical or a priori" readings of Black bodies, but she also appeals to Muñoz's notion of queer futurity, to express a materiality that exceeds the historical materialization of Black bodies—a materiality beyond historical constructions of sex, gender, race, and sexuality.[16] The last few paragraphs of her essay inhabit rather than resolve this tension: the tension between the desire to affirm the creative works of Black bodies and the desire for eros to figure radical futures and inform corporealizations that disrupt the politics of recognition that figure Black bodies like Trayvon Martin as devoid of subjectivity beyond their threatening corporeality. As Manigault-Bryant describes, historical materializations of Blackness have alienated Black persons from their bodies. However, she refuses to allow Black eros to be an escape from those violent/violating materializations of Blackness in an anti-Black world. Black eros resists eros as estrangement from histories of bodily becomings. And yet, Black eros is not simply becoming through these histories.

I read Manigault-Bryant's holding together of the queer futurity of eros and the affirmation of identity in #BlackLivesMatter as a prophetic warning: that dwelling on fabulations of Black subjectivity in an anti-Black world for the sake of a radical disruption is a venture that risks missing the radical creativity of a Black community connected in/by/through eros. Therefore, what I find most helpful for thinking through the tensions of difference as historical manifestations on the one hand and an abstract concept of ahistorical material becomings on the other is that Manigault-Bryant thinks eros as a disruptive and creative force for confronting and resisting an anti-Black world and its effects on corporealizations of Blackness.[17] An ethics that thinks materiality only in terms of radical alterity participates in anti-Blackness. Manigault-Bryant's Black eros pushes a reading of desire as being in one's own flesh, at once beyond the specificities of historical materializations of difference and in its midst. The appeal to a radical alterity and materiality of desire that I have developed in this book is not only an ethical interrogation of subjectivity (by way of an appeal to alterity) but also one that is materially always already in relation to, without being the negative/negation of, the symbolic. The materiality and alterity of this desire is therefore always in relation to the materialization of differences in the sociocultural order as a radically othered space and time. Lips, I insist, are just such a materiality.

My appeal to lips as rhetorical and yet also material (without being reduced to the inert matter of metaphysics) constitutes an effort to walk the line between absolute divisions between the real and the imagined, between a certain nature-and-culture distinction, between, relatedly, a concreteness of living and the fabulations of life.[18] Furthermore, the materiality of the lips functions rhetorically because it displays historical specificity relative to the symbolic. As such, we cannot think the materiality of the lips without thinking through their rhetoricity. And I would argue that the rhetoric of the lips, while I hope it speaks to a radically other desire, functions because it invokes the feminine as the mark of a body whose "death" or freezing in the inertness of matter is the possibility of the symbolic. I would also suggest that the feminine is not the only mark of such death; Blackness has a history that marks bodily deaths, and as such it offers another rhetorical space for interrogating the occlusion of materialities necessary for the symbolic to function. And as Manigault-Bryant suggests and will be discussed later in this chapter, this historical specificity of actual Black deaths and its relation to Black motherhood further speaks to the entanglement of intersectional demands and ontological possibility.

Manigault-Bryant's challenge serves as an important reminder about the promise and risk of investing in desire as a relation of dehistoricized materialities. By her reasoning, thinking a radical eros as an ethical relation of some presymbolic proximity of difference can seem too far removed from the politics of everyday relations. And her challenge to the radicality of eros is part of a broader conversation in critical theories of race in which the philosophical prioritization of alterity in ethics risks positing a universal other that is always already the consequence of a politics that determines the capacity to be recognized as an other.

The Visibility of the Other:
Psychoanalysis, Race, and the Question of Presence

As I see it, thinking the ethical and political together as questions of the alterity and materiality of the other means considering othered desire as always in relation to and apart from representations of the symbolic in the social order. I therefore want to take a brief detour into psychoanalytic framings of desire in conjunction with questions of race, racism, and racialization as a means to examine the structure of desire as it relates to the symbolic. Therefore, in this section, I consider what it means to think the white supremacy of desire as another way to articulate the anti-Blackness of metaphysics.

Psychoanalysis prioritizes sexual difference, or as Irigaray would argue, the illusion of sexual difference, as the basis of the social order. And psychoanalysis traditionally frames race as part of the social order, such that race is not eternal, transcendent, or ahistorical in any way. Kalpana Seshadri-Crooks offers a psychoanalytic reading that holds to psychoanalysis's prioritization of sexual difference while also contending with race as a question of the ethical, not just political, other. In *Desiring Whiteness: A Lacanian Analysis of Race*, Seshadri-Crooks walks this line by arguing that race is based on an economy of visibility in which the master signifier, which signifies the impossible fantasy of union, is white and phallic.[19] Seshadri-Crooks carefully explores Lacanian concepts of desire, the real, fantasy, and the death drive in relation to racial representation in film and literature. In keeping with her focus on psychoanalysis, she maintains that sexual difference names an irreducible difference that is prior to signification. By framing sexual difference in Lacanian terms, Seshadri-Crooks insists that she is not interested in establishing a symmetry between sexual difference and race—an important move to avoid analogizing sexual difference and racial difference.[20] She is, however, invested in how the two concepts function in material and discursive ways "to gain access to desire or lack."[21]

Seshadri-Crooks focuses on signification in the formation of subjects. She wants to put forward a concept of race that neither reifies race nor suggests race is imagined, but one that understands the depth of the symbolic for the construction of the subject such that one can "confound" race in a way that disrupts its relation to the master signifier and seeks a "desubjectification" rather than a subjectivity of oneness that race promises. Her aim is ethical, insofar as it aligns with Lacan's notion of ethics—that is, as a response to the desire of the subject. As it regards race specifically, her goal, then, is to "address the question of ethics as it pertains to the desire of the subject who is constituted as a subject in relation to the law of racial difference."[22] Note, desire described here is not the radical presubjective desire to which I appeal, but I hope that becomes more evident when, later in this chapter, I return to the discussion of race in relation to ontology rather than subjectivity.

Seshadri-Crooks finds the vocabulary to articulate an ethics of race in Lacan. In Lacan's theory of subjectivity, one becomes a subject through the process of negotiating the symbolic realm available for representing one's desires. The becoming subject enters into linguistic relations to return to a condition of wholeness, to become whole by uniting the imaginary realm of the symbolic with the Real of desire (here is he is drawing on Freud's understanding of the Real). But Lacan suggests there is a fundamental failure here. He proposes that the sexuate constitutes a binary that is inherently divided such that the Real can never be whole. This is also the basis for Lacan's notion of the split subject. Insofar as representation requires a movement toward sameness, discourses of sexual difference attempt to represent an irreducible difference of desire. But this irreducibility, this fundamental asymmetry of the sexuate, means that there is no oneness to represent. Representation, as a movement toward wholeness, cannot make sense of sexual difference.[23] Signification feeds, therefore, on an illusion or fantasy of wholeness. It is at this point of failure of signification to represent the binary of sexual difference that the subject negotiates its relation to its desire and lack of capacity to represent that desire in full. This movement of signification to wholeness does not stop because of this failure; rather this structure of representation Lacan describes opposes meaning with desire in a way that makes the Real of sex opposed to relation in the symbolic.

Note that here he is describing the system of linguistic representation in relation to a psychoanalytic understanding of the Real. As such, representation is a fact of communication and relation; therefore, this "failure" does not change the fact that humans communicate in and through language. Yet language still moves toward wholeness, so the unity to which representation is ordered is a whole that is only half of the whole. And the half of the whole to which signification returns is the masculine half. Because sexual difference is not representable, subject formation thus involves an inherent failure of signification. There is always an unknowing or misrecognition of the self's desire in the becoming of a subject. Lacan thus depicts the relationship between desire and representation as one of lack.

For Seshadri-Crooks, sexual difference, as unrepresentable, marks an absence. The trace of this absence is replaced with an "inaugural signifier" that, within the realm of signification, is reducible to itself. The phallus has served as the inaugural signifier of sex in a social order that forgets sexual difference. Whiteness, she claims, is the "inaugural signifier of race" in a way that is structurally similar to the phallus as the inaugural signifier of sex. Put differently, whiteness represents the Oneness that the symbolic realm is unable to achieve in sexual difference.[24] As a master signifier, whiteness "establishes a structure of relations, a signifying chain that through a process of inclusions and exclusions constitutes a pattern of organizing human difference" to secure a relationship to the promise of wholeness of Being.[25] Racial differences, like sex differences, thus efface the occlusion of the irreducible sexual difference that is annihilated in becoming subjects through the symbolic order. Because race emerges through the symbolic realm of identification, there is no radical other to whiteness or to the phallus; there are only projections of an Other who is an other of the same. Ironically, the subject's investment in race is an effect of the subject's insecurity about this symbolic origin of race.[26]

Seshadri-Crooks's effort to explain race as an effect of a master signifier holds together a perennializing of the psychoanalytic description of the process of becoming with a historicization of the master signifier as white and phallic. Central to her suggestion that race has been figured in relation to whiteness is her depiction of the regime of visibility. To the extent that race involves the visibility of certain physical markers (hair, skin tone, etc.), the existence of such markers—indeed their visibility as such—provides an assuredness that race is not simply discursive.[27] She writes: "The bodily mark, which (like sex) seems to be more than symbolic, serves as a powerful prophylactic against the anxiety of race as a discursive construction. We seem to need such a refuge in order to preserve the investment we, as a society, make in the signifier of Whiteness." Visibility thus involves an entire practice of racial looking that promises the subject wholeness. So yes, race "matters" literally and figuratively because it is part of a regime wherein visibility is necessary to its recognition, and recognition is essential to its being. Because race belongs to a practice of visibility that involves a seeing and being seen through an entire regime of social, cultural, political, and psychic realities, society has an "investment" in race as constitutive of our subject position in relation to others in ways that make the regime of race and its visible markers difficult, and perhaps even undesirable, to surrender. And her notion of the visibility of race speaks to the particularity of embodiments that produce existential anxiety with respect to the symbolic order.

Seshadri-Crooks confronts the visibility of race in which subjectivity is invested to offer the possibility of undermining racialized embodiments. She espouses an "adversarial aesthetics" as a turning of the regime of visibility upon itself and locates this adversarial aesthetics in artistic, cinematic, and literary uses of the visual to expose the underlying anxiety of racial referents.[28] As Seshadri-Crooks insists, troubling the illusion of Oneness that associates Being with whiteness requires "confound[ing] racial signification by stressing the continuity, the point of doubt among the so-called races, to the extent that each and every one of us must mistrust the knowledge of our racial belonging."[29] I read this confounding as a disidentification with whiteness that recasts the chain of signification in a way that resists the desire for wholeness as oneness.[30]

This framing of race as operating within a regime of visibility that is always already constituted through a Lacanian depiction of sexual difference resonates with Irigaray's framing of intersectional differences as distinct from the presymbolic alterity of the sexuate. For Seshadri-Crooks, as for Irigaray, race, sex, and gender are structural positions of this relative belonging; they are not ontological in a way that makes them analogous to sexual difference.[31] Assigning priority to sexual difference means that the self and other, and the possibility of an ethical interrogation of Being, occur prior to the question of race. As such, she continues to prioritize sexual difference such that confronting the whiteness and phallocentrism of visibility does not attend to the violence that structures visibility itself. There is no doubt that for Lacanian psychoanalysis, the question of sex as a question of sexual difference is separate from, and more fundamental than, questions of race or sexuality.[32] But is the forgetting of sexual difference alone really what allows whiteness and the phallus to be in the same position with respect to the illusion of oneness as wholeness? What might be the othered desire to desire for whiteness?

To pursue these questions, I turn to Afropessimist engagements with psychoanalysis. I will consider Afropessimist criticisms of ontology to trouble the prioritization of sexual difference as the basis for psychoanalytic interrogations of the visible, and I will turn to Black feminist rethinkings of perception as a way to reimagine touching lips as a new imagining of desire. The aim is to rethink materiality and alterity apart from metaphysical reductions to ground a new way of becoming self and other through a multiple, ambiguous, fleshy desire that is truly other than a phallocentric desire for whiteness.

Afropessimism and Psychoanalysis: The Ethics and Politics of Ontology

Notwithstanding its diversity, the Black radical tradition thinks Black life in relation to history, advocating the possibility of transformation of Black social life in civil society apart from the specter of the Transatlantic Slave Trade that has dominated the history through which Black life has been analyzed and imagined. The focus in much of the Black radical tradition has been tied to political perspectives of philosophical questions about freedom, agency, ethics, and subjectivity. Broadly conceived, Afropessimism refers to a discourse that theorizes Black life at once in relation to and beyond the specter of the Transatlantic Slave Trade by exposing an even more fundamental antagonism that exceeds the specificity of historical events: anti-Blackness.[33]

Afropessimist theorizing traces its most immediate origins to the work of literary critical theorist and writer Hortense Spillers. Spillers's famous essay "Mama's Baby Papa's Maybe: An American Grammar Book" has been described by Black feminist historian Sadiya Hartman as a "prism" through which an entire generation of Black thought emerges.[34] Spillers's work contends that race is a social and historically constructed category; however, something much more insidious lies beneath, something that cannot be redressed with political action.[35] Spillers attends to race without transcendentalizing it by refusing the hard and fast distinction between identity as either public or private, social *or* belonging to the constitution of the subject via relation to the unconscious.[36] In balancing the rejection of race as transcendental while also addressing its deeply psychic impacts, Spillers gestures to a space of identity that is not governed by racialization but is related to it nonetheless.

Despite the nuances among theorists associated with Afropessimism that have come to the fore, including different theoretical imaginings of Black life and the extent to which the historical figures, or doesn't, in their work, their discourses tend to converge around the idea that anti-Blackness is not a social issue like racism; rather, anti-Blackness envelops the sociality of reason itself.[37] Anti-Blackness is part of the history of thought and thought about being, of metaphysics and ontology—the very ideas that structure space and time, ideas about agency and freedom as well as ethics and responsibility. It is this challenge to thought itself as intertwined with the condition of anti-Black violence—captivity (enslavement and incarceration)—that leads to Jared Sexton's particular use of "ontological captivity" to describe the extent to which ontology is embroiled in anti-Blackness as a form of capture.[38] And what makes Afropessimism a "pessimism," as Sexton suggests, is its relentless interrogation of this space of anti-Blackness as the rhetorical, political, and historical space through which any sort of thought extends. Andrés Fabián Henao Castro writes that for Afropessimism, "It is anti-Blackness that makes something historically recognizable and thus makes what is materially transformable equally dependent on not addressing the violence of anti-Blackness as perhaps the sole violence that exceeds the materiality through which it is enacted."[39]

One of the most significant contributions of Afropessimism is its focus on thinking politics and ethics together by using psychoanalysis to think a certain psychic interiority of Black life in relation to an idea of Black social life that informed the Black radical tradition's political emphasis on coalition building. Indeed, Spillers critically adapts psychoanalysis, using especially Lacanian conceptualizations of the Symbolic, the imaginary, and the Real, to explain that race presents as an interplay of the "public' and "private" in a cultivation of self as an "interior subjectivity."[40] In the face of the history of racism in psychoanalytic discourse and study, Afropessimism has used psychoanalysis to explore the social and historical constructions of race (and the effects of racism as part of this construct) as entangled with deeper and more fundamental questions of ethics and politics, including asking not simply how one becomes a subject but also where one stands relative to the social and historical order—that is, to ask what one's possibility is of becoming.

In diagnosing anti-Blackness and, in some cases, considering a possibility of Black life that does not recapitulate anti-Blackness, Afropessimism has reenvisioned psychoanalysis to critique what Calvin Warren calls the "concealment" of Blackness as a question "buried deeply beneath layers of metaphysical violence . . . within the history of ontology."[41] As the language of concealment suggests, the question of the visual is an important component of such analysis because it attempts to confront the reliance on visibility as making something materialize differences in order to make them present. Furthermore, concealment gestures to the ways race has functioned within a regime of visibility to occlude the violence behind assertions of Black agency and freedom. Returning to Seshadri-Crooks's work, we could argue that psychoanalysis provides a language to analyze the prioritization of visibility in relation to desire. I will therefore critically examine visibility as entangled with a racialization of materiality that extends from anti-Blackness, and I will advocate a subjectivity born of touch beyond visibility in order to refuse anti-Blackness. But in service of this argument, I will first outline Afropessimist depictions of anti-Blackness as a more fundamental interrogation of thought about being, including efforts to think through the question of ethics while also thinking through the question of history to assert becoming beyond Being.

One of the most influential thinkers for the field described as Afropessimism, Frank Wilderson III uses the language of psychoanalysis to analyze regimes of visibility and explain the universal human subject as an anti-Black subject. In his *Red, White and Black: Cinema and the Structures of US Antagonisms*, Wilderson writes that Blackness is "a structural position of non-communicability in the face of all other positions" in a way that links Blackness to nonbeing. Referencing the Lacanian adaptation of Freudian concepts, Wilderson writes that "the 'antagonism' between Black and Human supersedes the 'antagonism' . . . in libidinal economy."[42] Wilderson insists that Blackness is so deeply entangled in the condition of Being and being labor in the world of whiteness that there is no possibility of reconciliation.[43] According to Daniel Barber, in Wilderson, anti-Blackness is the ground of being such that the grammar that structures the world itself, the grammar of "being, analogy, communication, possibility"—and I might add "hope"—is already based in an incoherency of the violence of anti-Blackness, such that this language cannot provide meaning. Barber writes, "This is to say that being—or the possibility thereof—grounds itself not through its own coherence, but through an enactment of power that is staged by antiblack violence. Power precedes grammatical ground."[44] In this emphasis on the incommensurability of Black life with an anti-Black world, there is only Black social death. Wilderson's depiction of anti-Blackness frames Black life as something that cannot be thought within an anti-Black order. His turn to the question of Black social death critiques interrogations of Being for forgetting the violation of Black bodies upon which ethics is constructed.[45] Here, ethics is not divorceable from the historical. Wilderson prioritizes the political as the lens for engaging historical violations of Black bodies that constitute the antefoundation for a culture and society of a white symbolic order.

In "The Violence of Presence," Wilderson and Patrice Douglass assert that Blackness is a fundamental violence or antagonism that makes Black (non)being possible.[46] Critiquing Jasbir Puar's *Terrorist Assemblages: Homonationalism in Queer Time*, Wilderson and Douglass argue that categories of race, gender, and sexuality are "genres of the subject" that, like genres or disciplines, establish their own epistemological spheres.[47] And thinking these genres together in terms of their "mergers, overlaps, and divergences of their competing and coalescing concerns, does not interrogate the parameters that suture race and sexuality as categories, and life and death as legible modes of existing and suffering within those categories."[48]

The critique of Wilderson and Douglass is also their call to attend to the metaphysics of presence that makes legibility, visibility, and subjectivity possible.[49] The pair concludes, "We need to imagine metaphysical violence rather than a metaphysics that violence destroys. We need to think metaphysically through social death and the figure of the slave."[50] The point that Douglass and Wilderson raise is that anti-Blackness is a deeply pervasive condition of sociality; however, transformation is possible by thinking through the structural violence of anti-Blackness, through the social death. For Wilderson, because social death is a construct, thinking through the anti-Blackness of social death is meant to imagine an other world and other way of knowing, a revolution of thought.

As part of the lineage of Afropessimism, part of Calvin Warren's stunning work involves theorizing the pervasiveness of anti-Blackness in a way that challenges the possibility of thinking about Black freedom and Black personhood through the lens of liberal philosophical or political ideas of the human.[51] For Warren, such ideas are grounded in anti-Blackness as the condition of possibility for metaphysics and ontology, or as he calls it, "ontometaphysics."[52] In "Black Nihilism and the Politics of Hope," Warren troubles the liberalism he views as embedded in the Black radical tradition's focus on anti-Blackness as a historical problem that can be transformed through politics, arguing that the realm of politics is an insufficient space from which to interrogate universal appeals to Being.

Warren suggests that the very idea of political action and transformation is entangled with anti-Blackness at the level of the psychic. He describes a fundamental violence that structures the myth of America and its narrative of exceptionalism and freedom through autonomy. He argues that the promise of Black subjectivity in America is a "perverse" relationship between the political discourse that promises equality as a means to restore the Black bodies which political, social, and cultural realities have rendered ontologically fractious/divided. In making the myth of America, Black bodies are necessarily divided, and the politics that cuts becomes the politics that promises to heal.

Because of this duplicity of the idea of America, political recognition for Black persons is founded on an unrealizable hope—that is to say on the hope of becoming a subject that one can never actually be.[53] "The Political, we are told, provides the material substance of our hope; it is within the Political that we are to find, if we search with vigilance and work tirelessly, the 'answer' to the ontological equation—hard work, suffering, and diligence will restore the fractioned three-fifths with its alienated two-fifths and, finally, create One that we can include in our declaration that 'All men are created equal.' "[54] Hope, as a promise of full participation in being, as a future-oriented concept, thus participates in and perpetuates anti-Blackness; it ties being with a political subjectivity that is constituted through anti-Blackness.[55]

Warren adapts Lacan's reconceptualization of Freud's drive and fantasy to explain the psychical, social, and political workings of this self-annihilating political hope for Black persons. Warren argues that because participation in politics does not result in meaningful change in the system, or "concrete transformations of anti-blackness,"[56] participation becomes a means without an end.[57] He adds, "The ends isn't just a constant unrealized disappointment; the ends is an expectation of an 'impossible object.'"[58] It is precisely in this sense of the "expectation of an 'impossible object'" that political hope is, in a Lacanian sense, fantasy. It is the "cruel attachment" to that ideal that keeps Black persons chasing the fantasy.[59]

The attachment and movement toward the fantasy strengthen "the very anti-black system that would pulverize black being."[60] Warren argues that this self-annihilating pursuit of the impossible is like the Lacanian notion of drive (which differs from desire). His analogy, drawing on Lacan's reading of Freud, implies that the drive for a wholeness that doesn't actually exist (a concept I explore more later) amounts to a complicity in one's own undoing. He uses psychoanalysis to frame political hope in relation to the symbolic order of becoming that always involves a certain annihilation or, at the very least, what Lacan would call a "misrecognition." The promise of Black subjectivity is thus pursued through an anti-Black symbolic in which one becomes complicit in the annihilation of Blackness. Political recognition for people of color is thus founded on an ahistorical object, on the promise of becoming a subject through a "cruel attachment to the means of subjugation."[61]

Warren argues that messages of political hope, in which the myth of American democracy perpetuates itself, weaponize the "spiritual" hope of the psychoanalytically framed subject. Put another way, political hope harnesses the self-annihilating movement of the death drive to sustain the illusion of an ever-retreating horizon of change. In this construction of subjectivity, Black "subjectivity" emerges by participation in an anti-Black symbolic order. Warren turns to the proposition of Black nihilism as a philosophical position of radical resistance to the violence that the myth of political hope enacts on Black bodies. Emancipation, he writes in *Ontological Terror*, "does not restore the ontological relation upon which freedom is predicated."[62] Put differently, an enunciation of the emancipation of enslaved persons does not return a wholeness to a two-thirds ontology. "Black nihilism," on the other hand, offers a theoretical framework for exposing how the logic of the political entraps Black lives in the pursuit of a hope that is tied to an unrealizable, ahistorical object—an ideal of Black justice that has never existed.[63]

Against the notion that this nihilism amounts to a passive despair, Warren suggests, "Black Nihilism is a 'demythifying' practice, in the Nietzschean vein, that uncovers the subjugating strategies of political hope and de-idealizes its fantastical object."[64] Warren's notion of practice involves a radical rejection of politics in order to refuse the perverse logic of political hope that, in Lacanian terms, would inform the lack of Black bodies and structure desire in terms of that cruel attachment to their subjugation. Warren's Black nihilism (and Afropessimism more broadly) would suggest that participating in the social, cultural, and political life of a white world means reifying a white projection of Black difference and therein reenacting anti-Black violence as the structure of the symbolic. I will revisit this point later, as it returns us to Manigault-Bryant's concern that thinking through desire may be too abstract to be useful for troubling the precarity of Black embodiment.

Despite their varied framings of the relationship between anti-Blackness and the questions of history, ethics, and politics, the Afropessimist theorizing of Wilderson and Warren (as well as Sexton and Moten, whom I will discuss below) linger in a problem that some would argue is ignored by Irigaray's return to an ontology of sexuation based in natality: the problem of anti-Blackness as constitutive of Being, regardless of whether anti-Blackness is viewed as historically constituted or radically ahistorical eternal violence. And Irigaray's interrogation of ontology—as an embodied alterity—beyond Being does not change the violation, unto death, that is the basis for a world in which she can even begin to interrogate Being. Here, I heed the words of Henao Castro, who writes, "From the slave ship, the plantation, the reservation, the prison, the detention center, the penal colony, and the concentration camp to the ways in which injurious signifiers fix the body and arrest its mobility, ontological difference should be unthinkable outside a confrontation with its material conditions of possibility and impossibility."[65] Can there be a relational ontology that does not hold flesh captive? To answer this, I turn to the question of othered fleshy desires that have been occluded in assigning ontological priority of sexual difference.

Rethinking Pessimism as Desire

Seshadri-Crooks's reading of race does not adequately speak to the psychic captivity of Black bodies to which Warren gestures. Race may be a construction of an illusion of desire for whiteness as wholeness, but what of the desires in its wake? Warren frames the self-annihilating pursuit of the fantasy as constructed not simply through a desire for whiteness but through a violent anti-Blackness. As I read Warren, and as I will read the Afropessimisms of Wilderson and Sexton, the assertion that the symbolic operates through anti-Blackness is not just about whiteness as a master signifier, but it is also about Blackness as marking a violation that precedes the forgetting of nonwhite bodies. This is a question of the violation that makes the very concept of Being possible and the metaphysical violence that structures the relation of the psychical, spiritual, and material in the constitution of subjectivity. My challenge to psychoanalytic representations of race is Irigarayan in its focus on othered desire, but it is also inspired by Afropessimism's interrogation of the concealment of the question of Blackness as the antefoundation of ontometaphysics. I am therefore interested in the constitutive absence of/in referents to difference in an anti-Black, and I would argue also phallocentric, symbolic. I am appealing to the question of the violation of difference that occurs in order for difference to be signified (even as a failure of signification or catachresis)—a violation of difference upon which regimes of visibility and discourse, as well as racialized, gendered, sexed, and sexualized embodiments are built.

Arguably more constructive and less totalizing in his diagnosis than Warren and Wilderson, Fred Moten appeals to aesthetics and Black social life more broadly to interrogate subjectivity. As part of his decades-long efforts beginning with his landmark *In the Break: The Aesthetics of the Black Radical Tradition*, Moten uses aesthetic experiences—particularly of music and poetry—to hold together questions of thinking, being, representation, and perception.[66] Part of this criticism includes his diagnosis of the ways ontology has been bound with imperialism and anti-Blackness of the ocularcentrism of the visual. Moten expands his early critiques of ontology, insisting that representational thinking about Being always assumes an object apart from which it will define itself.[67] Moten writes that there is a "pathology of blackness against which all representations of blacks, blackness, or (the color) black take place,"[68] a pathology constructed in relation to the Being of white man:

> What if the value of that absence or excess is given to us only in and by way of a kind of failure or inadequacy—or, perhaps more precisely, by way of a history of exclusion, serial expulsion, presence's ongoing taking of leave—so that the nonattainment of meaning or ontology, of source or origin, is the only way

to approach the thing in its informal (enformed/enforming, as opposed to formless), material totality? Perhaps this would be cause for black optimism or, at least, some black operations. Perhaps the thing, the black, is tantamount to another, fugitive, sublimity altogether.[69]

Moten's theorizing of the gap between binary positions of presence-absence, being and nonbeing, leads him to suggest that a certain refusal of ontology is the very possibility of some other materiality of Blackness. As Moten suggests, the refusal of ontology occurs through disruptions of materiality, disruptions that occur through deconstructions of perceptions of materiality, challenging especially the ocularcentrism of the visible.[70]

In "Blackness and Nothingness," an essay whose title confronts Afropessimist associations of Blackness with negation, non-Being, and Black death, Moten articulates the positions of Black optimism and Afropessimism as alternative trajectories on the same plane.[71] Their relationship is "asymptotic"—that is to say, they are a line and a curve that never meet but constitute one another's limits. The relationship is one of an "intimate nonmeeting" that is an "impossibility of touching in mutual radiation and permeation."[72] This asymptotic relationship of two ways of embodying life in an anti-Black world are the conditions of "black radicalism/black social life."[73] For Moten, these two ways of responding to an anti-Black world must in fact be held together. Moten writes that there is a way that "black life . . . is irreducibly social; that, moreover, black life . . . is lived . . . in the burial ground of the subject by those who, insofar as they are not subjects, are also not . . . 'death bound.' "[74] In the sense that it is a space of relation within the context of an impossible existence, Black social life evokes a way of being—not a naively optimistic way of being—beyond the living and dying of a white world. In this way, Moten intimates a way for conceiving the relationship between Black optimism and Afropessimism as the theoretical positions through which Black life must be thought.

Significantly, Moten here does not speak of Black life in terms of the sort of hope that Warren would condemn; rather, he speaks in terms of othered desire. I interpret the otheredness of this desire in Moten's insistence on thinking through that which materially exists as "the air of the thing that escapes enframing."[75] Between the discursive positions of optimism and pessimism about Blackness in an anti-Black world, there is an othered desire, constituted not in relation to anti-Blackness but in relation to otherness. In a telling conclusion about the gravity of this desire, Moten ends his essay with an historicization of anti-Black violence that also appeals to a desire that transcends such history. He turns to the most gruesome hold of the slave ship as an origin through a fantasy that absorbs, disturbs, and haunts the "wake work" of writers like Christina Sharpe and Saidiya Hartman in their attempts to think Blackness and Black life and lives.[76] Moten suggests that there might still emerge from this terror a different capacity for desire. He explicitly asks, "What if blackness is the name that has been given to the social field and social life of an illicit alternative capacity to desire?"[77] Might this alternative capacity to desire be thought in terms of Black living beyond the temporalities (historical vs. eternal) of an anti-Black metaphysics?

One of the key points of Moten's robust theoretical and poetic work that I want to raise as it relates to the work of this chapter is that he challenges the idea that interrogations of Being must *begin* from *either* the political *or* the ethical. He writes, "The lived experienced of blackness is, among other things, a constant demand for an ontology of disorder, an ontology of dehiscence, a para-ontology whose comportment will have been (toward) the ontic or existential field of things and events."[78] My effort to think the materiality and alterity of desire is an effort not simply to advocate ethical interrogation of being but to interrogate ethics itself, as well as the very idea of what it means to speak of an other—to press the *question* of ontological appeals.

Irigaray's work is relevant to the disruption of ontology and metaphysics (or ontometaphysics) because she engages in an interrogation of the violation that makes relationality within the symbolic, including the discourse of ontology, possible. Indeed, as discussed in chapter 1, Irigaray's *Ethics of Sexual Difference* challenges the ethical turn in phenomenology on the basis that it cannot begin to posit difference until it confronts the annihilation of embodied differences that render discursive differences possible. Irigaray's critique of Levinas's turn to the prediscursivity of the ethical moment, for example, attests to the impossibility of thinking the ethical without thinking through the sociocultural framework underpinning his assertions of alterity. Irigaray argued that Levinas's turn to the sexually different couple as the nexus of relation could never ground alterity because such a relation of sexual difference has not yet been thinkable in Western discourse, including philosophy. And, Irigaray insisted, Levinas's portrayal of the couple evidenced this unfortunate reality. I rehearse this as a reminder that I read Irigaray as drawing on the sociocultural order as a symptom of selfsame thought while also insisting therein that one cannot interrogate that structure as though from an outside—hence the emphasis on constitutive absence.

As it pertains to Irigaray's work, the erasure of the difference in sexual difference is prior to and constitutive of the subject's relation to the social while also being absent from it in any real way. In the context of her work, race is a category of difference within a system that promises Being through the sacrifice of sexual difference as a more radical extradiscursive alterity. Irigaray has been condemned by many critics for her unapologetic prioritization of sexual difference as gesturing to alterity, over other differences, including racial difference—and in some ways deservedly so. But briefly bracketing Irigaray's insufficient engagements with questions of racial difference to which I will return, I want to begin by re-emphasizing that sexual difference does not operate in the same genres of the subject like race, gender, and sexuality. Irigaray describes the sexuate as that which is sacrificed in the discourses of difference and differentiation, including political discourses, that constitute the sociocultural order. My interpretation of Irigaray's sexuate is that of an irreducible difference violated through the very positing of sexual difference upon which phallic oneness is based. Violence, or as Irigaray notes, sacrifice, structures such a world. The sexuate, by this reading, constitutes an irreducible difference that is incommensurable within the phallocratic order. And herein lies a resonance between Irigaray's sexual difference and the anti-Blackness of Afropessimist discourses: both anti-Blackness and sexual difference name the conditions for the near totalizing movement of selfsameness.

The sexuate and Blackness share a relation to the selfsame symbolic as a constitutive absence.[79] As Henao Castro writes, "Afropessimism, one could say, puts anti-Blackness in relation to racial differences in the same structural position into which psychoanalysis puts sexual difference in relation to gender differences: these are not differences, properly speaking, but differences that condition the possibility for difference to be recognized, while remaining excluded from it."[80] The psychoanalytic framing of the social order and its related structuring of the discourse of Being as expressed in Irigaray's work resonates with Afropessimism's use of psychoanalysis to describe the pervasiveness of anti-Blackness. There is a potentially totalizing description of the violence of the sociosymbolic framework in this depiction. The forgetting of sexual difference as an annihilation of "female sexuality" and the radical violence of anti-Blackness are figured as the conditions of a sociosymbolic world of all discourses (political, scientific, philosophical, religious, etc.) wherein Being is constituted. And if one reads philosophies of racial and sexual difference together, there is no way of being that is not always already in relation to the logic of sameness in the symbolic order, a logic that moves toward oneness of a white phallus.

The gravity of Afropessimist interpretations of the violence of the social order—especially the "pulverizing" of bodies whose annihilations are the conditions of differences within that order—have further shaped my interpretation of Irigaray's work. I would argue that throughout history and across cultures, there are multitudes of bodies whose potential for individuation has been pulverized because there was no space or time for their othered desires within the prevailing order. The line of questioning I want to push is how the othered desire of lips might refuse the totalizing force of phallocentrism in a way that also speaks to Afropessimist assertions about anti-Blackness. Might we argue for an irreducible ambiguity of othered desire as the possibility of embracing the unthought and the unrepresentable within the dominant social and symbolic order? Might the fecundity of such desire refuse a notion of living that is attached to the whiteness and phallocentrism of Being? And, in its fecundity, might such a desire refuse Being beyond negation—beyond lack and non-Being?

Returning to Moten's question, then, about whether Blackness is the name given to the social life of an illicit alternative capacity to desire, I want to consider the illicitness of desire in Irigaray—the multiplicity of pleasures that threatens the selfsame desire of a masculine imaginary. Moten's description of the response to anti-Blackness in terms of theoretical "intimate nonmeeting[s]" and the "impossibility of touching in mutual radiation and permeation" calls to mind Irigaray's language of the lips.[81] Insofar as the work of sexual difference has focused on articulating desire beyond a desire for oneness, there is a horizon for thinking about a praxis emerging from the space beyond the dichotomies of being or nonbeing, beyond life or death. Just as Moten describes the asymptotic relation of Afropessimism and black optimism, a terminology with which he says he is "reticent[ly]" associated, life happens beyond the absolute negation.[82] Similarly, the touching folds of Irigaray's labial lips gesture beyond lack and beyond the promise of representation. Lips are thresholds of desire, where coming into being is always in apposition to a singular subject and the discourse that grounds its desire for oneness. Desire here is a dwelling beyond the limits of either pessimism or optimism; it is dwelling in the ambiguity and multiplicity of desire itself, continuously generated in the dynamism of becomings; it is, perhaps, that relation between the erotic as power and survival in Audre Lorde's work.

Survival: Desire and Living beyond Hope

In a blog post with thefeministwire.com, Alexis Pauline Gumbs thinks through the concept of survival in relation to institutional violations of Audre Lorde's and June Jordan's dignity. Lorde's and Jordan's respective university employers denied them access to medical leave and other medically related accommodations as they battled cancer. Gumbs spells out a cruel real-ity (the hyphen invoking Hortense Spillers's interrogation of the presymbolic Real and a social reality in Lacanian psychoanalysis): regardless of how famous one is, how many accolades one receives, how hard one works, Black women's identity in a white academy is tied up in the expendability of their bodies and their labor.

But instead of concluding with lamentation for the deaths of Jordan and Lorde, Gumbs closes her piece with a certain exaltation in suffering's midst. Referring to Lorde's "A Litany for Survival," Gumbs locates promise in survival, thinking it as "intentional living with the memory" of ances-tors, with the "promise," or "covenant," that binds the living and ancestral communities. And in an act of "living with the memory," Gumbs writes, "I decided that Audre Lorde is right. Survival is a promise. . . . It is a promise that I make with my currently breathing body to the ancestors who move through it. It is a promise I make in honor of the deaths that make this clarity not only possible, but unavoidable. Survival is a promise."[83] Note this "promise" is not white civil society's perverse hope of false possibility. Promise invokes a different futurity than hope because it reframes the present and the future in relation to a past embodied covenant. Survival is a living with agency and is yet also beyond intention, in the psychic and social space and time of Black community as a space of promise. Gumbs describes the embodiedness of survival as abiding in a promise that is in some ways unintentional, or as she says, "unavoidable." Gumbs writes, "Sur-vival is what some Black women do in the academy, not because they are barely alive, but because we are not supposed to do it, and sometimes we do it anyway."[84] Black women's survival is resistance because it affronts the death of Black women's bodies and the occlusion of Black women's labor. Gumbs's reading of the institutional injustices Jordan and Lorde faced in their fights with cancer, when juxtaposed with the two women's illustrious academic careers, highlights the white supremacy and patriarchy found in institutions and the threat that Black women's survival poses. In a reflection of Black desire as that space beyond the either/or of Black social life or Black death, their acts of dying are acts of living; dying becomes the continuation of their survival-as-promise.

Gumbs's invocation of survival-as-promise speaks to Manigault-Bryant's efforts to walk the line between addressing broad-based historical and institutional injustices perpetrated on Black bodies and the need for a radical queer eros that would destabilize the materialities of difference that inform universals-as-singular (and therein bolster the white supremacy and cisheteronormativity that enable those injustices in the first place). For Manigault-Bryant, in the face of anti-Blackness, a complicated eros of Black bodies that transcends identification emerges in the face of the repetition of Black deaths that mark the purported "colorblindness" of US justice and "civil" society (and indeed the world). In this sense, Manigault-Bryant's invocation of the #BlackLivesMatter movement as a response to Trayvon Martin's death reveals the creative power not of identity but of survival.

Manigault-Bryant's words bear repeating: "If we are honest in our historical ontology, then we must also face the fact of history past and present that there are some bodies in our midst—including those that look like mine—where history past and present does not recognize or acknowledge the possibility of eros—as life, as askesis, as freedom, as political possibility, or as love."[85] Manigault-Bryant's call for "eros—as life, as askesis," resounds with both Gumbs's survival as a resistance and promise and Moten's suggestion that "black life . . . is lived . . . in the burial ground of the subject by those who, insofar as they are not subjects, are also not . . . 'death bound.'"[86] And read in relation to Lorde's emphasis on the erotic that opens this chapter, we might add that survival-as-promise is erotic living—living in the irreducibility of eros as a decolonized or other ontology.[87]

Irigaray suggests that desire aspires toward transcendence, as an aspiration toward a certain "wholeness" beyond oneness—a fecundity constituted through relation.[88] And while Irigaray's continued description of aspiration toward transcendence as a universal aim of becoming remains problematic, as I read it, desire thought through the question of sexual difference is not meant to displace desire in an idealized transcendent of some singular concept, idea, or God that recapitulates the subject's desire for selfhood. Rather, it is a notion of the irreducible multiplicity of eros, like the lips, whose touching is the condition for their closing that is always also an opening, an interval, a gap—a refusal of self-originating oneness. Eros is fecund and indeterminate. Its "ontological" condition is one of radical indeterminacy that is never self-originating, of a dynamic flux that reimagines wholeness apart from oneness. We may call this flux *disruption* or *instability*—terms that evoke a sense of anxiety—but the point is that this perhaps-strange eros (to invoke Lynne Huffer) is dynamic—it is living in all its complexities. It is to desire in relation, desire in the anticipation of touching without consuming, reaching toward the other without grasping.[89]

Drawing on this indeterminacy of desire alluded to by both Moten and—though she arguably forecloses it—Irigaray, and as lived in Audre Lorde's and June Jordan's acts of survival, I propose that thinking through the questions of sexual difference and Blackness (i.e., not gender or race) as constitutive absences of selfsameness invokes a robust concept of desire as the basis of becoming. This type of different desire might offer the sort of generative "ante-foundation" or "ontolog[ical] underground" that Moten searches for in walking the line between optimism and pessimism—desire as "the irreparable disturbance of ontology's time and space."[90] Might dwelling in, inhabiting, this desire be precisely the type of existence without standing to which Moten refers? And rather than thinking of this "ante-foundation" as a space of nothingness that is a space of despair, perhaps it is more accurately a space, gap, or interval of the touching lips. Taking Warren's critique of the anti-Blackness of ontology seriously, what would it mean if the unthought could be reimagined as a fecund relationality of materiality and alterity, where touching beyond the visible is the occasion for alterity to give rise to perception and recognition?[91] Perhaps such a concept of desire could be a better category for thinking about resistance than either participation in politics or rejection of the political.

Touching Elsewhere: The Racialization of Mat(t)er and Rethinking Desire between Lips

REIMAGINING SENSE PERCEPTION IN THE BECOMING OF SELF AND OTHER

Afropessimist focus on the concealment of Blackness—as a deeper anti-Black metaphysical violence that Wilderson and Douglass have identified—remains unaddressed by Irigaray's riVileging of sexual difference. With this occlusion, Irigaray's appeal to sexuation—and therein my appeal to desire—risks participating in the matricidal violence she critiques. After all, Irigaray locates the aspiration to transcendence of desire between two as a powerful and hopeful dimension of what it means to be human, as long as that desire is rooted in the specificity of one's flesh and moves between this fleshiness and aspiration—without an end.[92] But if theorizing the specificity of flesh-iness as condition of alterity recapitulates a history of the racialization of metaphysics and, therein, matter, then this desire must be interrogated in relation to anti-Blackness. And this Irigarayan foundation of my own emphasis on othered desire must therefore be thought through the question of the anti-Black violence of metaphysics and its role in ordaining the whiteness of the at-least two who can be in ontological relation. I therefore want to hold conversations about sexual difference and Afropessimism together in order to confront the phallocentrism and anti-Blackness of selfsame desire.

In this section, I first turn to Irigaray's emphasis on touching between two who are irreducible to each other to conceive a relationality that dis-rupts the empiricist framing of sense perception, which prioritizes visibility. Such a notion of touching beyond visibility posits an alternative to the metaphysics of presence. I end this section with a return to Afropessimist interrogations of dehistoricized ontologies to emphasize that touching, while it must be thought apart from the phallocentrism of the regime of visibility, demands a consideration of the racialization of matter in order to conceive relations beyond the anti-Blackness of the regime of visibility. Only then, I argue, can the material specificity of an irreducible two be imagined in the fullness of their desire.

According to Irigaray, we cannot imagine subjectivity without think-ing through how relationality between self and other has been framed in philosophical discourse. She argues that the history of Western philosophy prioritizes presence: philosophical framings of knowledge emerge through perceiving what is available, where availability is cast as presence. Perception occurs through the senses. But the senses have been privileged, she contends, in ways that recapitulate the conviction that what is known is what is sensed and what is sensed is what is present. In this recursive loop, relations are a prioritization of presence, a metaphysical construct of space and time that reinforces a selfsame notion of subjectivity.

For Irigaray, the prioritization of presence in philosophy has meant that humans are alienated from being in or inhabiting their own fleshiness because there are modes of perception that are occluded. Prioritization of presence also prevents us from relating to alterity through our flesh, the proof of which is evident in the ways sensory knowledge is distanced from the specificities of human fleshiness. For instance, Irigaray argues that even in transcendental philosophy, which attempts to make space for alterity, sight remains the privileged sense for relation. Responding to Levinas's prioritization of the face-to-face encounter (discussed at some length in chapter 1), Irigaray, in addition to phenomenologists like Merleau-Ponty and later Jean-Luc Marion, who were similarly interested in the ethical aspects of perception, has argued that privileging sight reinforces a metaphysics of presence. In a face-to-face encounter, alterity is a matter of being seen. Such an encounter places the possibility of alterity not in relation but in a reductive perception—that is, one sees something such that it is seen. Irigaray explicitly frames visibility as a symptom of a phallocentric symbolic that occludes the "unimaginable woman." "Surely man favors the visual because it marks his exit from the womb? His victory over the maternal power and his opportunity to overcome a mother whom he experiences as amorous, formless, a pit, a chasm in which he risks losing his form?"[93] Here, alterity must be recognizable in order to exist.

In contrast to such a construction of the other, and a relation to that other that remains oriented around self-perception, Irigaray insists that difference must be allowed to be "sensible and alive" beyond the instruments of representation of the other, which includes moving beyond the metaphysical discourse used to articulate sense perception.[94] Touch is the possibility of such a way of knowing. However, Irigaray insists that because sexuate difference has never been thought through, theories of touch have continued to promote a masculine epistemology of the senses. Even twentieth-century phenomenological theories of touch theorize the other's presence through an externalization of their flesh from the flesh of the self.

For example, Irigaray argues that Merleau-Ponty's appeal to an invisible fleshy touching in *The Visible and the Invisible* still relies on the economy of visibility for its framing.[95] She contends that even touch must be thought differently in order to be conceived beyond the visible; it must be thought through the question of sexual difference such that it remains irreducible. In the poetic prologue to *To Be Two*, Irigaray meditates on the importance of the space and time of a certain desire, love, and wonder that would allow two to exist (not as two ones, but as two always in relation), prioritizing what is not seen as that which maintains the space of unknowing necessary for these two to be two.[96]. It is touch that allows for this relation with an other who remains unseen and therein relatable while not fully perceived—to remain other in their wholeness. This is a distinct relation of space and time prior to language, "outside of all violence" of reduction; it is a touching beyond the regime of visibility.[97] And it is also this touching beyond the visible that Irigaray argues enables the proximity necessary for "re-touch" of "self-affection" such that "What the other sees does not reach the place or the presence to me, through which I preserve my own self."[98]

Irigaray's criticism of the ways the prioritization of the visible functions to reinforce a metaphysics of presence is all the more reason to turn to her lips, touching beyond the visible, as an embodied rhetorical critique of the metaphysics of presence. An embodied relation of the at-least two, lips, I have argued, gesture to a multiplicity of desire; their touchings challenge the interiority and exteriority and the verticality and horizontality of the space and time of a metaphysics of presence. Here, the other's becoming is always already part of the becoming of self, not external to the self. *Lips touch, and that touching is sensed regardless of whether or not they are seen.* One need not know if it is a top lip or bottom lip, a right lip or left lip, for that touching to be perceived; they disrupt such identification and directionality. And because they touch without needing to be seen, they challenge the priority of visibility in phenomenological perception, and therein, the metaphysics of presence. The irreducible difference to which the lips gesture and the generative desire of their relation do not need recognition within an economy of visibility. Lips suggest that being there is not the same as being seen. They want only to realize their touchings as constitutive of their mutual individuations.

This self-touching morphologically figured by the lips reimagines metaphysical determinations of materiality and discursivity to disrupt Western philosophical foundations of subjectivity and perception. Recall that Irigaray faults Hegel for positing human becoming as a potentially antagonistic movement between self-consciousness and the material world. Whereas in metaphysics, the material serves as that which must be reduced to knowledge in order to be overcome, the mode of perception that the lips invoke reimagines the dialectic beyond this antagonism—to rethink relation as desire rather than overcoming. Self-touching lips affront notions of interiority and exteriority and space and time that pit immanence and transcendence in oppositional terms, offering a sensible-transcendental mode of relation that refuses binaries for constructing theories of knowledge and subjectivity.[99]

As I have framed Irigaray's lipcentric interrogation of immanence and transcendence in chapters 1 through 3 in particular, the lips reimagine touch differently. Their touching beyond the economy of visibility gestures to a different mode of perception and therein a different way for conceiving both self and other. But is appealing to the touching of the lips beyond visibility sufficient to disrupt the white master signifier? In the remainder of this chapter, I argue that an appeal to lips as touching beyond visibility must also take into consideration the racialization of the very immanent-transcendent binary that Irigaray's touching beyond visibility is meant to transform.

THE RACIALIZATION OF MATTER

Philosopher and Irigaray scholar Rachel Jones has been a principal voice for thinking critical theories of race in relation to Irigaray's work. Jones's painstakingly careful and charitable readings of Irigaray inform her argument that despite Irigaray's "unsurpassed methodology of reading for constitutive silences," her reading of the indifference of the Western hegemonic myth of sexual difference never considers the racialization of this myth of sexual difference.[100] Jones more forcefully writes:

> My concern is thus less with what is said about race in Irigaray's texts and more with what is not said or attended to: with a met-aphorics of blackness that is invoked without critical reflection on its racialized connotations; or a call to parler femme that retains a universality apparently unmarked by race; or the positioning of sexual difference as "one of the major philosophical issues, if not the issue, of our age" that critiques the sexual indiffer-ence of the West without sufficiently thematizing its colonial, racializing history, which problematizes this "our" from the start.[101]

As Jones suggests, Irigaray's assertion that the maternal feminine is the constitutive absence of sexual difference and her appeal therein to the transformative power of female sexuality as the possibility of a new way of speaking of and between women occur without thinking of the "metaphorics of blackness" that constitute her theorizing.

Adding to Jones's assertions that Irigaray has not adequately theorized the racialization of the universal Being and the other that her sexual difference is meant to interrogate, I insist that there remains an implicit whiteness of *Irigaray's* lips. The materiality and alterity of the sexuate encounter is differ-entiated from a notion of matter and transcendence that is always already racialized. Therefore, positing the constitutive absence of the sexuate, and then deriving a notion of materiality and alterity from that sexuate without attending to the masculine and racialized immanence and transcendence apart from which the sexuate is imagined, participates in anti-Blackness. Put differently, theorizing lips through the question of sexual difference as a thinking through of what is constitutively absent from the social order, without thinking through other constitutive absences, risks reifying the colonial and anti-Black violence of thought.

Warren has called attention to the limits of Irigaray's efforts to challenge the metaphysics through a sexuate woman that is unthinkable and unrepresentable within the masculine symbolic because Irigaray's appeal to the sexuate hinges on the "abject Black Belly as the bridge to her Being."[102] Warren's accusation cuts deep and warrants, at the very least, a review of Irigaray's relation to the re-cognition that constitutes becoming in Hegel. As I have discussed, Irigaray has critiqued the dualism of immanence and transcendence that is essential to Hegel's understanding of the movement of consciousness. Irigaray argues that this dualism arises from an association of woman with reproduction, the maternal, the natural order—and therein with matter. Woman, matter, maternal, nature: all become reciprocal signifiers, interchangeable, as it were, in the positing of immanence. The woman as matter is opposed to the transcendent, the divine, and the eternal. This maternal feminine rendered as other is not other at all; she is the projection of a masculine worldview—a fiction that imagines immanence in order to posit immanence as that through which one can produce knowledge (through empiricism) and know oneself. But as Warren suggests, there is a Black maternal body that has been othered, and that othering is then occluded in the prioritization of sexual difference precisely because Irigaray's criticisms of Western philosophical and psychoanalytic depictions of materiality and transcendence ignore the racialization of this discourse.

As part her of literary criticism of the form of the novel as representative of "imperial Western humanism" that has "made possible the ongoing displacement of local knowledge (or culture-specific orders)," Zakiyyah Iman Jackson turns to Nalo Hopkinson's tropes of Blackness and African religion in *Brown Girl in the Ring* (1998) as figures that expose the reduction or "foreclosure of the black mater(nal)" in the production of the myth of history and its attending conceptions of immanence and transcendence.[103] Jackson's argument suggests that it is not simply the maternal that has been determined and delimited to project concepts of materiality and transcendence that serve selfsame models of subjectivity, as Irigaray would suggest. Rather, it is the myth of a Black mater(nal) and its "conjunctive abjection of black female gender and nullification of black maternity" that serves the selfsame representational function of language and the "orbiting discursive-material formations of knowledge and being."[104] And in similar fashion not only to Irigaray's positing of the feminine as the mark of a masculine representation of an nonrepresentable sexuate woman, but also to her assertion that invoking the feminine disrupts the notion of mimetic representation as an exact copy, Jackson contends that Black maternal figures disrupt the representational function of language. While connecting Jackson's readings of Black maternality to Irigaray's mimesis to the catachresis of Spivak's decolonial project is beyond the scope of this chapter, it is worth noting that the three theorists all read representations of the other as a trace of a forgotten other whose extradiscursive embodiedness is the possibility of disrupting the representational function of language.

Jackson refers to the "Black mater(nal)" to emphasize associations of maternality with matter as always already associations of Blackness to matter that render Blackness, Black female bodies, and Black motherhood as signifiers of a debased materiality. She highlights Hegel's dehumanizing racist descriptions of Africans with nature and his theorizing of transcendence in terms of the movement to overcome nature to return to spirit. Jackson emphasizes that Hegel's dialectic employs racial opposition as the means to posit the difference between immanence and transcendence. And she attends to this racialization of Hegel's dialectic in relation to the question of woman as the other to suggest that the Black maternal body is the other/matter/mater to be transcended in the movement toward becoming human.

Jackson proceeds from this theorization of racialization of materiality and transcendence to the problem of perception, suggesting that the Black mater(nal) is nonrepresentable (as opposed to unrepresented). Nonrepresentability is an effect of a world that posits the other through perceptions of difference materialized in representation. Here, the Black female signifies this myth of materiality and difference. But this nonrepresentability is, for Jackson, the possibility of "transform[ing] the terms of reality and feeling, therefore rewriting the conditions of possibility of the empirical."[105] In a move that is at least structurally/linguistically similar to Irigaray's turn to the sexuate other as a disruption of mimesis, Jackson writes that "a non-representationalist mode of reason or onto-epistemology—may hold the potential to unsettle hegemonic modes of racist reality and their constituent myths." She continues with the assertion that the "specter of the black mater(nal)—that is, nonrepresentability—haunts the terms and operations tasked with adjudicating the thought-world correlate or the proper perception of 'the world' such as hierarchical distinctions between reality and illusion, Reason and its absence, subject and object, science and fiction, and speculation and realism, which turn on attendant aporias pertaining to immanence and transcendence."[106] The Black maternal body, Jackson suggests, operates in a space of nonrepresentability that is also a space of potential transformation because it disrupts the very foundations of the real or imagined.

Jackson's appeal to nonrepresentability resonates with my characterization of Irigaray's appeal to the sexuate as an as-yet-unthought space for reimagining perception through touch—and it also connects to the position of the unthought. While these positions are not structurally the same, they appeal to a space beyond the dualism of immanence and transcendence—beyond the violence of metaphysics. The point I want to emphasize is that one must attend to both the gendering and racializing of materiality as the condition of possibility for perception in order to confront the anti-Black violence of metaphysics. If we posit a materiality of alterity of desire and ignore the racialization of matter apart from which we want to imagine such a materiality of alterity, we strip the lips of the multiplicity of desire that Irigaray herself heralds. I want to avoid recapitulating an ontology that universalizes and neutralizes materiality.

Jackson's above critique effectively substantiates, in Irigarayan terms, the gauntlet Warren throws Irigaray's way. While Irigaray's invocation of a sensible transcendental attempts to overcome the hierarchy of transcendence over immanence by positing a mode of relation that could ground a nonreductive, nonselfsame way of dwelling in the world together—beyond the reductive economy of phallocentric representation—Irigaray posits this relation by disrupting a materiality signified exclusively by a maternal feminine; she ignores the racialization of materiality. As such, the extradiscursive materiality of Irigaray's sexuate couple participates in the occlusion of the Black mater(nal). Furthermore, Irigaray's notion of the sexuate couple does not trouble the racialization of the ontological she attempts to reimagine. In fact, her ontologization of sexual difference risks rendering the very idea of Black sexuality an impossibility and promotes a willful ignorance of the "metaphysical infrastructure privileging being's vicious anti-Blackness."[107] If the Black mater(nal) is the condition of possibility for a grammar of ontology, Irigaray's appeal to an extradiscursive natural materiality might still "rel[y] on a problematic material reductionism . . . secured by the idea of race," as Jackson suggests.[108]

Heeding the words of Jackson, Warren, and Jones, I acknowledge the impacts of Irigaray's insufficient theorizing of racialization in her otherwise quite radical notion of materiality to determine what might be retrievable from her appeal to a different, relational mode of sensory perception, thinking, and knowing. While I have chosen to appeal to lips rather than Black maternity, I insist that both are efforts to reimagine the relation between thought and perception beyond sense/sensory/sensation becoming reduced to meaning through empiricism. As Irigaray suggests in "When Our Lips Speak Together," she does not want the sense of the lips to become "their" meaning—that is, she does not want the multiplicity of desire of touching lips to become reduced to the senses as empirically constructed.

Could attendance to racialization engender lips that offer an onto-epistemological framework that disrupts anti-Blackness? Could Black lips be a means to think embodiment differently in order to change the way knowledge emerges? Can we imagine embodiment as an appeal to flesh that is beyond bodies as historical material facts or an ahistorical transcendental universalized alterity—both crises that render bodies figments to be easily absorbed in the project of the history of philosophy toward sameness? Would such an ontoepistemological framework address the tensions between the ethical and the political interrogations of Being as effects of an insufficiently theorized notion of desire?

Black feminist interrogations of the regime of visibility/invisibility challenge what could otherwise amount to a dangerous neutrality of a morphology of lips that doesn't take racialization into consideration. Perhaps refiguring the sensory perception of touch through an appeal to a desire of Black lips could attend to the social-political context in which bodies (in philosophy) and their sexuality (in psychoanalysis) have been significations of a determinate, phallic, and anti-Black symbolic. And insofar as Irigaray's sexuate is not gender, Black lips are not racialized; rather, they might serve to disrupt the racialization of the selfsame dialectic as Jackson imagines it. And in their desire, Black lips might offer a new symbolic to signify otherwise than through selfsame representation.

Jared Sexton remarks that the task for Afropessimists is "how to theorize and to politicize violence in the midst of violence, to indicate the wetness of water while being submerged in it."[109] The Black feminist theorists I invoke from this point forward interrogate cinema as well as art and photography to disrupt the phallocentrism and whiteness of visibility. In thinking through images, these theorists are indicating the "wetness of water while being submerged in it" to expose visual representation as part of the violence of metaphysics, offering ways to appeal to the constitutive absence of those who are beyond invisibility and visibility. They are cultivating a labial logic of touch.

From Visible Matter to Touching in Shadows

Amber Jamilla Musser's work on race and psychoanalysis analyzes visual representations while refusing the anti-Blackness of the regime of visibility and its attending "vicious anti-Blackness" of metaphysics.[110] Describing her own work as occupying the space of a "yes, and" in relation to Afropessimism, Musser examines the associations of both Blackness and the feminine with materiality to articulate a different mode of becoming in and through the "amorphous quality of fleshiness that Hortense Spillers argues was assigned to the 'captive body.' "[111] In *Sensational Flesh*, Musser attends to what she sees as Fanon's antagonism to women's sexuality and psychoanalysis's antagonism to race to conceive an othered sexuality. Specifically, Musser challenges the white phallocentrism of psychoanalysis by examining the association of Black bodies with matter, describing whiteness as an affective state. Following her interpretation of Freud's reading of moral masochism as occurring in the formation of the superego, Musser suggests that "the biological and suffering can be read as sensations of becoming-black" and argues that such a reading of "becoming-black" is essential to the becoming of "white (masochistic) liberal sub-jectivity."[112] Musser effectively rethinks the "pathology of black-ness" described by Moten as a pathology of whiteness that is an effect of the selfsame movement of subjectivity in a white colonial world. Following her critical reading of Fanon's revision of the Hegelian relationship of recognition to subjectivity, Musser argues that the association of the Black body, and the Black male body as described by Fanon, not only casts that body as object but as an atomized, biological, and dismembered body.

Musser's reference to the dismembered body should feel familiar to readers of Irigaray, since the latter has long argued that women have been reduced to a reproductive body—casting woman as a particular function while also limiting her access to her own transcendence. The point I want to emphasize is that in both Fanon and Irigaray, alienation from one's body as a site of becoming means that one does not have access to their own sexuality. This is not to say that the alienation from the body described by Fanon and Irigaray is the same; Irigaray describes women's alienation from their bodies through a history of discursive violence and mostly allusions to its effects, not, like Fanon, through a history of discursive *and* physical violence. Musser attends to this violence by turning to Black and brown bodies to signify an "affective fleshiness" that exceeds the white phallocentric discourse of sexuality.[113]

In *Sensual Excess*, her follow-up to *Sensational Flesh*, Musser theorizes "brown jouissance": a fleshy pleasure beyond sexuality as a genre of a white phallocentric psychoanalytic representation of desires and pleasures. The turn to "brown jouissance" challenges white phallocentric reductions of Black women's sexuality to reproduction and labor, offering a non-Oedipal reading of the maternal feminine. As part of this effort, Musser draws on Irigaray's language of labial lips to think Black women's sexuality beyond violation—in other words, to think Black women's sexuality not simply as a constitutive absence of anti-Black symbolic. Highlighting how Irigaray's lips gesture to a jouissance that is dynamic and fluid, and how that fluidity engenders a subjectivity that refuses the stasis toward which egoism aspires, Musser writes: "In the ambiguity that Irigaray announces we can see the possibility of jouissance in the way that the labia mobilize oscillations between interiority and exteriority and subject and object. This is to say that the labia function as a marker of flesh's liquidity—formulated here through conversational excess—because they call attention to the movement and materiality of the body while also evacuating a stable 'I.' "[114]

Musser adds that Lynne Huffer's reading of Irigaray's lips provides a way to think alterity as emerging through the relationality of eros. But Musser also insists upon the materiality of the lips as engendering a "spatial mode of thinking fleshiness."[115] This materiality as the condition of relation in the symbolic is essential to Irigaray's "labial economy" because it allows for what Musser refers to as a "dialogical formation of the self that operates in and through proprioception."[116] As Musser suggests that proprioception, "allows us to ask what it means to mobilize the oscillation between touching/not touching in conjunction with categories of social difference."[117] In other words, the labial economy is always in relation to the sociality of becoming even while pleasures exceed that economy. As such, the labial economy gestures to a materiality and desire beyond the whiteness and phallocentrism of metaphysics and sexuality. Musser does not address directly the whiteness of Irigaray's lips; rather, she focuses her attention on the Black vulva as indicative of the porosity of self-other relations to which the labial economy gestures.

Not unlike Irigaray's call to disassimilate the feminine from the history of philosophy, Musser suggests analyzing the play of presence and absence of the Black vulva in representations of sexuality within the field of the social and cultural in order to "find black and brown maternal absence"—suggesting "Brown jouissance" is a "project of recovery and survival."[118] Emphasizing that it is the sensual that gives access to this elsewhere place of that which exists and yet is absent, Musser adds, "In finding permutations of selfhood that exceed the 'I,' we come close to the missing matter of these black and brown mothers."[119] As it regards the violence undergirding a racialized metaphysics, touching, retheorized through Musser's notion of Brown jouissance, gestures to an embodied space and time of sensation that is elsewhere than the field of visibility. Musser concludes by examining invocations of lesbian touch in Audre Lorde's poetry. She contends that Lorde's Black lesbian lovers touch in a way that is always already political because it challenges "epistemologies of sexuality." Musser doesn't dwell on touch, but following this reading of Lorde, she does turn again to Irigaray (by way of Denise Ferreira da Silva). And in this return to Irigaray, she advocates a reading of the radical potential of Irigaray's appeal to an othered female sexuality, insisting that the female lover in Irigaray's work develops "the power of the body and its materiality through a reordered sensorium and sensuality."[120]

In *Between Shadows and Noise*, Musser further pushes this question of representation of Black women's sexuality in relation to modes of sense perception and ways of knowing and therein becoming.[121] Here, she critically analyzes visual representations of Black femininity, especially art and cinematic portrayals of Black women and girls. Maintaining focus on the constitutive absence that is named by the unthought, the undercommons, or the fugitivity of Afropessimism, Musser advocates a fleshy thinking, or "body work" to create space for a sensual knowledge from which to engage in critique. She acknowledges that touch must be imagined beyond the light/dark and invisible/visible binary, and therefore uses the term *shadow* rather than *darkness* to resist the light/dark dichotomy of the regime of visibility that reinforces the whiteness of the master signifier of psychoanalysis.

The shadow presents a space for grappling with the psychic "underlying processes of repression, disavowal, and denial and their embeddedness in ontological and epistemological systems of valuation."[122] Musser writes: "The term shadow is used to separate 'light' from 'dark,' offering language not only for an optic phenomenon, but a system of value that would prioritize light, equating it with transparency, rationality, and 'enlightenment,' leaving the concept of the shadow to signify something that is either deliberately hidden from view (usually in a malevolent fashion), disavowed, or repressed; think of shadow terms, governments, processes, archives."[123] If, as Irigaray suggests, one must think through sexual difference to arrive at a different concept of irreducible difference that imagines being in the specificity of one's body in relation to others and apart from the violence of metaphysics, including reductive biological empiricism, Musser shows that thinking through the racialization of sense perception would first be necessary before approaching any relational theory of fleshy desire to be possible. Could a theory of lips touching in shadows prioritize a materiality of becoming through/from elsewhere—cultivating becoming in a space and time "beyond" the violence of metaphysics without ignoring that violence and its implications for living in an anti-Black society?[124] What if we think the lips themselves as occupying the position of the unthought that stands apart from anti-Blackness? I want to frame labial logic as a thinking through the materiality of difference beyond anti-Blackness of visibility, arguing ultimately that lips have the potential to gesture toward a relationality capable of confounding the regimes of identification within an anti-Black social and symbolic order.[125] Black labial logic opens possibilities of embodied desire that refuse the anti-Black violence of metaphysics.

If to see is effectively to grasp in thought, the visual eliminates the possibility of eros. Unlike the face-to-face encounter that prioritizes the visual, I argue that a logic of Black lips becomes a model for touching in shadows, preventing one from becoming the object of another's gaze.[126] The lips are a morphology that touches without grasping, refusing to be the reflective visible surface of a flat mirror upon which subject-object relations can be constructed. In their touching in shadows, beyond a binary of light and dark, lips evoke a becoming through desire beyond the "being" of presence or nonbeing of absence, a becoming from a space that is radically other, unthought, and untheorized.[127] But the unthought does not appear as unthought. Its absence appears as marked by a master signifier. As Irigaray's mimesis would suggest, the appearance of woman in the "feminine" is not the arrival of the unthought, nor, I would add, is the appearance of Blackness given in racialization the unthought. The unthought is not available in acts of representation, except as a trace of its invisibility and unrecognizability, its silence.

This does not mean that the unthought or nonrepresentable is a position of lack such that desire would be a wanting that reinscribes a subjectivity that moves toward sameness. It does mean, however, that the unthought are not recognized or heard in and through their desires. Such desire, with all its generative force, always in movement, could perhaps be a better category for thinking about resistance to the violence of metaphysics.[128] To get to othered desire, then, is to think through desire without letting the materiality of its alterity get trapped in the anti-Black reduction of flesh that would ignore the racialized conditions upon which ontology often turns. This is why an adversarial aesthetics of Black lips is needed—a Black labial logic achieved by thinking through the "nonrepresentable" and "unthought" position of those whose bodies have been associated with matter to bolster the transcendent promise of political representation in a white, phallocentric world.[129]

My invocation of Black lips is precarious and must be considered carefully in relation to the complex entanglements of Black desire and the alienations of Black bodies from Black identity in an anti-Black world in order to avoid recapitulating the selfsame desire of a white phallocentric symbolic. My turn to Black lips here is not therefore a reinvocation of a

Black mater(nal) as a signification of racialized biological reproduction. Black lips gesture to the nonrepresentable desire whose pleasurable touchings have been annihilated by carceral ontologies that hold flesh captive, to borrow from Warren's "ontological terror." My appeal to Black lips is also an appeal to think the political not as an extension or effect of the ethical but to think the politics that encumber ethical propositions in order to imagine a different mode of relation. Desire must be thought more radically, not simply through sexual difference but alongside the question of Black desire as a position of the unthought.

Unfortunately, despite espousing the irreducibility of their fleshy boundaries, Irigaray can't seem to allow *her* lips to make space for *these* lips. So while Irigaray's lips are structurally helpful for thinking the discursive representation of certain bodies as inert matter, disembodied from the psychic and spiritual self, Black lips allow rethinking the racialization of matter more by disrupting the colonizing whiteness of desire that underlies any discourse of embodiedness and prediscursivity. Dwelling in the specificities of flesh beyond societal and political racializations vis-à-vis a white phallocentric symbolic imagination, a Black labial logic reimagines even the Irigarayan touching lips in terms of a Black desire—in a materiality of desire beyond the penetrative and antipenetrative framework of heterosexism beyond the tyrannical touch of white hands on Black bodies.[130] This sort of disruptive thinking through the space of touching lips and the touching of Blackness beyond either life or death, this space of desire of a Black labial logic, I would argue, is profoundly evident in Saidiya Hartman's work.

An Ethics of Black Lips: Touching in Shadows and the Desire of the Unthought

Saidiya Hartman's interrogations of history's reliance on archival evidence is instructive for reimagining the lives of those whose lives have been unthought, yet no less lived, in the construction of history and in the prioritization of presence as visibility.[131] As Hartman also explains in "Venus in Two Acts," the cultural historian's attempt to give voice to the disinherited through the archival record is an inherently flawed process.[132] Hartman exposes the double bind of doing historical work on enslaved persons, noting that there are a host of ethical and political reasons one should want to reconstruct narratives about enslaved persons in order to foreground their silenced voices. And yet she notes the problem of recreating stories of Black women's subjectivity from fragments of an archive that always already represents a white phallic imaginary. In the 2003 interview of Hartman, "The Position of the Unthought," Wilderson praises Hartman's work, writing that she walks the fine line, or "split[s] the hair," between the discursive and the preconscious perspectives of subjectivity.[133] Wilderson's reading of Hartman through the psychoanalytic framework points to the fact that thinking through the position of enslaved persons as unthought means refusing the subject as either cultural or natural, free or determined, constructed or essential.[134]

Hartman's work exposes the violence of presence, institutionalized in the archive, as the condition for legibility, visibility, and intelligibility. But by reading the archives as artifacts for interpretation that hide as much as they tell, and by recovering narratives of enslaved persons by thinking through their archival marks and the traces of their effacements, Hartman considers the question of history as one of the tension between concepts of the historical as real versus the literary as imagined. Hartman's masterful genre-bending book, *Wayward Lives, Beautiful Experiments: Intimate Histories of Social Upheaval*, engages this question of history by making history itself an art. Indeed, *Wayward Lives* invokes and evokes the unthought materiality of Black lives through a literary reading of the historical that confronts the reductive processes by which Black bodies have become the debased matter upon which American history and with it the promise of political hope (I would add) have been constructed.

Turning to photographs and other archival research to reconstruct a narrative of the figures in the photos, Hartman invokes the limits of representation in order to search beyond them. Through this archival work, she creates glimpses of whole persons that, like acts of love, reach toward, without reductively grasping at, their lives. Hartman describes how early twentieth-century photographs of life in the "Black Quarter" were taken primarily by social-service organizations, depicting Black life in ways that served their "scientific" motives. "The photographs coerced the black poor into visibility as a condition of policing and charity, making those bound to appear suffer the burden of representation."[135] Such depictions placed Black life in a particular mode of being, reducing its complexities, its loves, and its traumas. These photographs do not so much depict as occlude the Black life that was lived, as Hartman puts it, in the hallways, those spaces of transition between rooms that are rarely depicted in these photographs "documenting" Black life.

Hartman's book is rich with examples that imagine the "Beautiful experiments in living free," as a space of Black eros.[136] In one of her most poignant portrayals, "A Minor Figure," she resurrects the story of a young girl who is known by a photograph of her nude body. Hartman meditates on the life of the young girl as follows:

> Fragments of her life are woven with the stories of girls resem-
> bling her and girls nothing like her, stories held together by
> longing, betrayal, lies, and disappointment. The newspaper article
> confuses her with another girl, gets her name wrong. . . . The
> photograph taken of her in the attic studio is the one that is
> most familiar; it is how the world still remembers her. Had her
> name been scribbled on the back of the albumen print, there
> would have been at least one fact that I could convey with a
> measure of certainty, one detail that I would not have to guess,
> one less obstacle in retracing the girl's path through the streets
> of the city.[137]

Hartman's suggestion that "Fragments of her life are woven with the stories of girls resembling her and girls nothing like her" is a statement about the way the archive has erased the specificity of the lives of young Black women, rendering them objects of history, objects of a particular portrayal of reality. The archive is an exercise in sameness: the archive itself is a racialized materialization, and it further reduces the differences of embodied experiences to a more cohesive, universalized singular narrative.

But Hartman is not just confounding history as a form of representation; she is also interrogating the regime of visibility through which racialization and racial belonging operate. The girl's specificity has been transcendentalized in the promise of facticity that the photograph suggests. As Hartman adds, this one image will be "how the world still remembers her," the specificity of her complexity whittled down to an image that perpetually subjects her to the white male gaze of history (at least for now). There is no "fact" here. And Hartman knows this. The "obstacle in retracing the girl's path" will always escape her.

The archival project to recover that specificity becomes not unlike chasing the fantasy that will "pulverize" her Black body in the name of history. In this very practice of thinking through the unthought, specifically in her dialogical engagement with the regime of visibility that informs racial belonging, Hartman invokes the intimacy and ethics of desire as a self-undoing—a continuous reaching toward the other at the risk of undermining any certainty of one's own exercise. This self-undoing is not a living or dying; it is a reimagining of living and dying in the graveyard of the subject. The forgetting of the nameless young girl (the ease with which she and so many others are erased by being confused with other girls, all rendered the same) is like forgetting the maternal origin in Irigaray's critique of psychoanalysis.[138] Annihilation of her memories becomes the means to establish an illusion of wholeness. That whole is a narrative of "the" historical that at once reflects and reproduces a particular image/representation of race relations. In the case of the "minor figure," the young Black girl remains nameless.

Hartman challenges representations of Black bodies not simply to deconstruct and reconstruct new representations but also to imagine a new way of relating to the limits of discourse altogether. She confounds sexual, gendered, and racial constructions of the white phallic master signifier, through dynamic and irreducible reincarnations of Black life. Her "intimate histories" dwell in the space of the unthought, refusing the dichotomy of the real versus the imagined, thinking through the materializations of Black bodies in order to get beyond those materializations to create "a dream book for existing otherwise."[139] New becomings emerge from those who touch in the shadows, in the hallways, where their sites of pleasure are multiple and their thresholds of touch mean their desire is irreducible.[140] The result is, once again recalling Shesadri-Crooks, a truly adversarial aesthetics—one that locates agency within the materiality of desire, within the art of survival (as living and as living memory). Hartman's work exemplifies how thinking through desire is itself an experiment with freedom—not the freedom of political identity, or of self-avowed autonomy, and certainly not the notion of hopeful freedom pushed by the false promises of politics—but the freedom of a radical materiality of alterity, of dynamic relations of wayward lives beyond the inertness of matter ascribed to Black female bodies in a white phallocentric world. Instead of exemplifying bodies as ontological lack, Hartman positions the archives' Black lives as the "unthought."

There is a useful intervention to be made by way of feminist psychoanalytic theory, which helps rethink the ontological equation beyond reduction. As Seshadri-Crooks notes, the whole was perhaps never whole. It has always been an illusion of wholeness that we chase (an illusion of wholeness that haunts any search for origins). If the ontological equation capitulates to an idea that being is ideally singular, the irreducible, unthought being refuses singularity. The position of the unthought confronts wholeness as an illusion, whether that wholeness is the illusion of a single preconscious nature (ontology) or a single discursive, political identity in which we freely partake.

Hartman reincarnates Black lives through the unthought such that their disruptions do not depend on their lack, on their mutilations and fractures/fractions of wholeness, on their participation in nonbeing or partial being.[141] She gestures to an other materiality of desires that subvert the regime of visibility. She thinks the Black lives that are never just nonwhite, that are always more than the whiteness of the whole. They are more than the oneness of the phallus. But they are also more than partial, more than lack—they are dynamic, irreducible, indeterminate, and fecund. The logic of relation to which her work gestures is a logic of a freedom of desire—of desire beyond visibility, of Black lips touching elsewhere to remake worlds.

My appeal to an ontology of othered desire has been an effort to assert a materiality and alterity that refuse reductions to foundations for thinking politics. The material-discursive tension is a problem of representation, and the challenge of thinking the ontological and intersectional together is the mark of a prior sacrifice of a prediscursive desire of the unthought. That desire of the unthought is not finally reducible to a particular body, but the trace of the unthought is no less marked in discourse. Put more precisely, the materiality of unthought desire is not sexed, nor is it raced; however, sex and race are the traces of its alienation in/by the representational function of the symbolic. It is those marks, those photographs, those archives, those representations that must be mined in order for disassimilation to occur.

Chapter 6

Horizons of Touch

Desire and a Reimagined Anthropos

In "Uses of the Erotic: The Erotic as Power," Audre Lorde draws attention to the Greek Eros as the "personification of love in all its aspects—born of Chaos." Here, Lorde insists upon the dynamic power that swirls about the erotic as "the sharing of joy, whether physical, emotional, psychic, or intellectual."[1] Lorde's suggestion that the erotic must be reclaimed for women, especially Black women, to cultivate their personhood suggests there is a way of becoming that is based in a deeply embodied relationality that is itself embedded in desire. Like Irigaray's emphasis on a jouissance reimagined through a multiplicity of pleasures beyond phallocentric reductions, Lorde too describes the sharing that generates eros's power in terms of its dynamic, energetic movement. She says, "It flows through and colors my life with a kind of energy that heightens and sensitizes and strengthens all my experience."[2]

Lorde's *Sister Outsider* was published in 1984, the same year that Irigaray's *An Ethics of Sexual Difference* was published in French. Despite their innumerable differences, Lorde and Irigaray belong to a generation of women whose articulation of their identity as women, and in Lorde's case, as a self-proclaimed "Black lesbian feminist,"[3] was a political act that, I argue, extended from their appeals to an irreducible an ontology of desire—from an imminent energy that transcends reductions in discourse. So, while the erotic is the possibility of a different epistemological framework, it is much more than a way of knowing. The erotic, as Lorde and Irigaray use it, appeals to a certain mode of being, of a deeper reality, of an energy, and even an "electrical charge."[4] In theorizing desire, and in particular the sexual dimensions of desire as belonging to a certain untapped energy, these early feminist works attempted to reimagine the landscape of thought in relation to the materiality of embodied living. They recognized that how one conceives embodiedness informs how one relates to space and time, to the world, to thought, to the notion of the subject, of the human, and one's others.

Early feminist emphases on embodiment, like that introduced by Simone de Beauvoir, with whom Lorde was philosophically engaged, and expanded upon by thinkers such as Lorde and Irigaray, challenged the philosophical foundations for thinking matter as posited through a universal subject who was always already masculine.[5] These turns to an embodiment that wasn't white, European, and male, disrupted representational thinking and the uninterrogated discursive mapping of/to reality, including the universalization of a single narrative about who the subject was and how it was constituted—a strange bedfellow with the postmodernist theories that would ultimately deconstruct bodies altogether. But the disruptive body has returned, and this time as an answer to the radical destabilization of corporeality. To this end, recent feminist turns to materialism are in part an effort to confront the arbitrariness of discourse—the ways discourse itself can make the world. If bad postmodernism leads to a posttruth world in which claims are always relative, then materialism would seem a way to ground existence in specificity. And such grounding in specificity is especially important for feminist politics.

But in the wake of poststructuralism and deconstruction's monumental theoretical interventions, an appeal to materiality requires a certain contextualizing of materiality itself—a thinking through the conditions through which materiality is theorized. The landscape of contemporary thought about materialism has moved far from a Marxist historical dialectic. There has been greater acknowledgment, even in fields like theoretical physics, that there are systems of relation that exceed what we think we know about matter itself. In critical theory, this reexamination of materiality includes developments in speculative realism as well as new materialism.

"New materialism" has become an increasingly popular field for thinking through the contingencies and specificities of life that poststructuralism (in particular) has rendered abstract, while also thinking the question of alterity that prevents new materialism from falling back into essentialism. "New materialism" rethinks assumptions about what constitutes the human and its limits by bringing the ethical to bear on the political, and vice versa, as it aims to theorize the radicality of contingencies and specificities. Among feminist philosophical retheorizings of materiality through this twenty-first-century paradigm, Rosi Braidotti's nomadic theory and Elizabeth Grosz's rethinking of incorporeality are especially notable because, I would argue, their engagements with materiality, and posthuman discourse more broadly, ensue from their early engagements with Irigaray sexual difference.[6] Although Grosz and Braidotti represent different approaches to the question of materiality, which I discuss later, I think they share an interest (sometimes more implicit than others) with Irigaray in thinking through desire.[7] In fact, I read the materiality and alterity of Irigarayan desire not simply as a coincidental resonance but as a harbinger of the current debates in the overlapping fields of posthumanism and new materialism.

Situated in relation to the linguistic adaptation of psychoanalysis and the ethical turn in phenomenology, Irigaray interweaves the materiality of desire and its representation in the symbolic realm in a way that links the disruption of "the whole problematic of space and time" to this project of interrogating the human subject (and even the subject as human).[8] Braidotti frames Irigaray's rethinking of the space and time of the subject as part of an antihumanist tradition that opens the door for thinking her work in relation to posthuman feminism and the turn to new materialism, notably its emphasis on the relationality in processes of materialization. Following the new materialist emphasis on the relationality of differences in the process of mattering, I argue that Irigarayan desire, particularly with its appeal to a sensible transcendental, insists on the importance of relationality, not just as an ethic between humans, but also as a principle of ethical relation that reimagines the limits of humanity.

In this chapter, I read both the materiality and the alterity of Irigaray's sexual difference/sexuate as forerunners of new materialism. Following Anne Van Leeuwen's framing of the embodied alterity of the sexuate as offering what Braidotti calls an "incorporeal materiality" of Irigaray's "radical feminist bodily materialism," I consider how sexual difference (the sexuate) can become a means of deterritorializing the selfsame, androcentrism, anthropocentrism, metaphysics, and—to borrow from Sylvia Wynter—"biocentric" conceptions of embodiment that have mapped the limits of existence.[9] Expanding on Braidotti's description of sexual difference as the ever-expansive space for thinking through the semiotic-material tension and Elizabeth Grosz's positing of sexual difference as a fact of the potential for life itself, I focus more closely on the ethics of desire as that which animates and ensures difference and therefore enables the material-transcendental relation to remain "touching" (a proximity that is at once a meeting and an interval) in and through difference. And here, I read Irigaray's sexuate as an important reminder that while thinking beyond the human is important, a post-Anthropocene might require a new theory of the anthropos that takes seriously the irreducible difference that conditions life as well as the desire that makes life worth living.

Today and for the foreseeable future, we are faced with the effects of a globally warmer planet that will produce increasingly hostile environments, which will in turn increase competition for resources and lay bare our societal entanglements with nature. So I ask, how do we live in an entangled, dying world? Can there be an ontoethics of an entangled anthropos that thinks the specificity and contingency of living and of responding—an affirmative, erotic chaos able to confront the destructive forms of chaos that surround us?[10] To begin to respond to these questions, I will argue that dwelling in the desire of the glorious slit is erotic—beyond notions of becoming as either absolute freedom or obligation, beyond guilt or innocence, beyond presence and absence, beyond the real and the imagined; the ethical is about an earnest relation with the ambiguity of desire as the mark of a perpetual touching that never grasps. Here the gap between at least two, who are also always not selfsame Ones, need not be figured as a wound but as the space of perpetual transformations.

I conclude by rethinking the possibility of touch beyond androcentric and even biocentric notions of matter. To depict the dynamism of touch beyond the passivity and activity binary of psychoanalysis and beyond the inert unspirited matter of metaphysical dualisms, I therefore turn to Karen Barad's interpretation of quantum physics as the foundation for a theory of agential realism. Barad contends that agential realism is "an epistemological-ontological-ethical framework that provides an understanding of the role of the human and nonhuman, material and discursive, and natural and cultural factors . . . thereby moving such considerations beyond the well-worn debates that pit constructivism against realism, agency against structure, and idealism against materialism."[11] And to articulate a certain responsibility (and response-ability) even in the midst of radical relationality,[12] I place Barad's notion of touch, conceived within this agential realist framework, in relation to Irigaray's lips to inform a more robust concept of material becomings that refuses an anthropocentric (white and phallic) nature-culture distinction and therein opens space for embodied relations in and with all others, at once beyond the human and in the midst of the specificities of human becomings.

Decapitating Subjects: From Self/Other to Same/Other

Iris van der Tuin has noted that feminist new materialisms constitute a relatively new heterogeneous, multigenerational, interdisciplinary, and geographically diverse field of study that has emerged out of multidisciplinary conversations surrounding questions about the agency of matter. Its various iterations involve the intersection of ideas not only within new materialism but also within animal studies, feminist science studies, and affect theory and queer theory. In light of this heterogeneity, feminist criticisms and critical adaptations of new materialisms abound.[13] Evelien Geerts couches new materialism as deepening poststructuralist disruptions of binary logics that devalue the corporeal while also disrupting the human-centeredness of materiality. Geerts writes, "Heavily invested in rethinking the dualist, somatophobic underpinnings of both modern and (some) poststructuralist thought, new materialisms spotlight the entanglements between the material and the discursive-cultural, whilst pushing the poststructuralist critique of the über-rational, modern human subject even further by revaluing the agential capacities of the subject's embodied materiality and of all the matter that surrounds us."[14]

In its heterogeneity, new materialism presents challenges for feminist philosophy and politics on multiple fronts. New materialist efforts to contest human-centered, and in some cases biologically centered, discourses of matter have been of particular concern for feminists. Clara Fisher notes that abstractions of materiality risk undermining the corporeality upon which decades of feminist work (and I would add especially liberal feminism) is based. Fisher writes, "For many new materialists, contemporary theorising adversely presents bodies as abstractions and removes the 'fleshiness' of corporeal existence from the feminist critical lens."[15] Sara Ahmed has criticized new materialism not primarily on theoretical grounds but on principle. Her critique highlights the tension between the field's oft-unacknowledged feminist theories of embodiment that are foundational to its theorizing. Ahmed argues that many prominent new materialist theorists ignore the long history of critical feminist engagements with the body, as though new materialism is doing something "new" without grounding itself in specific feminist cases that would necessitate its "newness."[16] I will discuss some of the theoretical challenges posed by new materialism later in this chapter; however, to construct a nuanced and constructive foundation for interrogating these theories, I first want to advance Ahmed's concern by elevating the significance of Irigaray's work for new materialism.

To frame Irigaray in relation to new materialism, I begin by thinking her critique of the selfsame as bound with the question of embodiment and the problem of sexual difference. Irigaray's work, and much feminist work broadly speaking, has critiqued the maleness of the universal subject.[17] As I have discussed throughout this book, the need for a new subjectivity, at least in Irigaray's thought, requires at least two (sexuate). This at least two of the sexuate gestures to the irreducibility of difference that must be at the heart of any ethical relation and the becoming of an ethical subjectivity. That the question of subjectivity has dominated the Anthropocene is evidence of the centrality of the human to our thought worlds. And Irigaray too is aware of this entanglement of subjectivity and anthropocentrism. Her notion of the sexuate is not exclusive to human becoming; rather, for many forms of life differentiation is required for generation. And Irigaray has explicitly made room for the possibility of more than two sexes; she has continued—even in her recent *On The Mediation of Touch*—making space for the possibility of more than two sexes. The point in her work has always been, though, that the sexuate is irreducible and not determined by its relation to culture. Irigaray's sexuate, I contend, makes space for the posthuman while also emphasizing the uniqueness of human sexuate becoming. And indeed, Braidotti places Irigaray in the posthuman legacy, describing her as part of an "anti-humanist" feminist tradition that thinks the symbolic and material together without essentializing nature on the one hand or rendering it an abstraction of culture on the other.

Broadly, posthumanism challenges the philosophical priority of the human subject for thinking life. In *Nomadic Subjects*, Braidotti asserts that contemporary feminist philosophy arrives posthumanism by way of two major methodological responses to the humanist, or modernist, prioritization of universals and the dualisms that enable such universals: the posthumanist and antihumanist approaches. Humanism here is characterized by the prioritization of the human subject, which is posited philosophically in universal terms. Postmodernity, which includes post*humanist*[18] and antihumanist critiques, throws such universals into question. And poststructuralism deconstructs modernity's assumed relationship between language and representation, pointing to the inconsistencies and erasures internal to processes of meaning making. The nondualistic, relational models of becoming posited in poststructuralism—especially in late-twentieth-century Continental thought—disturb the boundaries of identity that mark being human in the world. And within the world of "posts," posthumanist and antihumanist *feminist* methodologies attend specifically to internal contradictions of gender, sex, and sexuality constitutive of a universal subjectivity.

For the posthumanist, socially constructed categories generate the material conditions for universals and the possibility of the self. As a critique of modernity's figment of the neutral universal subject, the posthumanist feminist approach to the question of subjectivity exposes norms and universals as constructed through social, political, and historical conditions that enable a particular difference to take precedence over another. In short, a posthumanist approach emphasizes the ways a particular idea of the human becomes the spokesperson for all humanity. Braidotti puts Judith Butler in this camp and argues that Butler's emphasis on social constructivism, or in Butler's terms a sociocultural matrix, risks figuring bodies as matter being carried along in human history.[19]

Braidotti identifies the antihumanist as a second major feminist methodological approach for challenging traditional Western philosophical and theological models of the subject. Unlike posthumanist feminists, the antihumanists move beyond the language of constructed differences that support subject/object or self and other distinctions to a broader examination of the processes of differentiation that enable sameness and difference. This antihumanist turn to the processes of differentiation is representative of much of the Continental feminist philosophical and psychoanalytic tradition. Also implicit in this antihumanist work is the relationship to phenomenology, in particular, a phenomenological emphasis on the ethical implications of humanist epistemologies. As I have discussed previously, the ethical turn in phenomenology, particularly through the work of Levinas, raised early questions about the relationship between sameness and otherness in the formation of subjectivity. The subject here is no longer about an I that assumes the I exists but about the movement toward sameness that secures the idea of the *I* as identical to the *I* itself. In terms that resonate with linguistic psychoanalytic interpretations of the ethical calamity of such a subjectivity, one could say that the movement of the humanist and/or modern subject is one in which identity involves the annihilation of difference in order to secure the illusion of wholeness.

It is at this intersection (or collision) of the psychoanalytic with phenomenology at the point of ethics that Irigaray becomes particularly significant for foregrounding posthumanism as a necessarily political, ethical, and philosophical enterprise. The materiality and alterity offered in the desire that Irigaray's lips evoke refuse the passivity attributed to matter, the related association of women with matter, and women's sexuality with passivity—resonating with new materialist feminist concerns. Since I agree here with Braidotti about the significance of Irigaray's legacy, let me take a moment to frame Irigaray as belonging to an antihumanist vein of thinkers who have complicated the false dichotomy between sameness and otherness through the question of embodiedness by way of the ethical turn in transcendental phenomenology.

Thinking Materiality of Alterity beyond Sameness: The Sensible Transcendental

Anne Van Leeuwen frames new materialists as inheritors of transcendental phenomenology vis-à-vis Irigaray, arguing that Irigaray's reconceptualization of materiality is a precursor for new materialist theorizing. Transcendental phenomenology, as it emerges through Husserl, emphasizes the immanence of philosophical inquiry. It is committed to a certain science of discovery through a transcendental method. Van Leeuwen frames new materialists' critical view of phenomenology as follows: As an inquiry into how things appear, phenomenology is incapable of thinking difference. Phenomenology "contain[s] the emergence of difference within the purview of sameness or identity."[20] The appearance of the other depends on my perception such that my perception becomes foundational to the other's becoming. In this instance, transcendence is reduced to immanence because that which transcends my consciousness remains dependent on my consciousness as an uninterrupted selfsame truth. New materialist calls for reimagining materiality read through the ethical thrust of their disruptions of modern subjectivity situate the field in relation to the ethical turn in phenomenology of which Irigaray is part. Irigaray has, after all, similarly criticized the transcendental method on the basis that it reduces immanence to foundation. As discussed in chapter 5's criticism of the regime of visibility, for example, Irigaray has argued that philosophical perception has been constructed in relation to a notion of sense as an extension of a phallogocentric notion of the self.

Reading Irigaray's use of the sexuate in *Sharing the World*, Van Leeuwen contends that Irigaray's appeal to sexuate difference refuses the reduction of immanence to foundation that would typify a reductive transcendental method. Van Leewen notes that Irigaray posits sexuate difference as a dynamic becoming of difference and that this dynamism is a consequence of an at-least two who are prior to perception, in the phenomenological sense. Irigaray rethinks sense perception by emphasizing the need to rethink both alterity and materiality in relation to a sexuate "horizon of sense." Van Leeuwen adds that it is precisely because of this focus on alterity that the sexuate as a "ground" of difference in Irigaray is not reducible to a new universal. Van Leeuwen writes, "The appearance of irreducible alterity and the existence of at least two worlds as contemporaneous . . . suggests that she does not appeal to the recognition of alterity as a foundation for a difference of worlds."[21] Rather, sexuate difference is always relational; it is in a dynamic process of becoming, such that "the appearance of alterity is coextensive with the disclosure of a horizon of sense that, in virtue of the persistence of alterity, remains fundamentally open or equivocal (i.e., 'irreducible to a single world')."[22] As Van Leeuwen's reading of Irigaray suggests, Irigaray disrupts the "foundational" status of immanence and posits sexuation as the very possibility of radical alterity—constituting a revision of phenomenological perception.[23]

Irigaray's emphasis on rethinking alterity as the horizon of sense refuses a dialectic of recognizing/collapsing that alterity through sameness and, I would add, places Irigaray in the Levinasian phenomenological tradition. Like Emmanuel Levinas, her work reimagines a subjectivity in which selfhood is not constituted through a movement of sameness. This work shifts the conversation from the constitution of self-other distinction to the ethics of the economy of sameness through which differentiation emerges. So what is the significance of this rethinking of embodiment as a relation to alterity?

As Van Leeuwen describes it, Irigaray's notion of sense is not a static given to be experienced in a particular way, but it is, following Beauvoir, a condition of disclosure.[24] For Irigaray, the materiality of alterity is critical to a phenomenology that does not elide difference with sameness—it is critical for a subjectivity that is not constituted through the annihilation of the difference of the other. But in order for this materiality of alterity to avoid the return to foundation, it must be sexuate. Irigaray famously dubs this notion of becoming through materiality and alterity the "sensible transcendental." As I have suggested in previous chapters, the sensible transcendental emerges as a critical response to what Irigaray contends is Western culture's dissociation of body and spirit, or immanence and transcendence more broadly. Diagnosing the failure of "our age" to cultivate sexual difference, she writes, "It is surely a question of the dissociation of body and soul, of sexuality and spirituality, of the lack of passage for the spirit, for the god, between the inside and the outside, the outside and the inside, and of their distribution between the sexes in the sexual act."[25]

In contrast to this separation, the sensible transcendental, as "the material texture of beauty," holds together these traditionally separate realms and reimagines the structure of relations beyond binaries, including the metaphysical ascriptions of verticality to transcendence and horizontality to immanence. Read this way, the sensible transcendental disrupts the distinctions of metaphysics.[26] As Irigaray suggests in *Ethics*, in the space of relation between the irreducible two, there is "a *birth* into a transcendence . . . still in the world of the senses . . . still physical and carnal, and already spiritual."[27] Irigaray's insistence is that without sexual difference, there can be no ethics, no relation to alterity. And that alterity is possible only through a rethinking of its relation to the sensible world. But the sensible transcendental is not a collapsing of one into the other. It is not a movement through negation of difference. Anne Caldwell emphasizes that the sensible transcendental is a "conceptual mediation [that] never loses its relation to matter and difference."[28] For Irigaray, the sensible transcendental promises a remaking of both materiality and transcendence that defies altogether the sacrificial economy by which subjectivity and social life itself are established through the exclusion or sacrifices of the materiality of difference.[29] As such, her sensible transcendental is part of a rethinking of dialectics beyond the movement of sameness.[30] It intertwines "abstraction and materiality in order to insist on the need to retain the otherness of the other," as the very foundation of ethical relation in Irigaray.[31]

The sensible transcendental conjures multiple dimensions of Irigaray's project in regard to thinking the feminine and materiality beyond sameness. Tamsin Lorraine's *Irigaray and Deleuze* explores the term in relation to Irigaray's efforts to establish a divine feminine in order to enable women to provide a mirror to themselves for their own becoming.[32] Because of its association with Irigaray's thinking of the divine, religious studies and theology scholars have often focused on the importance the term holds for valuing immanence in the relation to God that doesn't return God to masculine sameness.[33] Philosophers have often emphasized the significance of Irigaray's sensible transcendental for rethinking materiality beyond its relation to the inertness of matter, finitude, and incompleteness.[34] But whether one emphasizes the alterity of immanence or the immanence of alterity, the term holds together immanence with radical alterity beyond signification. Rosi Braidotti has called this a "nonhierarchical or horizontal transcendence,"[35] emphasizing its disruption of the spatial and temporal dimensions of subjectivity.[36] So when we read Irigaray's notion of the sensible transcendental, we must keep in mind that she is thinking beyond metaphysical distinctions while also being conscientious about the importance of safeguarding alterity.[37] The sensible transcendental ensures that sexuate difference is always in a dynamic becoming in and with one's embodied others. It gestures to the materiality and alterity of relationality, which refuses binary oppositions as well as the illusion of wholeness that results from positing difference within the selfsame structures of a symbolic.

Irigaray's sensible transcendental illuminates the type of perception that her notion of touch elicits. Irigaray has expanded upon her notion of touch over the years, and she has framed her concepts of touch and matter by critiquing everything from Ancient Greek philosophical uses of *phusis* and *dunamis* to Merleau-Ponty's notion of perception. What I want to underscore, though, is that Irigaray's notion of touch is not a phenomenology of touch in any traditional sense. Irigaray emphasizes sexuation as a condition of human existence, such that all humans are born of two, and this two is only the beginning. Prior to discourse, our bodies are in relation to themselves and other bodies and other spaces, inside and outside, through touch. Thus, in relation to the phenomenological emphasis on becoming through perception, touch is not something I simply do; I become in and through touching. And, importantly, for Irigaray, this ontological relation is also ethical because it is the possibility of being in relation to others.

Irigaray, Deleuze, and Antihumanism

In the humanist tradition, binary thinking and its axes of differentiation (to borrow from critical theory), such as assexualization/racialization/naturalization, frame human interactions with each other and with the world. These polar arrangements of differences effectively map the territory and the limits of that world in oppositional terms. Braidotti insists that Irigaray's reimagining of sexual difference in terms of relationality, which refuses reductions to the either/or of axial thinking, situates her squarely in the antihumanist tradition and therefore makes her a precursor to posthumanism.[38] And Braidotti further reads Irigaray's reimagining of the immanent and transcendent and of materiality and spirit in the sensible transcendental as part of a broader notion of relational becoming that resonates with Gilles Deleuze and Félix Guattari's emphasis on rhizomatic relations and with feminist adaptations of their work.

In contrast to the mapping that structures relations through limits, Deleuze and Guattari's language of rhizomes draws on the nonhuman, vegetal world for thinking relationality; it reaches in and through the ground of being literally and figuratively to embody and represent interconnectedness.[39] By emphasizing the interwovenness of differences as part of dynamic processes of holding earth/ground/being together, rhizomatic thinking shows that territory is not an inevitable or inert thing. It reveals that territory is created through territorialization, a process of making the ground or territory that constitutes the limits of being.[40] Through rhizomatic thinking, one can decolonize the notion of territory, in effect deterritorializing the space and time of human and nonhuman relations. This ungrounding, or deterritorialization of territory, Braidotti says, characterizes the antihumanist response.

Relationality, conceived in terms of a deep, radical interconnectedness like that exhibited in rhizomes, deconstructs a static ontology and locates ethics in an embodied relationality prior to the representations of difference in language. In so doing, it engenders a monist rather than dualist notion of becoming. And yet, the monism is decidedly "nondeterministic"[41] in a manner that paves the way for rethinking "accepted ideas about what constitutes the boundaries of our common humanity."[42] Braidotti writes the following about the consequences of the Irigarayan (and Deleuzian) relational models of the subject: "The categorical distinction that separated the Human from his naturalized others has shifted, taking the humanist assumptions about what constitutes the basic unit of reference for the 'human' into a spin."[43] Theirs is a disruption based on interconnection that affirms radical difference as the possibility of a new commonality of beings in the world together—it is, according to Braidotti, a new monism—a principle of relationality as that which becomes unifying but does so by virtue of its plurality and dynamism. By this reading, the antihumanist developments represented both in Irigaray's work and in Deleuzian feminist work emphasize an embodied relationality of difference that, in conjunction with posthumanist feminist thinkers, foreground the posthuman conditions for reimagining matter itself as constituted in, by, and with, or alongside, difference rather than deterministically constitutive of difference. And this relationality challenges the limits of what constitutes the human to the extent of deposing the Anthropocene.[44] But where does this deposition leave us, particularly as it relates to politics?

Sexual Difference and Nomadic Subjectivity

Consistent with postmodern feminist deconstruction, particularly the branch that claims an antihumanist Deleuzian legacy, Braidotti advocates the radical destabilization of truth claims that a focus on difference enables. She empha-sizes, however, that Irigaray's relationality and Deleuze's rhizomatics do not sufficiently trouble the power of binary thinking and its manifestation of racial and sexual injustices. Within its exposure of the "internal contradic-tions" of binary thinking, rhizomatic thought becomes so deterritorialized, potentially so nomadic, that it has no ground from which to stake ethical and political claims. Binary thinking may be disrupted, but its power to reterritorialize is not. To this end, Braidotti argues that a rhizomatic emphasis on the transversing and traversing of territory does not dislodge or disrupt the traditional dialectical model of thinking in terms of axes of difference. So while rhizomatic thought deterritorializes by revealing inescapable inter-connectedness, rhizomatics can also imply a certain relativism with regard to relationality that does not offer a space of resistance to the economy of sameness that underlies binary thinking. After all, radical deterritorialization undermines the notion of ground, rendering ground itself a space-time of relation and thereby undermining the specificity of materiality in particu-lar times and spaces (and interior/exterior) upon which subjectivity relies. Braidotti attempts to find a way to affirm the radicality of rhizomatic deterritorialization with the focus on the particularities of embodiment that one gets in Irigaray.

Braidotti's own posthuman theory of nomadic feminism critically adapts both Irigaray's relational becoming and Deleuzian rhizomatics as an alterna-tive to the binary thinking that maps the Anthropocene as human versus nonhuman territories. In her nomadic feminism, the space-time of matter itself becomes relational. Rather than conceiving of difference along axes of sexualization, racialization, naturalization, and so on, she refuses the either/or thinking of axial thinking. Nomadic feminism shifts conversations within feminism away from either social constructivism or essentialism; it redirects the question of sexual difference away from either male or female difference, from either biology or culture, from either materiality or discursivity.

Though sexual difference theory has been marginalized because of the difficulty of conceptualizing it within a cisheteronormative discursive frame-work, Braidotti's own work continues to take sexual difference seriously as a space for thinking through the dynamism of embodied living. Her notion of sexual difference is not unlike Irigaray's sexuate in that they share an emphasis on a prediscursive materiality of irreducible difference that is the ground of life.[45] But unlike Irigaray's sexuate, Braidotti's emphasis on sexual difference has been the basis for a more decidedly feminist posthuman philosophical ethic. In *Nomadic Theory*, Braidotti articulates different philosophical and political theorizations of sexual difference. Here, she explores Irigaray's psychoanalytically informed critique of sexual (in)difference as the basis of metaphysical discourse, as well as Moira Gatens and Genevieve Lloyd's depiction of sexual difference as a nondualistic embodied fact that structures all subjectivity. Here, there is no universal singular subjectivity, but a philosophy of the subject based on a new monism, where the (nonuniversal) monism holds that all subjects partake in sexual difference as a ground of embodied activity. Braidotti also examines Claire Colebrook's Deleuzian-inspired reading of sexual difference as a fundamentally ethical concept.

Braidotti explains the ways in which key feminist thinkers of sexual difference imagine sexual difference for their projects and for feminism and politics: "For Irigaray, the metaphysical question of sexual difference is the horizon of feminist theory; for Grosz (1994), it is the precondition; for Butler (1993), it is the limit of the discourse of embodiment; for Braidotti (1994b), it is a negotiable, transversal, affective space. The advantage of a Deleuzian approach is that the emphasis shifts from the metaphysics to the ethics of sexual difference."[46] After having articulated the different theories of sexual difference and their implications for feminist thought and politics, Braidotti writes that despite their divergences, these theories share an emphasis on sexual difference as a concept beyond sameness. She concludes her discussion of the different theories of sexual difference by appealing to desire. Here, Braidotti elides desire with "sexuality as the vital force that deterritorializes gender and its binary system."[47]

Braidotti's return to the importance of sexuality "beyond gender" contends that the relationality sexual difference offers is a relationality of a nonmetaphysical, posthuman corporeality of desire that nomadic feminism demands.[48] Her nomadic theory thus reads sexual difference as an "affective space" that insists on materiality in a way that rhizomatic thinking alone cannot.[49] "A nomadic process of sexual differing is a permanent fracture, and it's a block of becoming positioned outside the gender system, which mobilizes untapped forces and energies and sets them to the task of sustaining processes of deterritorialization."[50] Herein, I think Braidotti captures my own sense of how the sexuate operates in Irigaray (note that Braidotti uses the term *sexual difference* as an already retheorized concept beyond metaphysics). Braidotti writes as follows: "Sexual difference is just an embodied and embedded point of departure that signals simultaneously the ontological priority of difference and its self-organizing and self-transforming force. The ontology of becoming allows difference to emerge as radical immanence, i.e., as creative evolution. . . . This emphasis on the productive nature of desire and the view of sexuality as the vital force that deterritorializes gender and its binary system is the signature of nomadic feminism."[51] Braidotti's emphasis on the ontology of becoming, rather than an ontology of being, prioritizes the embodiedness of relations beyond the relations figured through subjectivity. As a "self-organizing and self-transforming force," difference disrupts debates, such as the one between autonomy and responsibility, that are effects of a subjectivity based in identification. I want to think beyond a dialectic of sameness, as well as beyond the metaphysics of sexual difference and beyond an ontology of sexual difference as a metaphysical concept.

But I would argue that linkage of desire with sexuality, even beyond heterosexism, is better captured in the language of the eros of desire rather than in "sexuality," even if explicitly disconnected from the discursivity of gender that shapes heterosexism. My move to desire, as part of a presymbolic but not extrasensible relation that disrupts metaphysics, follows the trajectory Braidotti makes possible within Irigaray's work—but it does so without the problematic historicity of sexuality, including its immersion in cisgendered and therein heteronormative thinking that cannot be easily sidestepped just by saying or thinking so. Irigarayan desire, like that evoked in "that glorious slit" which is an opening and a self-enclosure, which is a touch and an asymptotic relation, moves/dwells/inhabits/thrives beyond metaphysics, in the space-time of the unthought. A call for an ontology of othered desire is just such an effort to describe an ethics beyond sexual difference, an ethics of the radical difference that constitutes relationality—an ethics that decades of thinking through sexual difference and its relation to metaphysics, to ontology, to politics, makes possible.[52]

The Virtuality of Matter

Braidotti argues that interest in the virtuality of matter has led to an emphasis less on what matter actually is and more on matter as a question of mattering as a process of becoming.[53] Along these lines, Luciana Parisi has taken up the question of mattering to think materiality as indeterminate and as the possibility of becoming.[54] In *Abstract Sex*, Parisi attributes the dynamism of difference to both the affective and the symbolic dimensions of embodied living. Drawing on Guattari's notion of "schizogenesis" and "mixed semiotics that combines the virtual (indeterminate) and the actual domains," [55] Parisi emphasizes differentiation as a dynamic process (semiotic and asemiotic) that occurs through the processes of becoming, where materiality offers the condition and possibility of that becoming.[56] Also invoking Spinoza's "ethics-ethology of nature," Parisi refers to this dynamic materiality as "hypernature" to emphasize the intensity of interconnectedness "of all bodies." [57] Parisi describes hypernature as a "continuum [that] delineates the potential becomings of matter: the power of nature-matter-body to mutate, to be affected by new assemblages of bodies (a bacterium, a human being, an egg cell, a microchip) that in turn affect the organization of society, culture, economics and politics."[58] Regarding Parisi's theory of matter as depicted in hypernature, Braidotti notes, "Difference emerges as pure production of becoming-molecular and the transitions or stratifications are internal to the single process of formation or of assemblage."[59] For Parisi, difference is not merely the fabric of sociality; it is the fabric of becoming, of existence itself. [60]

Parisi's work turns to questions of technological automation in a way that holds together the question of materiality with the desire for transcendence that characterizes cultural representations. She does so by resisting the binary logic that would render matter either imagined or real, either substantive or discursive.[61] Parisi considers automated computations of modern technology to examine the conditions of thought itself in order to reimagine a sensible realm beyond cognition and the representational frameworks that inform cognition.[62] As Braidotti writes, in Parisi's focus on automation and computation to disrupt semiotics, "The emphasis falls . . . on the micropolitics of relations, as a posthumanist ethics that traces transversal connections among material and symbolic concrete and discursive lines and forces."[63] In *Contagious Architecture*, for example, Parisi uses architectural theory and computational theory to investigate the relationship between ethics, politics, and the actualization or production of abstract thought that occurs in automation to posit the possibility of a way of "thinking" beyond representation. Automation includes algorithms that operate independently of logic and are instead based purely on computational relationships between the actualization of space or the production of abstract thought that occurs in computation. The most abstract of concepts that cannot be thought in human cognition can be actualized through algorithms, and these algorithms become the possibility of new spaces.[64] Parisi suggests that algorithms offer a way of thinking that exceeds the limits of human cognition and operate independently of human decision making; the nonhuman materialize the unthought. Thus, the most abstract of concepts that cannot be thought in human cognition can be actualized through algorithms, and these algorithms become the possibility of new spaces for thinking—and, I would add, potentially new ontologies.

Algorithms have become so sophisticated that they are no longer simply applications of existing knowledge but create their own representational frameworks. Parisi points to the ways algorithms in facial-detection software incorporate processes of differentiation that "impart a de-naturalization of what we know."[65] As an example, Parisi points to artist Shinseungback Kimyonghun's 2013 art installation, *Cat or Human*, which applied cat facial-recognition algorithms to recognize humans and human facial recognition algorithms to distinguish cats from humans. The mixups or failures in which the algorithm wrongly identifies cat or human indicate that algorithms assemble and interpret data differently in ways that confound human categories.

Today, Parisi acknowledges, "networks" of algorithms are confronting the primacy of abstract theorization, which was long the purview of philosophy. Turning to Deleuze's reflections on how cinema involves an automation that disrupts representational thinking and the space and time of semiotics meaning, Parisi suggests that automation of algorithms can radically disrupt thinking if we let it. She writes, "As non-human thought above all exposes pre-individual, prerepresentational affects and percepts, it also manifests itself through the fallibility of reasoning and the inability to think of the whole."[66] It is this inability to think the whole that becomes instructive: the whole was never real; it was always representation, always tied to the semiotic.

Parisi's appeal to virtuality is part of her criticism of human-centered philosophy. She casts the problem of a human-centered philosophy as its aim toward truth. Human-centered philosophy is teleological such that the aims of the philosophy become the justification for what it means to be human.[67] Virtuality therefore confronts philosophy for theorizing reality as a truth. The world of the virtual is the possibility of reality if we understand reality as part of the fabulation of living.[68] For Parisi, we need to rethink how philosophy distinguishes between theoretical and practical knowledge. We need to consider ways that automation works and to understand what it can teach us—ways it can show us how to think the horizon of thought. As she puts it, automation shows us that "practical knowledge has shifted from a function of demonstration to the transcendental task of knowing how, involving the speculative becoming of practical knowledge in and through its functions."[69]

In the case of computational or automated thinking, procedural activities have exposed a transcendentalism embedded in logical procedures themselves. Parisi is asking us to look toward this disruption of the automated thinking as a challenge to our own ways of bifurcating knowledge between thinking the known (instrumental thinking) and thinking the unknown (theorizing) in order to make thinking "toward the unthought" possible.[70] I take Parisi to be attempting to achieve a way to think about the relationality of becoming as an acknowledgment of both the indeterminacy of what it means to be human and the materiality of existence as bound to the transcendence of becoming. Essential to this focus on interconnection and relationality is a notion of the space-time of materiality that itself becomes relational. Materiality is in relation to the virtual, not entirely unlike the relation of the sensible transcendental as a disclosure of alterity that is also the horizon of worlds.

Parisi's new materialism prioritizes the medium of thought as the condition of thought, but her focus on the computational to disrupt the binary schemas of materiality doubtless risks recapitulating the primacy of thought over enfleshed bodies. My reservation is that her materialism is so tied up in a computational medium that it becomes challenging to conceive any sort of human agency or responsibility beyond the project of thinking. Still, her challenge is important inasmuch as she wants to reimagine a way of thinking (and a way of rethinking human-machine interactions) that transcends an aim toward a goal or end.[71] This work therefore offers opportunities for considering what it means to speak of posthuman futures. Parisi's petition for a "media ontology" attempts to prioritize a way of approaching being that decenters the human and endeavors to move beyond a notion of becoming as a never-ending abstract process or an outcomes-based telos. She wants "the futurity of thinking to enter the procedures of thoughts."[72]

Importantly, however, Parisi does not simply praise technology as a substitute for life itself; rather, she insists that these processes of actualization are coextensive with the human. Recalling Braidotti's description of Parisi's "mixed semiotics," this relation between the human and the nonhuman at the limits of what constitutes what we think is human (i.e., cognition, creativity, and so on) also transforms humans' relationship to the limits of their worlds.[73] Charitably reading Parisi's project in light of her effort to reimagine the sensible beyond a totalizing concept of cognition and recognition, perhaps we might take her challenge not to ask what it means to think without the human but rather to think a new nonhuman-centered "human," a new "Anthropos" altogether. This invites us to rethink agency and responsibility in relation to a horizon of materiality and alterity that opens us toward the *unthought* (a term Parisi also uses) and prompts consideration of desire as a truly other sensible transcendental—as the possibility of becoming that is a mattering beyond the human but also that remains relevant to the question of what it means to think about being human.

Becoming Undone: Toward an Incorporeal Materiality

A longtime reader of Irigaray, Elizabeth Grosz considers the entanglements of philosophy, ethics, and politics in theorizing not just subjectivity, but life itself. In *Becoming Undone*, Grosz argues that thinking beyond the human is a necessary move to acknowledge contemporary crises. Specifically, Grosz's notion of becoming undone critically adapts the dynamic not-Oneness of Irigaray's idea of becoming. For Grosz, becoming undone prioritizes a willingness to accept the inevitability and uncontrollability of transformations. In an interview published in *Qui Parle* in 2016, she adds that our becomings are so entangled with other becomings that we are "part of the domain of becoming."[74]

The trick, Grosz acknowledges, is how one rethinks the fractiousness of this becoming undone into a "creativity and politics" rather than allowing it to constitute an overwhelming anxiety.[75] As Braidotti writes of Grosz's work (taking a jab at Butler), becoming undone doesn't mean that radical alterity ends in radical "undecidability."[76] Taking up the mantle of new materialist concerns in a critical way, Grosz's recent focus on incorporeality deconstructs the opposition of materiality and ideality that risk making becoming undone a totalizing spiral of despair subject to perpetual reterritorializations (to borrow from Braidotti's language). The incorporeal locates an "ethics that is indissolubly also an ontological politics" in its resistance of the opposition of materiality and ideality, as well as in its attempt to deal with specificity.

In *The Incorporeal*, Grosz turns to the Stoics to rethink ontology itself in a way that disrupts rather than represents what is known. Although she does not address Irigaray at any length in the book, she does reference Derrida, Irigaray, and Deleuze together as thinkers of a certain type: those attempting to think nondichotomously about thought and the world such that they think the relationship between ontology, ethics, and politics together.[77] But in Grosz's focus on the "incorporeal conditions of corporeality," I see a resonance with Van Leeuwen's reading of Irigaray's sensible transcendental as positing a relationship between "the appearance of alterity belong[ing] to the very disclosure of a world, understood as a horizon of sense."[78] Grosz is attempting, like Irigaray, to reimagine the ontological in relation to the ethical but with an acknowledgment that one must somehow respond to the radical undoing that results. On the one hand, I read Grosz's becoming undone as moving away from Irigaray by thinking becoming as a certain deconstruction of the subject rather than a reconstruction. On the other hand, her notion of incorporeality is calling for a certain reconstruction through uncertainty and ambiguity that is not unlike Irigaray's notion of desire. I think it is helpful here to examine the relationship between Irigaray's reading of materiality and her reframing of desire to transform the space of tension from one of loss and lack to one of relational fecundity in the touching gap of lips.

Despite the nuances, genealogical differences, and aims of Braidotti's nomadic feminism, Pheng Cheah's nondialectical materialism, Parisi's mixed semiotics, or Elizabeth Grosz's becoming undone, all of these thinkers are in some way contending with something that Irigaray has contended with: what it means to imagine the subject as not-One, even in and of itself. And these theorizations have all asserted the primacy of a certain embodiedness (even beyond human embodiments) as the "horizon of sense . . . ineluctably inscribed by the opening of irrecuperable alterity."[79] I therefore return to Irigaray to think the difference of the at least two who are always not-One in terms of the nonconsuming and nonanxious, albeit ambiguous, desire between and sustaining them in the dynamism of their at-least-twoness.

The Mattering of Desire

As I have noted before, in *An Ethics of Sexual Difference*, Irigaray begins by arguing that ethics will require a new age altogether—one in which space and time and the very conception of subjectivity in relation to space and time would have to be reimagined. Importantly, she adds, implicitly invoking Aristotle, that this remaking includes an "evolution or transformation of forms, of the relations of *matter* and *form* and of the interval *between*."[80] In other words, the change in space and time involves a rethinking of materiality and immaterial or extramaterial realms. The interval names the relation between form and matter in this regard—between the potentiality typically ascribed matter and its fulfillment in form. The interval is the space of relation that determines whether these differences are seen as oppositional or as something else altogether.

Two sentences after calling for rethinking form and matter, Irigaray writes, "*Desire* occupies or designates the place of the *interval*. Giving it a permanent definition would amount to suppressing it as desire. Desire demands a sense of attraction: a change in the inter-relations of nearness or distance."[81] She suggests that the space between matter and form, the space between immanence and transcendence that shapes their relation and the borders of these very concepts, is a space of desire. Irigaray is clear, however, that naming the space desire does not mean that desire will have been thought through; quite the opposite. She continues: "Our age, which is often thought to be one in which the problematic of desire has been brought forward, frequently theorizes this desire on the basis of observations of a moment of tension or a moment in history, whereas desire ought to be thought as a changing dynamic whose outlines can be described in the past, sometimes in the present, but never definitively predicted."[82]

As an integral dimension of Irigaray's concept of ethics, desire designates the space of relation that shapes the two or more who are in relation to one another. How desire is configured determines how we establish the limits of bodies (conceptual and/or fleshy). Shortly following the previous passage, Irigaray draws a parallel between Freud's concept of sublimation and physics to insists that, in order for women to become subjects apart from masculine phallic desire, desire itself must be rethought apart from a sense of attraction and repulsion that reinforces the disconnect between things. She insists that thinking of desire as a relation based in lack has placed woman on the side of perpetual motion with respect to her own becoming. She writes, "In terms of contemporary physics, it could be said that she remains on the side of the electron, with all that this implies for her, for man, for their encounter."[83] Irigaray describes how an electron rotates around an axis that has a positive and negative charge. Her point: if there is only one axis, even if that axis would seem to offer difference (in the form of opposite charges), these oppositions belong to the single axis, such that all things rotate around it ceaselessly. For something truly different or other to occur, it must have its own access and its own charges. A "double pole of attraction and support" is needed to "ensur[e] the separation that articulates every encounter and makes possible speech, promises, alliances."[84]

Significantly, Irigaray concludes her introduction to *Ethics* with a section that petitions readers to *think* the "link" between "masculine and feminine" as "horizontal and vertical, terrestrial and heavenly."[85] In the midst of her commandment to think these realms, including the divine and the flesh, Irigaray invokes the crossing lips (to which I refer in chapter 3), "where the borders of the body are wed in an embrace that transcends all limits—without, however, risking engulfment."[86] The thread of desire is woven through Irigaray's critique of the separations perpetrated by metaphysics to her call for reuniting these separations anew (without collapsing one into the other). Let us retrace the thread as I have presented it: we have gone from Irigaray's call to think through sexual difference, to her demand that a new space-time-place must be imagined through a new concept of desire; to her insistence upon of a mode of relation that is dynamic but not centrifugal, and finally to the image of the lips.

Lips figure Irigaray's emphasis on the sexuate as a not-Oneness through their embodied, multiple desire. As fleshy, corporeal figurations of two that are never just one, lips constitute a dynamic "ground" for thinking about becoming beyond the Oneness of being. If Irigaray's sexuate difference is an irreducible difference that portends the dynamism of materiality and alterity, lips figure this dynamism in the flesh. This not-Oneness does not devolve into a crisis of becoming based on experience of lack. It is an experience of the fullness of desire that could inform a new ethical horizon. Braidotti explains:

> This humbling experience of not-Oneness, far from opening the doors to relativism, anchors the subject in an ethical bond to alterity, to the multiple and external others that are constitutive of that entity which, out of laziness and habit, we call the "self." The split, or the not-one nature of the subject, entails the recognition of a prediscursive structure of the "self," of a necessary loss of that which is always already there—an affective, interactive entity endowed with intelligent flesh and an embodied mind. The totality and the always-already-thereness of the corporeal self is that which must become foreclosed, and thus remain inaccessible to the reduced, but more cantonal unit that will become the socialized subject. As such, the totality and priority of the enfleshed corporeal subject—rooted in desire—is that which remains unthought at the heart of the thinking subject, because it is what drives him/her in the first place.[87]

As Braidotti suggests, in Irigaray, the "corporeal subject" is "rooted in desire." I would add that we might think the complexity of this desire as that space of the glorious slit of "La Mystérique." It is enfleshed, like desire in the lips. It is the desire of a deconstructive embrace that is also the possibility of new worlds. At issue for Braidotti, for Grosz, and for perhaps Parisi is not the alterity of Irigaray's desire, or even the remaking of materiality, but the question of what it means to live in this not-Oneness, in the space of becoming undone, in nomadism. This is in many ways a question of agency. And this agency cannot be reduced to the desire for control, lest it descend into autocracy and individualism.

Moving beyond Irigaray's investments in notions of "nature" and the natural or "biological,"[88] I hope to have shown that Irigaray's invocations of touching lips offer a notion of materiality born of othered desire that lends itself to new materialism.[89] And though I have thus far insisted that Irigaray's work remains relevant to that school of thought, I do think there are dimensions of new materialism that might help us parse Irigaray's lips in ways that will elucidate a more robust theory of desire that can speak to this question of agency and ethics together. The space and time of the sexuate, figured in the lips, marks an irreducible difference that reimagines materiality and alterity in terms of becomings, not unlike new materialist rethinkings of matter as relational. Notions of incorporeality and virtuality have reframed matter as a question of mattering—of manifestations, as well as materializations through relation beyond a notion of corporeality as fixed in the space and time of metaphysics or a dialectics of sameness.

Rethinking Materiality through Touch

"Agential realism" designates a field built around Karen Barad's innovative work on the question of mattering in new materialism.[90] Barad uses the term to describe her brand of justice-minded new materialism, which establishes a distinct performativity that does not render matter a complete abstraction. Barad's agential realism looks to inhuman matter in quantum physics as a means for reimagining relationality and focuses on how touching has the capacity to transform realities such that materiality is reconceived in desire.[91] Trained as a theoretical physicist, Barad conceives her philosophical engagements with quantum mechanics as an effort to articulate the entanglements of "human and nonhuman, material and discursive, natural and cultural factors in scientific and other practices."[92] As the quote suggests, Barad is invested in questions of living that, I would argue, have occupied Irigaray, as well as Braidotti, Grosz, and other feminists interested in ethics and materiality. Barad's consideration of the virtual as a site of possibility for what are otherwise impossible becomings involves a new way of thinking about the dynamism of materiality. Perhaps most importantly for the purposes of this book, she investigates the question of materiality as a question of touching.

In "On Touching," Barad argues that Democritean physics has long understood touch in terms of electromagnetic interaction. In this explanation, the sense one has of touching is a perception of the negative energy of the object's repulsion—again, differences have been ascribed to matter to inform a certain balance or symmetry that reinforces that relation as one of opposition. But Barad argues that quantum mechanics understands this notion of touch differently. Drawing on quantum field theory, Barad explains that electrons are the outer limits of atoms. They effectively create the limits of touch. But electrons are an infinite space of self-generating energy—they emit the virtual particles known as photons and reabsorb them. Here, the relation is not one of opposition but of touching. To borrow from Irigaray, we might say electrons, as described by Barad, double onto themselves, in a self-touching that is the very possibility of a proximity of touching others. Barad suggests that touch can therefore be reframed in terms of a certain relation not of opposites but of indeterminacy, an indeterminacy that I would argue resonates with the asymmetry of sexuate difference.

Barad insists that quantum field theory therefore offers an understanding of touch that rethinks the idea of the virtual not as immaterial but in terms of a different notion of matter, constituted, no less, through that different framing of touching. Here, the different concept of touching gives rise to the virtual as a space for conceiving a different sort of materiality.[93] Regarding the radical implications of this touching, Barad writes the following:

> Particles no longer take their place in the void; rather, they are constitutively entangled with it. As for the void, it is no longer vacuous. It is a living, breathing indeterminacy of non/being. The vacuum is a jubilant exploration of virtuality, where virtual particles—whose identifying characteristic is not rapidity (despite the common tale explaining that they are particles that go in and out of the vacuum faster than their existence can be detected) but, rather, indeterminacy—are having a field day performing experiments in being and time. That is, virtuality is a kind of thought experiment the world performs. Virtual particles do not traffic in a metaphysics of presence. They do not exist in space and time. They are ghostly non/existences that teeter on the edge of the infinitely fine blade between being and nonbeing. Admittedly, virtuality is difficult to grasp. Indeed, this is its very nature. To put it concisely, virtual particles are quantized indeterminacies-in-action.[94]

Barad's emphasis on the virtual as existing beyond the metaphysics of presence and the constraints of space and time, at some sort of "difficult to grasp" (except perhaps through the touching of thought) "edge of the infinitely fine blade between being and nonbeing" is evocative of the sexuate as I have elaborated it throughout this book. And though she does not reference Irigaray, Barad's depiction of touch quoted above resonates with Irigaray's desire, which fills the space of relation in sexuate difference. One could easily interweave Irigaray's terminology here, just as in the description of touching hands. The vacuum is lack that is transformed into fecundity. The virtual particles are like the materiality of alterity of sexuate difference. They do not traffic in the metaphysics of presence. They do not exist in space and time. They are like angels and mucous,[95] the infinitely fine interval between being and nonbeing. Admittedly, this sexuate difference is difficult to grasp because it demands and depends upon an irreducible openness; it is like eros that reaches but cannot be grasped. The materiality and alterity of sexuate difference is dynamic indeterminacies in action; it is radical desire. I will return to this point shortly.

How does this virtuality intersect with desire as the space of relation, of touching? As Barad describes the virtual in the article "Transmaterialities," matter is transformative and transformed in and through its proximity, its desire. In her discussion of the virtual, Barad writes, "Matter is caught up in its own and others' desiring fields. It cannot help but touch itself in an infinite exploration of its (im/possible) be(com)ing(s). And in touching it/self, it partners promiscuously and perversely with otherness in a radical ongoing deconstruction and (re)configuring of itself."[96] Matter here is in a process of mattering, continuously, in relation. In its "ongoing deconstruction," we might suggest, borrowing from Grosz, that matter involves a continuous becoming undone that is always interwoven with infinite other undoings. And importantly, desire is not a thing; it is "a field." That is to say, it is a space-time (beyond space and time) of proximity. Desire is a matter of touching.

Barad continues by reframing the "agency" of matter in relation to desire in the virtual. And I quote Barad at length here in order to capture the poetics of her thought experiment as a form of touching itself.[97]

> Matter is a wild exploration of trans* animacy, self-experimentations/ self-re-creations, not in an autopoietic mode, but on the contrary, in a radical undoing of "self," of individualism. Ever lively, never identical with itself, it is uncountably multiple, mutable. Matter is not mere being but its ongoing un/doing.

> Nature is agential trans*materiality/ trans-matter-reality in its
> ongoing re(con)figuring, where trans is not a matter of changing
> in time, from this to that, but an undoing of "this" and "that,"
> an ongoing reconfiguring of spacetimemattering in an iterative
> reworking of past, present, future integral to the play of the
> indeterminacy of being-time.[98]

Despite the tensions between Barad's and Irigaray's projects, I find in
Barad's language and the eros of its poetics an echo of Irigaray's early depiction
of the touching lips and its allusions to the relationship between the plurality
of desires and a dynamic relationality constitutive of multiple becomings.[99]
The interrogations of matter in the virtual particles of Barad's quantum field
theory signal a materiality of extradiscursive difference that would provide
space and time for asymmetrical becomings—becomings that refuse difference as opposite, opposition, or reversal. Similarly, Irigaray's portrayal of this
sort of difference beyond the space and time of metaphysics, in the intimate
self-touching of lips, as an embodiment that is shared and sharing in and
of itself, opens a path for a deep relationality of being that is not bound to
mattering in phallocentric or even biocentric discourse in order to be real.

For both thinkers, touch gestures toward a notion of materiality that is
transformative in and through its proximity as a threshold of desire. Barad,
referring to incorporeal particles of quantum theory, not lips, mind you,
writes the following: "Matter is an enfolding, an involution, it cannot help
touching itself, and in this self-touching it comes in contact with the infinite
alterity that it is. Polymorphous perversity raised to an infinite power: talk
about a queer intimacy! What is being called into question here is the very
nature of the 'self,' and in terms of not just being but also time."[100] I read in
Barad's rethinking of matter as a process of mattering that echoes Irigaray's
assertion in *Ethics* that ethics will require a new thinking of space and time,
of interiority and exteriority, of immanence and transcendence. What if we
thought of Irigaray's sensible transcendental as "an ongoing reconfiguring of
spacetimemattering in an iterative reworking of past, present, future integral
to the play of the indeterminacy of being-time?"[101]

The Horizon of Touch:
Rethinking Sexual Difference and New Materialism

Feminist philosopher Stacey Moran cautions that physicists can explain
how particles relate, but they cannot speak to generation of matter itself.

Moran specifically critiques Barad's notion of "entanglement" as insufficient for theorizing materiality because it ignores this gap. Referring to quantum theory's concept of "quantum decoherence," Moran argues that this gap in theory "complicates, rather than settles, the ontology of such materials."[102] Entanglement alone, she contends, cannot address "the thorny questions of how power is organized among those entities."[103] And perhaps this rather humbling reading of quantum physics is the feminist one we need to think the agency of matter in relation to the fleshiness of desire.

So, while Barad is useful for articulating a new materiality that takes seriously relationality of matter, Barad's turn to particles relating without thinking generation borders on an abstraction of touching that risks being rendered a "neutral" desire—which for Irigaray is never neutral. It is in regard to this problem of neutrality that Slavoj Žižek has suggested that new materialism attempts to posit alterity without thinking through sexual difference.[104] I take Žižek's point, which also serves as a major point of emphasis as a reminder that the question of sexual difference regrounds radical abstractions of materiality. And I would add that Irigaray's sexuate, particularly because of its grounding in her reimagined notion of desire, offers a uniquely important contribution to the ethical and political implications of virtual mattering or incorporeal corporealities. Her sexuate remains an irreducible yet also indeterminate difference that holds materiality and alterity together, as a horizon, without collapsing one into the other.

Scholarship that thinks sexual difference in the manner of new materialism, and Irigaray with Barad specifically, is increasing—and largely out of the concerns with politics that prompted the return to materiality in the wake of postmodern disruptions.[105] Alison Stone's work frames Irigaray's interest in the question of materiality as tied to the question of agency. I agree with Stone and would argue that Irigaray's ethics and politics attempt to attribute agency to materiality without the snares of identity that one finds in liberal notions of autonomy.[106] Gail Schwab too makes an important argument about the importance of desire for Irigaray's refiguring of the subject in this regard.[107] But Stone also asserts that Irigaray relies on a relationship of the feminine to matter that she cannot undo because the feminine becomes a mark of the something that might be able to imagine and become differently from the selfsame.[108] Stone, referencing Barad's work, appeals to the need consider the relationship between physiological impacts and processes of materialization, understood as cultural processes. As Stone frames the dilemma, there would be an inherent paradox in the use of sexuate difference as a means to render materiality indeterminate;

however, I have insisted throughout this book that this sort of paradox is a dilemma of *reading* Irigaray; it is not Irigaray's dilemma.

In their 2016 article, Evelien Geerts and Iris van der Tuin also place Barad's work in conversation with Irigaray's notion of sexual difference. Claiming a practice of "diffractive reading" that draws on both Donna Haraway's work and on Barad's adaptation of it as "intra-action," Geerts and van der Tuin suggest that Irigaray offers an example of a feminist reading of mutual recognition of one's alterity that takes sexual difference into account.[109] Here Geerts and van der Tuin are reading Irigaray's disruption of representation as a reflection of the one. They contend that Barad's notion of "intra-action" similarly moves away from a "representationalist ontology and epistemology where the knowing subject, the object that is being represented, and the produced representations or knowledge are seen as separately existing entities."[110] And in this regard, we might return again for support to Van Leeuwen's argument about Irigaray's reframing of phenomenology, even if Van Leeuwen might demand a rethinking of the language of "recognition." In either case, this recognition, or perhaps making space for the alterity of the other, is what leads Geerts and van der Tuin to Barad's description of two hands touching in "On Touching" to intimate the place of sexual difference in her work. For readers of Irigaray, this touching may seem familiar:

> When two hands touch, there is a sensuality of the flesh, an exchange of warmth, a feeling of pressure, of presence, a proximity of otherness that brings the other nearly as close as oneself. Perhaps closer. And if the two hands belong to one person, might this not enliven an uncanny sense of the otherness of the self, a literal holding oneself at a distance in the sensation of contact, the greeting of the stranger within? So much happens in a touch: an infinity of others—other beings, other spaces, other times—are aroused.
>
> When two hands touch, how close are they? What is the measure of closeness? Which disciplinary knowledge formations, political parties, religious and cultural traditions, infectious disease authorities, immigration officials, and policy makers do not have a stake in, if not a measured answer to, this question?[111]

It's rather surprising that Geerts and van der Tuin don't examine Irigaray's touching lips here, given the fact that they are interested in the question of sexual difference in Irigaray and the disruptive capacity of touch in Barad. As I see it, the two hands touching that Barad describes invoke and evoke the lips in the language of proximity and otherness, as well as the "holding oneself at a distance" that connotes Irigaray's interval and the "stranger within" that resonates with Irigaray's notion of woman being other unto herself.[112] To riff on Barad, in order to attend more clearly to the plurality of desire that the sexuate engenders, I offer you as follows: "When two [lips] touch, how close are they?"[113] I do think Barad's notion of the virtual shares much with Irigaray's sensible transcendental and might be useful for framing the sort of radical touching that Irigaray's lips invoke—where touchings are mutually constitutive of their differences and their pleasures, of self and Other, "touching it/self."[114] This is a touching that transforms distinctions between the incorporeal and corporeality, the material and the discursive, and reimagines these relationships in terms of entanglements, of nondialectical, nonteleological desire of becomings. To borrow from Barad, which I have argued is to borrow from Irigaray, this is a relational ontology of intra-active touch.[115]

Barad's turn to the inhuman realm of the virtual is a means to imagine a relational ontology that does not privilege the human. "What if it is only in facing *the inhuman—the indeterminate non/being non/becoming of mattering and not mattering*—that an ethics committed to the rupture of indifference can arise?"[116] Irigaray's touching lips point to the limits of the human and yet also to a reminder that there is still something of the human that might be reimagined rather than abandoned altogether.[117] As Irigaray writes in *Vegetal Being*, there is a "risk" involved in returning to human touchings.[118] The lips remind us that the context of touching matters: lips are fleshy, but, I add, they are not the instrumental hands of a phallocentric phenomenology or a dehistoricized virtuality. Perhaps by thinking the virtual in relation to the fleshy self-affection of touching lips, we might locate a reimagined Anthropos based in a responsibility to the radical alterity of materiality, both distinctly human and beyond.

In, *Sharing the Fire*, Irigaray writes that the "call of the other already lies" in touch. But for Irigaray, the desire that enables touching is a desire cultivated by dwelling in one's own flesh.[119]

> Only the flesh of the other, as a flesh present to us, can give us back our self-affection. Self-affection of the other can bring us back to our own self-affection in particular through touch, because in this touch a call of the other already lies. As such it reminds us of the properties of life, in particular of its link with

226 | Desire beyond Identity

the other. However, if we have not opened in ourselves the void
space that the respect for the difference of the other involves,
we do not perceive all that their touch tells to us.[120]

In *Sharing the Fire*'s emphasis above on the importance of desire, incarnation,
and the possibility of dwelling together, Irigaray's suggestion that we have to
be "opened in ourselves" in order to "perceive all that their [the other's] touch
tells to us" strikes me as reminiscent of the lips, whose self-affection would
be a condition of sexuate desire—marked by an openness of that glorious
slit that is the occasion for a touch that is erotic in its most corporeal and
ambiguous sense. And though Irigaray's multiple invocations of lips in *On
the Mediation of Touch* appear as part of a list of touchings (of hands, souls
of feet, and eyelids), I maintain that the lips figure desire in relation to the
history of these questions of ethics, ontology, and subjectivity, uniquely.

Conclusion

At the end of her essay on Irigaray and Sartre, Gail Schwab writes that the
worlds that Irigaray's sexuate desire are meant to open up are to be shared,
but because of their irreducibility, they are never fully available to one
another. "Part of the tragic paradox of [Irigaray's] *Sharing the World* is that
we are forever alienated from that other world the other sees and in which
the other dwells."[121] Despite this paradox, Schwab says there is "an opening
that would allow us both egress from our own world and entrance into
another—totally new and previously unimagined and unimaginable—where
we can go together."[122] I am drawn by Schwab's words in particular because
they speak not only to the radical remaking of worlds that Irigaray demands
but also to the importance of thinking the space of irreducible difference as
reconfiguring desire as an opportunity for a new freedom. Here the idea of
"freedom" is reimagined; it is no longer "to lift oneself above nature with
the help of a God who is 'hidden,' necessary but hidden."[123] Irigaray does
not pretend that thinking the permanent fracture of sexual difference in
terms of a horizon will be easy. And Schwab suggests that the paradoxical
"sharing" is tragic. It's tragic because we still haven't figured out how to
desire differently.

Can we read the gap of the irreducibility of the sexuate not as a permanent fracture but, with Irigaray, as a shared horizon, as a possibility of
becomings in order to desire differently? Can we read the lips as ushering

in a different desire altogether that might reshape even Irigaray's notion of sharing as offering the "separation and alliance" that speaks to a certain relational freedom?[124] Perhaps the glorious slit, this vulnus/vulva (to borrow from "La Mystérique") may be a source of fracturing our becomings, but it need not simply be a wound, the opening that must be violently sutured. It is a gap ensconced by labial folds, touching lips.

Beyond the binary or otherwise identitarian arrangements of gender, race, and sexuality, lips figure a new materiality that emerges in the spaces where discourses and bodies (and the discourse of bodies) fail us. The slit transforms the wound into a space of eros in the full ambiguity of its differential relation and yet also in the specificity of its fleshiness. There is no suture here, no bridge from one to the other, as though the depths are reducible to a single crossing. There is only touching that reimagines the relation of that which has been rendered a wound, a lack, and an absence, toward a new fecund fragmentation that refuses universalization. This is desire cultivated by the lips in their infinite nonmeeting that figures the singularities of becomings as always in relation (as always at least two) and the threshold between them that occasions their pleasure. The importance of thinking the desire is that it gestures to the generativity of relations between us—a relationality that depends on our shared existence and the space and time of a world we create through our proximity.

My intent has been to return to touching lips to locate a reading of Irigarayan embodiment not as a raw material or resource, not simply as the stuff of history, nor as the potential through which one achieves transcendence, but rather as a condition of relationality in alterity, in the asymmetry of difference and the ambiguity therein of desire. I hope that this reading allows for a reimagining of matter as a dynamic field of desire, based in the proximity of differences, that opens a space for thinking the radical alterity of relationality that constitutes a robust shared existence.

Notes

Introduction

1. I offer my gratitude to one of my anonymous readers for helping me clarify the flow of my argument.

2. Irigaray continues to use both *sexual difference* and *sexuate difference*, noting that she prefers the term *sexuate*. In this book, I use both terms but invoke *sexuate* when I want to emphasize the uniqueness of her philosophy of sexual difference as distinct from the tradition of occluding sexual difference.

3. Though Lacan looms large in Irigaray's work, Laura Roberts reminds us that both Margaret Whitford and Michelle Boulous Walker have explored other influences on Irigaray's psychoanalytic lens, including Melanie Klein, Donald Winnicott, and Cornelius Castoriadis. See Laura Roberts, *Irigaray and Politics: A Critical Introduction* (Edinburgh: Edinburgh University Press, 2019), 4, 10.

4. Maggie Nelson, *The Argonauts* (Minneapolis: Graywolf, 2015), 62.

5. My invocation of relational ontology borrows from Emma Jones, who has elaborated the relationality that constitutes an ontology of the sexuate in Irigaray. Jones offers an especially nuanced reading of Irigaray's project as distinct from both Heidegger's and Lacan's divergent understandings of ontology. See Emma R. Jones, *Being as Relation in Luce Irigaray* (New York: Springer, 2023).

6. A more contemporary trend in Irigaray studies that follows a more generous engagement with Irigaray made possible by decades of work fostered by the Irigaray Circle. See https://www.irigaray.org.

7. See Christos Hadjioannou, "Can Our Being in the World Remain in the Neuter?," in *Towards a New Human Being*, ed. Luce Irigaray, Mahon O'Brien, and Christos Hadjioannou (New York: Springer, 2019), 195.

8. See Lynne Huffer, *Are the Lips a Grave? A Queer Feminist on the Ethics of Sex* (New York: Columbia University Press, 2013).

9. Throughout this text, I use the asterisk with the term *trans** to gesture to the multiplicity of histories and experiences, including in some instances an

anti-identitarianism, that *trans* names. For additional discussion related to the use of *trans**, see Katy Steinmetz, "The Oxford English Dictionary Added 'Trans.': Here's What the Label Means," *Time*, April 23, 2018, https://time.com/5211799/what-does-trans-asterisk-star-mean-dictionary/.

10. State-level bathroom bills that require people to use the restroom corresponding to the gender assigned to them at birth provide one example.

11. Sara Ahmed, *Living a Feminist Life* (Durham, NC: Duke University Press, 2017), 158.

12. Calvin Warren, "Improper Bodies: A Nihilistic Meditation on Sexuality, the Black Belly, and Sexual Difference," *Palimpsest* 8, no. 2 (2019): 42.

13. See Emily Anne Parker's insightful explanation of Irigaray's concept of nature, which rejects the mechanized notion of nature in scientific discourse. See *Elemental Difference and the Climate of the Body* (New York: Oxford University Press, 2021), 82–83.

14. Irigaray refers to the "at least two" of women's pleasure that marks women's sexuation at several points in *This Sex*. For example, early in the text, Irigaray chastises Western culture for denying space for women's pleasure by casting her as lack, and then reminds the reader that woman has "that contact of *at least two* (lips) which keeps woman in touch with herself, but without any possibility of distinguishing what is touching and what is touched." Luce Irigaray, *This Sex Which Is Not One*, trans. Catherine Porter (Ithaca, NY: Cornell University Press, 1985), 26. For an overview of critical interpretations of Irigaray's notion of the sexuate, see Rebecca Hill, "The Multiple Readings of Irigaray's Concept of Sexual Difference," *Philosophy Compass*, 11 (2016): 390–401.

15. bell hooks, *Writing beyond Race: Living Theory and Practice* (New York: Routledge, 2012), 190.

16. Hortense Spillers, "Critical Theory in Times of Crisis," *South Atlantic Quarterly* 119, no. 4 (2020): 683.

17. Anne Carson, *Eros the Bittersweet: An Essay* (Princeton: Princeton University Press, 2014), 171.

18. Louis A. Ruprecht Jr., *Reach without Grasping: Anne Carson's Classical Desires* (New York: Lexington, 2022), xvii.

19. Luce Irigaray, *The Mediation of Touch* (Cham, Switzerland: Palgrave MacMillan, 2024), 204.

20. See Judith Butler, "Bodies That Matter," in *Engaging with Irigaray: Feminist Philosophy and Modern European Thought*, ed. Carolyn Burke, Naomi Schor, and Margaret Whitford (New York: Columbia University Press, 2013), 141–73.

21. I adopt the language of queer in its radical sense of disruption—as a naming of a space beyond the categories of sex and gender—though I insist the disruption is not simply a negation of normativity. I read queer as a space generated not through self-naming as much as a materialization of alterity, and with

José Esteban Muñoz, as a temporality different from "straight" historical time and disruptive of the politics of recognition. See the special issue of *Differences: A Journal of Feminist Cultural Studies* 26, no. 1 (2015), and José Esteban Muñoz, *Cruising Utopia, 10th Anniversary Edition: The Then and There of Queer Futurity* (New York: New York University Press, 2019).

22. Jared Sexton, *Black Men, Black Feminism: Lucifer's Nocturne* (Cham, Switzerland: Palgrave Macmillan, 2018), 79.

23. Fred Moten, "Blackness and Nothingness (Mysticism in the Flesh)," *The South Atlantic Quarterly* 112, no. 4 (2013): 737–80.

24. Frank Wilderson III, *Red, White and Black: Cinema and the Structure of U.S. Antagonisms* (Durham, NC: Duke University Press, 2010), 58.

25. Parker, *Elemental Difference*, 276.

26. Jacques Derrida, "At This Very Moment in This Work Here I Am," trans. Ruben Berezdivin, in *Re-Reading Levinas*, ed. Robert Bernasconi and Simon Critchley (Indianapolis: Indiana University Press, 1991), 14.

27. Spillers, "Critical Theory in Times of Crisis," 683.

Chapter 1

1. Luce Irigaray, *An Ethics of Sexual Difference*, trans. Carolyn Burke and Gillian C. Gill (Ithaca: Cornell University Press, 1993), 5.

2. Understanding this desire in the fullness of its potential to move beyond Irigaray's own commitments requires an appreciation for the ways Irigarayan desire is set apart from the genealogy of thinkers who have informed her work.

3. Throughout this book, I will use both the terms *sexual difference* and the *sexuate* to refer to the irreducible difference prior to discourse, as both terms appear in Irigaray's work.

4. Jacques Lacan, "The Mirror Stage as Formative of the *I* Function as Revealed in Psychoanalytic Experience," in *Écrits: A Selection*, trans. Alan Sheridan (New York: Tavistock, 1977), 92.

5. Lacan, "The Mirror Stage," 78.

6. Jacques Lacan, "A Love Letter," in *Feminine Sexuality: Jacques Lacan and the École Freudienne*, ed. Juliet Mitchell and Jacqueline Rose (New York: Norton, 1983), 151.

7. Lacan, "A Love Letter," 150.

8. Carolyn Burke offers a more detailed history of Irigaray's relationship to Lacan. See "Irigaray through the Looking Glass," *Feminist Studies* 7, no. 2 (1981): 288–306.

9. Ewa Plonowska Ziarek, "Toward a Radical Female Imaginary: Temporality and Embodiment in Irigaray's Ethics," *Diacritics* 28, no. 1 (1998): 63.

10. For a more robust reading of Irigaray's project in relation to Lacan's, see Elizabeth Weed, "The Question of Style," in *Engaging with Irigaray: Feminist Philosophy and Modern European Thought*, ed. Carolyn Burke, Naomi Schor, and Margaret Whitford (New York: Columbia, 1994), 79–110. See also Maggie Berg, "Luce Irigaray's 'Contradictions': Poststructuralism and Feminism," *Signs* 17, no. 1 (1991).

11. Since Lacan has articulated the structure of a symbolic order in relation to a masculine imaginary (which he nonetheless deems neutral), any "Other" to this subject is already inscribed in the masculine subject's discursive universe; whether in the assignment of roles within the domestic sphere or in language about God, the subject was always masculine. Except for her assertion that the phallus is not a neutral signifier, Irigaray is in many ways not saying anything structurally different from Lacan here. Her emphasis on the need to overcome this reality is what makes her such an important reader of Lacan. See Irigaray, *Ethics*, 6–7.

12. Luce Irigaray, *Éthique de la différence sexuelle* (Paris: Les Éditions de Minuit, 1984), 59.

13. Irigaray, *Ethics*, 93.

14. Irigaray, 55.

15. Irigaray, 126.

16. For an in-depth analysis of Irigaray's reception and interpretation of Levinas, see Tina Chanter's "Levinas and the Question of the Other," in her *Ethics of Eros: Irigaray's Re-writing of the Philosophers* (New York: Routledge, 1995), 170–224.

17. While recognition by the other is necessary to Hegel's formulation of the subject, that recognition is arguably not a movement of the other toward the self but a reflection of the self projected onto the other and returned to the self.

18. Emmanuel Levinas, *Totality and Infinity: An Essay on Exteriority*, 3rd ed. trans. Alphonso Lingis (Norwell, MA: Kluwer, 1991), 77.

19. Emmanuel Levinas, *Totality and Infinity*, 174.

20. Luce Irigaray, "Questions to Emmanuel Levinas," in *The Irigaray Reader*, ed. Margaret Whitford (Malden, MA: Blackwell, 1992), 181.

21. For further discussion of Levinas's use of the erotic in relation to questions of embodiment, and Irigaray's related criticisms, see Irina Poleshchuk, "Unfolding Flesh towards the Other: Levinas' Perspective of Maternity and the Feminine," *Problemos* 84 (January 2013): 138–52.

22. Poleshchuk, "Unfolding Flesh," 142.

23. As noted in the introduction, Irigaray's references to an "at least two" of the lips elicits the multiplicity of women's pleasure as a non-assimilative model of desire. And this "at least two" of the lips extends to an "at least two" of sexual difference. Rebecca Hill emphasizes the complexity of this move in relation to Irigaray's interlocutors as both a multiplicity of sexuate persons and the potential for multiplicity in their sexuate individuations. See Hill, "The Multiple Readings," 393–94.

24. Ziarek, "Toward a Radical Female Imaginary," 60.

25. See John D. Caputo, "Dionysus vs. the Rabbi," in *Against Ethics: Contributions to a Poetics of Obligation with Constant Reference to Deconstruction* (Bloomington: Indiana University Press, 1993), 42–68.

26. For a comprehensive reading of Hegel and Irigaray on the questions of immanent relations and transcendence, see Rawlinson, *The Betrayal of Substance: Death, Literature, and Sexual Difference in Hegel's Phenomenology of Spirit* (New York: Columbia University Press, 2021). See also Rawlinson's 'Opening Hegel's Autological Circle: Irigaray and the Metaphysics of Sexual Difference' in *What is Sexual Difference? Thinking with Irigaray*, ed. Rawlinson, Mary C., and Sares, James (New York: Columbia University Press, 2023): 39–58.

27. Roberts, *Irigaray and Politics*, 86–107.

28. The position of lack alludes to the Hegelian subject's movement toward self *re*-cognition through an emptying oneself of that which one is not. See Alison Stone, "Hegel and Twentieth-Century French Philosophy" in *Nature, Ethics and Gender in German Romanticism and Idealism* (London: Rowman & Littlefield Publishers, 2018), esp. pp. 261–65.

29. Levinas's own philosophy is a direct response to what he viewed as the problem of immanence that resulted from Hegel's positing of subjectivity as movement to return to a transcendent truth. Levinas contended that Hegel's philosophy does not begin with transcendence but results in a philosophy that posits transcendence through a process of subjectivity. For Levinas, the implications of Hegel's thought were that philosophy had become a philosophy of immanence—positing thought about alterity only in relation to a movement of the subject.

30. Luce Irigaray, *To Be Two* (New York: Routledge, 2001), 109.

31. Irigaray is adamant that the lips she invokes are not the lips of Merleau-Ponty's phenomenology—lips that she argues are subjected to the economy of visibility that "neutralizes them by removing them from the singularity of their source." Irigaray, *To Be Born: Genesis of a New Human Being* (Cham, Switzerland: Palgrave Macmillan, 2017), 26.

32. Irigaray, *Ethics*, 18.

33. Irigaray, 18.

34. Rachel Jones, *Irigaray*, 145.

35. Irigaray, *Ethics*, 16.

36. For Irigaray's own depiction of morpho-logic see Luce Irigaray *Je, Tu, Nous: Toward a Culture of Difference* (New York: Routledge, 1992), 59.

37. This transcendence is not "a projection into the distance or into the beyond." Irigaray, *To Be Born*, 39. For more on the philosophical foundations of Irigaray's sensible transcendental, see Joanna Hodge's depiction of the indispensability of both Kant's distinction between the sensible and intelligible *and* Heidegger's framing of the relation between the ontical and ontological for interpreting the sensible transcendental. Hodge, "Irigaray reading Heidegger,"

in *Engaging with Irigaray: Feminist Philosophy and Modern European thought*, ed. Carolyn Burke, Naomi Schor, Margaret Whitford (New York: Columbia, 1994), 203–4.

38. Athena V. Colman, "Tarrying with Sexual Difference," in *Horizons of Difference: Rethinking Space, Place, and Identity with Irigaray*, ed. Ruthanne Crapo Kim, Yvette Russel, and Brenda Sharp (Albany: State University of New York Press, 2022), 26.

39. Penelope Ingram, *The Signifying Body: Toward an Ethics of Sexual and Racial Difference* (Albany: State University of New York Press, 2009), 26.

40. Irigaray, *Ethics*, 13.

41. Irigaray, 216–17.

42. Irigaray, 216.

43. Irigaray, *Mediation of Touch*, 269–71.

44. Rebecca Hill writes, Irigaray's most careful and sympathetic readers recognized that parler-femme is literal and metaphoric,serious and playful." (391) For more Irigaray and interpretating *parler femme* see Rebecca Hill, "Multiple Readings," 391–92. Note that *l'écriture féminine* is most often associated with Hélène Cixous's coining of the phrase; however, it can also be thought in relation to Irigaray's broader efforts to use language to institute a different symbolic order altogether. For a description of this distinction, see Rachel Jones, *Irigaray: Towards a Sexuate Philosophy* (Malden, MA: Polity, 2011), 34.

45. Irigaray, *Ethics*, 13.

46. For insights into this criticism of Irigaray's appropriations of Buddhism and Yoga, see Sokthan Yeng, "Irigaray's Alternative Buddhist Practices of the Self," *Journal of French and Francophone Philosophy* 22, no. 1 (2014): 61–75.

47. Toril Moi refers to this mimetic process in Irigaray as "double mimesis." However, Moi does not believe double mimesis can shake itself free from the dangers of essentialism. *Sexual/Textual Politics: Feminist Literary Theory* (New York: Routledge, 2002). Among others, Naomi Schor has also discussed the mimetic process in Irigaray in terms of double mimesis. Naomi Schor, "This Essentialism Which Is Not One: Coming to Grips with Irigaray," in *Engaging with Irigaray: Feminist Philosophy and Modern European Thought*, ed. Naomi Schor, Carolyn Burke, and Margaret Whitford (New York: Columbia University Press, 1989), 76.

48. I owe this observation to Louis Ruprecht Jr., who alerted me to the fact that the Greek masculine accusative of *eros* is distinguishable from the word for question only by an accent that occurs in speech but not in writing.

49. James Sares, "Irigarayan Ontology and the Possibilities of Sexual Difference," in *Horizons of Difference*, ed. Crapo Kim (Albany: State University of New York Press, 2022), 118.

50. Sares, 119.

51. Irigaray, *To Be Born*, 99.

52. Irigaray, 38.

53. Irigaray, *Sexes and Genealogies*, 59.

54. Luce Irigaray, "Dreaming of a Truly Democratic World," *Sophia* 61 (2022): 106.

55. Irigaray, 107.

56. Irigaray, 106.

57. See Irigaray, *Mediation of Touch*, esp. 271–75.

58. Irigaray, 105.

59. Parker, *Elemental Difference*, 106.

60. Irigaray, *To Be Born*, 103.

61. Irigaray, 41.

62. I owe this important clarification about singularity to a prompting by an anonymous reader.

63. See Adriana Cavarero, *Horrorism: Naming Contemporary Violence* (Columbia, 2011 [2009]). See also Cavarero's description of this work in Silvia Benso, *Viva Voce: Conversations with Italian Philosophers* (Albany: State University of New York Press, 2017). Instead of framing the condition of singularity and/or individuation as "vulnerability or exposure" as Fanny Söderbäck describes Cavarero's work, I argue desire is about space and time of living in the world with other as ambiguous and fraught with tension of response and responsibility. Fanny Söderbäck, "Singularity in the Wake of Slavery: Adriana Cavarero's Ontology of Uniqueness and Alex Haley's *Roots*," *Philosophy Compass* 15, no. 7 (2020): 1–16, 9.

64. Jean-Luc Nancy, "Of Being Singular Plural" in *Philosophy of Communication*, ed. Briankle G. Chang, and Garnet C. Butchart (Cambridge, MA: MIT Press, 2012), 580.

65. Irigaray's notion of the sexuate two as necessary for life is for her not the same as saying the sexuate is necessary for reproduction. Indeed, she wants to separate life from reproduction. The at-least-twoness is a condition of living.

Chapter 2

1. Irigaray, *Ethics*, 5.

2. I focus on Irigaray's early references to the language of incarnation in *Ethics* here to attend to the question of salvation and the role that lips play in such a soteriology; however, Irigaray also takes up the language of incarnation in other works, notably in *Marine Lover of Friedrich Nietzsche, Sexes and Genealogies*, and more recently *The Mediation of Touch*, and an article "God Becoming Flesh, Flesh Becoming Divine," in *Continental Philosophy Review* 56, no. 4 (2023): 505–16.

3. I capitalize *Incarnation* when referring to the specific incarnation of Jesus as Christ and to theologies of that incarnation in the Christian tradition. I will not capitalize *incarnation* when referring to it more generally. Similarly, I will capitalize *Crucifixion* when referencing the crucifixion of Jesus as foundational for Christian theologies.

4. This book was in its final stages of revision when Irigaray's *The Mediation of Touch*, was released. I turned to *Mediation* in the copyedit stage of my writing and

was struck by the timeliness of my reflections in relation to Irigaray's. In *Mediation*, Irigaray revisits themes of incarnation and touch, transcendence and desire from her life's work, ideas I have long traced in her work, and explicitly in this book, to articulate the materiality and alterity of desire. Irigaray has repeatedly emphasized touch as a primary mode of relations constitutive of the self and others, and in *Mediation* she holds touch together with her emphasis on sexuation as part of what it means to be human as "natural beings" in their "singularities." (74–75). Biblical studies scholars often argue that the authors of the prophetic texts of the Hebrew Bible wrote in the exilic or even postexilic period, in other words, they were issuing warnings to future generations about the very realities they were living (rather than predicting those realities). In the context of the pandemic and postpandemic world that frames *Mediation*, Irigaray's extended meditation on touch at this stage in her work feels prophetic.

5. For further exploration of the cross-disciplinary applications of Irigaray's work in the study of religion as well as sources on Irigaray and religion see *Irigaray, Religion, and Embodiment: Commemorating the Fiftieth Anniversary of "Speculum de l'autre femme,"* a special issue of the journal of *Body and Religion*, Wesley N. Barker and Emily Holmes, guest editors (forthcoming, late 2024).

6. Invoking the language of labia and vulva (as well as the womb), Irigaray at once articulates the reduction of women to procreative sex *and* refuses that reduction of her desire. See Jones, *Irigaray,* 142–44. With multiple sites of pleasure, women find pleasure with or without sex, with or without procreation.

7. Although I concentrate on the relationship of lips to the language of the Incarnation, there are other tropes in Irigaray for thinking materiality beyond the discourse of matter, including the breath.

8. For an overview of the earliest and most influential receptions of Irigaray among Christian feminist theologians, see Elsa Kunz, "What Difference Does It Make? Early Reception Stories about Luce Irigaray's Writing on Divine Women," *Journal of Feminist Scholarship* 23 (2023): 24–38.

9. My reading is not interested in the accuracy of Irigaray's appropriations of Christian theology and imagery; getting embroiled in a normative philosophical critique of Irigaray prevents the reader from engaging with her ideas and her vision of an ethical mode of relation that are capable of cultivating a different world.

10. This list is far from exhaustive. Emily Holmes and I offer a more complete, though not exhaustive overview of Irigaray's engagements with religion as well as of the landscape of receptions of her work in a forthcoming introduction to a special issue of *Body and Religion.*

11. Scholars Amy Hollywood and Anne-Claire Mulder have offered some of the most sustained and in-depth explorations Irigaray's remaking of immanence and transcendence using religious imagery. See A.-C. Mulder, *Divine Flesh, Embodied Word: "Incarnation" as a Hermeneutical Key to a Feminist Theologian's Reading of Luce Irigaray's Work* (Amsterdam: Amsterdam University Press, 2006), and Amy

Hollywood, "Deconstructing Belief: Irigaray and the Philosophy of Religion," *The Journal of Religion* 78, no. 2 (1998): 230–45.

12. For a useful contemporary tracing of Irigaray's reception in Christian theology see, "What Difference Does It Make? Early Reception Stories about Luce Irigaray's Writing on Divine Women." *Journal of Feminist Scholarship* 23, no. 23 (2023): 24–38.

13. See "Divine Women" in *Sexes and Genealogies*, 57–72.

14. Irigaray, *Sexes and Genealogies*, 58.

15. Irigaray, 58.

16. Irigaray, 58.

17. Irigaray, 72.

18. Irigaray, 61.

19. Irigaray, 61.

20. See Irigaray's emphasis on individuation as distinct from individualization in *The Mediation of Touch*, 250–54.

21. Ada S. Jaarsma, "Irigaray's *To Be Two:* The Problem of Evil and the Plasticity of Incarnation," *Hypatia* 18, no. 1 (Winter 2003): 48.

22. Irigaray, *This Sex*, 30.

23. Irigaray, *Sexes and Genealogies*, 69.

24. The verse that foregrounds the theology of Incarnation in Catholic theology is from the Gospel of John, which reads, "And the *Word became flesh* and lived among us, and we have seen his glory, the glory as of a father's only son, full of grace and truth." John 1:14 New Revised Standard Version–Catholic Edition. Emphasis added.

25. Ann-Marie Priest, "Woman as God, God as Woman: Mysticism, Negative Theology, and Luce Irigaray," *Journal of Religion* 83, no. 1 (2003): 19.

26. Though I have discussed this text at some length in previous publications, "La Mystérique" remains a complex and rich resource for Irigaray studies. See Wesley N. Barker, "Thresholds of Touch: Revisiting the Mat(t)er of the Body in the Work of Luce Irigaray," *Body and Religion* 4, no. 1 (2020): 105–29. See also "A Theology of Lips: Beyond the Wounding of Desire," in *Horizons of Difference: Rethinking Space, Place, and Identity with Irigaray*, ed. Ruthanne Crapo Kim, Yvette Russell, and Brenda Sharp (Albany: State University of New York Press, 2022), 139–68.

27. Barker and Holmes, "Introduction: Irigaray and Religion."

28. See Tina Beattie, *God's Mother, Eve's Advocate* (London: Bloomsbury, 2002). See also the chapter "The Female Body and Religious Practice in the Later Middle Ages," in Carolyn Walker Bynum, *Fragmentation and Redemption: Essays on Gender and the Human Body in Medieval Religion* (New York: Zone Books, 1991), 181–238.

29. Janet Martin Soskice, *The Kindness of God: Metaphor, Gender, and Religious Language* (New York: Oxford University Press, 2008).

30. Amy M. Hollywood, "Beauvoir, Irigaray, and the Mystical," *Hypatia* 9, no. 4 (Fall 1994): 160–61.

31. According to Irigaray's criticism, the tradition represents women with breast and vagina—both associated with reproduction (nursing and penetration). These are the associations that she will harness and reframe in order to think the fleshy sites as sites of pleasure.

32. Irigaray, *Speculum*, 199–200. The ellipsis is original.

33. This emphasis on kissing elicits what Elizabeth Grosz has referred to as a "homo-sexuate" pleasure that emerges in and through the lips as figures of feminine desire and the possibility of women's subjectivity. Elizabeth Grosz, "The Hetero and the Homo: The Sexual Ethics of Luce Irigaray," in *Engaging with Irigaray: Feminist Philosophy and Modern European Thought*, ed. Carolyn Burke, Naomi Schor, and Margaret Whitford (New York: Columbia University Press, 1994): 336.

34. In the essay's first appearance in English, Carolyn Burke translates the line "Ton sang devenu leur sens" as "Your blood translated to their senses." Irigaray, Luce, and Carolyn Burke. "When Our Lips Speak Together." *Signs: Journal of Women in Culture and Society* 6, no. 1 (1980): 69; Catherine Porter's later translation reads, "Your blood becomes their meaning." I prefer Porter's translation here because—in addition to its allusions to the generation of becoming and its resonance with what Lee Edelman says is an entanglement of sex and meaning in Lacan's use of *sens*—it captures the language of sacrifice more clearly. Irigaray, *This Sex*, 205. For more on Lacan's use of *sens* see Lee Edelman, *Bad Education: Why Queer Theory Teaches Us Nothing* (Durham: Duke University Press, 2023).

35. Although Catherine Porter translates "Entre nous" as "Among us," I prefer "Between us," which invokes the specificity of the interval of lips as having borders that constitute a distinct place of their own that touch to engender a space between them. See Luce Irigaray, *Ce sexe qui n'en est pas un* (Paris: Les Éditions de Minuit, 1977), 212.

36. Irigary, *This Sex*, 212. In the French, Irigaray's structuring of this scene is even more evocative, as the phrasing in this paragraph is cut short into a series of mostly one- to three-word sentences.

37. Irigaray, 28.

38. Irigaray, 29.

39. See Irigaray's suggestion that space for men and women needs to be reimagined. *Ethics*, 11–12. See also her engagement with Spinoza on the relationship of space to the ethics of "God." *Ethics*, 83–94.

40. Irigaray, *Speculum*, 200.

41. Irigaray, 199. Irigaray's words evoke the medieval representations of Christ as a nurturing, lactating, and/or nursing mother. Compare footnote 31.

42. Irigaray, 200.

43. Irigaray, 200.

44. Kathryn Stockton, " 'God' between Their Lips: Desire between Women in Irigaray and Eliot," *Novel* (Spring 1992): 354.

45. Irigaray, *Speculum*, 200.

46. Butler, "Bodies That Matter," 155; Irigaray, *This Sex*, 179.

47. Irigaray, *Speculum*, 200.

48. Hollywood is critical of this shift as abandoning the penetrative dimension of pleasure as though it were an exclusively masculine enterprise.

49. Amy Hollywood, *Acute Melancholia and Other Essays: Mysticism, History, and the Study of Religion* (New York: Columbia University Press, 2016), 172.

50. Butler, "Bodies That Matter," 158; Butler also quoted in Hollywood, *Acute Melancholia*, 172.

51. Hollywood, *Acute Melancholia*, 187.

52. Hollywood, 188.

53. Lynne Huffer has turned to Foucault's references to fisting in order to rethink penetrative sexual practices as offering a queer praxis that redefines penetration. But I think Irigaray is attempting to offer something more than understanding women's pleasure as a new radical sexuality of sorts. Irigaray, or at least lips, reimagine the relationality beyond the grounds for a feminist politics or a queer politics toward a new order altogether.

54. See Anne Caldwell, "Transforming Sacrifice: Irigaray and the Politics of Sexual Difference," *Hypatia* 17, no. 4 (2002): 16–38.

55. See Anne Caldwell's discussion of Irigaray's interpretation of Plato's allegory of the cave. "Transforming Sacrifice," 24.

56. Butler, "Bodies That Matter," 158.

57. Irigaray, *This Sex*, 206.

58. Irigaray, 77. See also Butler's discussion of the relationship between this " 'elsewhere' of female pleasure" and matter in Irigaray's reading of Plato's portrayal of the feminine and the form/matter binary in "Bodies That Matter," especially 149–65. Emphasis in original.

59. Irigaray, *This Sex*, 74.

60. Irigaray, 77.

61. Irigaray, 77. Emphases original.

62. Irigaray, *Ethics*, 17.

63. Irigaray, 18.

64. Irigaray, 18.

65. Irigaray, 18–19.

66. Irigaray, 18.

67. Irigaray, 18.

68. In Renaissance art, the *ostentatio genitalium* (showing of genitals) represents a fixation on Jesus's maleness, which, as Leo Steinberg suggests in *The Sexuality of Christ in Renaissance Art and in Modern Oblivion*, restores the potentiality of human sexuality. Steinberg claims that images offer a subtlety of representation that words alone do not. I contend Irigaray invokes the materiality of flesh in her writing to

create fleshy words that play with the space between the real and the specular. Leo Steinberg, *The Sexuality of Christ in Renaissance Art and in Modern Oblivion*, 2nd ed. (Chicago: University of Chicago Press, 1996).

69. John 1:1, New Revised Standard Version.

70. The absence of the wound is a rejection of the sacrificial economy, and the placing of the lips on the cross is a refiguring of the sacrificial economy—though I think the wound could be reimagined apart from the sacrificial economy, but only after matter has been transformed apart from metaphysics.

71. We could view God otherwise as beginning (alpha) and end (omega): an eternal return. Here, the space-time of the Christian story looks more like Hegel's dialectic of consciousness.

72. Irigaray, *This Sex*, 77.

73. Roberts, *Irigaray and Politics*, 94.

74. *This Sex*, 77.

75. Irigaray, *This Sex*, 31.

76. Irigaray's lips on the cross take on the mediating quality of mucous, membranes, and angels. See Gail M. Schwab, "Mother's Body, Father's Tongue," in *Engaging with Irigaray: Feminist Philosophy and Modern European Thought*, ed. Carolyn Burke, Naomi Schor, and Margaret Whitford (New York: Columbia University Press, 1994), 351–78. This connection between lips, angels, and mucous as gesturing to the importance of interval thinking is also suggested when Irigaray refers to the lips as "the threshold that gives access to the *mucous*." Irigaray, *Ethics*, 18.

77. For a discussion of matter as potentiality in Aristotelian notions of form and matter, and Irigaray's critique of such concepts, see Rebecca Hill, *The Interval: Relation and Becoming in Irigaray, Aristotle, and Bergson* (New York: Fordham University Press, 2012). See also Butler's discussion of form/matter in both Plato and Aristotle in "Bodies That Matter," especially 149–61.

78. Irigaray, *This Sex*, 77.

79. Irigaray, 77.

80. John 1:14, referring to Jesus, reads, "The Word became flesh and dwelt among us."

81. The original French reads as follows: "L'entrée dans la demeure, ou le temple, où l'un et l'autre s'inviteraient à avoir accès, aussi au divin." *Éthique de la Différence Sexuelle* (Paris: Les Éditions de Minuit 1984), 191.

82. *La demeure*, as a place of living or settling, suggests inhabiting. Though Irigaray uses the noun *demeure* instead of the verb *habiter* in this instance, the sense of dwelling invokes the Greek σκηνόω (*skénoó*), which conveys the sense of dwelling as both literally inhabiting a place and God's relationship to the tabernacle. Hence, Irigaray implicitly and playfully references the significance of the living together of the divine and the human in another space-time of an ethical future—in her later work, perhaps even a dwelling of the divine and an otherwise incarnate sexuate other, beyond the human.

83. Irigaray, *Sharing the Fire*, 13.

84. Butler, "Bodies That Matter," 155.

85. Anne Carson, *Eros the Bittersweet: An Essay* (Princeton: Princeton University Press, 2016), 171.

Chapter 3

1. The impositions of gender binaries perpetrated in the *language* of sexual difference (in the illusion of that difference) mean that some bodies and bodily desires remain sublimated in order to "make sense" within the masculine symbolic.

2. See Lee Edelman, *Bad Education: Why Queer Theory Teaches Us Nothing* (Durham, NC: Duke University Press, 2023).

3. This reading of trans* does not cover debates and tensions within trans* and feminist theories. For a good introduction, see *Transgender Studies Reader*, ed. Susan Stryker and Stephen Whittle (New York: Routledge, 2006).

4. This chapter is not meant to elide feminist, queer, and trans* identifications, as though the embodied desires of their discursive traces were the same. Rather, it is an attempt to think these identifications in relation to the problem/question of sexual difference.

5. Mitchell Damien Murtagh's work is particularly notable among new voices for thinking through the radicality of sexual difference as a resource for trans* theory. Murtagh defends sexual difference against transphobia through an incisive engagement with the perpetually contested grammar of sexual difference in Irigaray's ontology. Mitchell Damien Murtagh, "The Onto-Ethics of Transsexual Difference," in *What Is Sexual Difference? Thinking with Irigaray* ed. Rawlinson, Mary C., and Sares, James (New York: Columbia University Press, 2023): 227–50.

6. As noted in the introduction, I use the term *queer* in this chapter in a broad sense to capture an embodied strangeness and estrangement from the sociocultural norms of a phallocentric, heteronormative symbolic imagination. *Queer* speaks to how disidentifications, not reidentifications, operate—and to the way that desire proves to be constantly disruptive of identities. In this emphasis on queer as marking an *embodied* strangeness, I offer a modified version of Edelman's use of queer as an "empty marker of a stigmatized otherness to communitarian norms, thus preserving its force as something that thwarts the straightness of intelligibility." Edelman, *Bad Education*, 20. Edelman might push me to ask, "Embodiments of what exactly?"

7. Michel Foucault, *History of Sexuality Vol. 1: The Will to Knowledge*, trans. Robert Hurley (New York: Vintage, 1990), 78.

8. Foucault, 11.

9. Foucault, 8–11.

10. Foucault, 159.

11. Michel Foucault: *History of Sexuality Vol. 3: The Care of Self* (New York: Vintage, 1988), 51.

12. Foucault, 55.

13. Foucault, 55.

14. Foucault, 61.

15. Foucault, 64.

16. See Foucault, 66.

17. This is a very different sort of pleasure from *voluptas.* This pleasure, via experience of the self and hence always available, is not from the outside, is not excited from other sources, and therefore, "is not undermined by the fear of loss." It is not contingent or uncertain.

18. Foucault, *History of Sexuality Vol. 3*, 67.

19. Foucault, 5–6.

20. For example, Niki Kasumi Clements's examination of how *Confessions of the Flesh* relates to Foucault's treatments of Christianity in volumes 2–4 has reignited questions about the processes of cultivation and subjectivation and its implications for differentiating a religious ethics of pleasure from religious moralizing. Niki Kasumi Clements, "Discussing the Discipline: Foucault's Christianities," *Journal of the American Academy of Religion* 89, no. 1 (2021): 3.

21. José Esteban Muñoz, *Disidentifications: Queers of Color and the Performance of Politics* (Minneapolis: University of Minnesota Press, 1999), 11.

22. Muñoz turns to the psychic and affective realms to explain the condition of performativity as resistance, and he describes "brown depression" as a space of resistance to the subject that externalizes the other in its own becoming and that features others with whom one stands in relation in this performativity. Others are not external threats; they are materialities of alterity through which one has the feeling of wholeness of recognition and belonging without having to abide in the illusion that one is whole through separation from others. Drawing on Klein and Eve Kasofsky Sedgwick, Muñoz describes this performativity as reparative performance—"a form of reparation grounded in love for the object." (683) See "Feeling Brown, Feeling Down: Latina Affect, the Performativity of Race, and the Depressive Situation," *Signs: Journal of Women in Culture and Society* 31, no. 3 (2006), https://doi.org/10.1086/499080.

23. See Luce Irigaray and Noah Guynn, "The Question of the Other," *Yale French Studies* 87 (1995): 11. I owe my thinking on Irigaray's critique of liberalism to Caldwell's "Transforming Sacrifice," 24. Irigaray repeatedly warns that any universal is never neutral, and positing a universal or idea as neutral comes at the expense of acknowledging particularities, the materiality of difference.

24. Muñoz, "Feeling Brown," 684. This quote emerges from Muñoz's engagement with an art installation by Nao Bustamante.

25. Munoz's 2009 book *Cruising Utopia* is adamant that the space of alterity is not another universal; it is material, and the particularities of its materiality—one might say the embodiments of alterity—are the possibility of antinormative performativity.

26. Butler's own work demonstrates a sustained investment in thinking an ethical subjectivity that can empower marginalized subjects within their particularities rather than relegate them to universalized abstractions (simply as others). Butler takes up the question of materiality in Irigaray's work more recently in the chapter "Sexual Difference as a Question of Ethics: Alterities of the Flesh in Irigaray and Merleau-Ponty," in Butler, *Senses of the Subject* (New York: Fordham University Press, 2015), 149–70. Butler has also discussed their debt to Irigaray in an interview with Elizabeth Grosz and Pheng Cheah, "The Future of Sexual Difference: An Interview with Judith Butler and Drucilla Cornell," *Diacritics* 28, no. 1 (1998): 19–42. Butler also has an extended consideration of Irigaray on the question of ethics and politics in *Antigone's Claim* (New York: Columbia University Press, 2000).

27. Butler has recently stated in several interviews and publications that they prefer to use the pronouns *they/theirs*.

28. Contemporary theories of performativity are divergent, but they extend from various adaptations of Foucault's early work. Eve Kosofsky Sedgwick is eminent in this lineage as an inheritor of Foucault's legacy.

29. Butler's performativity is often read as being insufficiently agential; however, I read it in relation to their emphasis on the opacity and frailty of human subjectivity. See respectively *Giving an Account of Oneself* (New York: Fordham University Press, 2005), and *Precarious Life* (New York: Verso, 2004). In light of the entanglement of performativity with the psychic and social demands of life, I still think Butler's performativity resonates with the agency of desire toward which I am driving in this book.

30. Positing the fullness of feminine desire in its refusal to be fixed does not render desire as a potentiality for something else, such as a true essence or, in Aristotelian terms, the form of a thing versus its matter. Rebecca Hill articulates a construction of desire in Irigaray that emerges in *An Ethics of Sexual Difference*, through a careful reading of Irigaray and Aristotle on the question of matter and the feminine. See Rebecca Hill, *The Interval: Relation and Becoming in Irigaray, Aristotle, and Bergson* (New York: Fordham University Press, 2012). In this regard, Irigaray's use of desire to refigure matter is not unlike the work that Derrida does in terms of the relation of matter to iterability and the gift of time. See Pheng Cheah, "Nondialectical Materialism," *Diacritics* 38, nos. 1/2 (2008): 149.

31. Butler, "Bodies That Matter," 158.

32. This quote is a critique in reference to Irigaray's chapter in *Ethics* on Merleau-Ponty. Judith Butler, "Sexual Difference as a Question of Ethics: Alterities of the Flesh in Irigaray and Merleau-Ponty," in *Feminist Interpretations of Maurice Merleau-Ponty*, ed. Dorothea and Gail Weiss Olkowski (University Park: Pennsylvania State University Press, 2006), 108.

33. Though Alison Stone is critical of Butler's refusal to consider natural or physical specificities, Stone's critique of Irigaray's thinking of matter is similar here

to Butler's in its acknowledgment of a paradox in Irigaray's writing on matter. As Stone frames the dilemma, there would be an inherent paradox in the use of sexuate difference as a means to render materiality indeterminate. I insist that this sort of paradox is a dilemma of *reading* Irigaray; it is not Irigaray's dilemma. Alison Stone, *Luce Irigaray and the Philosophy of Sexual Difference* (Cambridge, UK: Cambridge University Press, 2006), 36.

34. Butler, *Bodies That Matter*, 143.

35. Indeed, Irigaray's emphasis on the materiality of alterity as the space-time of desire of a sexuate couple does attempt to transcend the historical specificity of the symbolic.

36. Matter itself has a history, and that history is intertwined with the ways certain differences, such as sexual difference, are endowed with certain attributes, such as passivity and receptivity. Any concept of prediscursive difference owes its proximity to the symbolic to discursive constructs of matter and alterity, space and time.

37. Butler, *Bodies That Matter*, 143.

38. As discussed in regard to Amy Hollywood's criticism of Irigaray's lips, with the exception of their associations with the wound of Christ in "La Mystérique," Irigaray depicts lips as touching in a way that resists the language of penetration (attributing the language of penetration to a masculine notion of heterosexual desire). Her focus on touching lips is thus an effort to rethink desire apart from phallocentrism.

39. Alison Stone presses Butler on the question of natural or ontological differences, suggesting that Butler's statement that "sex is not natural" skirts the question of physical specificity. Butler, however, rejects being submitted to the question, which they contend would dehistoricize the matter of the physical and natural.

40. Penelope Ingram offers a useful intervention here insisting on the possibility of material signification that does not just think matter as a discursive construction—which Ingram adds constrains ways of thinking through questions of race and gender. See *Signifying Body*, 41.

41. Whereas Butler ends with a critique that raises the question of what it means to think about materiality, Salamon actually begins to think that materiality. Gayle Salamon, *Assuming a Body: Transgender and Rhetorics of Materiality* (New York: Columbia University Press, 2010), 131–33.

42. Salamon, 137.

43. Salamon, 137–38.

44. Salamon, 138.

45. See especially Parker's depiction of Irigaray's "two-sex" model. Parker, *Elemental Difference*, 63–78.

46. Stone's reading of Butler informs her reading of Irigaray, and she ultimately argues that sexual difference and sexed duality are not compatible insofar as sexual difference is based in a dynamic relationality. I agree with Stone on this point. Penelope Deutscher and Mary Beth Mader have both challenged Stone's reading of

Irigaray as perhaps too generous in this regard. See Alison Stone, *Luce Irigaray and the Philosophy of Sexual Difference*. See also the conversation between Deutscher, Mader, and Stone published in *Differences: A Journal of Feminist Cultural Studies* 19, no. 3 (2008). The conversation includes the following articles: Alison Mary Beth Mader, "Somatic Ontology: Comments on Alison Stone's Luce Irigaray and the Philosophy of Sexual Difference," 126–38; Penelope Deutscher, "Recastings: On Alison Stone's Luce Irigaray and the Philosophy of Sexual Difference," 139–49; Stone, "Unthought Nature: Reply to Penelope Deutscher and Mary Beth Mader," 150–57.

47. In Maggie Berg's terms, "If the 'horizon' of identity continually disappears, this does not mean . . . that 'there is no one to emancipate'; rather, it means that the subject is oriented by desire toward half-glimpsed alternatives." Berg, "Contradictions," 70.

48. Although I do not intend to exclude the womb, I do think the lips deemphasize reproduction in ways that I find more useful for imagining liberative sexuate morphologies, particularly for queer temporalities.

49. Maggie Berg notes Irigaray's disruptive resonance with Foucault. See "Contradictions," 69.

50. Lynne Huffer, Maternal Pasts, *Feminist Futures: Nostalgia, Ethics and the Question of Difference* (Stanford: Stanford University Press, 1998), 24.

51. Note that the title itself, referencing the association of the maternal with origins and masculine nostalgia, invokes the question of history as entrenched in the discourse of a phallocentric symbolic.

52. Huffer, *Maternal Pasts*, 59.

53. Huffer, *Are the Lips a Grave?*, 124.

54. Huffer, *Maternal Pasts*, 24.

55. Huffer, 123.

56. I think what Huffer grasps about Irigaray is that the materiality of alterity is not the same as the ethical other of the philosophical tradition. And yet one is responsible to both. In Irigaray, there can be no ethics without desire.

57. After all, nostalgia, for Huffer, implies a particular relation to one's history that freezes that history in relation to a pining of the present, a freezing that is antithetical to the ethical performativity of narrative that a queer feminist desubjectivation enacts.

58. Huffer, *Maternal Pasts*, 249.

59. To ask whether the lips are a grave is to raise a question about the lips as a question—instead of a declaration that might reduce the lips to a moralizing force. Instead, Huffer *asks* a question of the lips and answers with a question: "Or are they?"—answering in a way that speaks the desire to meet the lips with the eros they deserve.

60. Huffer's third book in her trilogy on Foucault, *Foucault's Strange Eros* (New York: Columbia University Press, 2020), does not engage Irigaray's work in an explicit or sustained way.

61. Huffer cautions the reader about the self-referential tendencies of queer theory and queer collectivity. See especially *Are the Lips a Grave?*, 67.

62. Huffer, 21.

63. Huffer, 86.

64. Huffer, 86.

65. Huffer's reading of Foucault leads to her consideration of the split between queer and feminist issues as based in differing conceptions of power (productive or repressive)—with potentially devastating consequences for both camps. See Huffer, *Are the Lips a Grave?*, 91–117.

66. Huffer, 53. See also footnote 36 on 196.

67. Huffer, 87.

68. Huffer, 5.

69. Huffer views the exploration and action of Foucault's desubjectivation as a historicization of the relationship between sexuality and morality by interrogating the process of moralizing. *Are the Lips a Grave?*, 30.

70. Huffer, 30.

71. Huffer, 33.

72. Huffer differentiates the notion of alterity in Foucault from that found in Levinas in order to articulate their different conceptions of transcendence, situating Foucault's alterity within the sociohistorical.

73. The antisocial thesis in queer theory is represented in various forms in the works of Leo Bersani, Janet Halley, and Lee Edelman, for example. For an overview, see Robert L. Caserio, Lee Edelman, Judith Halberstam, José Esteban Muñoz, and Tim Dean, "The Antisocial Thesis in Queer Theory." *Proceedings of the Modern Language Association* 121, no. 3 (2006): 819–28. In opposition to antisocial theory, see Ellis Hanson, "The Future's Eve: Reparative Reading after Sedgwick," *South Atlantic Quarterly* 110, no. 1 (2011): 101–19. Huffer writes that, contrary to those queer theorists who read Foucault as radically antisocial, the question of ethics is for Foucault always a question of the self in relation to the other. Huffer, *Mad for Foucault*, 246–47. See also the special issue of *Differences: A Journal of Feminist Cultural Studies*, which includes Edelman's response to Huffer's critiques of his work.s

74. Huffer, *Mad for Foucault*, 253.

75. Huffer, 246–47.

76. Bersani calls attention to the prioritization of the phallus as heterosexual desire, contending as well that anal sex acts as a refusal of the redemptive privilege granted to heterosexual sex—a form of radical resistance to the moralizing sexuality of redemptive heterosexual sex. Huffer's title *Are the Lips a Grave?* at once considers the lips as rejecting the moralizing tendencies of heterosexual sex and registers criticisms that Irigaray's work is "antithetical to Bersani's anal repudiation of redemptive sex." Huffer, in positing this question, is cautiously considering the lips as disrupting heterosexual desire of penetrative sex acts. *Are the Lips a Grave?*, 34.

77. Huffer, 47.

78. Huffer, 124.

79. Huffer, 130.

80. Huffer, 32.

81. Huffer is critical of both Muñoz and Bersani here. She contends that the assertion that "subversive" sex acts are "subversive" devolves into a new moralizing sexuality, making them part of power-knowledge as one deploys them in the name of freedom. In contrast, Huffer provides a notion of performativity that is inherently relational and antifoundationalist, feminist and queer, turning to narrative performance to let the fist "becom[e] something other than itself." Huffer, 68, 78. This performativity has become an explicit part of Huffer's work in the last decade. See "Mysterics: Extinction and Emptiness" in Rawlinson and Sares, *What Is Sexual Difference?*, 372–476.

82. Huffer, *Mad for Foucault*, 253.

83. This would be an ethics without the violence of moralizing, perhaps a possibility of genealogy, of history without nostalgia.

84. Vicki Kirby, "Transgression: Normativity's Self-Inversion," *Differences: A Journal of Feminist Cultural Studies* 26, no. 1 (2015): 96–116.

85. Athena Colman, "Tarrying with Sexual Difference," in *Horizons of Difference: Rethinking Space, Place, and Identity with Irigaray*, ed. Ruthanne Crapo Kim, Yvette Russell, and Brenda Sharp (Albany: State University of New York Press, 2022), 34.

86. Colman, Irigaray Circle, Karen Burke Panel. Reykjavik, Iceland, June 7, 2024. See also Jules Gill-Peterson, *Histories of the Transgender Child* (Minneapolis: University of Minnesota Press, 2018).

87. Stephen Seely, "Sexual Difference in/and the Queer beyond of Ethics," *Feminist Formations* 29, no. 3 (2017): 168.

88. By thinking the lips as a form of desubjectivation, we locate an alterity inherent in their embodiedness of an othered desire. But could this render the lips passive, incapable of a queer feminist politics? Is the lips' refusal of identity agential in any way, or is it simply ontological? The question of the political viability of the lips remains.

89. I borrow the term *radical immanence* from Rosi Braidotti in "Of Bugs and Women: Irigaray and Deleuze on the Becoming-Woman," in *Engaging with Irigaray: Feminist Philosophy and Modern European Thought*, ed. Carolyn Burke, Naomi Schor, and Margaret Whitford (New York: Columbia University Press, 1994), 122. Braidotti notes she owes the term to Anne-Claire Mulder, who elaborates on Irigaray's sensible transcendental to rethink the notion of Incarnation in Christianity. See Anne-Claire Mulder, *Divine Flesh, Embodied Word: "Incarnation" as a Hermeneutical Key to a Feminist Theologian's Reading of Luce Irigaray's Work* (Amsterdam: Amsterdam University Press, 2006).

90. Slavoj Žižek is noticeably absent from this conversation—but he is useful in relation to Irigaray for his insistence on the need to think sexual difference. See Judith Butler, Slavoj Žižek, and Ernesto Laclau, *Contingency, Hegemony, Universality: Contemporary Dialogues on the Left* (London: Verso, 2000). Žižek argues that Lacan's point in discussing the Real as an ahistorical "limit of historicization/

resignification" is that "every historical figuration of this limit is itself contingent and, as such, susceptible to a radical overhaul."(221). In regard to Irigaray's lips, we might suggest that figuration of the lips as an "ahistorical limit of historicization/ resignification" means the lips are always in a dynamic relation to an insistence on the contingencies of the historical (221).

91. Caldwell, "Transforming Sacrifice," 21. Recall from chapter 1 that the positing of a universal as neutral inherently involves an occlusion of the particularities of material existence. After all, Irigaray insists the universal is never neutral.

92. Irigaray, *Mediation of Touch*, 74.

93. Nelson, *The Argonauts*, 62–63. Irigaray's essay "When Our Lips Speak Together" was part of the women's- and gender-studies canon throughout the 1990s and early 2000s in the United States, making its appearance in multiple feminist theory readers of that era. Nelson thus invokes a moment that many women who have ever taken a feminist theory course may have had.

94. Fanny Söderbäck's work is particularly instructive here for exploring this question of the temporality opened up by Irigaray's materiality. In *Revolutionary Time*, Söderbäck focuses on Irigaray's remaking of the maternal and material together as a remaking of time, one that reaches back to the maternal as forgotten origin—but that in this reaching back, also occurs through the body as a dynamic present. Söderbäck's reaching back to the maternal is not the queer time of desire that I contend lips engender; Söderbäck's reading of Irigaray highlights prioritization of generation in Irigaray's notion of materiality. Söderbäck, *Revolutionary Time: On Time and Difference in Kristeva and Irigaray* (Albany: State University of New York Press, 2019), esp. 185, 242.

95. Söderbäck, *Revolutionary Time*, 265.

96. Note that while porosity is an important dimension of this refiguring of inside and outside, it involves a certain passivity that is part of the touching, but not all of it.

97. Muñoz, *Cruising Utopia*, 17.

98. Universals transform the plurality of specificities into fixed singularities, suspending them in transcendence. This rhetorical question therefore recalls Caldwell's insistence, raised at the beginning of this section, that Irigaray's turn to materiality challenges universals as part of a sacrificial economy.

99. Here I am borrowing and playing on Maggie Berg's term *lipeccentric*. "Contradictions," 65.

100. Braidotti, *Nomadic Subjects*, 164.

Chapter 4

1. Spivak's Derridean-inspired critical homage to Foucault insists that Foucault's notion of power does not afford a notion of resistance that can be considered

in relation to individual freedom. See Gayatri Chakravorty Spivak, *Outside in the Teaching Machine* (New York: Routledge, 2009 [1993]), 27–57. Given the link to Foucault, it is no surprise that this assessment is not limited to postcoloniality; it resonates too with Lee Edelman's interrogation of negative ontologies that use the historicity of woman and Black being to assert their nonbeing. See *Edelman's* introduction to *Bad Education*.

2. Spivak, "More on Power/Knowledge," 48.

3. Spivak, 48.

4. In psychoanalytic terms, this failure to enact its claim mirrors the failure in mimesis that reveals the illusoriness of its wholeness.

5. Julietta Singh, *Unthinking Mastery: Dehumanism and Decolonial Entanglements* (Durham, NC: Duke University Press, 2017), 82.

6. Although Irigaray's lack of attention to postcolonial positions may make her seem an unlikely conversation partner for decolonial thought, Spivak's intellectual formation in feminist theory, literary theory, and deconstruction result in their overlap. Spivak engages Irigaray as part of her criticism of Western feminism and psychoanalysis in "French Feminism in an International Frame" (177–78). Spivak's homage to Foucault and Derrida (including their mutual though different reliance on Heidegger) continue to suggest a deep resonance with Irigaray's investment in thinking through the ontological and ontic in relation to questions of ontology, epistemology, and power. For more on the question of ontology, see Gayatri Chakravorty Spivak, *Teaching Machine*, especially pp. 27–57, 158–92.

7. Irigaray has been read in relation to questions of coloniality for over a decade. Rebecca Hill, Sabrina Hom, Ruthanne Kim, Shaireen Rasheed, and Laura Roberts, Stephen Seely, and Irene Watson are notable for their sustained decolonizing engagements, though they vary on their interpretations of the limits of the sexuate as the lens for this work. See especially Sabrina L. Hom "Between Races and Generations: Materializing Race and Kinship in Moraga and Irigaray," *Hypatia* 28, no. 3 (2013): 419–35; Ruthanne Soohee Crapo Kim, "A Feminist and Decolonial Approach to Kinship: An Ambiguous and Ambivalent Account," *Philosophy Compass* 19, no. 2 (2024); Fabiane Ramos and Laura Roberts. "Wonder as Feminist Pedagogy: Disrupting Feminist Complicity with Coloniality," *Feminist Review* 128, no. 1 (2021): 28–43; Shaireen Rasheed "Islam, Sexuality, and the 'War on Terror': Luce Irigaray's Post-Colonial Ethics of Difference," *American Journal of Islam & Society* 31, no. 1 (2014): 1–15; Stephen D. Seely, "Irigaray between God and the Indians: Sexuate Difference, Decoloniality, and the Politics of Ontology," *The Australian Feminist Law Journal* 43, no. 1 (2017): 41–65.

8. Spivak refers to the term *decolonization* as a "convenient and misleading word" that is meant to signify the displacement of colonialism, but that must remain under contestation in order to avoid becoming colonialism's inverse (which amounts to neocolonialism). See Spivak's discussion of Mahasweta Devi's fiction

as a way to think beyond feminist and Enlightenment subjectivity and political agency. *Teaching Machine*, 49.

9. Gayatri Chakravorty Spivak, "Echo," *New Literary History* 24, no. 1 (1993): 17–43. This essay was republished in Gayatri Chakravorty Spivak, *The Spivak Reader* (New York: Routledge, 1996). All citations for this chapter will cite the essay from *New Literary History*.

10. Spivak, "Echo," 19.

11. Ovid, *Metamorphoses: The New, Annotated Edition*, trans. Rolfe Humphries (Indianapolis: Indiana University Press, 2018), 67.

12. Ovid, *Metamorphoses* (Humphries), 67.

13. Ovid, 67.

14. See Spivak on deconstruction in Sara de Jong and Jamila M. H. Mascat, "Relocating Subalternity: Scattered Speculations on the Conundrum of a Concept," *Cultural Studies* 30, no. 5 (2016): 717–29.

15. Spivak, "Echo," 17.

16. Ovid, "The Story of Echo and Narcissus," in *Metamorphoses*, book 3, trans. A. S. Kline (Ann Arbor, MI: Ann Arbor Editions, 2004), 75. Rolfe Humphries's translation reads Juno's punishment as follows: "The tongue that made a fool of me will shortly have shorter use, the voice be brief hereafter" (Ovid/Humphries, 68).

17. Ovid, *Metamorphoses* (Kline), 75. See also Humphries's translation: "Echo always says the last thing she hears, and nothing further." Ovid, *Metamorphoses* (Humphries), 69.

18. Spivak, "Echo," 23. The term *respondent* is Spivak's term, not Ovid's.

19. I am indebted to my former professor, Claire Nouvet, for introducing me to Spivak's Echo and for informing my analysis of it—fundamentally shaped the trajectory of my work. See "An Impossible Response: The Disaster of Narcissus," *Literature and the Ethical Question*, ed. Claire Nouvet, *Yale French Studies* 79 (1991): 103.

20. In Ovid's telling, Juno sought Tiresias to arbitrate between Juno and Jupiter (Jove). But when Tiresias sides with Jove, Juno punishes Tiresias by making him blind. In his blindness, however, Tiresias gains the "power to tell the future." See "The Story of Tiresias" in *Metamorphoses* (Humphries), lines 316, 67.

21. Spivak, "Echo," 30.

22. Ovid, *Metamorphoses* (Humphries), 69.

23. Spivak, "Echo," 27. Note that fugis is translated as "flee," "fly," and "run," depending on the translation.

24. In Latin, the line reads "'quid' inquit 'me fugis,'" or "Why," he asked, "do you run from me?" Ovid, *Metamorphoses*, vol. 1, trans. Frank Justus Miller (G. P. Putnam's sons, 1916), lines 383–84, 150. I incorporate Miller's translation, which includes the Latin version of the text.

25. Spivak, "Echo," 26.

26. Spivak, "Echo," 24–25. Note the second-person singular imperative of fugere is fuge.

27. Echo repeats/reports back (*reportat*) the ends of voices heard, or as Humphries translates it "the last thing she hears." The Latin is "tantum haec in fine loquendiingeminat voces auditaque verba reportat." Ovid, *Metamorphoses* (Miller), lines 368–69, 149.

28. Spivak, "Echo," 24–25.

29. Clair Nouvet, CPLT 751: Theories of Subjectivity, class lecture, Emory University, Atlanta, GA, November 11, 2003.

30. The "law" of the text, as rules of grammar and syntax, and the law of the gods, given in the punishment, function simultaneously in this imprisonment of the feminine in language and in Echo's double dispossession.

31. Spivak, "Echo," 26.

32. For Derrida, *la différance* denotes a space and time of the gap between the implicit and explicit, between signs and signification—a result of and testament to the ways in which meaning is established through the differential relationship between terms. Spivak also suggests that Echo's position exceeds the limits of Derrida's reading of the absent interlocutor. See Spivak, "Echo," 27.

33. Spivak, 27.

34. Spivak, 24.

35. Spivak, 26.

36. Spivak, 32.

37. Ovid, *Metamorphoses* (Miller), 151.

38. See Ovid, *Metamorphoses* (Humphries), lines 372–403, 70.

39. Both stories prove tragic, and both reflect an unreturned desire. For Narcissus, his self-love meant he was unable to open to the other on the other's terms. Echo was unable to love on her own terms, in her own way, because she could only love Narcissus in a way that always returned that love to him. Echo's desires could not be spoken for an echo has no addressee. Her voice does not communicate anything. It only returns the desire, in and off the tongue of the other.

40. Echo's deferred response, which is a "truth not dependent on intention" (24), undoes the promises of narcissistic self-knowledge, in which one receives back the perfect image of the self one has put forward for the other to return. Narcissus cannot immediately experience the response to his desire. He cannot receive the image of himself that he wants. Echo becomes an indication of Narcissus's lack of self-knowledge. Spivak, 24–25.

41. By drawing attention to Echo, Spivak asserts the need to reconsider resistance and to view the postcolonial ethic as an ethic of risk in which the reward may simply be a response that refuses to respond, even if one refuses to respond in spite of one's self.

42. Spivak, *Teaching Machine*, 64.

43. Roberts, *Irigaray and Politics*, 109.

44. Roberts, 109.

45. Roberts, 110.

46. See Spivak, *Teaching Machine*, 32.

47. Roberts, *Irigaray and Politics*, 121.

48. Fionola Meredith asserts that the perceived crisis of postmodernity is one in which "marginalized" persons are either nonsubjects, in accordance with their own marginalized experiences, or miming subjects, who couch their experiences in terms of predetermined dominant worldviews. Meredith insists this crisis of perception is unnecessary, arguing instead for a postmetaphysical self that emerges through a paradigm of writing toward otherness, wherein those who are marginalized speak through their indeterminacy and uncertainty, beyond the seemingly either/or of false dichotomies. See *Experiencing the Postmetaphysical Self: Between Hermeneutics and Deconstruction* (New York: Palgrave Macmillan, 2005), 2–3.

49. Spivak reads Ovid's Echo to demonstrate that this crisis of representation can be seen in the inability of a normative masculine discourse of justice and punishment to account for the marginalized subaltern other it seeks to punish. Spivak not only creates space for Echo's voice; she also shows that it is within the aporia of the condition of the subaltern that the intentionality of the juridical subject is shattered.

50. Reading Fanon's interpretation of unveiled Algerian women "passing" as pro-European to disguise their revolutionary aims, Diana Fuss emphasizes Fanon's notion of the "nonmimetic," as imitation without identification. Irigaray's mimetic writing is similar in that it is disruptive and embraces a certain performance. However, only if we read catachresis and mimesis as actions (as deliberate writings/deconstructions) can this fit with Fuss's emphasis on the importance of intentionality for political resistance. Fuss warns against Fanon's essentializing of Black femininity that "masquerade is a natural function of femininity"—an important reminder to tread lightly in the movement from politics to ontology in order to avoid rendering woman or the colonized as lack. Diana Fuss, *Identification Papers: Readings on Psychoanalysis, Sexuality, and Culture* (New York: Routledge, 1995), 152, 151.

51. Homi Bhabha depicts mimicry itself as a colonizing tool and not just an effect or consequence of colonizing, identitarian discourse. Citing Lacan's description of mimicry as camouflage, Bhabha suggests that colonial mimicry is a means to establish an Other (within the sociocultural order) who is not same but also not allowed to be in accordance with their difference—with the ironic effect of "pos[ing] an immanent [*sic*] threat to both 'normalized' knowledges and disciplinary powers," which itself prompts a need for "surveillance." Consistent with Irigary's and Spivak's discussions, Bhabha focuses on the problem of mimicry as reflective of an "interdictory desire" as "a discourse uttered between the lines and as such both against the rules and within them." But unlike Irigaray and Spivak, Bhabha's focus is not on the colonized using mimicry but on the way mimicry functions to support a logic of identity rather than undermine it. Homi Bhabha, "Of Mimicry and Man: The Ambivalence of Colonial Discourse," in *Tensions of Empire: Colonial*

Cultures in a Bourgeois World, ed. Frederick Cooper and Ann Laura Stoler (Berkeley: University of California Press, 1997), 153, 157.

52. Spivak's reading of Echo's and women's utterances reflects an interest in the deconstruction of linguistic structures, as seen, for example, in Kristeva's "The System and the Speaking Subject" or Irigaray's use of the term *la parole* to refer to women's speech, and more famously, *parler femme* to denote speaking woman/women's way of speaking as a different language meant to disrupt the stasis (selfsameness) of masculine language (*le langage*). Spivak's assertion that the catachresis is a crisis of Echo's speech/utterance also gestures toward significations through disruption of homogeneity and stasis of the selfsame masculine language and the colonizing tongue.

53. Irigaray observes differences between utterances by her male and female patients. She documents the structure of sentences given by male analysands as follows: "*I wonder if I am loved* or *I tell myself that perhaps I am loved.*" In contrast, she says women typically phrased the topic in terms of an actual question, asking, "*Do you love me?*" The male subject does not engage an other addressee or listener but "speaks to himself." The self-doubt of his "wonder" can only be resolved by the subject (I) itself. Female subjects' question, though, "presents the message as ambiguous." The women render themselves objects in the grammatical structures they use. The addressee, the *you* in the "D*o you love me?*" is the subject on which the *me* relies for a response (i.e., "yes" or "no") that would give meaning to the question; woman's identity is bound to the response of the subject of her inquiry (you). *Irigaray, An Ethics of Sexual Difference*, 134–35.

54. Note that disruption to this totality does not come from an outside; rather, resistance looks much more like Irigaray's efforts to disassimilate the feminine from masculine discourse and seems to belong to the embodiedness of alterity that cannot materialize in discourse, entailing a certain agency that is not the agency of volition. Spivak locates disruption not in the "nature" of Echo but in the failure of the system to enact a complete enclosure. Here, Echo is a sort of victim (violated) but is also the condition of the possibility of resistance.

55. Echo has been written in the feminine and subjected to a narrative (and juridical order) in which the feminine cannot be the same in her own difference. Her words cannot be spoken and allow the text to continue in the manner it intends, according to the punishment it has imposed on her. She cannot say, "me fugis," without speaking in the masculine tongue, which would disrupt the gendered nature of language; Ovid then cloaks this violence of her impossible position with a second violence by speaking for her. The feminine must be excluded for the narrative to continue its trajectory toward the wholeness of meaning making. But this exclusion of the feminine in language is what I would argue leads to the alienation of the nymph from her body—suggesting that women's orientation to the law is an effect of language, but not necessarily that her orientation to language is ontological.

56. Spivak's depiction of the "pre-ontological ontic level of the everydayness of the being" in Foucault and Derrida is useful for thinking through the complex relationship between ontology and catachresis. The reference to a preontological ontic

suggests modes of being that are indeterminate insofar as they are not trapped in ontology as a discourse of origins and being. In her chapter on Foucault in *Outside in the Teaching Machine*, Spivak asserts that the ontico-ontological defies liberalism's notion of the ethical subject (see 41–47). If we apply this assertion to her reading of Echo, Echo's preontological ontic reality is an aporia that would recast ethics apart from the liberal/modern subject whose subjectivity emerges through egoistic self-projection. Put differently, Echo exists in her difference, whether or not that difference is prior to her naming and her subjection to the law. Ovid must deal with her after all. Her unintended deferred response gestures to the space and time (and irreducible difference) in the aporia prior to any reduction of her being.

57. Johanna Oksala, *Foucault, Politics, and Violence* (Evanston: Northwestern University Press, 2012), 16.

58. This is Spivak's secondary description of the preontological ontic. See *Outside in the Teaching Machine*, 38.

59. Oksala, *Foucault, Politics, and Violence*, 18.

60. There is space in Irigaray's notion of embodiment that I think can tend to the historically situated genres of subjectivity. Since she talks about mining the tradition for the erasures of women and the use of the feminine, the symbolic would not really be a totality for her. The selfsameness of a phallocentric symbolic is not the only way to imagine the world. Accordingly, Irigaray turns to sexuation as the foundation of another mode of relation, a new language, and a new way of becoming. The problem as I see it is that Irigaray does not submit her own imaginings of relation to the same test to which she submits Heidegger and Levinas in pointing to these thinkers' universalization of their own difference.

61. Andrés Fabián Henao Castro, "Ontological Captivity: Toward a Black Radical Deconstruction of Being," *Differences* 32, no. 3 (2021): 89.

62. Henao Castro, 89.

63. Spivak criticizes Western intellectual institutions broadly for their neo-imperialism. But even in her homage to Foucault and Derrida, she contends that intellectual work, no matter how elegant in its descriptions and responsible in its aims, is not the same as performing the labor of the subaltern. Spivak, *Teaching Machine*, 51.

64. Sumit Chakrabarti describes Spivak's deconstructive readings as "arbitrary and interventionist" in a way that is meant to "subvert the hegemonic formations of Western historiography." Chakrabarti uses the term *affirmative deconstruction* to describe these efforts, which I think captures the aim of Spivak's work but oversimplifies the depth of her deconstruction. This oversimplification will also be what allows Chakrabarti to say Homi Bhabha's postmodern engagements are "more complex." Sumit Chakrabarti, "Moving beyond Edward Said: Homi Bhabha and the Problem of Postcolonial Representation," *International Studies* 14, no. 1 (2019).

65. Spivak suggests that deconstructive critique itself is perhaps the best way to avoid the pull of the ontic that would simply be a "ruse" of colonizing logic and its manifestations in the "politics of difference." Spivak, *Teaching Machine*, 53.

66. Singh, *Unthinking Mastery*, 30.

67. Singh, 31.

68. Singh, 97–98. Singh draws on Mark Sanders's definition of complicity, in which opposition involves a participation in the thing it opposes. See Mark Sanders, *Complicities: The Intellectual and Apartheid* (Durham, NC: Duke University Press, 2002).

69. Zaynab Shahar explicitly links Singh's project with Spivak's work. See Zaynab Shahar, "Fear, Flight, and Freedom: On Anti-Colonial Countermasteries and Ontological Insecurities," *Horizontes Decoloniales=Decolonial Horizons* 1 (2019): 165–96.

70. Shahar, 169.

71. Shahar, 169.

72. Shahar draws on Maria Lugones and on the affective dimensions of the colonizer-colonized relationship and the political "weaponiz[ing]" of affect—and on Lugones and Nelson Maldonado-Torres to focus on the way "indifference" is perpetuated in colonial and anticolonial discourse. Shahar, 183. For Maldonado-Torres, this indifference is ontological; for Lugones it is not. Shahar notes that for both theorists, indifference is reproduced in countermastery narratives. See Shahar, 180–87.

73. Shahar, 185.

74. Shahar is reading Walter Mignolo, *The Darker Side of Western Modernity: Global Futures, Decolonial Options* (Durham, Duke University Press, 2011), 136.

75. Halberstam urges the reader to reimagine failure in relation to queer spaces in order to consider "what happens when failure is productively linked to racial awareness, anticolonial struggle, gender variance and different formulations of the temporality of success." Judith Halberstam, *Queer Art of Failure* (Durham, NC: Duke University Press, 2011), 92.

76. Shahar, "Fear, Flight, and Freedom," 189.

77. Shahar, 168, 185, 190.

78. Shahar writes, "Understanding foundational anti-colonial discourses and texts as queer failures might yield the sort of queer-feminist knowledge production Lugones and other decolonial feminists believe is possible. Such a departure would require more than decolonial enunciation that declares texts and thinkers as queer failures. It would require rereading foundational texts and discourses with the desire to deconstruct the affective politics of mastery. . . . [not] to merely ascertain what was done wrong but to better understand how foundational political affects have their hauntologies in the present." Shahar, 190–91.

79. Ahmed, *Willful Subjects* (Durham, NC: Duke University Press, 2014), 174.

80. Ahmed, 1.

81. Ahmed, 174.

82. Ahmed on Gramsci, 174. For an excellent collection that covers multiple dimensions of the Italian political theorist's thought and life, including his critical adaptations of Marx that emerged from during his initial imprisonment in 1929, see Davide, Caddedu, ed., *A Companion to Antonio Gramsci: Essays on History and Theories of History, Politics and Historiography* (Boston: Brill 2020).

83. Ahmed, *Willful Subjects*, 175.

84. Ahmed's notion of willfulness is related to her emphasis on embodiedness as more than a voluntary political decision. Willfulness is an embodied position of "holding on" that reverberates in Alexis Pauline Gumbs's interpretation of "survival" in Audre Lorde's work and as part of the Black radical tradition, wherein embodied survival abides in promise (not unlike Ahmed's discrete sense of optimism) that is in some ways unintentional, or as Gumbs says, "unavoidable." Alexis Pauline Gumbs, "The Shape of My Impact," *The Feminist Wire*, October 12, 2019, https://thefeministwire.com/2012/10/the-shape-of-my-impact/.

85. As I have mentioned previously, Irigaray's *The Mediation of Touch* was published while this manuscript was in its final stages of post-reader-report revisions. And while I regret that timing prohibited me from fully engaging *Mediation of Touch*, I would point the reader to Irigaray's extensive discussion of affect, desire, and self-affection in *Mediation* as promising for future investigations of Irigarayan desire in relation to Ahmed's affect.

86. Willfulness looks a bit like a subjectivity that is not tied up in the language of voluntary political acts that reinforce identity. The efforts of willful subjects are therefore not resisting through a self-naming that could be reabsorbed by the political.

87. What is this body that Echo loses in her pining? There are multiple ironies in writing about and referencing the materiality of a nymph within a text afforded the status of a "classic" in literature. There are many displacements between the discursive representations and the corporeal that highlight the ways bodies, and materialities more broadly, are imagined. The body Echo will lose is a materialization of her difference according to the law of the text. The law gives her a body that it can then punish and take from her.

88. Irigaray uses the terms *feminine* and *female imaginary* at various points in her work, including her clear assertion about her project in *This Sex,* where she describes her work as both a retraversal of the masculine imaginary in order to (re)discover ((*re)trouver*) the feminine imaginary (l'imaginaire féminin). See Irigaray, *Ce Sexe*, 159; *This Sex*, 164.

89. Serene Khader articulates the tensions between many Western feminist and transnational feminist perspectives as an unnecessary tension between universalism and relativism. Opting for what she calls a "nonideal universalism," Khader rethinks feminist efforts to work toward gender justice without reifying those approaches in some new universal. Khader, *Decolonizing Universalisms: A Transnational Feminist Ethic* (New York: Oxford University Press, 2019). My rethinking of the position of the excluded beyond a position of lack, and yet within the condition of the double bind, is similarly an effort to reframe the very notion of relativism beyond its relation to the universal as a singular concept. See also Khader's response to the symposium on her book, with Linda Alcoff, Sunaina Arya, and Olúfẹ́mi O. Táíwò: Serene Khader, "Introduction: Symposium on Serene J. Khader's *Decolonizing Universalism: A Transnational Feminist Ethic,*" *Journal of Global Ethics* 16, no. 3 (2020): 343–48.

90. Her materiality was effaced in and through the repeated violations of her difference as she was subjected to the law; the violations of her difference allowed the law to posit its self-sufficiency, to encapsulate its logic and the logic of a selfsame subject.

91. Spivak concludes her engagement with the question of power and resistance in Foucault and Derrida by turning to Bengali writer Mahasweta Devi. "More on Power/Knowledge," 24. Having lived through India's independence movement, Spivak describes her as a "citizen of a recently decolonized 'nation.'" "More on Power/Knowledge," 53. Spivak suggests this subject position means that Mahasweta's writing constitutes an epistemic space that is outside (not a mere reversal of) the colonizing logic of imperialism that gets reinscribed in the language of nationhood. Her portrayal of Mahasweta resonates deeply with her depiction of Echo, whose relation to catachresis is unintentional, whose position is one of relation to "justice done" that also disrupts and creates a space beyond a simple reversal of the colonizing logic of identity.

92. We can describe this radical materiality, returning to Irigarayan terms, as the possibility of a proximity of relations. I am reading materiality as the prediscursive (or extradiscursive) materiality of alterity that constitutes Irigarayan desire, the materiality of Echo for which the law cannot account that enacts the catachresis, or the materiality in Lorde's survival that redefines "intentional" living in relation to the irreducible space and time of the memory of ancestors.

93. Michalinos Zembylas reads affect theory in relation to Spivak, focusing on the prediscursive dimensions of postcolonial embodiment. Michalinos Zembylas, "Revisiting Spivak's 'Can the Subaltern Speak' through the Lens of Affect Theory: Can the Subaltern Be Felt?" *Qualitative Research Journal* 18, no. 2 (2018): 115–27.

94. Ahmed, *Willful Subjects*, 175.

95. But unlike Ahmed's formulation, this willfulness does not hold on as though the willful subject ever has or fully knows what she wants. Ahmed specifically insists it is the subject who is not fully aware that opposes the figment that a subject ever does know (is self-coinciding). *Willful Subjects*, 175.

96. Ahmed's turn to affect, like that of Berlant, imagines a subject who is not a fully knowing subject but rather one who becomes and even "feels" in relation to a complex sociopolitical and cultural matrix.

97. Irigaray's notion of breath provides a dynamic ontology that also gestures to unintentionality as possibility.

98. See Clare Hemmings, "Affect and Feminist Methodology, Or What Does It Mean to Be Moved?" in *Structures of Feeling: Affectivity and the Study of Culture*, ed. Devika Sharma and Frederik Tygstrup (Boston: De Gruyter, 2015), 148.

99. Braidotti emphasizes the distinction between the will and desire in psychoanalysis in order to articulate Irigaray's unique sense of embodiment and its significance for politics, emphasizing that representation here "is not merely a cultural scheme but also fulfills an ontological function." *Nomadic Subjects: Embodiment and*

Sexual Difference in Contemporary Feminist Theory, 2nd ed. (New York: Columbia University Press, 2011), 103. One cannot simply will oneself to change because the imprint of the symbolic itself is embodied. Desire, unlike will, captures the unrepresented force of relations. In this way, desire is perhaps a more useful concept than willfulness for capturing Ahmed's efforts to think beyond the self-identical political and still think in terms of a prepolitical possibility of agency—one that does not demand political recognition.

100. Luce Irigaray, *Sharing the Fire: Outline of a Dialectics of Sensitivity* (New York: Springer, 2020), 14.

101. Sara Ahmed writes that ontology is only pure ontology "if we strip subjects and objects of any attributes." *Living a Feminist Life* (Durham, NC: Duke University Press, 2017), 156.

102. See Irigaray, *Sharing the Fire*, 35.

103. Irigaray, 10.

104. Irigaray, 1.

105. Irigaray's work presents a framework for a dynamic, "decolonized" ontology of the ambiguity and irreducibility of desire as a way to think an embodied alternative to becoming without participating in the logic of sameness.

106. See Lauren Berlant's work on affect in *Cruel Optimism* (Durham, NC: Duke University Press, 2011). In particular, consider the way one participates in affect and how through repetition, affective structures are created.

107. Here I borrow from Audre Lorde's notion of Black women's survival a certain resistance in and of itself.

108. This approaches Berlant's notion of the suffering of the everyday or the ordinariness of suffering.

109. Recalling Meredith's search for writing through the double bind to engender a postmetaphysical subject, the dynamic ontology reveals itself in the unintentional failures of mimesis, or in the catachresis of Echo's narrative.

Chapter 5

1. Kathryn Gines, "From Color-Blind to Post Racial," *Journal of Social Philosophy* 41, no. 3 (2010): 379. Gines explains that the use of the term *postracial* is too frequently a means of occluding the effects of racism and erasing racialization in name and acting thereby as a means of undermining the capacity of those impacted by racist structures and institutions to name race as the main or even contributing factor in discriminatory policies and practices. Joseph Winters also takes up the question of the postracial as it is entangled with American exceptionalism. See *Hope Draped in Black: Race, Melancholy, and the Agony of Progress* (Durham, NC: Duke University Press, 2016), 187–235.

2. This brings up another thread in this book: the question of history and its role in producing and reproducing norms and occluding differences, and therein, the difficulty of appeals to historicization and the reliability of history as a source for liberatory discovery.

3. #SayHerName developed in response to the lack of attention media gave to the deaths of Black women. See the African American Policy Forum, https://www.aapf.org/sayhername, which documents the timeline and circumstances of these deaths. Jared Sexton briefly frames #SayHerName in relation to #BlackLivesMatter to think through the stakes of Afropessimist contestations of coalition building and how anti-Blackness informs Black social life, including heteronormative and phal-locentric forms of representation. See Jared Sexton, "Afro-Pessimism: The Unclear Word," *Rhizomes* no. 29 (2016): 5–8.

4. Braidotti, *Nomadic Subjects*, 97.

5. My invocation of Irigaray's decolonizing ontology in the previous chapter attempts to reimagine the "predicament" (to borrow from Spivak) of colonized, gendered, and radicalized subject positions in terms of the fecundity of that palpable ambiguity of desire.

6. Irigaray's early use of mimesis, is especially helpful for challenging the prioritization of visibility (the perception of what is seen/recognized) as constitutive of presence (which ultimately has implications for challenging the politics of presence).

7. Christos Hadjioannou, "Can Our Being in the World Remain in the Neuter?," in *Towards a New Human Being*, ed. Luce Irigaray, Mahon O'Brien, and Christos Hadjioannou (New York: Springer, 2019), 195.

8. Manigault-Bryant interrogates the relationship between politics of Black subjectivity and eros as that relationship pertains to racialization and the Black body. Though she does not specifically deal with the question of sexual differ-ence, Manigault-Bryant does engage the intersectional corporealities of gendered subject positions that I would argue result from representations of sexual differ-ence. LeRhonda S. Manigault-Bryant, "Where Black Bodies Lie: Historiography, Race, and the Place of Eros," *Theology & Sexuality*, 22, no. 3 (2016): 165–74.

9. Manigault-Bryant, 168.

10. Manigault-Bryant, 168.

11. Manigault-Bryant insists that eros is especially complicated for Black bodies and Black sexuality, largely due to the significance Black religions play in the cultivation and sustaining of Black community. Manigault-Bryant, 168.

12. Manigault-Bryant, 168–69.

13. Manigault-Bryant, 169.

14. Manigault-Bryant, 169.

15. Emphasis is original. Manigault-Bryant, 171.

16. Manigault-Bryant, 171.

17. See also Manigault-Bryant's "A 'Club' No Black Woman Wants to Join: Confronting the Aftermath of Black Death," *Black Perspectives*, July 19, 2016, https://www.aaihs.org/confronting-the-aftermath-of-black-death/.

18. I gesture here to Saidiya Hartman's notion of "critical fabulation" as the work of relational narration that she uses to attend to the singularities of the unthought—work that will be discussed at the end of this chapter.

19. Here, I want to draw attention to a thoughtful consideration of race within the psychoanalytic framework that prioritizes sexual difference, consistent with Lacan, and yet also thinks the idea of wholeness that structures selfsame desire as white *and* phallic. In no way am I suggesting that the discourse of race is synonymous with Afropessimist conceptions of Blackness as Black death. Rather, I want to consider what a reading of whiteness as constitutive of selfsame desire can offer for thinking an ontology of Blackness beyond racial representations and a sexuate beyond representations of sex, gender, and sexuality.

20. In thinking through race as signified by whiteness, she does not think Blackness presymbolically in the way that Wilderson, Warren, Sexton, or even Moten does.

21. Kalpana Seshadri-Crooks, *Desiring Whiteness: A Lacanian Analysis of Race* (New York: Routledge, 2000), 3.

22. Seshadri-Crooks, 103.

23. It is because the relationship of sexual difference is unrepresentable that Lacan also says woman is "not whole," and that "woman" does not signify anything. See seminar XX in *Ecrits*. See also Seshadri-Crooks, *Desiring Whiteness*, 140–41.

24. Seshadri-Crooks thus understands race as bound to an unethical structure that reduces difference to sameness and veils that reduction through a signification of differences bound to whiteness.

25. Seshadri-Crooks, *Desiring Whiteness*, 3.

26. Seshadri-Crooks follows Lacan here to suggest that representation effectively places the subject in the chain of signification in a way that gives the subject its meaning. Seshadri-Crooks, 105.

27. Here, she frames both visibility and discursivity as part of the symbolic more broadly.

28. Seshadri-Crooks, *Desiring Whiteness*, 131, 144. Seshadri-Crooks offers a brilliant analysis of Scott McGehee and David Siegel's 1993 film *Suture*, which she notes follows the structure of desire as framed by Lacan's reading of Freud's law of the (dead) father. Here, a Black man and a white man are cast as identical twins, the two visibly raced bodies portrayed as the same. Seshadri-Crooks argues that the film's literal identification of these racialized bodies is the occasion for "misidentification" because the film refuses the viewer's notion of racial difference as a construct. She explains the implications of this refusal of the "logic of racial gestalt implicit in both resemblance and similitude" as modes of representation. The difference is something the viewer sees but is being told no one else sees. Seshadri-Crooks, 125.

29. Seshadri-Crooks, 12.

30. She continues with a quote from Lacan, focusing on bodily jouissance as that foundation of the "living body" (Lacan, Seminar 20, 24). Seshadri-Crooks, *Desiring Whiteness*, 125.

31. Irigaray's prioritization of sexual difference over other types of difference has everything to do with her critical adaptation of the Lacanian model for understanding the becoming of subjects through the symbolic order. Writing on Irigaray's understanding of sexual difference and the ways in which women constitute a space of "relative" belonging to culture and politics, Rosi Braidotti notes an opening for engaging race and sex as structural positions. Braidotti suggests that in regard to the power of racism and misogyny as constitutive of societal organization and institutions, "woman or the person of color as 'Other' is constructed as 'different from' the expected norm: as such she or he is both the empirical referent for and the symbolic sign of pejoration." Braidotti, *Nomadic Subjects*, 97.

32. Edelman, *Bad Education*, 171.

33. See Lewis Gordon's critical engagement with the philosophical presuppositions of and what he deems paradoxes in Afropessimist thought. Lewis Gordon, *Freedom, Justice, and Decolonization* (New York: Routledge, 2021). See especially pp. 73–84.

34. Hortense Spillers, Saidiya Hartman, Farah Jasmine Griffin, Shelly Eversley, and Jennifer L. Morgan, "'Whatcha Gonna Do?': Revisiting 'Mama's Baby, Papa's Maybe: An American Grammar Book': A Conversation with Hortense Spillers, Saidiya Hartman, Farah Jasmine Griffin, Shelly Eversley, & Jennifer L. Morgan," *Women's Studies Quarterly* 35, no. 1/2 (2007): 299–309.

35. See Hortense Spillers, "All the Things You Could Be by Now, If Sigmund Freud's Wife Was Your Mother: Psychoanalysis and Race," *Boundary* 2, no. 23 (1996): 80.

36. Spillers, "84.

37. Note that some theorists hyphenate *anti-Blackness* and others do not. Lewis Gordon, who is critical of Afropessimism, suggests that *antiblackness*, unhyphenated, more accurately captures the efforts of Afropessimist theory to challenge the notion that anti-Blackness is an antagonism that emerges in the world—and that the unhyphenated variant points instead to a more fundamental antagonism that is the condition of worlding itself. Gordon, *Freedom, Justice, and Decolonization*, 75. In this chapter, I primarily use anti-Blackness, consistent with most of the Afropessimist theorists I am citing.

38. Sexton traces Afropessimism to the history of pessimism in philosophy and explains it in relation to the ethical and political. See Jared Sexton, "Affirmation in the Dark: Racial Slavery and Philosophical Pessimism," *The Comparatist* 43, no. 1 (2019): 90–111. Henao Castro argues that the idea of "ontological captivity" is present in DuBois prior to Heidegger, with whom the term is most often associated. Henao Castro, "Ontological Captivity," 96.

39. Henao Castro, "Ontological Captivity," 104.

40. Spillers, "All the Things," 84.

41. Calvin Warren, *Ontological Captivity: Blackness, Nihilism, and Emancipation* (Durham: Duke University Press, 2018), 29.

42. Wilderson, *Red, White, Black*, 26.

43. Wilderson, 26.

44. Daniel Colucciello Barber, "The Creation of Non-Being," *Rhizomes: Cultural Studies in Emerging Knowledge*, 29 (2016), http://www.rhizomes.net/issue29/barber.html.

45. Afropessimism often employs Lacanian psychoanalytic concepts to articulate a notion of Blackness as a position radically opposed to prevailing liberal notions of freedom and justice. Frantz Fanon is seminal to this work: "I came into this world anxious to uncover the meaning of things, my soul desirous to be at the origin of the world, and here I am an object among other objects. Locked in this suffocating reification, I appealed to the Other so that his liberating gaze . . . would give me back the lightness of being I thought I had lost." Frantz Fanon, *Black Skin, White Masks* (New York: Grove, 2008), 89. Fanon explains the ways in which language constitutes the field of becoming; insofar as the colonized Black body must speak the language of the colonizer to come into being, it is always a misspeaking that involves a disavowal of one's Blackness. As Fanon suggests in the context of French Algeria, to try to speak French "properly" recapitulates colonizers' construction of Blackness and Black speech as the absence of culture, as other than civilization. There can in fact be no social origin for those whose identity has been fabricated/created through the imposition to respond to the address of another as the condition for being recognized, as the condition for social being.

46. Patrice Douglass and Frank Wilderson, "The Violence of Presence," *Black Scholar* 43, no. 4 (2014): 117–23, 117–18.

47. Douglass and Wilderson note that they borrow this language of genre from Sylvia Wynter, in particular her depiction of genre in "*ProudFlesh* Inter/views: Sylvia Wynter," *ProudFlesh New Afrikan Journal of Culture, Politics, and Consciousness*, no. 4 (2006). See footnote 5 in Douglass and Wilderson, "The Violence of Presence," 122.

48. Douglass and Wilderson, 118.

49. In their reading of Elaine Scarry's *The Body in Pain: The Making and Unmaking of the World* (New York: Oxford University Press, 1985), Wilderson and Douglass assert that the violence of torture is aimed at destroying the metaphysics of presence that constitutes the subject's "being," though there is a more fundamental (physical and psychological) violence at work: Black death is the ground of metaphysics, such that torture has been "deracinated." And this deracination means that the adjudication, or the psychic and social redressing, of such violence, as well as the "metaphysical renewal" of healing, is impossible for Black persons.

50. Wilderson and Douglass, "The Violence of Presence," 122.

51. Calvin Warren, *Ontological Terror: Blackness, Nihilism, and Emancipation* (Durham, NC: Duke University Press, 2018). Lee Edelman emphasizes Warren's distinction between queerness as "unfreedom" and Blackness as "non-ontological" as setting him apart from Wilderson's work. However, Edelman ultimately argues that Warren nonetheless, "like Wilderson, links Blackness as ontological impossibility to the foreclosure from subjectivity of those who embody it catachrestically," Edelman, *Bad Education*, 103.

52. Warren uses this term repeatedly in *Ontological Terror* to describe the tradition of interrelatedness of ontology and metaphysics in terms of their questions and assumptions about being and knowing, including the ways metaphysics structures materiality around "ontological imagining around differences." Warren, *Ontological Terror*, 33.

53. Warren, "Nihilism," 221.

54. The "ontological equation" refers to the three-fifths compromise of 1783, which counted enslaved persons in the United States as three-fifths of a person for taxation and representation purposes. But this "compromise" is not simply a political calculation; the equation cuts to the very being of Blackness in America. Warren, "Nihilism," 216.

55. Hope participates in anti-Blackness not unlike the ways that narratives of independence participate in colonialism.

56. Warren is drawing on Grant Fared's work on electoral politics here. Warren, "Nihilism," 221.

57. Warren, 221.

58. Warren, 221.

59. Warren, 221.

60. Warren, 221. In *Ontological Terror*, Warren expands upon his notion of Black being as an impossibility within ontometaphysics. Warren's reading of "Black being" as providing the "ontological labor . . . in an antiblack world" means that ontology and metaphysics are both fundamentally antithetical to Black existence. He writes, "Black being is the evidence of an ontological murder, or onticide, that is irrecoverable and irremediable." In this language of onticide, I find echoes Irigaray's assertions that a certain matricide undergirds thought about ontology. Warren adds, "Ultimately, I propose that the Negro Question is a proper metaphysical question, since the Negro is black and black(ness) has always been a terror for metaphysics." Warren, *Ontological Terror*, 27–28.

61. Warren, "Nihilism," 221.

62. Warren, *Ontological Terror*, 100.

63. Warren, "Nihilism," 221.

64. Warren, 221. Emphasis added.

65. See also Henao Castro's incisive description and critique of the relationship between the ontological, ethical, and political in Calvin Warren's work. Henao Castro, "Ontological Captivity," 85–113.

66. Fred Moten, *In the Break: The Aesthetics of the Black Radical Tradition* (Minneapolis: University of Minnesota, 2003), 90–91.

67. See Moten's critical turn to the distinction between thing (Ding) in Heidegger and an object in order to elaborate a way of thinking the nearness and distance of fugitivity that does not resubmit Blackness to an object for representational thinking. Fred Moten, "The Case of Blackness," *Criticism* 50, no. 2 (Spring 2008): 177–218.

68. Moten, 177.

69. Moten, 177.

70. Moten hints at the complex questions of materiality and perception as potentially representative and disruptive of this pathology of Blackness. See, for example, his textual engagement with James Baldwin's interpretation of the effects of Emmet Till's death and the publication of the gruesome image of Till's body as speaking to an "ontological impulse" while also disrupting ontology through the multidimensionality of resoundings that exceed the visual image (196). See also his reference to artist and philosopher Adrian Piper's invocation of the term *visual pathology*, to elaborate the criticism of the ocularcentrism of the visual (233–51). Though she ignores race as an ontological question(ing), Irigaray's turn to touching beyond the visible is her effort to challenge this ocularcentrism of visual. But in relation to Moten, much more is to be considered on the relation between touch and the sonorous. For more on Irigaray and the sonority of the visual, see Sarah Hickmott's innovative work in *Music, Philosophy and Gender in Nancy, Lacoue-Labarthe, Badiou* (Edinburgh: Edinburgh University Press, 2020).

71. Moten, "Blackness and Nothingness," 778.

72. Moten, 778. For a framing of Black optimism as in relation to rather than opposed to Afropessimism, see also Jonathan Howard, "To See the Earth before the End of the Antiblack World," *Souls* 22.2, no. 4 (2020): 292–314.

73. Moten, "Blackness and Nothingness," 778.

74. "Death bound" refers to Abdul JanMohamed's "Death bound subject." Moten, "Blackness and Nothingness," 739.

75. Moten, "The Case of Blackness," 182.

76. In *The Undercommons*, Moten also discusses the fantasy in the hold. There he and Stefano Harney argue that the Transatlantic Slave Trade is the foundation of the "ambition" of "[modern] logistics." (36). In one of the most poetically beautiful and also provacatively disturbing lines that recalls Moten's previously mentioned interrogation of phenomenological perception and also gestures (as I see it) to the lips, Moten writes of the experience of the hold as follows: "Having defied degradation the moment becomes a theory of the moment, of the feeling of a presence that is ungraspable in the way that it touches. This musical moment—the moment of advent, of nativity in all its terrible beauty, in the alienation that is always already born in and as parousia—is a precise and rigorous description/theory of the social life of the shipped, the terror of enjoyment in its endlessly redoubled folds." Stefano

Harney and Fred Moten, *The Undercommons: Fugitive Planning and Black Study* (New York: Minor Compositions, 2013), 36.

77. Moten, "Blackness and Nothingness," 778. Emphasis added.

78. Moten, "The Case of Blackness," 187.

79. Edelman frames Afropessimism and feminist projects (through Wilderson and through Irigaray by way of Catherine Malabou) as structurally similar with respect to Lacan's depiction of the Real and the symbolic order. Edelman, however, is critical of projects that risk prioritizing "ontological negations of a totalized world" (9), arguing that these efforts to draw on "woman" or "Black" as "unbearable Real of ontological negation" (16–17) continue to rely on some sort of affirmation of their "oneness" that "preserve[s] that world" (17). See Edelman, *Bad Education*, 1–43. For further analysis of Edelman's reading of Afropessimism, see Joseph Winters, "Queer Negativity and Racial Antagonism: Edelman, Afro-Pessimism, and the Limits of Recognition," in *Lee Edelman and the Queer Study of Religion*, ed. Kent L. Brintnall, Rhiannon Graybill, and Linn Marie Tonstad (New York: Taylor & Francis, 2023).

80. Henao Castro, "Ontological Captivity," 104.

81. Moten, "Blackness and Nothingness," 778. Since I have focused in previous chapters on the ways Irigaray's visceral language confounds metaphysical distinctions and on how lips specifically usher in a different temporality, I offer two examples here of the many found throughout Irigaray's work that gesture to a space of dwelling beyond metaphysics. First, playing with the semiotics of female flesh, Irigaray writes, "Woman, insofar as she is a container, is never a closed one. . . . The boundaries touch against one another while still remaining open. . . . The touch of one's body at the threshold." Irigaray, *Ethics*, 51. And in another example regarding the trope of the lips, she writes that these are also thresholds, "gathered one against the other but without any possible suture. . . . They offer a shape of welcome but do not assimilate, reduce, or swallow up." Irigaray, *Ethics*, 19. The concept of suturing in Irigaray and Black studies would be a topic worthy of future book. Seshadri-Crooks discusses Lacan's concept of suture, noting parenthetically that Lacan refers to it "briefly," in Seminar 11. *Desiring Whiteness*, 105.

82. Moten, "Blackness and Nothingness," 738.

83. Gumbs, "The Shape of My Impact."

84. I refer to Lorde's and Jordan's as acts of dying rather than murders in order to emphasize the unique subject position of survival and to allocate that agency rightfully within Lorde and Jordan as subjects. My work shares engagements similar to that of Rachel Jones. Unsurprisingly, Rachel Jones's essay "Sexual Difference in the Black Atlantic" also takes up the language of survival in the context of Black feminist thought. Rachel Jones, "Sexual Difference in the Black Atlantic," in *What Is Sexual Difference?*, ed. Mary Rawlinson and James Sares (New York: Columbia University Press, 2023), 270.

85. Emphasis of Greek is original. Manigault-Bryant, "Where Black Bodies Lie," 171.

86. Moten, "Blackness and Nothingness," 739.

87. Following the previous chapter's discussion of Spivak's, Singh's, and Ahmed's decolonization of subjectivity-as-identity, I would argue that Gumbs's reference to Black women's survival in academic institutions evokes a subjectivity beyond intention, beyond recognition as "a self-fulfilling movement of intent toward identity." Because it involves a temporality of desire, survival highlights the embodiedness of agency beyond intention and/or volition (understood as acts of autonomy that inform political identifications). It points to a certain agency of Black women's embodiments that exists because it exists (by existing—existing here is not passive).

88. Irigaray, *Sharing the Fire*, 99.

89. Anne Carson describes the dynamic enterprise of collection and division that defines Socratic thought in terms of eros. She writes, "A thinking mind is not swallowed up by what it comes to know. It reaches out to grasp something related to itself and to its present knowledge. . . . In any act of thinking, the mind must reach across this space between known and unknown, linking one to the other but also keeping visible to difference. It is an erotic space." Carson reads Sappho and Plato to attend to the relationship between wooing and knowing, respectively, noting that for both the poet and the philosopher, grasping an object or idea results in a reduction of the very difference needed to keep wooing and knowing erotic. *Eros the Bittersweet*, 171.

90. Moten on Chandler in "Blackness and Nothingness," 739.

91. I locate Warren's warning about politics and his subsequent turn to the relationship between the political and ontological to articulate the possibility of thinking Blackness a resonance to my insistence that discursive identifications, which includes political identifications, are symptoms of a more fundamental reduction of the alterity of materiality. But, I will add, there is a difference between positing this larger problem and thinking about how such a problem can be posited as such: the political—not as the institutions and practices of politics but rather as a sphere of relation in the social order—is the unavoidable context through which my thought emerges. I do not view the political as the condition of thought but as the context of thinking.

92. Irigaray, *Mediation of Touch*, 324.

93. Irigaray, *Sexes and Genealogies*, 59.

94. Irigaray, *To Be Two*, 9, 13.

95. Irigaray suggests that Merleau-Ponty's thinking of touch, even in his invocation of lips touching, does not account for the doubling of the lips (vertical and horizontal) of the "flesh of the feminine. See Irigaray, *Ethics*, 166.

96. Evoking Levinas's face-to-face encounter to reframe the ethical apart from visibility, Irigaray writes, "Looking at the other, respecting the invisible in him, opens a black of blinding void in the universe. Beginning from this limit, inappropriable by my gaze, the world is recreated. I inhabit it, but the entirety of its truth is not mine; since it is not completely known to me, it remains sensible

and alive. . . . We can remain together if you do not become entirely perceptible to me, if a part of you stays in the night." Irigaray, *To Be Two*, 8.

97. Significantly, Irigaray insists that this is a relationship of fleshy sensibility and transcendence that is multidimensional. After all, she asks, "Would a vertical transcendence not rob us of this third dimension beginning from which we approach each other as different others? Others in flesh and spirit?" As Irigaray imagines it, the relation of the interval of desire that allows two to be two resists the separation of space in terms of verticality and time in terms of the horizontal. Irigaray, *To Be Two*, 9, 13.

98. Irigaray, *Mediation of Touch*, 322.

99. In *Sharing the Fire*, Irigaray refers to a "dialectics of sensitivity" to emphasize the movement of desire as a disruption of metaphysical renderings of sense perception to overcome subject-object thinking. See especially chapters 2 and 3 in *Sharing the Fire*, 7–54. Bracketing the differences between Irigaray's invocations of these two concepts (i.e., sensible transcendental and dialectics of sensitivity), I interpret both references as a relation of, in, and through desire in order to rethink perception. And perception is related to representation because the symbolic order, of which representation is part, is the making sense of perception through reduction.

100. Rachel Jones, "Sexuate Difference in the Black Atlantic: Reading Irigaray with Hartman," in *What Is Sexual Difference?: Thinking with Irigaray*, ed. Mary C. Rawlinson, and James Sares (New York: Columbia University Press, 2023), 256.

101. Jones, 256.

102. Calvin Warren, "Improper Bodies: A Nihilistic Meditation on Sexuality, the Black Belly, and Sexual Difference," *Palimpsest* 8, no. 2 (2019): 42. This critique also illicits further discussion about Irigaray's failure to think the history of experimentation on Black and Brown women in the development of the speculum in her critique of specularization in *Speculum* that are beyond the scope of this chapter.

103. Zakiyyah Iman Jackson, "Sense of Things," *Catalyst: Feminism, Theory, Technoscience* 2, no. 2 (2016): 7, 3.

104. Jackson, "Sense of Things," 7. Jackson footnotes Derrida's framing of différance in *Of Grammatology* and *Margins of Philosophy* as the foundation of her depiction of the Black mater(nal) as "constitutive yet absent" in the myth making of Western imperialism. Hopkinson, Jackson argues, makes this "constitutive yet absent" present beyond visibility. Note that Jackson refers to the invisibility of this "constitutive yet absent" marked by the Black mater(nal); however, I would argue that the constitutive yet absent is better read as beyond the regime of visibility rather than reducing it to the inverse, or invisibility.

105. Jackson, 10.

106. Both the previous quotation and this one are from Jackson, "Sense of Things," and 5–6 respectively.

107. Warren, "Improbable," 36.

108. Jackson, "Sense of Things," 20.

109. Jared Sexton, *Black Men, Black Feminism: Lucifer's Nocturne* (Cham, Switzerland: Palgrave Macmillan, 2018), 80–81.

110. Warren, "Improbable, 36.

111. Musser, *Sensual Excess,* 9.

112. Musser, *Sensational Flesh*, 98.

113. Musser, *Sensual Excess*, 9.

114. Musser, 29.

115. Musser, 29.

116. Musser, 29.

117. Musser, 29.

118. Musser, 172.

119. Musser, 172.

120. Musser, 176. The association of female sexuality with excess must be understood not as external but as the constitutive absence. It is not simply what escapes because the flesh is captive. But it is, as Musser suggests, a consequence of living in difference in the "amorphous quality of fleshiness" of the captive body.

121. The very title of the book evokes an elsewhere of sensation that echoes her turn to the Black maternal body in the conclusion of *Sensual Excess* to think non-Oedipal modes of perception. Amber Jamilla Musser, *Between Shadows and Noise: Sensation, Situatedness, and the Undisciplined* (Durham, NC: Duke University Press, 2024).

122. Musser, *Between Shadows and Noise*, 4.

123. Musser's discussion of noise is beyond the scope of this project. Her attempt, though, to examine "what lies beneath representation"—an attempt that includes a deeply moving and theoretically provocative reading of chimerism—is fruitful for thinking difference in and through the multiplicity of one's flesh, and her sensual knowledge is not unlike a labial logic.

124. Asking this question entails and leads to many others, not the least of which is whether shadows offers a transvaluation of the economy of the visual and its valuations; and might lips reimagine the radicality of Eros for thinking Black life toward mutual survival that resists anti-Black and colonial worlds?

125. Just as Seshadri-Crooks's claims that adversarial aesthetics uses the mediums of writing and film to disrupt the regimes of representation, we can frame Irigaray's use of woman to confound representational thinking (to disrupt relationships between signifiers and referents as well as resemblances and disembodied similitudes) as a praxis of an othered, unthought desire.

126. Ruthanne Crapo Kim beautifully invokes Irigaray's reimagining of sense perception beyond the visible as an opportunity to think the racialization of sense making. Kim focuses on the womb as representative of Irigaray's turn to images of "dark places" that are part of this reimagining to locate an antiracist and decolonizing logic available in Irigaray's thought. See Ruthanne Crapo Kim, "Creolizing

Place, Origin, and Difference: The Opaque Waters between Glissant and Irigaray," *Hypatia* 37, no. 4 (Fall 2022): 765–83. My project turns to Irigaray's lips rather than wombs to invoke the self-affection of self-touching; and my invocation of Musser is an attempt to think beyond the dichotomies of light and dark that govern visibility and inform the racialization of matter.

127. As noted in chapter 1, the lips are meant to remake the metaphysics of space and time of the vertical and the horizontal (respectively); as chapter 3 suggests, this is also the possibility of a queer temporality.

128. I do not envision resistance as passively attributed to particular bodies in some essentialized way. In relation to the sociality of being, I think of resistance here in a manner closer to Joseph Winters's depiction (drawing on Mikhail Bakhtin) of the dual movement of centripetal and centrifugal forces that at once generate conformity and disruption. The major difference, however, in my thinking of resistance through Irigaray is in the turn to a presocial, presymbolic order of the sexuate, which gestures toward those "divergent desires" prior to any "divergence" from the social; the turn to a dynamic ontology of desire attempts to reimagine the relation to the social order altogether. In that sense, returning to ontology becomes a truly radical move. See Joseph Winters, *Hope Draped in Black*, 143–44.

129. While turning to Black materiality presents a fruitful engagement with Irigaray, I also think the queerness of the lips, especially in their capacity to elicit a self-touching, speaks to the need for an eros of bodies to be distinct in their touching apart from whiteness (just as for Irigaray, the sexuate would involve a self-touching distinct from reductions of the feminine to a masculine imaginary).

130. The critique of white hands on black bodies extends beyond the abuses of enslavement, policing, and carceration. See Janell Hobson's discussion of critics' interpretations of Nicki Minaj's *Anaconda* video exposes the ways white representations of beauty delimit the potential defiance and intellectual power of Black women's eros. While Minaj's critics were describing her video as pornographic, "Minaj's posts challenged viewers to consider her erotic appeal, sexual agency, and ironic performativity." Janell Hobson, "Remnants of Venus: Signifying Black Beauty and Sexuality," in *Women's Studies Quarterly* 46, no. 1/2 (2018): 105–20.

131. Saidiya Hartman, *Lose Your Mother: A Journey along the Atlantic Slave Route* (New York: Farrar, Straus and Giroux, 2007). Rachel Jones offers a careful and thoughtful analysis of Irigaray's notions of maternality in relation to Hartman's work and its implications for reading Black materiality and maternality that is irreducible to negation. Jones uses Emanuela Bianchi's depiction of the "elsewhere" of matter to link Irigaray and Hartman. See Jones, "Sexual Difference," 255, quoting from Emanuela Bianchi, *The Feminine Symptom: Aleatory Matter in the Aristotelian Cosmos* (New York: Fordham University Press, 2014), 240.

132. Saidiya Hartman, "Venus in Two Acts," *Small Axe : A Journal of Criticism* 12, no. 2 (2008): 1–14.

133. Frank B. Wilderson, "The Position of the Unthought: An Interview with Saidiya V. Hartman conducted by Frank B. Wilderson, III," *Qui Parle*, 13, no. 2 (2003): 184.

134. Hartman writes, "On one hand, the slave is the foundation of the national order, and, on the other, the slave occupies the position of the unthought." Wilderson, "The Position of the Unthought," 185.

135. Hartman, *Wayward Lives, Beautiful Experiments: Intimate Histories of Social Upheaval* (New York: Norton, 2019), 21.

136. I use the term *eros* rather than *desire* more broadly here to reflect Audre Lorde's insistence on the creative power of the erotic as a life force that expresses an interrelationality of body and spirit, of community and selfhood, beyond its reductions to a libidinal economy.

137. Hartman, *Wayward Lives*, 13–14.

138. Hartman, 13.

139. Hartman, xv.

140. Fanny Söderbäck highlights the importance of singularities that Hartman's recoveries engender, casting them as "narratives as care." Fanny Söderbäck, "Narration as a Practice of Care in the Wake of Violence: Adriana Cavarero's Narrative Theory and Saidiya Hartman's Critical Fabulation," *Journal of Italian Philosophy* 7 (2024): 88–126. I appreciate Söderbäck's approach; however, I hope that I have emphasized that I view this work as a labial logic more akin to survival.

141. The pattern of alienation of self and return to wholeness articulated in Hegel emerges. The being who aspires to wholeness originates from wholeness. If one concedes to this notion of being as a condition of wholeness from which one has been alienated and to which one must return, Black bodies, as ontologically divided, are excluded from ever becoming anything other than partial beings. And to be partial being in a world where being is synonymous with wholeness is to not be at all.

Chapter 6

1. Audre Lorde, "Uses of the Erotic," in *Sister Outsider: Essays & Speeches by Audre Lorde* (Trumansburg, NY: Crossing, 1984), 55.

2. Lorde, 57.

3. Lorde, 59.

4. This connection between the political and the ontological is evident in Lorde's articulation of consciousness as being shaped by the social and cultural life of a "european-american male tradition." Lorde, "Uses of the Erotic," 59.

5. Braidotti writes that for Irigaray, ethics is a recognition of alterity, and politics is about the representation of the unrepresented through memory and creativity to bring "the other of the Other into representation." Braidotti, *Nomadic Subjects*,

101. Braidotti's words about memory and creativity as the means to represent the unrepresented bring to mind Audre Lorde's essay "Uses of the Erotic," in which Lorde insists that the erotic has been separated from its "most vital areas of our lives" and that we must reclaim this erotic as a shared space of "creative energy." Lorde's emphasis is on reclaiming eros as the "creative power" "born of Chaos." Lorde, "Uses of the Erotic," especially pages 54–55.

6. Among feminist theorists offering innovative readings of materiality and the limits of the human who also consider the question of sexual difference through an Irigarayan genealogy are Alison Stone, Claire Colebrook, Iris Van der Tuin, and Evelien Geerts. Catherine Malabou does not figure prominently in my analysis; however, she too engages sexual difference by way of Irigaray and, to a greater extent, Derrida. See Catherine Malabou, *Changing Difference* (Malden, MA: Polity, 2011). Rachel Jones has explored the relevance of Jane Bennett's notion of "vital materiality" for conceptualizing the ethics of sexual difference for dwelling in the world with human and non-human others. Rachel Jones, "Vital Matters and Generative Materiality: Between Bennett and Irigaray," *Journal of the British Society for Phenomenology* 46, no. 2 (2015): 156–72. For an overview of feminist new materialisms particularly in relation to questions of epistemology and ontology (and onto-ethico-epistemology) with which I am engaged in this book, see Gill Jagger, "The New Materialism and Sexual Difference," in *Signs: Journal of Women in Culture and Society* 40, no. 2 (2015): 321–42. Jagger's article offers a clear framing of the concerns of new materialism in relation to poststructuralism, including demarcating these returns to materiality from Butler's notion of matter in relation to performativity. Susan Hekman's work connects the philosophical and theological dimensions of these questions of materiality and offers general insights for the significance of these conversations for feminist theology more broadly. Much work remains to be done in this area, but I find Hekman's efforts a good starting point for revisiting the materiality of Irigaray's self-claimed onto-theology. See, for example, Hekman, "Feminist New Materialism and Process Theology: Beginning the Dialogue," in *Feminist Theology* 25, no. 2 (2017): 198–207; and "Divine Women? Irigaray, God, and the Subject," in *Feminist Theology* 27, no. 2 (2019): 117–25. For Irigaray's distinct vision of onto-theology see Irigaray, *Mediation of Touch*, especially pp. 258–61.

7. I want to continue to think through various interests/investments: the posthumanist disruptions of ontology, the antihumanist positing of a materiality of difference prior to discourse (that posthumanists might say reontologizes matter), and the decolonial, radical queer, and Afropessimist critiques (as well as Irigaray's critique) of preontological violations of difference. Returning to the relationship between materiality and ethics as the responsibility to think beyond sameness confronts the otherwise impossible choice between prioritizing either materiality or discursivity all the way down. My hope is that desire offers a source for creative becoming as well as for critiquing power without fixing that becoming or critique upon a logic of identity (i.e., an ethics of radical desire in which the materiality

of alterity is the possibility of deterritorialization, and the possibility therein of expansive, irreducible, multidimensional touchings).

8. Irigaray, *Ethics*, 7.

9. In biocentrism, material relations are thought almost exclusively in terms of human relations, where the human and human relations are always already delimited by white, phallocentric, and biological reductions of matter. Wynter's assertion that that metaphysics is rooted in a biocentric notion of materiality, combined with questions about the racialization of matter raised in Afropessimism, raises significant challenges for thinking morphology without thinking about corporeality beyond the human. Emily Anne Parker turns to Irigaray's elemental difference to gesture toward this space without the pitfalls of the language of the sexuate and its encumbrances in psychoanalytic reductions and renditions of sex and sexuality. See Parker, *Elemental*, especially pp. 27–101.

10. Thanks to Katy Scrogin for helping me wordsmith this reconnection to Lorde.

11. Karen Barad, *Meeting the Universe Halfway: Quantum Physics and the Entanglement of Matter and Meaning* (Durham, NC: Duke University Press, 2007), 26.

12. Barad thinks materiality in terms of proximal relations and is therefore particularly useful for expanding concepts of materiality beyond the human and the corporeal.

13. Iris van der Tuin, "New Feminist Materialisms," in *Women's Studies International Forum* 34, no. 4 (2011): 271–77. This heterogeneity of new materialism and its particular feminist iterations and/or intersections with feminism have been represented in critical edited volumes. See the following: Stacy Alaimo and Susan Hekman, eds., *Feminist New Materialisms: Material Feminisms* (Indiana University Press, 2008); Diana Coole and Samantha Frost, eds. *New Materialisms: Ontology, Agency, and Politics* (Duke University Press, 2010); Rosi Braidotti, Felicity Colman, and Iris van der Tuin, *Methods and Genealogies of New Materialisms* (Edinburgh: Edinburgh University Press, 2023).

14. Aurora Hoel and Sam Skinner, "Curated Panel: 'Genealogies and Apparatuses of New Materialist Production' Aurora Hoel and Sam Skinner with contributions from Jelena Djuric, David Gauthier, Evelien Geerts, Sofie Sauzet and Maria Tamboukou," in *Methods and Genealogies of New Materialisms*, ed. Rosi Braidotti, Felicity Colman, and Iris van der Tuin van (Edinburgh: Edinburgh University Press, 2023): 112.

15. Clara Fischer, "Revisiting Feminist Matters in the Post-Linguistic Turn: John Dewey, New Materialisms, and Contemporary Feminist Thought," in *New Feminist Perspectives on Embodiment*, ed. Clara Fischer and Luna Dolezal (Cham: Springer, 2018), 84–85.

16. Ahmed accuses both Karen Barad and even Elizabeth Grosz in this regard. I take Ahmed's point, which Van Leeuwen echoes, to be that new materialism forgets the debt that is owed to Irigaray and science feminism. However, it's important

to note that Grosz has had a long history of writing and teaching on Irigaray. See Sara Ahmed, "Open Forum Imaginary Prohibitions: Some Preliminary Remarks on the Founding Gestures of the 'New Materialism,'" *The European Journal of Women's Studies* 15, no. 1 (2008): 23–39.

17. Rosi Braidotti, *Nomadic Theory: The Portable Rossi Braidotti* (New York: Columbia University Press, 2011), 132–33.

18. I emphasize *humanist* here to clearly distinguish the posthumanist challenges of subjectivity from the contemporary posthuman critiques of prioritizations of the human in thought.

19. Braidotti is particularly critical of Butler on the grounds that Butler does not take seriously a certain inescapability of materiality. Braidotti, like Grosz, thinks there are material differences (whether we call them "sexual" or "sexuate") that condition life itself. And for human life, those conditions remain. Even if we can generate life in a lab, that life requires at least two whose irreducible difference to each other is the possibility of generation. *Nomadic Theory*, 140.

20. Anne Van Leeuwen, "The Possibility of Feminist Phenomenology," *Journal of Speculative Philosophy* 26, no. 2 (2012): 475.

21. Van Leeuwen, 480.

22. Van Leeuwen, 480.

23. Van Leeuwen, 474.

24. Van Leeuwen, 481.

25. Irigaray, *Ethics*, 15.

26. Irigaray invokes the term *sensible transcendental* in the introduction to *Ethics*, and it will serve as the foundation for her rethinking of both the metaphysical and dialectical. *Ethics*, 32.

27. Irigaray, *Ethics*, 82. Emphasis added.

28. Caldwell turns to Irigaray's notion of fluid elements as a remaking of materiality in its difference as the condition of relations. Reading Irigaray's critique of Plato's allegory of the cave, Caldwell notes that for Irigaray, "the philosopher's progression from the material shadows of the cave to the bright world of ideas effaces the interdependence and interval that connects two domains." This ignoring of the passage from material to the intelligible renders the two in opposition. Materiality is always, therefore, that which must be overcome to achieve the order of ideas, of concepts, of intelligibility in its highest, transcendent form. The sensible transcendental would be a new way of imagining the relation of materiality to the transcendent that would respect the passageway, the threshold, such that there is no opposition of inside and outside, only continuous movement "shaped by a logic of fluids rather than solids." Anne Caldwell, "Transforming Sacrifice," 16–39.

29. Chanter writes that the term "conflates categories that traditionally philosophers have kept apart." I disagree with Chanter's use of the term conflate, as I think Irigaray specifies that this is a relational space, not a collapsing. Based on her reading of the eros of Irigaray's work, I think Chanter would agree that this is

not a simple collapsing or conflation—but she uses the term *conflate* nonetheless. Chanter, *Ethics of Eros*, 180.

30. In her examination of Spivak's reading of Irigaray on Levinas, Laura Roberts emphasizes Irigaray's reimagined dialectic of sexuate becoming to the sensible transcendental. Roberts, *Irigaray and Politics*, 125.

31. Chanter, *Ethics of Eros*, 180.

32. Tamsin Lorraine, *Irigaray and Deleuze: Experiments in Visceral Philosophy* (Ithaca, NY: Cornell University Press, 2018). See especially pp. 67–75.

33. I find that Emily Holmes's recent work on breath as the sensible transcendental is particularly innovative for complicating the idea of incarnation in terms of becomings. Her essay "The Age of Spirit" is particularly insightful in its troubling of the Christian trinitarian notion of time and her use of Irigaray's adaptation of the trinitarian imagery to recast the present apart from historical time. See Emily A. Holmes, "The Age of the Spirit: Irigaray, Apocalypse, and the Trinitarian View of History," in *Thinking Life with Luce Irigaray: Language, Origin, Art, Love*, ed. Gail M. Schwab (Albany: State University of New York Press, 2020), 211–26.

34. Both Braidotti and Grosz have reimagined the sensible transcendental in relation to new materialism. See also *Thinking Life*.

35. Rosi Braidotti, *Nomadic Theory*, 200. See also Braidotti, *Nomadic Subjects*, 91.

36. In challenging the relationship between the immanent and transcendent and between interiority and exteriority, the sensible transcendental remakes the very structures by which self and other are constituted. This rejection of binarisms and axial thinking is fundamental to understanding the materiality and alterity of the sexuate in Irigaray's work. And I will ultimately contend that the desire generated by this irreducible indeterminacy of the sexuate offers a dynamic new materiality beyond a determined notion of anthropocentric corporeality.

37. It is this concern with safeguarding alterity in conceiving the sensible transcendental that situates Irigaray in relation to Levinas. Chanter adds that Irigaray's sensible transcendental is similar to Levinas's explication of the paradox of an otherworldly freedom and materiality or what he will later refer to as "sensibility." Chanter, *Ethics of Eros*, 173, 180.

38. Braidotti, *Nomadic Theory*, 132.

39. Gilles Deleuze and Félix Guattari, *A Thousand Plateaus: Capitalism and Schizophrenia*, trans. and ed., Brian Massumi (New York: Continuum, 2004 [1980]) 7, 22–23. There's no doubt that the language of rhizomes, particularly as developed in *A Thousand Plateaus* and in *Anti-Oedipus*, has become one of the most enduring, and perhaps even hackneyed, concepts of Deleuze and Guattari's legacy. Still, rhizomes remain a critical model for feminist new materialisms. See Jerry Aline Flieger's exploration of Deleuze and Guattari's notion of rhizomes in relation to mimesis in *A Thousand Plateaus*. Flieger, "Becoming-Woman: Deleuze, Schreber, and

Molecular Identification," in *Deleuze and Feminist Theory*, eds. Ian Buchanan and Claire Colebrook (Edinburgh: Edinburgh University Press, 2000), 38–85.

40. Deleuze and Guattari, *A Thousand Plateaus*, 358–59.

41. Braidotti, *Nomadic Theory*, 134.

42. Braidotti, 130.

43. Braidotti, 134.

44. Dethroning the universal Man or divine king is also a dethroning of Oedipus Rex and the oedipal narrative as the foundational structure of desire. The play on cutting or beheading the phallocentric narrative is intentional. Karen Barad frames her onto-ethical project of "agential realism" as a play on the cutting that falsely dichotomizes materialities. There is also an important connection to *Antigone* here. When Irigaray revisits the play in *To Be Two*, she contrasts Creon's life to the complex interconnectedness of Antigone's life—refusing distinctions between love, religion, family, and even neighbor. "Creon builds his kingdom on an empty space with an abstract logic, with the use of force and terror, with the self-conferral of right which will be the law for others. . . . He thinks that he can substitute a power made possible by artifice for a respect for traditions, for the earth, and for the citizens." Irigaray, *To Be Two*, 78. Irigaray's meditation on *Antigone* in *To Be Two* is part of her broader interrogation of the problem of neutrality (103–12) and of the forgetting of sexual difference that cuts us off from/alienates us from the natural world and our own flesh (see "Prologue," 1–16).

45. Here, I adopt the language of sexual difference in accordance with sexual-difference theory. These references to sexual difference (in contemporary sexual difference theory) are akin to Irigaray's notion of the sexuate insofar as it gestures toward a primary, irreducible difference (not a discursive difference). Irigaray's use of the sexuate is more specific in its embroilment with psychoanalysis.

46. Braidotti, *Nomadic Theory*, 146.

47. Braidotti, 148.

48. Braidotti, 140.

49. Braidotti, 146.

50. Braidotti, 148.

51. Braidotti's lines follow her overview of sexual difference theory, in which she points to a shared interest in the question of becoming. Braidotti's portrayal of these conversations of sexual difference theory explicitly resonate with the posthumanist and antihumanist genealogy she articulates in the book. In particular, her intertwining of the language of ontology, materiality, and evolution echoes notions of becoming in Irigaray and in Deleuze (and Guattari's), "creative involution." For an exploration of Deleuze and Guattari's "creative involution" as an adaptation of Henri Bergson's creative evolution that informs becoming, see Mark Hansen, "Becoming as Creative Involution?: Contextualizing Deleuze and Guattari's Biophilosophy," *Postmodern Culture* 11, no. 1 (2000).

52. Braidotti notes that Colebrook's notion of the body is "an incorporeal complex assemblage of virtualities." Here, the incorporeal becomes a means to rethink the limits of materiality beyond the corporeality of the human. Braidotti, *Nomadic Theory*, 147.

53. The notion of the virtual in discourses of new materialism and posthuman thought can most readily be traced through Deleuze. And in his 1968 *Difference and Repetition*, Deleuze frames the distinction between the real and the virtual in Lacan, emphasizing that what separates the two for Lacan is that the real has a relation to place or being somewhere. Gilles Deleuze, *Difference and Repetition* (New York: Bloomsbury, 2004), 101–3. I would suggest mapping Deleuze's reading of Lacan's alignment of the virtual with placelessness and of the real with place onto Irigaray's reading of woman and man respectively within the masculine symbolic. The placelessness of woman would render her in relation to the lack of the virtual. However, unlike Lacan, I would argue that Irigaray's constructive theorization of an *irreducible* sexuate that is also *indeterminate*—and with this theorization an assertion that the irreducible sexuate would have place/space-time for oneself while also holding space-time for the sexuate other (see especially Irigaray on Spinoza in *Ethics*, 88–94)—explicitly opens onto the landscape of new materialist theories that reimagine the virtual beyond lack and placelessness, and in relation to sexual difference.

54. Braidotti, *Nomadic Theory*, 136.

55. Braidotti, 136.

56. Luciana Parisi, *Abstract Sex: Philosophy, Bio-Technology, and the Mutations of Desire* (London: Continuum, 2004), 196.

57. Parisi, 196.

58. Parisi, 196.

59. Bracketing the complexities of the genealogy of theories of matter, mattering, materiality, form, and the like, feminist posthumanism attributes the dynamism of difference to both the affective and the symbolic dimensions of embodied living. Braidotti, *Nomadic Theory*, 136.

60. For Parisi, the dynamism of difference is an assemblage that thinks feminine desire in relation to "technology and nature through immanent (without negation) relations of affect between biodigital body-sex and the biophysical and biocultural organization of the body." Parisi's emphasis on relation without negation resonates with Irigaray's emphasis on a becoming of subjects beyond a dialectics of negation. Parisi, *Abstract Sex*, 196.

61. As noted above, in so doing, she shifts conversations within feminism away from either social constructivism or essentialism; she also shifts the question of sexual difference away from either male or female difference, from either biology or culture, from either the material or the discursive.

62. Luciana Parisi, "Media Ontology and Transcendental Instrumentality," in *Theory, Culture & Society* 36, no. 6 (2019): 96.

63. Braidotti, *Nomadic Theory*, 136.

64. See Parisi's discussion of algorithms and their relation to aesthetics in the section "Algorithmic Aesthetics," Luciana Parisi, *Contagious Architecture: Computation, Aesthetics, and Space* (Cambridge, MA: MIT Press, 2013), 66–70.

65. Parisi, "Media," 99.

66. Parisi, 108.

67. Parisi, 97.

68. Here, I playfully invoke Deleuze's use of Henri Bergson's notion of "fabulation," which has become an important term in critical theory for thinking of the literary quality of becoming. See "Literature and Life," *Critical Inquiry* 23, no. 2 (1997): 227–28.

69. Parisi, "Media," 121.

70. Parisi, 106.

71. Parisi, 97.

72. Parisi, 120.

73. See Parisi's rethinking of the relationship between users and computational models and their varying views of the dynamic between perception and cognition (31–32). See also her discussion of soft thought especially its relation to human cognition (175–76) in Parisi, *Contagious*.

74. Elizabeth Grosz and Simone Stirner, "All Too Human: A Conversation with Elizabeth Grosz," *Qui Parle* 25, no. 1–2 (2016): 22.

75. In relation to Braidotti's concerns, we might suggest that Grosz is attempting to locate a response to the destabilization of subjectivity and the deterritorialization of relations in a way that does not leave life in the lurch to be reterritorialized by global capitalism.

76. Braidotti, *Nomadic Theory*, 131.

77. Elizabeth A. Grosz, *The Incorporeal: Ontology, Ethics, and the Limits of Materialism* (New York: Columbia University Press, 2017), 132.

78. Van Leeuwen, "The Possibility of Feminist Phenomenology," 480.

79. Van Leeuwen, 481.

80. Irigaray, *Ethics*, 7.

81. Irigaray, 8.

82. Irigaray, 8.

83. Irigaray, 9.

84. Irigaray, 9.

85. Irigaray, 17.

86. Irigaray, 18.

87. Emphasis added. Braidotti, *Nomadic Subjects*, 112.

88. See Luce Irigaray and Carol Mastrangelo Bové, "Le Sujet de La Science Est-Il Sexué?/Is the Subject of Science Sexed?" *Hypatia* 2, no. 3 (1987): 65–87. When asked by Stephen Pluháček and Heidi Bostic about her previous admonitions of science, Irigaray distinguishes between a natural "biological economy" and the

discourse of science. She says, "It cannot be harmful to woman to discover the reality of her biological economy. What harms her is to be subjected to a science which is not appropriate for her, or to be reduced to a simple nature. . . . It is also important that they [women] not accept being reduced to a pure body, or a pure nature, whether it be by inertia or by submission to the other." Luce Irigaray, *Conversations* (London: Bloomsbury, 2008), 6.

89. And I would add that it is no coincidence that Pheng Cheah has long (I think) been one of the best readers of the radical potential in Irigaray's thought.

90. Agential realism is a burgeoning field built around Barad's use of the term to reference her brand of new materialism, which establishes a performativity that does not render matter a complete abstraction. Barad's agential realism specifically looks to inhuman matter in quantum physics as a means for reimagining relationality, "a transdisciplinary theory" that "offers an understanding of the world's ongoing materialization" (1–2). Its proponents view agential realism as "an *ethico-onto-epistemological* endeavor" that includes "research practices . . . entangled with ethics, accountability, and responsibility" (2). In an interview with Barad in *Dialogues on Agential Realism*, Barad says that her passion for justice drives her scholarly work. As I read it, Barad's investment in justice is what makes her work prioritize the possibility of a certain agency attributable to the real specificities of existence (119–21). See Malou Juelskjær, Helle Plauborg, and Stine W. Adrian, *Dialogues on Agential Realism: Engaging in Worldings through Research Practice* (New York: Taylor & Francis, 2021).

91. In this chapter, because Barad is an interlocutor, I refer to touching when emphasizing the dynamism and multiplicity that is touching and being touched. Barad favors touching as distinct from earlier scientific renderings of touch; however, Irigaray uses the language of both touch and touching, and even "touching upon" focusing on touch as a sensory mediation that reimagines sensory perception beyond receptivity or activity, and especially beyond sight. In this sense, she conceives touch much differently from the scientific depictions of touch as oppositional, which are effects of representing the reductiveness of masculine desire. In contrast to this reduction, Irigaray insists that touch is an openness "the means through which I can be in communication with myself, with the other(s) and with the world." Irigaray, *Mediation of Touch*, 60. For "touching upon" see *I Love to You: Sketch of a Possible Felicity in History*, trans. Alison Martin. New York: Routledge, 1996, 124–26. When not discussing Barad directly, I employ both touch and touching in relation to Irigaray's work.

92. Barad, *Meeting the Universe Halfway*, 25.

93. Barad writes, "Quantum field theory allows for something radically new in the history of Western physics: the transience of matter's existence. No longer suspended in eternity, matter is born, lives, and dies. But even more than that, there is a radical deconstruction of identity and of the equation of matter with essence in ways that transcend even the profound un/doings of (nonrelativistic) quantum

mechanics. Karen Barad, "On Touching—the Inhuman That Therefore I Am," *Differences* 23, no. 3 (2012): 209.

94. Barad, 210.

95. Irigaray, *Ethics*, 17.

96. Karen Barad, "Transmaterialities: Trans*/Matter/Realities and Queer Political Imaginings," *GLQ: A Journal of Lesbian and Gay Studies* 21, no. 2 (2015): 411.

97. Barad frames the materiality of thinking—of thought experiments—as touching. Barad, "On Touching," 207–8.

98. Barad, "Transmaterialities," 411.

99. In their "diffractive reading," Evelien Geerts and Iris van der Tuin discuss Irigaray's sexual difference in terms of her carnal ethics as an example of a feminist account of mutual recognition of one's alterity that takes sexual difference into account. This mutuality is what then moves them to Barad's work on touch, even if they interestingly don't talk about the lips and the touching that occurs there. Additionally, they offer up Barad's description of two hands touching in "On Touching" in order to intimate the place of sexual difference in Barad's work. See Evelien Geerts and Iris van der Tuin, "The Feminist Futures of Reading Diffractively: How Barad's Methodology Replaces Conflict-Based Readings of Beauvoir and Irigaray," *Rhizomes: Cultural Studies in Emerging Knowledge* 30 (2016): 26–43.

100. Barad, "On Touching," 213.

101. Barad, "Transmaterialities," 411.

102. Stacey Moran, "Quantum Decoherence," *Philosophy Today (Celina)* 63, no. 4 (2019): 1052.

103. Moran, 1058.

104. See Žižek's charting of contemporary revisionings of sexual difference in "The Non-All, or, the Ontology of Sexual Difference" in conjunction with his engagement with Barad in "The Ontology of Quantum Physics," in *Less Than Nothing: Hegel and the Shadow of Dialectical Materialism* (New York: Verso, 2012).

105. Thinking Irigaray in relation to physics is not accidental—it is an extension of her philosophical engagement with *physis*, and the question of materiality as a question of nature and culture. Irigaray has engaged the sciences as part of her broader critique of metaphysics and is characteristically sweeping in her assessment of science as a phallocentric discourse. In her essay "Is the Subject of Science Sexed?" Irigaray argues that the discourse of matter in physics, as with other scientific discourses, is encumbered by the phallocentric logic of sameness. She suggests that physics, in its ever-increasing axiomatic descriptions of matter not visible to the subject, further alienates matter from the senses. This, she says, deepens the chasm between matter and the value of sensory perception, further disembodying scientific knowledge. Significantly, however, Irigaray very briefly mentions that quantum field theory, in its concern with the mechanics of fluids, has the potential to reimagine the "imperceptibility" of matter in its dynamism and infinity. She adds that this potential is lamentably foreclosed by the focus on

discovery, which privileges a certain "solidity" or selfsameness of scientific discourse. It is worth noting that Irigaray follows this critique of science by invoking both the mirror stage and the problem of the dream of symmetry, thereby implying a direct relation between the problem of representation (of the flatness of woman as empty mirror reflecting a masculine image of sameness) and the inability to imagine matter beyond metaphysics. See Luce Irigaray and Carol Mastrangelo Bové, "Le Sujet de La Science Est-Il Sexué?," 77, 78.

106. In her work on Islam, politics, and postcolonialism, Shaireen Rasheed frames Irigaray's sexual ethics as offering a different mode of self-identification that is both ethical in its reaching out to the other and can attend to the demands of politics. Rasheed reads the embodiedness of Irigaray's ethic as a means to "negotiate between an obligation for the other and the agency" that disrupts concepts about liberal citizenship. Shaireen Rasheed, "Islam, Sexuality, and the 'War on Terror': Luce Irigaray's Post-Colonial Ethics of Difference," *American Journal of Islam & Society (Online)* 31, no. 1 (2014): 13.

107. Schwab reads Irigaray's engagements with Sartre on the question of subjectivity in *Sharing the World* and in *To Be Two*, texts in which Irigaray insists on the importance of different desires as necessary for different worlds of becoming. Gail Schwab, "Freedom, Desire, and the Other: Reading Sartre with Irigaray," in *Thinking Life with Luce Irigaray: Language, Origin, Art, Love*, ed. Gail M. Schwab (Albany: State University of New York Press, 2020).

108. See Alison Stone, *Luce Irigaray and the Philosophy of Sexual Difference*, 35–37. Stone argues that notions of matter as indeterminate (and she identifies Braidotti in this vein) escape ontological essentialism but are subject to political essentialism because matter becomes passive. Indeterminate "(proto)-bodily matter" is susceptible to the "influence of cultural representation." Irigaray's contribution, as Stone sees it, is her insistence "that indeterminate matter first receives shape from form" and thus rejects the rendering of bodies as complete abstractions or passive shapes. Stone, *Luce Irigaray and the Philosophy of Sexual Difference* 36. See also Penelope Deutscher's argument that within Stone's interpretation of Irigaray's materiality there must be some*thing* able to imagine and capable of becoming differently in Deutscher, "Recastings," and Stone's reply to Mary Beth Mader and Deutscher in Stone, "Unthought Nature."

109. Geerts and Tuin, "The Feminist Futures of Reading Diffractively, 28.

110. Geerts and Tuin, 31.

111. Geerts and Tuin, 37. This is the opening passage of Barad's "On Touching," 206.

112. See Irigaray, *This Sex*, 28.

113. Note, I replace *hands* with *lips*. Barad, "On Touching," 206.

114. Barad, "Transmaterialities," 411.

115. Barad argues for a "relational ontology" and uses the term *intra-active* to depict this relationality to mark it as a performativity that does not "turn every-

thing (including material bodies) into words" *Meeting the Universe Halfway*, 133. Over the last decade, Barad has continued to expand upon this notion of relational ontology and intra-activity, framing intra-activity as a unique queer performativity. Intra-activity almost constitutes what we might call an ethical praxis insofar as it gestures beyond a human-centric world, toward "a commitment to being attentive to the activity of each critter in its ongoing intra-active engagement with and as part of the world it participates in materializing." Karen Barad, "Nature's Queer Performativity" part of the world it participates in materialzing." Karen Barad, *Qui Parle* 19, no. 2 (2011): 127. Barad has noted that she uses the slash as a gesture of intra-activity, emphasizing the performative ethical dimensions of her writing. And significantly, as it regards the question of Irigaray's refusal of binaries, Barad writes that she aims specifically to refuse binary logic. See footnote 9 in Karen Barad, "After the End of the World: Entangled Nuclear Colonialisms, Matters of Force, and the Material Force of Justice," *Theory & Event* 22, no. 3 (2019): 538.

116. Barad, "On Touching," 216.

117. For Irigaray, we must not abandon the possibility of unique embodiments of spirit that touch makes possible, Irigaray, *Mediation of Touch*, 237.

118. Luce Irigaray and Michael Marder, *Through Vegetal Being: Two Philosophical Perspectives* (New York: Columbia University Press, 2016), 56–62.

119. Irigaray, *Sharing the Fire*, 12.

120. Irigaray, 14.

121. Schwab, "Freedom, Desire," 191.

122. Schwab, 191.

123. Irigaray, *To Be Two*, 88.

124. Irigaray, arguing that although wonder is required for an ethics of sexual difference, it does not currently exist, writes, "This has never existed between the sexes since wonder maintains their autonomy within their statutory difference, keeping a space of freedom and attraction between them, a possibility of separation and alliance." Irigaray, *Ethics*, 13.

Bibliography

Ahmed, Sara. *Living a Feminist Life*. Durham, NC: Duke University Press, 2017. https://doi.org/10.1215/9780822373377.

Ahmed, Sara. "Open Forum Imaginary Prohibitions: Some Preliminary Remarks on the Founding Gestures of the 'New Materialism.'" *The European Journal of Women's Studies* 15, no. 1 (2008): 23–39. https://doi.org/10.1177/1350506807084854.

Ahmed, Sara. *Willful Subjects*. Durham, NC: Duke University Press, 2014. https://doi.org/10.1215/9780822376101.

Alaimo, Stacy, and Hekman, Susan, eds. *Feminist New Materialisms: Material Feminisms*. Bloomington: Indiana University Press, 2008.

Alcoff, Linda Martín. "Feminism." *The Journal of Speculative Philosophy* 26, no. 2 (2012): 268–90. https://doi.org/10.5325/jspecphil.26.2.0268.

Anderson, Reynaldo, and Charles E. Jones, eds. *Afrofuturism 2.0: The Rise of Astro-Blackness*. New York: Rowman & Littlefield, 2016.

Barad, Karen. "After the End of the World: Entangled Nuclear Colonialisms, Matters of Force, and the Material Force of Justice." *Theory & Event* 22, no. 3 (2019): 524–50. https://muse.jhu.edu/article/729449.

Barad, Karen. *Meeting the Universe Halfway: Quantum Physics and the Entanglement of Matter and Meaning*. Durham, NC: Duke University Press, 2007. https://doi.org/10.1215/9780822388128.

Barad, Karen. "Nature's Queer Performativity." *Qui Parle* 19, no. 2 (2011): 121–58. https://doi.org/10.5250/quiparle.19.2.0121.

Barad, Karen. "On Touching—the Inhuman That Therefore I Am." *Differences: A Journal of Feminist Cultural Studies* 23, no. 3 (2012): 206–23. https://doi.org/10.1215/10407391-1892943.

Barad, Karen. "TransMaterialities: Trans*/Matter/Realities and Queer Political Imaginings." *GLQ: A Journal of Lesbian and Gay Studies* 21, nos. 2–3 (2015): 387–422. https://doi.org/10.1215/10642684-2843239.

Barker, Wesley N. "A Theology of Lips: Beyond the Wounding of Desire." In *Horizons of Difference: Rethinking Space, Place, and Identity with Irigaray*, edited by Ruthanne Crapo Kim, Yvette Russel, and Brenda Sharp, 139–67. Albany: State University of New York Press, 2022. https://doi.org/10.1515/9781438488479.

Barker, Wesley N. "Thresholds of Touch: Revisiting the Mat(t)er of the Body in the Work of Luce Irigaray." *Body and Religion*, 4, no. 1 (2020): 105–29. https://doi.org/10.1558/bar.17861.

Benso, Silvia. *Viva Voce: Conversations with Italian Philosophers*. State University of New York Series in Contemporary Italian Philosophy. Albany: State University of New York Press, 2017. https://doi.org/10.1515/9781438463803.

Berg, Maggie. "Luce Irigaray's 'Contradictions': Poststructuralism and Feminism." *Signs: Journal of Women in Culture and Society* 17, no. 1 (1991): 50–70. https://doi.org/10.1086/494713.

Berger, Anne-Emmanuelle. "Sexing Differences." *Differences: A Journal of Feminist Cultural Studies* 16, no. 3 (2005): 52–67. https://doi.org/10.1163/156853011X578983.

Bergo, Bettina. "Ontology, Transcendence, and Immanence in Emmanuel Levinas' Philosophy." *Research in Phenomenology* 35, no. 1 (2005): 141–80. https://doi.org/10.1163/1569164054905474.

Berlant, Lauren. *Cruel Optimism*. Durham, NC: Duke University Press, 2011. https://doi.org/10.1215/9780822394716.

Bernasconi, Robert, and Simon Critchley. *Re-Reading Levinas*. Studies in Continental Thought. Bloomington: Indiana University Press, 1991.

Bersani, Leo. *"Is the Rectum a Grave?" and Other Essays*. Chicago: University of Chicago Press, 2010.

Bhabha, Homi. "Of Mimicry and Man: The Ambivalence of Colonial Discourse." In *Tensions of Empire: Colonial Cultures in a Bourgeois World*, edited by Frederick Cooper and Ann Laura Stoler, 152–60. Berkeley: University of California Press, 1997. https://doi.org/10.1525/9780520918085-006.

Boer, Karin de. "Hegel's Antigone and the Dialectics of Sexual Difference." *Philosophy Today* 47, no. 5 (2003): 140–46. https://doi.org/10.5840/philtoday200347Supplement18.

Boothroyd, Dave. "Labial Feminism: Body against Body with Luce Irigaray." *Parallax* 2, no. 2 (1996): 65–79. https://doi.org/10.1080/13534649609362025.

Boulous Walker, Michelle. "Nature, Obligation, and Transcendence: Reading Luce Irigaray with Mary Graham." *Sophia* 61, no. 1 (2022): 187–201. https://doi.org/10.1007/s11841-022-00907-2.

Boyce Davies, Carole. *Black Women, Writing and Identity: Migrations of the Subject*. New York: Routledge. Reprint, 1999.

Braidotti, Rosi. "Comment on Felski's "The Doxa of Difference": Working through Sexual Difference." *Signs* 23, no. 1 (1997): 23–40. https://doi.org/10.1086/495234.

Braidotti, Rosi. "Embodiment, Sexual Difference, and the Nomadic Subject." *Hypatia* 8, no. 1 (1993): 1–13. https://doi.org/10.1111/j.1527-2001.1993.tb00625.x.

Braidotti, Rosi. "Identity, Subjectivity and Difference: A Critical Genealogy." In *Thinking Differently: A Reader in European Women's Studies*, edited by Gabriele Griffin and Rosi Braidotti. New York: Palgrave Macmillan, 2002.

Braidotti, Rosi. *Nomadic Subjects: Embodiment and Sexual Difference in Contemporary Feminist Theory*. 2nd ed. New York: Columbia University Press, 2011.

Braidotti, Rosi. *Nomadic Theory: The Portable Rossi Braidotti*. New York: Columbia University Press, 2011.

Braidotti, Rosi. "Of Bugs and Women: Irigaray and Deleuze on the Becoming-Woman." In *Engaging with Irigaray: Feminist Philosophy and Modern European Thought*, edited by Naomi Schor Carolyn Burke, Margaret Whitford, 111–37. New York: Columbia University Press, 1994.

Braidotti, Rosi. *The Posthuman*. Malden, MA: Polity, 2013.

Braidotti, Rosi, Felicity Colman, and Iris van der Tuin. *Methods and Genealogies of New Materialisms*. 1st ed. Edinburgh: Edinburgh University Press, 2023.

Bray, Abigail, and Claire Colebrook. "The Haunted Flesh: Corporeal Feminism and the Politics of (Dis)embodiment." *Signs: Journal of Women in Culture and Society* 24, no. 1 (1998): 35–67. https://doi.org/10.1086/495317.

Bray, Karen. *Grave Attending: A Political Theology for the Unredeemed*. New York: Fordham, 2020. https://doi.org/10.5422/fordham/9780823286850.001.0001.

Breger, Claudia. "The Leader's Two Bodies: Slavoj Zizek's Postmodern Political Theology." *Diacritics* 31, no. 1 (2003): 73–90. https://doi.org/10.1353/dia.2003.0003.

Brintnall, Kent L., Rhiannon Graybill, and Linn Marie Tonstad, eds. *Lee Edelman and the Queer Study of Religion*. Oxford: Taylor & Francis, 2023.

Bühlmann, Vera, Felicity Colman, and Iris van der Tuin, "Introduction: New Materialisms: Quantum Ideation across Dissonance." In *Methods and Genealogies of New Materialisms*, edited by Rosi Braidotti, Felicity Colman, and Iris van der Tuin, 17–25. Edinburgh: Edinburgh University Press, 2023.

Burian, Peter H. "Gender and the City: Antigone from Hegel to Butler and Back." In *When Worlds Elide: Classics, Politics, Culture*, edited by J. P. Euben and Karen Bassi, 255–99. Lanham, MD: Lexington, 2010. https://doi.org/10.1093/acprof:oso/9780199673926.001.0001.

Burke, Carolyn. "Irigaray through the Looking Glass." *Feminist Studies* 7, no. 2 (1981): 288–306. https://doi.org/10.2307/3177525.

Butler, Judith. *Antigone's Claim: Kinship between Life and Death*. New York: Columbia University Press, 2000.

Butler, Judith. "Bodies that Matter." In *Engaging with Irigaray: Feminist Philosophy and Modern European Thought*, edited by Naomi Schor Carolyn Burke, Margaret Whitford, 138–73. New York: Columbia University Press, 1994.

Butler, Judith. *Gender Trouble: Feminism and the Subversion of Identity*. New York: Routledge, 1990.

Butler, Judith. *Giving an Account of Oneself*. New York: Fordham University Press, 2005. https://doi.org/10.5422/fso/9780823225033.001.0001.

Butler, Judith. "On Never Having Learned How to Live." *Differences: A Journal of Feminist Cultural Studies* 16, no. 3 (2005): 27–34. https://doi.org/10.1215/10407391-16-3-27.

Butler, Judith. *Precarious Life: The Powers of Mourning and Violence*. New York: Verso, 2004.

Butler, Judith. *The Psychic Life of Power: Theories in Subjection*. Stanford: Stanford University Press, 1997.

Butler, Judith. *Senses of the Subject*. New York: Fordham, 2015.

Butler, Judith. "Sexual Difference as a Question of Ethics: Alterities of the Flesh in Irigaray and Merleau-Ponty." In *Feminist Interpretations of Maurice Merleau-Ponty*, edited by Dorothea and Gail Weiss Olkowski. University Park: Pennsylvania State University Press, 2006.

Butler, Judith, Slavoj Zizek, and Ernesto Laclau. *Contingency, Hegemony, Universality: Contemporary Dialogues on the Left*. London: Verso, 2000.

Caddedu, Davide, ed. *A Companion to Antonio Gramsci: Essays on History and Theories of History, Politics and Historiography*. Boston: Brill, 2020.

Caldwell, Anne. "Transforming Sacrifice: Irigaray and the Politics of Sexual Difference." *Hypatia* 17, no. 4 (2002): 16–38. https://doi.org/10.1111/j.1527-2001.2002.tb01072.x.

Caputo, John D. *Against Ethics*. Bloomington: Indiana University Press, 1993 [Reprint 1999].

Caputo, John D. "Being Given: Toward a Phenomenology of Givenness (Review)." *Journal of the American Academy of Religion* 74, no. 4 (2006): 986–89. https://doi.org/10.1093/jaarel/lfl005.

Caputo, John D. *God, the Gift and Postmodernism*. Bloomington: Indiana University Press, 1999.

Carson, Anne. *Eros the Bittersweet: An Essay*. Princeton, NJ: Princeton University Press, 2014.

Carter, Jennifer. "On Peaceful Political Relations between Two in Luce Irigaray's Work." *Sophia* 61, no. 1 (2022): 219–238. doi: https://doi.org/10.1007/s11841-022-00919-y. https://doi.org/10.1007/s11841-022-00919-y.

Carter, J. Kameron. "Black Malpractice (A Poetics of the Sacred)." *Social Text* 37, no. 2 (2019): 67–107. https://doi.org/10.1215/01642472-7370991.

Carter, J. Kameron, and Sarah Jane Cervenak. "Black Ether." *CR: The New Centennial Review* 16, no. 2 (2016): 203–24. https://doi.org/10.14321/crnewcentrevi.16.2.0203.

Casalis, Matthieu. "Merleau-Ponty's Philosophical Itinerary: From Phenomenology to Onto-Semiology." *The Southwestern Journal of Philosophy* 6, no. 1 (1975): 63–69. https://doi.org/10.5840/swjphil1975619.

Caserio, Robert L., Lee Edelman, Judith Halberstam, José Esteban Muñoz, and Tim Dean, "The Antisocial Thesis in Queer Theory." *Proceedings of the Modern Language Association* 121, no. 3 (2006): 819–28. https://doi.org/10.1632/pmla.2006.121.3.819.

Cavarero, Adriana. *Horrorism Naming Contemporary Violence*. New York: Columbia University Press, 2011.

Cavarero, Adriana. *Stately Bodies: Literature, Philosophy, and the Question of Gender*. Translated by Robert de Lucca and Deanna Shemek. Ann Arbor: University of Michigan Press, 2002.

Chakrabarti, Sumit. "Moving beyond Edward Said: Homi Bhabha and the Problem of Postcolonial Representation." *International Studies* 14, no. 1 (2012): 5. https://doi.org/10.2478/v10223-012-0051-3.

Chanter, Tina. *Ethics of Eros: Irigaray's Rewriting of the Philosophers*. New York: Routledge, 1995.

Chanter, Tina. *Whose Antigone? The Tragic Marginalization of Slavery*. Albany: State University of New York Press, 2011. https://doi.org/10.1515/9781438437569.

Cheah, Pheng. "Mattering." *Diacritics* 26, no. 1 (1996): 108–39. https://doi.org/10.1353/dia.1996.0004.

Cheah, Pheng. "Nondialectical Materialism." *Diacritics* 38, no. 1/2 (2008): 143–57. https://doi.org/10.1353/dia.0.0050.

Cheah, Pheng. "Obscure Gifts: On Jacques Derrida." *Differences: A Journal of Feminist Cultural Studies* 16, no. 3 (2005): 41–51. https://doi.org/10.1215/10407391-16-3-41.

Cheah, Pheng, and Elizabeth Grosz. "Of Being-Two: Introduction." *Diacritics* 28, no. 1 (1998): 2–18. https://doi.org/10.1353/dia.1998.0003.

Cheah, Pheng, and Caroline S. Hau. *Siting Postcoloniality: Critical Perspectives from the East Asian Sinosphere*. Durham, NC: Duke University Press, 2022. https://doi.org/10.1215/9781478023951.

Cheah, Pheng, Elizabeth Grosz, Judith Butler, and Drucilla Cornell. "The Future of Sexual Difference: An Interview with Judith Butler and Drucilla Cornell." *Diacritics* 28, no. 1 (1998): 19–42. https://doi.org/10.1353/dia.1998.0002.

Cimitile, Maria C., and Elaine P. Miller, ed. *Returning to Irigaray: Feminist Philosophy, Politics, and the Question of Unity*. Albany: State University of New York Press, 2007.

Clements, Niki Kasumi. "Foucault's Christianities" *Journal of the American Academy of Religion* 89, no. 1 (2021): 1–40. https://doi.org/10.1093/jaarel/lfab024.

Coetzee, Azille, and Annemie Halsema. "Sexual Difference and Decolonization: Oyěwùmí and Irigaray in Dialogue about Western Culture." *Hypatia* 33, no. 2 (2018): 178–94. https://doi.org/10.1111/hypa.12397.

Cohoon, Christopher. "Coming Together: The Six Modes of Irigarayan Eros." *Hypatia* 26, no. 3 (2011): 478–96. https://doi.org/10.1111/j.1527-2001.2011.01190.x.

Colebrook, Claire. "A Cut in Relationality." *Angelaki* 24, no. 3 (2019): 175–95. https://doi.org/10.1080/0969725X.2019.1620469.

Colebrook, Claire. "Feminist Philosophy and the Philosophy of Feminism: Irigaray and the History of Western Metaphysics." *Hypatia* 12, no. 1 (1997): 79–98. https://doi.org/10.1111/j.1527-2001.1997.tb00172.x.

Colebrook, Claire. "From Radical Representations to Corporeal Becomings: The Feminist Philosophy of Lloyd, Grosz, and Gatens." *Hypatia* 15, no. 2 (2000): 76–93. https://doi.org/10.1111/j.1527-2001.2000.tb00315.x.

Colebrook, Claire. "Questioning Representation." *SubStance* 29, no. 2 (2000): 47–67. https://muse.jhu.edu/article/32249. https://doi.org/10.1353/sub.2000.0017.

Colebrook, Claire. "The Trope of Economy and Representational Thinking: Heidegger, Derrida and Irigaray." *Journal of the British Society for Phenomenology* 28, no. 2 (1997): 178–91. https://doi.org/10.1080/00071773.1997.11007196.

Colebrook, Claire. "What Is It Like to Be Human?" *Transgender Studies Quarterly* 2, no. 2 (2015): 227–43. https://doi.org/10.1215/23289252-2867472.

Colman, Athena B. "Tarrying with Sexual Difference." In *Horizons of Difference: Rethinking Space, Place, and Identity with Irigaray*, edited by Ruthanne Crapo Kim, Yvette Russell, and Brenda Sharp, 17–39. Albany: State University of New York Press, 2022. https://doi.org/10.1515/9781438488479.

Coole, Diana, and Samantha Frost. *New Materialisms*. Durham, NC: Duke University Press, 2020. https://doi.org/10.1215/9780822392996.

Cornell, Drucilla. "Derrida: The Gift of the Future." *Differences: A Journal of Feminist Cultural Studies* 16, no. 3 (2005): 68–75. https://doi.org/10.1215/10407391-16-3-68.

Cornell, Drucilla. *Transformations: Recollective Imagination and Sexual Difference*. New York: Routledge, 1993.

Craker, Tim. "Speaking Philosophy in the Voice of Another: Wittgenstein, Irigaray, and the Inheritance of Mimesis." In *Feminist Interpretations of Ludwig Wittgenstein*, edited by Naomi Scheman and Peg O'Connor, 65–94. University Park: Pennsylvania State University Press, 2002. https://doi.org/10.5325/j.ctv14gp7jh.9.

Davis, Noela. "New Materialism and Feminism's Anti-Biologism: A Response to Sara Ahmed." *The European Journal of Women's Studies* 16, no. 1 (2009): 67–80. https://doi.org/10.1177/1350506808098535.

De Jong, Sara, and Jamila M. H. Mascat. "Relocating Subalternity: Scattered Speculations on the Conundrum of a Concept." *Cultural Studies (London, England)* 30, no. 5 (2016): 717–29. https://doi.org/10.1080/09502386.2016.1168109.

Deleuze, Gilles. *Difference and Repetition*. New York: Columbia University Press, 1994.

Deleuze, Gilles, and Félix Guattari. *Anti-Oedipus: Capitalism and Schizophrenia*. New York: Viking, 1977.

Deleuze, Gilles, and Félix Guattari, *A Thousand Plateaus: Capitalism and Schizophrenia*, Translated and edited by Brian Massumi. New York: Continuum, 2004.

Dellamora, Richard. "Apocalyptic Irigaray." *Twentieth Century Literature* 46, no. 4 (2000): 492–512. https://doi.org/10.1215/0041462X-2000-1004.

Derrida, Jacques. *Adieu to Emmanuel Levinas*. Stanford: Stanford University Press, 1999.

Derrida, Jacques. "At This Very Moment in This Work Here I Am." Translated by Ruben Berezdivin. In *Re-Reading Levinas*, edited by Robert Bernasconi and Simon Critchley. Indianapolis: Indiana University Press, 1991.

Derrida, Jacques. "Interview: Choreographies: Jacques Derrida and Christie V. McDonald." *Diacritics* 12, no. 2 (1982): 10. https://doi.org/10.2307/464681.

Derrida, Jacques. *The Post Card: From Socrates to Freud and Beyond*. Translated by Alan Bass. Chicago: University of Chicago Press, 1987.

Derrida, Jacques. "Signature Event Context." In *Limited, Inc.* Evanston: Northwestern University Press, 1988.

Derrida, Jacques. "Women in the Beehive: A Seminar with Jacques Derrida." *Differences: A Journal of Feminist Cultural Studies* 16, no. 3 (2005): 138–57. https://doi.org/10.1215/10407391-16-3-139.

Derrida, Jacques. *Writing and Difference*. Chicago: University of Chicago Press, 1978.

Derrida, Jacques, and John D. Caputo. *Deconstruction in a Nutshell: A Conversation with Jacques Derrida*, Perspectives in Continental Philosophy. New York: Fordham University Press, 1997.

Deutscher, Penelope. "Looking Back at 'This Sex Which Is Not One': Post-De-constructive New Materialisms and Their (Sexual Difference)." In *What Is Sexual Difference? Thinking with Irigaray*, edited by Mary C. Rawlinson and James Sares, 79–100. New York: Columbia University Press, 2023. https://doi.org/10.7312/rawl20272.

Deutscher, Penelope. "Lynne Huffer's Are the Lips a Grave? Averting and Accentuating the Genealogical." *Differences: A Journal of Feminist Cultural Studies* 27, no. 3 (2016): 132–44. doi 10.1215/10407391-3696655. https://doi.org/10.1215/10407391-3696655.

Deutscher, Penelope. *A Politics of Impossible Difference: The Later Work of Luce Irigaray*. Ithaca, NY: Cornell University Press, 2002.

Deutscher, Penelope. "Recastings: On Alison Stone's Luce Irigaray and the Philosophy of Sexual Difference." *Differences: A Journal of Feminist Cultural Studies* 19, no. 3 (2008): 139–49. https://doi.org/10.1215/10407391-2008-013.

Douglass, Patrice, and Frank Wilderson. "The Violence of Presence: Metaphysics in a Blackened World." *The Black Scholar* 43, no. 4 (2013): 117.

Edelman, Lee. *Bad Education: Why Queer Theory Teaches Us Nothing*. Durham, NC: Duke University Press, 2023. https://doi.org/10.1215/9781478023227.

Edelman, Lee. "An Ethics of Desubjectivation?" *Differences: A Journal of Feminist Cultural Studies* 27, no. 3 (2016): 106–18. https://doi.org/10.1215/10407391-3696679.

Edelman, Lee. *No Future: Queer Theory and the Death Drive*. Durham, NC: Duke University Press, 2004. https://doi.org/10.1215/9780822385981.

Elliot, Patricia. 2010. *Debates in Transgender, Queer, and Feminist Theory: Contested Sites*. Farnham: Taylor & Francis Group. https://doi.org/10.4324/9781315576008.

Fanon, Frantz. *Black Skin, White Masks*. Translated by Richard Philcox. New York: Grove, 2008.

Faulkner, Joanne. "Voices from the Depths: Reading 'Love' in Luce Irigaray's 'Marine Lover.'" *Diacritics* 33, no. 1 (2003): 81–94. https://doi.org/10.1353/dia.2005.0014.

Fausto-Sterling, Anne. "Gender, Race, and Nation: The Comparative Anatomy of Hottentot Women in Europe, 1815–1817." In *Deviant Bodies*, edited by Jennifer Terry and Jacqueline Urla. Bloomington: Indiana University Press, 1995.

Feinberg, Leslie. "Transgender Liberation: A Movement Whose Time Has Come." In *The Transgender Studies Reader*, edited by Susan Stryker and Stephen Whittle. New York: Routledge, 2006.

Felski, Rita. *Beyond Feminist Aesthetics: Feminist Literature and Social Change*. Cambridge: Harvard University Press, 1989.

Felski, Rita. "The Doxa of Difference." *Signs: Journal of Women in Culture and Society* 23, no. 1 (1997): 1–21. https://doi.org/10.1086/495231.

Finley, Stephen, and Lori Latrice Martin. "The Complexity of Color and the Religion of Whiteness." In *Color Struck: How Race and Ethnicity Matter in the "Color-Blind" Era*. Rotterdam: Sense, 2017.

Fischer, Clara. "Feminist Philosophy, Pragmatism, and the 'Turn to Affect': A Genealogical Critique." *Hypatia* 31, no. 4 (2016): 810–26. https://doi.org/10.1111/hypa.12296.

Fischer, Clara. "Revisiting Feminist Matters in the Post-Linguistic Turn: John Dewey, New Materialisms, and Contemporary Feminist Thought." In *New Feminist Perspectives on Embodiment*, edited by Clara Fischer and Luna Dolezal, 83–102. Cham, Switzerland: Springer, 2018.

Flieger, Jerry Aline. "Becoming-Woman: Deleuze, Schreber, and Molecular Identification." In *Deleuze and Feminist Theory*, edited by Ian Buchanan and Claire Colebrook, 38–85. Edinburgh: Edinburgh University Press, 2000.

Foucault, Michel. *Archaeology of Knowledge and the Discourse on Language*. New York: Pantheon, 1972.

Foucault, Michel. *The History of Sexuality Volume 1: The Will to Knowledge*. Translated by Robert Hurley. New York: Vintage, 1990.

Foucault, Michel. *The History of Sexuality Volume 2: The Use of Pleasure*. Translated by Robert Hurley. New York: Vintage, 1985.

Foucault, Michel. *The History of Sexuality Volume 3: The Care of Self*. Translated by Robert Hurley. New York: Vintage, 1986.

Foucault, Michel. *The History of Sexuality Volume 4: Confessions of the Flesh*. New York: Pantheon Books, 2021.

Foucault, Michel. *Power/Knowledge: Selected Interviews and Other Writings 1972–1977*. Translated by Leo Marshall Colin Gordon, John Mepham, Kate Soper. Edited by Colin Gordon. New York: Pantheon 1980.

Freud, Sigmund. *Beyond the Pleasure Principle*. Newburyport: Dover, 2014.

Freud, Sigmund. *Collected Papers. Volume 1*. England: Hogarth and the Institute of Psycho-Analysis, 1953. https://hdl.handle.net/2027/uc1.31822005017363.

Freud, Sigmund. *Totem and Taboo: Resemblances between the Psychic Lives of Savages and Neurotics*. Translated by A. A. Brill. Warsaw, Poland: Ktoczyta, 2020. https://ebookcentral.proquest.com/lib/merceru/reader.action?docID=6247080.

Fuss, Diana. "'Essentially Speaking': Luce Irigaray's Language of Essence." *Hypatia* 3, no. 3 (1989).

Fuss, Diana. "Pink Freud." *GLQ* 2, nos. 1–2 (1995): 1–9. https://doi.org/10.1215/10642684-2-1_and_2-1.

Gallop, Jane. *Reading Lacan*. Ithaca, NY: Cornell University Press, 1985.

Geerts, Evelien, and Iris van der Tuin. "The Feminist Futures of Reading Diffractively: How Barad's Methodology Replaces Conflict-Based Readings of Beauvoir and Irigaray." *Rhizomes: Cultural Studies in Emerging Knowledge* 30 (2016): 26–43. https://doi.org/10.20415/rhiz/030.e02.

Gines, Kathryn. "From Color-Blind to Post Racial." *Journal of Social Philosophy* 41, no. 3 (2010): 370–84. https://doi.org/10.1111/j.1467-9833.2010.01504.x.

Goh, Irving. "Le Rejet of Luce Irigaray in *Through Vegetal Being*." *Differences: A Journal of Feminist Cultural Studies* 29, no. 3 (2018): 137–54. https://doi.org/10.1215/10407391-7266508.

Goh, Irving. "Touch Today: From Subject to Reject." *Substance* 40, no. 3 (2011): 115–29. https://doi.org/10.1353/sub.2011.0029.

Gordon, Lewis. *Freedom, Justice, and Decolonization*. Oxford: Taylor & Francis, 2020.

Grosz, Elizabeth. "Derrida and Feminism: A Remembrance." *Differences: A Journal of Feminist Cultural Studies* 16, no. 3 (2005): 88–94. https://doi.org/10.1215/10407391-16-3-88.

Grosz, Elizabeth. "The Force of Sexual Difference." In *Sex, Breath and Force: Sexual Difference in a Post-Feminist Era*, edited by Ellen Mortensen, 7–15. Lanham, MD: Lexington Books (a Division of Rowman & Littlefield), 2006.

Grosz, Elizabeth. "The Hetero and the Homo: The Sexual Ethics of Luce Irigaray." In *Engaging with Irigaray: Feminist Philosophy and Modern European Thought*, edited by Carolyn Burke, Naomi Schor, and Margaret Whitford, 335–50. New York: Columbia University Press, 1994.

Grosz, Elizabeth. *The Incorporeal: Ontology, Ethics, and the Limits of Materialism*. New York: Columbia University Press, 2017.

Grosz, Elizabeth. "Ontology and Equivocation: Derrida's Politics of Sexual Difference." *Diacritics* 25, no. 2 (1995): 10. https://doi.org/10.2307/465148.

Grosz, Elizabeth. *Sexual Subversions: Three French Feminists*. Winchester, MA: Unwin Hyman, 1989.

Grosz, Elizabeth. *Space, Time, and Perversion: Essays on the Politics of Bodies*. New York: Routledge, 1995.

Grosz, Elizabeth, and Simone Stirner. "All Too Human: A Conversation with Elizabeth Grosz." *Qui Parle* 25, no. 1–2 (2016): 17–33. https.://doi.org/10.5250/quiparle.25.1-2.0017.

Guenther, Lisa. "Being-from-Others: Reading Heidegger after Cavarero." *Hypatia* 23, no. 1 (2008): 99–118. doi:10.1111/j.1527-2001.2008.tb01167.x.

Gumbs, Alexis Pauline. "The Shape of My Impact," *The Feminist Wire*, October 12, 2019. https://thefeministwire.com/2012/10/the-shape-of-my-impact/.

Gumbs, Alexis Pauline. *Spill: Scenes of Black Feminist Fugitivity.* Durham, NC: Duke University Press, 2016. https://doi.org/10.1215/9780822373575.

Guy-Sheftall, Beverly, ed. *Words of Fire: An Anthology of African-American Feminist Thought.* New York: New Press, 1995.

Haas, Marjorie. "Fluid Thinking: Irigaray's Critique of Formal Logic." In *Representing Reason: Feminist Theory and Formal Logic,* edited by Rachel Joffe Falmagne and Marjorie Haas. Lanham, MD: Rowman & Littlefield, 2002.

Hagglund, Martin. "The Necessity of Discrimination: Disjoining Derrida and Levinas." *Diacritics* 34, no. 1 (2006): 40–71. https://doi.org/10.1353/dia.2006.0022.

Halberstam, Judith. *Queer Art of Failure.* Durham, NC: Duke University Press, 2011. https://doi.org/10.1215/9780822394358.

Hall, Lynda. "Passion(Ate) Plays "Wherever We Found Space": Lorde and Gomez Queer(Y)Ing Boundaries and Acting In." *Callaloo* 23, no. 1 (2000): 394–421. https://doi.org/10.1353/cal.2000.0024.

Hansen, Mark. "Becoming as Creative Involution?: Contextualizing Deleuze and Guattari's Biophilosophy." *Postmodern Culture* 11, no. 1 (2000). https://doi.org/10.1353/pmc.2000.0032.

Hanson, Ellis. "The Future's Eve: Reparative Reading after Sedgwick." *South Atlantic Quarterly* 110, no. 1 (2011): 101–19. https://doi.org/10.1215/00382876-2010-025. https://doi.org/10.1215/00382876-2010-025.

Halperin, David M. "One Hundred Years of Homosexuality." *Diacritics.* Ithaca, NY: Johns Hopkins University Press, 1986. https://doi.org/10.2307/465069.

Halperin, David M. *One Hundred Years of Homosexuality: And Other Essays on Greek Love,* New Ancient World Series. New York: Routledge, 1990.

Harney, Stefano, and Moten, Fred. *The Undercommons: Fugitive Planning and Black Study.* New York: Minor Compositions, 2013.

Hartman, Saidiya V. *Lose Your Mother: A Journey along the Atlantic Slave Route.* New York: Farrar, Straus and Giroux, 2007.

Hartman, Saidiya V. "The Position of the Unthought: An Interview with Saidiya V. Hartman conducted by Frank B. Wilderson, III," *Qui Parle* 13, no. 2 (Spring/Summer, 2003). https://doi.org/10.1215/quiparle.13.2.183.

Hartman, Saidiya V. "Venus in Two Acts." *Small Axe: A Journal of Criticism* 12, no. 2 (2008): 1–14. https://doi.org/10.1215/-12-2-1. https://doi.org/10.1215/-12-2-1.

Hartman, Saidiya V. *Wayward Lives, Beautiful Experiments: Intimate Histories of Social Upheaval.* New York: Norton, 2019.

Hegel, G. W. F. *Aesthetics: Volume 1.* Oxford: Oxford University Press, 1998.

Hegel, G. W. F. *Hegel's Lectures on the History of Philosophy*, volume 1. Translated by E. S. Haldane. New York: Humanities, 1955.

Hegel, G. W. F. *Phenomenology of Mind*. Translated by J. B. Baille. New York: Dover, 2012.

Hegel, G. W. F. *Phenomenology of Spirit*. Translated by A. V. Miller. Delhi: Motilal Banarsidass, 1998.

Hegel, G. W. F. *Philosophy of Nature*. Translated by A. V. Miller. New York: Oxford University Press, 2004.

Heidegger, Martin. *Being and Time: A Revised Edition of the Stambaugh Translation*. Edited by Joan Stambaugh and Dennis J. Schmidt. Albany: State University of New York Press, 2010.

Hekman, Susan. "Divine Women? Irigaray, God, and the Subject." *Feminist Theology* 27, no. 2 (2019): 117–25. https://doi.org/10.1177/0966735018814.

Hekman, Susan. "Feminist New Materialism and Process Theology: Beginning the Dialogue." *Feminist Theology* 25, no. 2 (2017): 198–207.

Hekman, Susan. *The Material of Knowledge: Feminist Disclosures*. Bloomington: Indiana University Press, 2010. https://doi.org/10.1177/0966735016678544.

Hemmings, Clare. "Affect and Feminist Methodology, Or What Does It Mean to Be Moved?" In *Structures of Feeling: Affectivity and the Study of Culture*, edited by Devika Sharma and Frederik Tygstrup, 147–58. Boston: De Gruyter, 2015. https://doi.org/10.1515/9783110365481.

Henao Castro, Andrés Fabián. "Ontological Captivity: Toward a Black Radical Deconstruction of Being." *Differences: A Journal of Feminist Cultural Studies* 32, no. 3 (2021): 85–113. https://doi.org/10.1215/10407391-9479702.

Hickmott, Sarah. *Music, Philosophy and Gender in Nancy, Lacoue-Labarthe, Badiou*. Edinburgh: Edinburgh University Press, 2020.

Hill, Rebecca. *The Interval: Relation and Becoming in Irigaray, Aristotle, and Bergson*. New York: Fordham University Press, 2012. https://doi.org/10.5422/fordham/9780823237241.001.0001.

Hill, Rebecca. "Interval, Sexual Difference: Luce Irigaray and Henri Bergson." *Hypatia* 23, no. 1 (2008). 10.1111/j.1527-2001.2008.tb01168.x.

Hill, Rebecca. "The Multiple Readings of Irigaray's Concept of Sexual Difference." *Philosophy Compass* 11, no. 7 (2016): 390–401. https://doi.org/10.1111/phc3.12331.

Hill Collins, Patricia. *Black Feminist Thought: Knowledge, Consciousness, and the Politics of Empowerment*. 2nd ed. New York: Routledge, 2000.

Hill Collins, Patricia. *Fighting Words: Black Women and the Search for Justice*. Minneapolis: University of Minnesota Press, 1998.

Hirsh, Elizabeth, Gary A. Olson, and Brulotte Gaeton. ""Je-Luce Irigaray": A Meeting with Luce Irigaray." *Hypatia* 10, no. 2 (1995): 93–114. https://doi.org/10.1111/j.1527-2001.1995.tb01371.x.

Hobson, Janell. "Remnants of Venus: Signifying Black Beauty and Sexuality." In *Women's Studies Quarterly* 46, no. 1/2 (2018): 105–20. https://doi.org/10.1353/wsq.2018.0010.

Hobson, Janell. *Body as Evidence: Mediating Race, Globalizing Gender*. Albany: State University of New York Press, 2012. https://doi.org/10.1515/9781438444024.

Hodge, Joanna. "Irigaray Reading Heidegger." In *Engaging with Irigaray: Feminist Philosophy and Modern European Thought*, edited by Naomi Schor Carolyn Burke, Margaret Whitford, 111–37. New York: Columbia University Press, 1994.

Hoel, Aurora, and Sam Skinner. "Curated Panel: 'Genealogies and Apparatuses of New Materialist Production' Aurora Hoel and Sam Skinner with contributions from Jelena Djuric, David Gauthier, Evelien Geerts, Sofie Sauzet and Maria Tamboukou." In *Methods and Genealogies of New Materialisms*, edited by Felicity Colman and Iris van der Tuin, 105–35. Edinburgh: Edinburgh University Press, 2023.

Hollywood, Amy. "Beauvoir, Irigaray, and the Mystical." *Hypatia* 9, no. 4 (1994): 158–85. https://doi.org/10.1111/j.1527-2001.1994.tb00654.x.

Hollywood, Amy. "Deconstructing Belief: Irigaray and the Philosophy of Religion." *Journal of Religion* 78, no. 2 (1998): 230–45. doi:10.1086/490179. https://doi.org/10.1086/490179.

Hollywood, Amy. *Sensible Ecstasy: Mysticism, Sexual Difference, and the Demands of History*. Chicago: University of Chicago Press, 2002. https://doi.org/10.7208/chicago/9780226349466.001.0001.

Hollywood, Amy. "That Glorious Slit: Irigaray and the Medieval Devotion to Christ's Side Wound." In *Acute Melancholia and Other Essays: Mysticism, History, and the Study of Religion*, 171–88. New York: Columbia University Press, 2016.

Holmes, Emily. "The Age of Spirit: Irigaray, Apocalypse, and the Trinitarian View of History." In *Thinking Life with Luce Irigaray: Language, Origin, Art, Love*, edited by Gail M. Schwab. Albany: State University of New York Press, 2020). https://doi.org/10.1515/9781438477831.

Holmlund, Christine. "The Lesbian, the Mother, the Heterosexual Lover: Irigaray's Recodings of Difference." *Feminist Studies* 17, no. 2 (1991): 283–308. https://doi.org/10.1111/j.1527-2001.2007.tb01154.x.

Honig, Bonnie. *Antigone, Interrupted*. Cambridge: Cambridge University Press, 2013.

Honig, Bonnie. "Antigone's Lament, Creon's Grief: Mourning, Membership, and the Politics of Exception." In *Political Theory* 37, no. 1 (2009): 5–43. https://doi.org/10.1177/0090591708326645.

Howard, Jonathan. "To See the Earth before the End of the Antiblack World." *Souls* 22.2, no. 4 (2020): 292–314. https://doi.org/10.1080/10999949.2021.2003622.

hooks, bell. "Essentialism and Experience." *American Literary History* 3, no. 1 (1991): 172–83. https://doi.org/10.1093/alh/3.1.172.

hooks, bell. *Writing beyond Race: Living Theory and Practice*. New York: Routledge, 2012.

Huffer, Lynne. *Are the Lips a Grave? A Queer Feminist on the Ethics of Sex*. New York: Columbia University Press, 2013.

Huffer, Lynne. *Foucault's Strange Eros*. New York: Columbia University Press, 2020.

Huffer, Lynne. "Luce Et Veritas: Toward an Ethics of Performance." *Yale French Studies*, no. 87 (1995): 20–41. https://doi.org/10.1515/9780804765091-007.

Huffer, Lynne. *Mad for Foucault Rethinking the Foundations of Queer Theory*. New York: Columbia University Press, 2010.

Huffer, Lynne. *Maternal Pasts, Feminist Futures: Nostalgia, Ethics and the Question of Difference*. Stanford: Stanford University Press, 1998.

Hull, Gloria T., Patricia Bell Scott, and Barbara Smith, eds. *All the Women Are White, All the Blacks Are Men, but Some of Us Are Brave: Black Women's Studies*. New York: Feminist Press at the City University of New York, 1982.

Ince, Kate. "Questions to Luce Irigaray." *Hypatia* 11, no. 2 (1996): 122–40. https://doi.org/10.1111/j.1527-2001.1996.tb00667.x.

Ingram, Penelope. "From Goddess Spirituality to Irigaray's Angel: The Politics of the Divine." *Feminist Review*, no. 66 (2000): 46–72. https://www.jstor.org/stable/1395832.

Ingram, Penelope. *The Signifying Body: Towards an Ethics of Sexual and Racial Difference*. Albany: State University of New York Press, 2008. https://doi.org/10.1515/9780791478370.

Irigaray, Luce. *Between East and West from Singularity to Community*. New York: Columbia University Press, 2002. https://ebookcentral.proquest.com/lib/mercer-u/reader.action?docID=909050.

Irigaray, Luce. *Ce sexe qui n'en est pas un*. Paris: Les Éditions de Minuit, 1977.

Irigaray, Luce. "Dreaming of a Truly Democratic World." *Sophia* 61 (2022): 105–15. https://doi.org/10.1007/s11841-022-00913-4.

Irigaray, Luce. *An Ethics of Sexual Difference*. Translated by Carolyn Burke and Gillian C. Gill. Ithaca, NY: Cornell University Press, 1993.

Irigaray, Luce. *Éthique De La Différence Sexuelle Critique*. Paris: Les Éditions de Minuit, 1984.

Irigaray, Luce. *Éthique de la différence sexuelle*. Paris: Les Éditions de Minuit, 1984.

Irigaray, Luce. *The Forgetting of Air in Martin Heidegger*. Translated by Mary Beth Mader. Austin: University of Texas Press, [1983] 1999.

Irigaray, Luce. *I Love to You: Sketch of a Possible Felicity in History*. Translated by Alison Martin. New York: Routledge, 1996.

Irigaray, Luce. *Je, Tu, Nous*. New York: Routledge, 1993.

Irigaray, Luce. Le corps—à—corps avec la mère. In *Sexes et parentés*. Les Éditions de Minuit, 1987.

Irigaray, Luce. *Marine Lover of Friedrich Nietzsche*. Translated by Gillian C. Gill. Ithaca, NY: Cornell University Press, 1991.

Irigaray, Luce. *A New Culture of Energy: Beyond East and West*. New York: Columbia University Press, 2021. https://doi.org/10.7312/irig17712.

Irigaray, Luce. "Questions to Emmanuel Levinas." In *The Irigaray Reader*, edited by Margaret Whitford. Malden, MA: Blackwell, 1992.

Irigaray, Luce. *Sexes and Genealogies*. Translated by Gillian C. Gill. New York: Columbia University Press, 1993.

Irigaray, Luce. *Sharing the Fire: Outline of a Dialectics of Sensitivity*. New York: Springer, 2020. https://doi.org/10.1007/978-3-030-28330-8.

Irigaray, Luce. *Sharing the World*. London: Continuum, 2008.

Irigaray, Luce. *Speculum of the Other Woman*. Translated by Gillian C. Gill. Ithaca, NY: Cornell University Press, 1985.

Irigaray, Luce. *Thinking the Difference: For A Peaceful Revolution*. New York: Routledge, 1994.

Irigaray, Luce. *This Sex Which Is Not One*. Translated by Catherine Porter. 6th ed. Ithaca, NY: Cornell University Press, 1985.

Irigaray, Luce. *To Be Born: Genesis of a New Human Being*. New York: Palgrave Macmillan, 2017.

Irigaray, Luce. *To Be Two*. New York: Routledge, 2001.

Irigaray, Luce. *The Way of Love*. New York: Continuum, 2002.

Irigaray, Luce, and Carol Mastrangelo Bové. "Le Sujet de La Science Est-Il Sexué?/ Is the Subject of Science Sexed?" *Hypatia* 2, no. 3 (1987): 65–87. https://www.jstor.org/stable/3810123.

Irigaray, Luce, and Carolyn Burke. "When Our Lips Speak Together." *Signs: Journal of Women in Culture and Society* 6, no. 1 (1980): 69–79. https://doi.org/10.1086/493777.

Irigaray, Luce, and Noah Guynn. "The Question of the Other." *Yale French Studies* 87, (1995): 7–19. https://doi.org/10.2307/2930321.

Irigaray, Luce, and Michael Marder. *Through Vegetal Being: Two Philosophical Perspectives*. New York: Columbia University Press, 2016.

Irigaray, Luce, Mahon O'Brien, and Christos Hadjioannou. *Towards a New Human Being*. Cham, Switzerland: Palgrave Macmillan, 2019. https://ebookcentral.proquest.com/lib/merceru/reader.action?docID=5730787.

Irigaray, Luce, and Stephen Pluháček. *Conversations*. London: Continuum, 2008. https://ebookcentral.proquest.com/lib/merceru/detail.action?docID=601789.

Irigaray, Luce, and Sara Speidel. "Veiled Lips." *Mississippi Review* 11, no. 3 (1983): 93–131. https://www.jstor.org/stable/20133925.

Jaarsma, Ada S. "Irigaray's *To Be Two*: The Problem of Evil and the Plasticity of Incarnation." *Hypatia* 18, no. 1 (Winter 2003). https://doi.org/10.1111/j.1527-2001.2003.tb00778.x.

Jackson, Zakiyyah Iman. "Sense of Things." *Catalyst: Feminism, Theory, Technoscience* 2, no. 2 (2016): 1–48. https://doi.org/10.1086/678190.

Jagger, Gill. "The New Materialism and Sexual Difference." *Signs: Journal of Women in Culture and Society* 40, no. 2 (2015): 321–42. https://doi.org/10.1086/678190.

Johnston, Tim R. "Questioning the Threshold of Sexual Difference: Irigarayan Ontology and Transgender, Intersex, and Gender-Nonconforming Being." *GLQ: A Journal of Lesbian and Gay Studies* 21, no. 4 (2015): 617–33. https://doi.org/10.1215/10642684-3123713.

Jones, Emma R. *Being as Relation in Luce Irigaray*. Cham, Switzerland: Springer, 2023.

Jones, Emma R. "The Future of Sexuate Difference: Irigaray, Heidegger, Ontology, and Ethics." *L'Esprit Créateur* 52, no. 3 (2012): 26–39. https://doi.org/10.1353/esp.2012.0037.

Jones, Rachel. *Irigaray: Towards a Sexuate Philosophy*. Malden, MA: Polity, 2011.

Jones, Rachel. "Irigaray and Lyotard: Birth, Infancy, and Metaphysics." *Hypatia* 27, no. 1 (2012): 139–62. https://doi.org/10.1111/j.1527-2001.2011.01236.x.

Jones, Rachel. "Sexuate Difference in the Black Atlantic: Reading Irigaray with Hartman." In *What Is Sexual Difference?*, edited by Mary Rawlinson and James Sares, 253–77. New York: Columbia, 2023.

Jones, Rachel. "Vital Matters and Generative Materiality: Between Bennett and Irigaray." *Journal of the British Society for Phenomenology* 46, no. 2 (2015): 156–72. https://doi.org/10.1080/00071773.2014.963343.

Joy, Morny. "Equality or Divinity: A False Dichotomy?" *Journal of Feminist Studies in Religion* 6, no. 1 (1990): 9–24. https://www.jstor.org/stable/25002120.

Juelskjær, Malou, Helle Plauborg, and Stine W. Adrian. *Dialogues on Agential Realism: Engaging in Worldings through Research Practice*. New York: Taylor & Francis, 2021.

Julien, Philippe. *Jacques Lacan's Return to Freud: The Real, the Symbolic, and the Imaginary*. Translated by Devra Beck Simiu; New York: New York University Press, 1995.

Käll, Lisa. "Traces of Otherness." In *Sex, Breath, and Force: Sexual Difference in a Post-Feminist Era*, edited by Ellen Mortensen. Lanham, MD: Lexington Books, 2006.

Kamuf, Peggy, ed. *A Derrida Reader: Between the Blinds*. New York: Columbia University Press, 1991.

Kamuf, Peggy. "To Follow." *Differences: A Journal of Feminist Cultural Studies* 16, no. 3 (2005): 1–15. https://doi.org/10.1215/10407391-16-3-1.

Keenan, Dennis King. "Irigaray and the Sacrifice of the Sacrifice of Woman." *Hypatia* 19, no. 4 (2004): 167–83. https://doi.org/10.1111/j.1527-2001.2004.tb00153.x.

Kelly, Siobhan M. "Multiplicity and Contradiction: A Literature Review of Trans Studies in Religion." *Journal of Feminist Studies in Religion* 34, no. 1 (2018): 7–23. https://doi.org/10.2979/jfemistudreli.34.1.03.

Khader, Serene J. *Decolonizing Universalisms: A Transnational Feminist Ethic*. New York: Oxford University Press, 2019.

Khader, Serene J. "Introduction: Symposium on Serene J. Khader's Decolonizing Universalism: A Transnational Feminist Ethic." *Journal of Global Ethics*, 16, no. 3 (2020): 343–48. https://doi.org/10.1080/17449626.2021.1876144.

Kim, Ruthanne Crapo. "Creolizing Place, Origin, and Difference: The Opaque Waters between Glissant and Irigaray." *Hypatia* 37, no. 4 (2022): 765–83. https://doi.org/10.1017/hyp.2022.52.

Kirby, Vicki. "Transgression: Normativity's Self-Inversion." *Differences: A Journal of Feminist Cultural Studies* 26, no. 1 (2015): 96–116. https://doi.org/10.1215/10407391-2880618.

Kozel, Susan. "The Diabolical Strategy of Mimesis: Luce Irigaray's Reading of Maurice Merleau-Ponty." *Hypatia* 11, no. 3 (1996): 114–29. https://doi.org/10.1111/j.1527-2001.1996.tb01018.x.

Kozel, Susan. "The Story Is told as a History of the Body: Strategies of Mimesis in the Work of Irigaray and Bausch" In *Meaning in Motion: New Cultural Studies of Dance*, edited by Jane C. Desmond, 101–109. Durham, NC: Duke University Press, 1997. https://doi.org/10.1215/9780822397281.

Kristeva, Julia. *Desire in Language: A Semiotic Approach to Literature and Art*. Translated by Thomas Gora, Alice Jardine, and Leon S. Roudiez. New York: Columbia University Press, 1980.

Kristeva, Julia. "Some Observations on Female Sexuality." *Annual of Psychoanalysis* 32, (2004): 59–68. https://doi.org/10.4324/9780203780633.

Kristeva, Julia. "The System and the Speaking Subject." In *The Kristeva Reader*, edited by Toril Moi, 24–33. New York: Columbia University Press, 1986.

Kunz, Elsa. "What Difference Does It Make? Early Reception Stories about Luce Irigaray's Writing on Divine Women." *Journal of Feminist Scholarship* 23, no. 23 (2023): 24–38. https://doi.org/10.23860/jfs.2023.23.03.

Lacan, Jacques. "A Love Letter." In *Feminine Sexuality: Jacques Lacan and the École Freudienne*. Edited by Juliet Mitchell and Jacqueline Rose. New York: Norton, 1983.

Lacan, Jacques. "The Mirror Stage as Formative of the I Function as Revealed in Psychoanalytic Experience." In *Écrits: The First Complete Edition in English*. Translated by Bruce Fink. New York: W. W. Norton, 2006.

Lacan, Jacques. "The Mirror Stage as Formative of the I Function as Revealed in Psychoanalytic Experience." In *Ecrits: A Selection*, translated by Alan Sheridan, 1–29. New York: W. W. Norton, 1977.

Lacan, Jacques. *Le Séminaire*. Livre 7: *L'éthique de la psychanalyse*. Paris: Seuil, 1959–60.

Lacan, Jacques. *The Seminar of Jacque Lacan*. Book 7: *The Ethics of Psychoanalysis*. Translated by J. A. Miller. New York: W. W. Norton, 1992.

Lehtinen, Virpi. *Luce Irigaray's Phenomenology of Feminine Being*. Albany: State University of New York Press, 2014. https://doi.org/10.1515/9781438451299.

LaMothe, Kimerer L. "Reason, Religion, and Sexual Difference: Resources for a Feminist Philosophy of Religion in Hegel's Phenomenology of Spirit." *Hypatia* 20, no. 1 (2005): 120–49. https://doi.org/10.1111/j.1527-2001.2005.tb00376.x.

Lee Kyoo. "Lipthink, Anyone? On, Lips Apart, Disagreeing with You . . . For a Queer Feminist Rectication?" *Differences: A Journal of Feminist Cultural*

Studies 27, no. 3 (2016): 119–31. doi 10.1215/10407391-3696667. https://doi.org/10.1215/10407391-3696667.

Leonard, Miriam. "Lacan, Irigaray, and Beyond: Antigones and the Politics of Psychoanalysis." In Vanda Zajko, and Miriam Leonard, *Laughing with Medusa: Classical Myth and Feminist Thought*. Oxford: Oxford University Press, 2006, 121–39.

Levinas, Emmanuel. "The Ego and the Totality." In *Emmanuel Levinas: Collected Philosophical Papers*. Dordrecth, Netherlands: Martinus Nijhoff, 1987.

Levinas, Emmanuel. *Ethics and Infinity: Conversations with Philippe Nemo*. Translated by Richard A. Cohen. Pittsburgh: Duquesne University Press, 1994.

Levinas, Emmanuel. "Meaning and Sense." In *Emmanuel Levinas: Basic Philosophical Writings*, edited by Simon Critchley, Adriaan T. Peperzak, and Robert Bernasconi. Bloomington: Indiana University Press, 1996.

Levinas, Emmanuel. *Otherwise than Being or beyond Essence*. Translated by Alphonso Lingis. Pittsburgh: Duquesne University Press, 2004.

Levinas, Emmanuel. "Substitution." In *Emmanuel Levinas: Basic Philosophical Writings*, edited by Simon Critchley, Adriaan T. Peperzak, and Robert Bernasconi. Bloomington: Indiana University Press, 1996.

Levinas, Emmanuel. *Time and the Other*. Translated by Richard Cohen. Pittsburgh: Duquesne University Press, 1987.

Levinas, Emmanuel. *Totality and Infinity: An Essay on Exteriority*. 3rd rpr. Norwell, MA: Kluwer Academic, 1991.

Levinas, Emmanuel. "The Trace of the Other." In *Deconstruction in Context: Literature and Philosophy*, edited by Mark C. Taylor. Chicago: University of Chicago Press, 1986.

Levinas, Emmanuel. "Transcendence and Height." In *Emmanuel Levinas: Basic Philosophical Writings*, edited by Simon Critchley, Adriaan T. Peperzak, and Robert Bernasconi. Bloomington: Indiana University Press, 1996.

Levinas, Emmanuel, and Sean Hand. "Reflections on the Philosophy of Hitlerism." *Critical Inquiry* 17, no. 1 (1990): 63–71. https://doi.org/10.1086/448574.

Levinas, Emmanuel, and Paula Wissing. "As If Consenting to Horror." *Critical Inquiry* 15, no. 2 (1989): 485–88. https://www.jstor.org/stable/1343597.

Lloyd, Moya. *Beyond Identity Politics: Feminism, Power, & Politics*. Thousand Oaks, CA: Sage, 2005.

Lorraine, Tamsin. *Irigaray and Deleuze: Experiments in Visceral Philosophy*. Ithaca, NY: Cornell University Press, 2018.

Lorde, Audre. *Sister Outsider: Essays & Speeches by Audre Lorde*. Trumansburg, NY: Crossing, 1984.

Lyotard, Jean-François. *The Differend: Phrases in Dispute*. Minneapolis: University of Minnesota Press, 1988.

McGehee, Scott, and David Siegel, directors. *Suture*. Samuel Goldwyn Company, 1993. 96 minutes.

Mader, Mary Beth. "Somatic Ontology: Comments on Alison Stone's Luce Irigaray and the Philosophy of Sexual Difference." *Differences: A Journal of Feminist Cultural Studies* 19, no. 3 (2008): 126–28. https://doi.org/10.1215/10407391-2008-012.

Malabou, Catherine. *Changing Difference*. Malden, MA: Polity, 2011.

Malabou, Catherine, and Ewa Plonowska Ziarek. "Negativity, Unhappiness or Felicity: On Irigaray's Dialectical Culture of Sexual Difference." *L'Esprit Créateur* 52, no. 3 (2012): 11–25. https://doi.org/10.1353/esp.2012.0035.

Manigault-Bryant, LeRhonda. "A 'Club' No Black Woman Wants to Join: Confronting the Aftermath of Black Death." *Black Perspectives*, July 19, 2016.

Manigault-Bryant, LeRhonda. "Where Black Bodies Lie: Historiography, Race, and the Place of Eros." *Theology & Sexuality* 22, no. 3 (2016): 165–74. https://doi.org/10.1080/13558358.2017.1329884.

Marion, Jean-Luc. "The Other First Philosophy and the Question of Givenness." *Critical Inquiry* 25, no. 4 (1999): 784–800. https://doi.org/10.1086/448946.

Marion, Jean-Luc. *Reduction and Givenness: Investigations of Husserl, Heidegger, and Phenomenology*. Translated by Thomas A. Carlson. Evanston: Northwestern University Press, 1998.

McCann, Rachel. "A Sensuous Ethics of Difference." *Hypatia* 26, no. 3 (2011): 497–517. https://doi.org/10.1111/j.1527-2001.2011.01207.x.

McDonald, Christie. "Notes on an Unfinished Question." *Differences: A Journal of Feminist Cultural Studies* 16, no. 3 (2005): 35–40. https://doi.org/10.1215/10407391-16-3-35.

McKittrick, Katherine. *Sylvia Wynter: On Being Human as Praxis*. Durham, NC: Duke University Press, 2015. https://doi.org/10.1215/9780822375852.

McNulty, Tracy. "Demanding the Impossible: Desire and Social Change." *Differences: A Journal of Feminist Cultural Studies* 20, no. 1 (2009): 1–39. https://doi.org/10.7312/mcnu16118.6.

Meltzer, Françoise. "Theories of Desire: Antigone Again." *Critical Inquiry* 37, no. 2 (Winter 2011): 169–86. https://doi.org/10.1086/657289.

Meredith, Fionola. *Experiencing the Postmetaphysical Self: Between Hermeneutics and Deconstruction*. New York: Palgrave Macmillan, 2005.

Merleau-Ponty, Maurice. *Phenomenology of Perception*. Translated by Donald A. Landes. New York: Routledge, 2012.

Merleau-Ponty, Maurice. *The Visible and the Invisible*. Translated by Claude Lefort. Evanston, IL: Northwestern University Press, 1968.

Mignolo, Water. *The Darker Side of Western Modernity: Global Futures, Decolonial Options*. Durham, NC: Duke University Press, 2011. https://doi.org/10.1215/9780822394501.

Miller, Elaine. "The 'Paradoxical Displacement': Beauvoir and Irigaray on Hegel's Antigone." *Journal of Speculative Philosophy* 14, no. 2 (2000): 121–37. https://dx.doi.org/10.1353/jsp.2000.0014.

Min, Anselm K. "The Trinity and the Incarnation: Hegel and Classical Approaches." *Journal of Religion* 66, no. 2 (1986): 173–93. https://doi.org/10.1086/487360.

Moi, Toril. *Sexual/Textual Politics: Feminist Literary Theory*. New York: Routledge, 2002. Taylor & Francis, 2002.

Mortensen, Ellen. *The Feminine and Nihilism: Luce Irigaray with Nietzsche and Heidegger*. Stockholm: Scandinavian University Press, 1994.

Mortensen, Ellen, ed. *Sex, Breath, and Force: Sexual Difference in a Post-Feminist Era*. Lanham, MD: Lexington Books, 2006.

Moten, Fred. "Black Op." *PMLA: Publications of the Modern Language Association of America* 123, no. 5 (2008): 1743–47. https://doi.org/10.1632/pmla.2008.123.5.1743.

Moten, Fred. "Blackness and Nothingness (Mysticism in the Flesh)." *South Atlantic Quarterly* 112, no. 4 (2013): 737–80. https://doi.org/10.1215/00382876-2345261.

Moten, Fred. "The Case of Blackness." *Criticism* 50, no. 2 (2008): 177–218. https://doi.org/10.1353/crt.0.0062.

Moten, Fred. *In the Break: The Aesthetics of the Black Radical Tradition*. Minneapolis: University of Minnesota, 2003.

Moten, Fred. "Notes on Sentient Flesh." *Comparative Literature Studies* 60, no. 1 (2023): 2–5. https://doi.org/10.5325/complitstudies.60.1.0002.

Moten, Fred. *The Universal Machine*. Durham, NC: Duke University Press, 2018. ProQuest Ebook Central. https://doi.org/10.1215/9780822371977.

Mulder, Anne-Claire. *Divine Flesh, Embodied Word: 'Incarnation' as a Hermeneutical Key to a Feminist Theologian's Reading of Luce Irigaray's Work*. Amsterdam: Amsterdam University Press, 2006.

Muñoz, José Esteban. *Cruising Utopia*. 10th anniversary ed.: *The Then and There of Queer Futurity*. New York: New York University Press, 2019.

Muñoz, José Esteban. *Disidentifications: Queers of Color and the Performance of Politics*. Minneapolis: University of Minnesota Press, 1999.

Muñoz, José Esteban. "Feeling Brown, Feeling Down: Latina Affect, the Performativity of Race, and the Depressive Position." *Signs: Journal of Women in Culture and Society* 31, no. 3 (March 2006): 675–88. https://doi.org/10.1086/499080.

Muraro, Luisa. "Female Genealogies." In *Engaging with Irigaray: Feminist Philosophy and Modern European Thought*, edited by Carolyn Burke, Naomi Schor, and Margaret Whitford, 57–78. New York: Columbia University Press, 1994.

Murtagh, Mitchell Damian. "An Onto-ethics of Transsexual Difference." In *What Is Sexual Difference?*, edited by James Sares and Mary Rawlinson, 227–50. New York: Columbia University Press, 2023. https://doi.org/10.7312/rawl20272.

Musser, Amber Jamilla. *Between Shadows and Noise: Sensation, Situatedness, and the Undisciplined*. Durham, NC: Duke University Press, 2024. https://doi.org/10.1215/9781478059097.

Musser, Amber Jamilla. *Sensual Excess: Queer Femininity and Brown Jouissance*. New York: New York University Press, 2018.

Namaste, Viviane. "Undoing Theory: The 'Transgender Question' and the Epistemic Violence of Anglo-American Feminist Theory." *Hypatia* 24, no. 3 (2009): 11–32. https://doi.org/10.1111/j.1527-2001.2009.01043.x.

Nancy, Jean-Luc. "Of Being Singular Plural." In *Philosophy of Communication*, edited by Briankle G. Chang and Garnet C. Butchart, 577–600. Cambridge, MA: MIT Press.

Nelson, Maggie. *The Argonauts*. Minneapolis, MN: Graywolf, 2015.

Nouvet, Claire. "An Impossible Response: The Disaster of Narcissus." *Yale French Studies*, no. 79 (1991): 103–34. https://doi.org/10.2307/2930248.

Oksala, Johanna. "From Sexual Difference to the Way of Breath." In *Sex, Breath, and Force: Sexual Difference in a Post-Feminist Era*, edited by Ellen Mortensen. Lanham, MD: Lexington Books, 2006.

Oliver, Kelly. "Antigone's Ghost: Undoing Hegel's Phenomenology of Spirit." *Hypatia* 11, no. 1 (1996): 67–90.

Oliver, Kelly. "Textures of Light: Vision and Touch in Irigaray, Levinas and Merleau-Ponty." *Hypatia* 16, no. 1 (2001): 106–8. https://doi.org/10.1353/hyp.2001. 0013. https://doi.org/10.1111/j.1527-2001.1996.tb00507.x.

Ovid. "Echo and Narcissus." In *Metamorphoses*. Book 3. Translated by Horace Gregory. New York: Signet Books, 2009.

Ovid. *Metamorphoses: The New, Annotated Edition*. Translated by Rolfe Humphries. Indianapolis: Indiana University Press, 2018.

Ovid. "The Story of Echo and Narcissus." In *Metamorphoses*. Book 3. Translated by A. S. Kline. Ann Arbor, MI: Ann Arbor Editions, 2004.

Parisi, Luciana. *Abstract Sex: Philosophy, Bio-Technology, and the Mutations of Desire*. London: Continuum, 2004.

Parisi, Luciana. *Contagious Architecture: Computation, Aesthetics, and Space*. Cambridge, MA: MIT Press, 2013.

Park, Linette. "Afropessimism and Futures of . . . : A Conversation with Frank Wilderson." *The Black Scholar* 50, no. 3 (2020): 29–41. https://doi.org/10.1 080/00064246.2020.1780863.

Parker, Emily Anne. *Elemental Difference and the Climate of the Body*. New York: Oxford University Press, 2021.

Parker, Emily Anne, and Anne van Leeuwen. *Differences: Rereading Beauvoir and Irigaray*. Oxford: Oxford University Press, 2017.

Perpich, Diane. "From the Caress to the Word: Transcendence and the Feminine in the Philosophy of Emmanuel Levinas." In *Feminist Interpretations of Emmanuel Levinas*, edited by Tina Chanter, 28–52. University Park: Pennsylvania State University, 2001.

Pitts-Taylor, Victoria, ed. *Mattering: Feminism, Science, and Materialism*. New York: New York University Press, 2016.

Plato. *The Symposium*. Translated by Christopher Gill. reissue, illustrated ed. New York: Penguin, 2003.

Poleshchuk, Irina. "Unfolding Flesh towards the Other: Levinas' Perspective of Maternity and the Feminine." *Problemos* 84 (January 2013): 138–52. https://doi.org/10.15388/Problemos.2013.0.1772.

Priest, Ann-Marie. "Woman as God, God as Woman: Mysticism, Negative Theology, and Luce Irigaray." *The Journal of Religion* 83, no. 1 (2003): 1–23. https://doi.org/10.1086/491221.

Rada, Michelle. "Overdetermined: Psychoanalysis and Solidarity." *Differences: A Journal of Feminist Cultural Studies* 33, nos. 2–3 (December 2022): 1–32. https://doi.org/10.1215/10407391-10124647.

Raschke, Debrah. "A Comment on 'Writing (with) Cixous.'" *College English* 50, no. 7 (1988): 822–25. https://doi.org/10.2307/377686.

Rasheed, Shaireen. "Islam, Sexuality, and the 'War on Terror': Luce Irigaray's Post-Colonial Ethics of Difference." *American Journal of Islamic Social Sciences* 31, no. 1 (2014): 1–15. https://doi.org/10.35632/ajiss.v31i1.291.

Rawlinson, Mary C. *The Betrayal of Substance: Death, Literature, and Sexual Difference in Hegel's Phenomenology of Spirit*. New York: Columbia University Press, 2021.

Rawlinson, Mary C. *Just Life: Bioethics and the Future of Sexual Difference*. New York: Columbia University Press, 2016.

Rawlinson, Mary C. "On Embodiment: Freud and the Concept of the Feminine." *Southwestern Journal of Philosophy* 10, no. 1 (1979): 190. https://www.jstor.org/stable/43155461.

Rawlinson, Mary C. "Opening Hegel's Autological Circle: Irigaray and the Metaphysics of Sexual Difference." In *What Is Sexual Difference? Thinking with Irigaray*, edited by Mary C. Rawlinson and James Sares, 39–58. New York: Columbia University Press, 2023. https://doi.org/10.7312/rawl20272.

Raymond, Janice. *The Transsexual Empire: The Making of the She-Male*. New York: Teachers College Press, 1994.

Richardson, William J. "Lacan and the Enlightenment: Antigone's Choice." *Research in Phenomenology* 24, no. 1 (1994): 25–41. https://doi.org/10.1163/156916494X00032.

Ripley, AJ. "'Feeling-Seeing' in *Transparent:* Using the Mirror to Reflect beyond In/Visibility." *GLQ: A Journal of Lesbian and Gay Studies* 27, no. 2 (April 2021): 201–31. https://doi.org/10.1215/10642684-8871663.

Robbins, Jill. "Visage, Figure: Reading Levinas's Totality and Infinity." *Yale French Studies*, no. 79 (1991): 135–49. https://doi.org/10.2307/2930249.

Rodemeyer, Lanei M. "Feminist and Transgender Tensions: An Inquiry into History, Methodological Paradigms, and Embodiment." In *New Feminist Perspectives on Embodiment*, edited by Clara Fischer and Luna Dolezal, 103–23. Cham, Switzerland: Springer, 2018. https://doi.org/10.1007/978-3-319-72353-2_6.

Roberts, Laura. *Irigaray and Politics*. Edinburgh: Edinburgh University Press, 2019.

Roberts, Laura. "Returning to Irigaray's Radical Materialism: Sexuate Difference, Ontology, and Bodies of Water." In *What Is Sexual Difference? Thinking with Irigaray*, edited by Mary C. Rawlinson and James Sares, 79–100. New York: Columbia University Press, 2023. https://doi.org/10.7312/rawl20272-007.

Roberts, Laura. "A Revolution of Love: Thinking through a Dialectic That Is Not 'One.'" *Hypatia* 32, no. 1 (2017): 69–85. https://doi.org/10.1111/hypa.12306.

Roberts, Laura, and Škof Lenart. "Thinking Politically with Luce Irigaray." *Sophia* 61, no. 1 (2022): 93–97. doi:https://doi.org/10.1007/s11841-022-00923-2. https://www.proquest.com/scholarly-journals/thinking-politically-with-luce-irigaray/docview/2657511016/se-2.

Royer, Michelle. *The Cinema of Marguerite Duras: Multisensoriality and Female Subjectivity.* Edinburgh: Edinburgh University Press, 2019.

Ruprecht, Louis A., Jr. *Reach without Grasping: Anne Carson's Classical Desires.* New York: Lexington, 2022.

Salamon, Gayle. *Assuming A Body: Transgender and the Rhteorics of Materiality.* New York: Columbia University Press, 2010.

Sanders, Mark. *The Intellectual and Apartheid.* Durham, NC: Duke University Press, 2002. https://doi.org/10.1215/9780822384229.

Sares, James. "Irigarayan Ontology and the Possibilities of Sexual Difference." In *Horizons of Difference*, edited by Ruthanne Crapo Kim, Yvette Russell, and Brenda Sharp, 117–36. Albany: State University of New York Press, 2022. https://doi.org/10.1515/9781438488479-008.

Schor, Naomi. "This Essentialism Which Is Not One: Coming to Grips with Irigaray." In *Engaging with Irigaray: Feminist Philosophy and Modern European Thought*, edited by Carolyn Burke, Naomi Schor, and Margaret Whitford, 57–78. New York: Columbia University Press, 1994.

Schwab, Gail. "Beyond the Vertical and the Horizontal: Spirituality, Space, and Alterity in the Work of Luce Irigaray." In *Thinking with Irigaray*, edited by Serene J. Khader, Sabrina L. Hom, and Mary C. Rawlinson. 77–98. Albany: State University of New York Press, 2011. https://doi.org/10.1515/9781438439181-005.

Schwab, Gail. "Freedom, Desire, and the Other: Reading Sartre with Irigaray." In *Thinking Life with Luce Irigaray: Language, Origin, Art, Love*, edited by Gail M. Schwab. Albany: State University of New York Press, 2020. https://doi.org/10.1515/9781438477831.

Schwab, Gail. "Mother's Body, Father's Tongue." In *Engaging with Irigaray: Feminist Philosophy and Modern European Thought*, edited by Naomi Schor, Carolyn Burke, and Margaret Whitford, 351–78. New York: Columbia University Press, 1994.

Schwab, Gail. "Previous Engagements: The Receptions of Irigaray." In *Engaging with Irigaray: Feminist Philosophy and Modern European Thought*, edited by Naomi Schor, Carolyn Burke, and Margaret Whitford, 3–14. New York: Columbia University Press, 1994.

Schwab, Gail. "Sexual Difference as Model: An Ethics for the Global Future." *Diacritics* 28, no. 1 (1998): 76–92. https://doi.org/10.1353/dia.1998.0007.

Schutte, Ofelia. "Irigaray on the Problem of Subjectivity." *Hypatia* 6, no. 2 (1991): 64–76. https://doi.org/10.1111/j.1527-2001.1991.tb01393.x.

Sedgwick, Eve Kosofsky. *Epistemology of the Closet*. Berkeley: University of California Press, 1990.

Sedgwick, Eve Kosofsky. *Tendencies*. 1st ed. New York: Routledge, 1994.

Seely, Stephen D. "Irigaray between God and the Indians: Sexuate Difference, Decoloniality, and the Politics of Ontology." *Australian Feminist Law Journal* 43, no. 1 (2017): 41–66. https://doi.org/10.1080/13200968.2017.1322024.

Seely, Stephen D. "Sexual Difference in/and the Queer Beyond of Ethics." *Feminist Formations* 29, no. 3 (2017): 163–71. https://doi.org/10.1353/ff.2017.0037.

Sexton, Jared. "Affirmation in the Dark: Racial Slavery and Philosophical Pessimism." *The Comparatist* 43, (2019): 90–111. https://doi.org/10.1353/com.2019.0005.

Sexton, Jared. "Afro-Pessimism: The Unclear Word." *Rhizomes*, no. 29 (2016). https://doi.org/10.20415/rhiz/029.e02.

Sexton, Jared. *Black Men, Black Feminism: Lucifer's Nocturne*. Cham, Switzerland: Palgrave Macmillan, 2018.

Sexton, Jared. "Unbearable Blackness." *Cultural Critique* 90, no. 90 (2015): 159–78. https://doi.org/10.5749/culturalcritique.90.2015.0159.

Shahar, Zaynab. "Fear, Flight, and Freedom: On Anti-Colonial Countermasteries and Ontological Insecurities." *Horizontes Decoloniales/Decolonial Horizons* 1 (2019): 165–96. https://doi.org/10.13169/decohori.5.1.0165.

Sharpe, Christina. "Black Studies: In the Wake." *Black Scholar* 44, no. 2 (2014): 59–69. https://doi.org/10.1080/00064246.2014.11413688.

Sharpe, Christina. *In the Wake: On Blackness and Being*. Durham, NC: Duke University Press, 2016. https://doi.org/10.1215/9780822373452.

Silverman, Kaja. *The Acoustic Mirror: The Female Voice in Psychoanalysis and Cinema*. Theories of Representation and Difference. Bloomington: Indiana University Press, 1988.

Seshadri-Crooks, Kalpana. *Desiring Whiteness: A Lacanian Analysis of Race*. New York: Routledge, 2000.

Singh, Julietta. *Unthinking Mastery: Dehumanism and Decolonial Entanglements*. Durham, NC: Duke University Press, 2017. https://doi.org/10.1215/9780822372363.

Sjöholm, Cecilia. *The Antigone Complex: Ethics and the Invention of Feminine Desire*. Redwood City, CA: Stanford University Press, 2004.

Sjöholm, Cecilia. "Crossing Lovers: Luce Irigaray's Elemental Passions." *Hypatia* 15, no. 3 (2000): 92–112. https://doi.org/10.1111/j.1527-2001.2000.tb00332.x.

Skiveren, Tobias. "New Materialism's Second Phase." *Criticism* 63, no. 3 (2021): 309–12. https://doi.org/10.13110/criticism.63.3.0309.

Söderbäck, Fanny. "Narration as a Practice of Care in the Wake of Violence: Adriana Cavarero's Narrative Theory and Saidiya Hartman's Critical Fabulation." *Journal of Italian Philosophy* 7 (2024): 88–126. https://research.ncl.ac.uk/italianphilosophy/currentissue/5.%20SODERBACK_Narration%20as%20a%20Practice%20of%20Care.pdf.

Söderbäck, Fanny. *Revolutionary Time: On Time and Difference in Kristeva and Irigaray*. Albany: State University of New York, 2019. https://doi.org/10.1515/9781438477015.

Söderbäck, Fanny. "Singularity in the Wake of Slavery: Adriana Cavarero's Ontology of Uniqueness and Alex Haley's Roots." *Philosophy Compass* 15, no. 7 (2020): 1–16. https://doi.org/10.1111/phc3.12685.

Söderbäck, Fanny, ed. *Feminist Readings of Antigone*. Albany: State University of New York, 2010. https://doi.org/10.1515/9781438432809.

Sophocles. Sophocles: *The Plays and Fragments*. Part 3: *The Antigone*. 2nd ed. Translated by R. C. Jebb. London: Cambridge University Press, 1891.

Spelman, Elizabeth V. *Inessential Woman: The Problems of Exclusion in Feminist Thought*. Boston: Beacon, 1988.

Spelman, Elizabeth V. "Woman as Body: Ancient and Contemporary Views." *Feminist Studies* 8, no. 1 (1982): 109–31. https://doi.org/10.2307/3177582.

Spillers, Hortense J. "'All the Things You Could Be by Now, if Sigmund Freud's Wife Was Your Mother': Psychoanalysis and Race." *Boundary 2*, 23, no. 3 (1996): 75–141. https://doi.org/10.2307/303639.

Spillers, Hortense J. "The Idea of Black Culture." *CR* 6, no. 3 (2006): 7–28. https://doi.org/10.1353/ncr.2007.0022.

Spillers, Hortense J. "Mama's Baby, Papa's Maybe: An American Grammar Book." *Diacritics* 17, no. 2 (1987): 65–81. https://doi.org/10.2307/464747.

Spillers, Hortense, Saidiya Hartman, Farah Jasmine Griffin, Shelly Eversley, and Jennifer L. Morgan. "'Whatcha Gonna Do?': Revisiting 'Mama's Baby, Papa's Maybe: An American Grammar Book': A Conversation with Hortense Spillers, Saidiya Hartman, Farah Jasmine Griffin, Shelly Eversley, & Jennifer L. Morgan." *Women's Studies Quarterly* 35, no. 1/2 (2007): 299–309. http://www.jstor.org/stable/27649677.

Spivak, Gayatri Chakravorty. "Can the Subaltern Speak?" In *Marxism and the Interpretation of Culture*, edited by Cary Nelson and Lawrence Grossberg, 271–316. Urbana: University of Illinois Press, 1988.

Spivak, Gayatri Chakravorty. "Echo." *New Literary History* 24, no. 1 (1993): 17–43.

Spivak, Gayatri Chakravorty. "French Feminism in an International Frame." *Yale French Studies* no. 62 (1981): 154–184. https://doi.org/10.2307/2929898.

Spivak, Gayatri Chakravorty. "Notes toward a Tribute to Jacques Derrida." *Differences: A Journal of Feminist Cultural Studies* 16, no. 3 (2005): 102–13. https://doi.org/10.1215/10407391-16-3-102.

Spivak, Gayatri Chakravorty. *Outside in the Teaching Machine*. New York: Routledge, 2009 [1993].

Steinberg, Leo. *The Sexuality of Christ in Renaissance Art and in Modern Oblivion*. 2nd ed. Chicago: University of Chicago Press, 1996.

Stockton, Kathryn Bond. "'God' between Their Lips: Desire between Women in Irigaray and Eliot." *Novel: A Forum on Fiction* 25, no. 3 (1992): 348–59. https://doi.org/10.2307/1345893.

Stone, Alison. *Being Born: Birth and Philosophy*. Oxford: Oxford University Press, 2019. https://ebookcentral.proquest.com/lib/merceru/detail.action?docID= 5896238.

Stone, Alison. *Luce Irigaray and the Philosophy of Sexual Difference*. Cambridge University Press, 2006. https://ebookcentral.proquest.com/lib/merceru/detail. action?pq-origsite=primo&docID=261153.

Stone, Alison. "Unthought Nature: Reply to Penelope Deutscher and Mary Beth Mader." *Differences: A Journal of Feminist Cultural Studies*, no. 3 (2008): 150–57. https://doi.org/10.1215/10407391-2008-014.

Taylor, Mark C., ed. *Deconstruction in Context: Literature and Philosophy*. Chicago: University of Chicago Press, 1986.

Thomas, Greg. "ProudFlesh Inter/views: Sylvia Wynter." *ProudFlesh: A New Afrikan Journal of Culture, Politics, and Consciousness*, no. 4 (2006).

Tuin, Iris van der "New Feminist Materialisms." *Women's Studies International Forum* 34, no. 4, (2011): 271–77. https://doi.org/10.1016/j.wsif.2011.04.002.

Van Leeuwen, Anne. "An Examination of Irigaray's Commitment to Transcendental Phenomenology in 'The Forgetting of Air' and 'The Way of Love.'" *Hypatia* 28, no. 3 (2013): 452–68. https://doi.org/10.1111/j.1527-2001.2011.01 257.x.

Van Leeuwen, Anne. "The Possibility of Feminist Phenomenology." In *Journal of Speculative Philosophy* 26, no. 2 (2012): 475. https://doi.org/10.5325/ jspecphil.26.2.0474.

Van Leeuwen, Anne. "Sexuate Difference, Ontological Difference: Between Irigaray and Heidegger." *Continental Philosophy Review* 43 (2010): 111–26. https:// doi.org/10.1007/з11007 010 9136 7.

Walton, Heather. "Extreme Faith in the Work of Elizabeth Smart and Luce Irigaray." *Literature and Theology* 16, no. 1 (2002): 40–50. https://doi.org/10.1093/ litthe/16.1.40.

Ward, Graham. "The Displaced Body of Jesus Christ." In *Radical Orthodoxy*, edited by Catherine Pickstock, John Milbank, and Graham Ward. New York: Routledge, 1999.

Ward, Graham. "Divinity and Sexuality: Luce Irigaray and Christology." *Modern Theology* 12, no. 2 (1996): 221. https://doi.org/10.1111/j.1468-0025.1996. tb00088.x.

Ward, Graham. "In the Name of the Father and of the Mother." *Literature and Theology* 8, no. 3 (1994): 311–27. https://doi.org/10.1093/litthe/8.3.311.

Warren, Calvin. "Black Nihilism and the Politics of Hope." *CR* 15, no. 1 (2015): 215–48. https://doi.org/10.14321/crnewcentrevi.15.1.0215.

Warren, Calvin. "Improper Bodies: A Nihilistic Meditation on Sexuality, the Black Belly, and Sexual Difference." *Palimpsest* 8, no. 2 (2019): 35–51. https://doi. org/10.1353/pal.2019.0017.

Warren, Calvin. *Ontological Terror: Blackness, Nihilism, and Emancipation*. Durham, NC: Duke University Press, 2018.

Weheliye, Alexander G. *Habeas Viscus: Racializing Assemblages, Biopolitics, and Black Feminist Theories of the Human*. Durham, NC: Duke University Press, 2014. https://doi.org/10.1215/9780822376491.

Whitford, Margaret. "Irigaray, Utopia, and the Death Drive." In *Engaging with Irigaray: Feminist Philosophy and Modern European Thought*, edited by Naomi Schor Carolyn Burke, and Margaret Whitford, 379–400. New York: Columbia University Press, 1994.

Whitford, Margaret. *Luce Irigaray: Philosophy in the Feminine*. New York: Routledge, 1991.

Wilderson III, Frank. *Red, White and Black: Cinema and the Structure of U.S. Antagonisms*. Durham, NC: Duke University Press, 2010. https://doi.org/10.1215/9780822391715.

Winters, Joseph. Hope *Draped in Black: Race, Melancholy, and the Agony of Progress*. Durham, NC: Duke University Press, 2016. https://doi.org/10.1215/9780822374084.

Wittig, Monique. *The Straight Mind and Other Essays*. Boston: Beacon, 1992.

Wynter, Sylvia. "The Ceremony Must Be Found: After Humanism." *Boundary 2* (1984): 19–70. https://doi.org/10.2307/302808.

Yeng, Sokthan. "Irigaray's Alternative Buddhist Practices of the Self." *Journal of French and Francophone Philosophy* 22, no. 1 (2014): 61–75. https://doi.org/10.5195/JFFP.2014.643.

Zembylas, Michalinos. (2018). Revisiting Spivak's "Can the Subaltern Speak" through the Lens of Affect Theory: Can the Subaltern Be Felt? *Qualitative Research Journal* 18, no. 2: 115–27. https://doi.org/10.1108/QRJ-D-17-00048.

Ziarek, Ewa Plonowska. "The Ethical Passions of Emmanuel Levinas." In *Feminist Interpretations of Emmanuel Levinas*, edited by Tina Chanter, 78–95. University Park: Pennsylvania State University, 2001.

Ziarek, Ewa Plonowska. "Toward a Radical Female Imaginary: Temporality and Embodiment in Irigaray's Ethics." *Diacritics* 28, no. 1 (1998): 60–75. https://doi.org/10.1353/dia.1998.0009.

Ziarek, Krzysztof. "Love and the Debasement of Being: Irigaray's Revisions of Lacan and Heidegger." *Postmodern Culture* 10, no. 1 (1999). https://doi.org/10.1353/pmc.1999.0035.

Žižek, Slavoj. *Interrogating the Real*. Edited by Rex Butler, and Scott Stephens. New York: Continuum, 2005.

Žižek, Slavoj. *Less than Nothing: Hegel and the Shadow of Dialectical Materialism*. New York: Verso, 2012.

Žižek, Slavoj. *The Sublime Object of Ideology*. New York: Verso, 1989.

Index

www.ingramcontent.com/pod-product-compliance
Lightning Source LLC
Chambersburg PA
CBHW021212270326
41929CB00010B/1089